16

How They Lived

How They Lived

An Annotated Tour of Daily Life through History in Primary Sources

Volume 2
1500 to the Present Day

James Ciment

Foreword by Robert André LaFleur

 GREENWOOD™

An Imprint of ABC-CLIO, LLC
Santa Barbara, California • Denver, Colorado

Library of Congress Cataloging-in-Publication Data

Names: Ciment, James.
Title: How they lived : an annotated tour of daily life through history in primary sources / James Ciment; foreword by Robert André LaFleur.
Description: Santa Barbara, California : Greenwood, an Imprint of ABC-CLIO, LLC, 2016-
Identifiers: LCCN 2015017582| ISBN 9781610698955 (hardback : v. 1) | ISBN 9781610698962 (ebook)
Subjects: LCSH: Civilization—History—Sources. | Civilization—History—Juvenile literature. | World history—Sources. | World history—Juvenile literature. | BISAC: HISTORY / World. | HISTORY / Study & Teaching.
Classification: LCC CB69.2 .C56 2016 | DDC 930.1—dc23 LC record available at http://lccn.loc .gov/2015017582

ISBN: 978-1-61069-895-5
EISBN: 978-1-61069-896-2

20 19 18 17 16   1 2 3 4 5

This book is also available on the World Wide Web as an eBook.
Visit www.abc-clio.com for details.

Greenwood
An Imprint of ABC-CLIO, LLC

ABC-CLIO, LLC
130 Cremona Drive, P.O. Box 1911
Santa Barbara, California 93116-1911

This book is printed on acid-free paper ∞
Manufactured in the United States of America

Contents

Contents

Contents

Contents

Contents

Contents

Contents

Part 15: The Rise of Nationalism: Late Eighteenth–Early Twentieth Centuries

Part 12:
The Emergence of Modern Europe

1500–1700 CE

2.12.1 A Venetian Ambassador's Description of Germany

Germany
1507

The customs and manners of this German nation are as follows: first, there are four kinds of persons—princes of the Empire, nobles, citizens of the free towns, and, lastly, the common people. The princes are in the habit of remaining in their own territories far from the court, where they support by their income, so far as they can, the nobles [knights] of the region. These princes are almost continually at strife with one another or with some of the free towns. If they are poor, they generally permit their retainers to attack and rob on the highways. They are naturally proud and insolent, and feel resentment toward any one who is able to rival them in any respect. They heartily hate the free towns, and all republics and free communities in general, especially the Swiss and our most exalted senate, for it seems to them that the Swiss have always shown themselves rebels toward the Empire and that your sublimities, paying little attention to their authority, hold much territory which they claim is not yours and which they believe should rightfully be divided among them.

Moreover the chief temporal princes are in the habit of leaving their principality to the eldest son and then providing for the rest of their children with other territories, bishoprics, or ecclesiastical benefices; so that if a duke has ten sons, all demand to be dukes like their father. The result is that there are an infinite multitude of counts, dukes, and margraves in Germany. . . . Consequently the greater part of the temporal princes are always ready to descend into Italy in order to provide, some their sons, some their brothers or nephews, with principalities. The ecclesiastical princes, on the other hand, and the free towns would prefer to live in peace and not waste their substance. The princes all live in abundance, but give more attention to drinking than anything else. They are miserably dressed, nor do they affect much ceremony in their courts.

The knights are accustomed to live in some castle far from a town, or at the court of some prince, or among the mountains in solitary regions. They live and dress wretchedly, hate the burghers, and are poor, but so proud that nothing in the world would induce them to engage in commerce. They are devoted to fighting; and when that is wanting they have nothing to do but to hunt or set to plundering on the highways. . . .

The burghers. The burghers of the free towns are all merchants. They live well but dress ill, although there are some very rich people among them. They maintain justice, desire peace, hate the knights heartily and fear the princes, and for this reason the cities form leagues among themselves. The towns are moreover at enmity each with its bishop on account of his desire to exercise the temporal as well as the spiritual authority over the town. This hostility is increased by the natural ill feeling between the burghers on the one hand and the knights and princes on the other, for the bishops are always chosen from among the knights and princes, since the canons, who have the right to elect the bishop, all belong by descent to the noble classes and not to the burghers.

The lower classes, whether subject to the princes or the free towns, are poor, wild by nature, do not fear to endanger their lives, and are very loyal to their lords. They are loath to exert themselves to earn anything, and the little they get they speedily drink up.

Source: Quirini, Giacomo. Excerpts from a letter to Maximilian I. In *Readings in European History*. Vol. II. Edited by James Harvey Robinson. Boston: Ginn and Company, 1906, pp. 35–37.

TIMELINE   2000 1900 1800 1700 1600 1500 1400 1300 1200 1100 1000 900 800 700 600 500 400 300 200 100 1 BCE

What You Need to Know

The report excerpted here was written by a Venetian ambassador known as Quirini to the court of the Holy Roman Emperor Maximilian I in 1507.

For virtually all of their history until the nineteenth century, the German-speaking peoples of north-central Europe have not known political unity, other than a brief time under the rule of Charlemagne in the first half of the ninth century. Charlemagne's legacy, the Holy Roman Empire, offered only a patina of centralized government. Instead, what is now Germany was divided into a collection of small principalities, duchies, and other political entities. While England, France, and Spain slowly coalesced in the late Middle Ages and Renaissance period into unified kingdoms, Germany remained torn by petty warfare among its many rulers. After 1519, and Martin Luther's break with the Catholic Church, the region no longer even had the unity provided by a common religion, as various princes aligned themselves either with the Catholic Church or Protestant reformers. These sectarian divisions would lead to the Thirty Years' War in the first half of the seventeenth century, arguably the bloodiest conflict in European history before the twentieth century.

A Closer Look

The ambassador begins with a description of the political disunity that was the Holy Roman Empire in the sixteenth century. He notes that inheritance customs meant that every son of a duke insisted on retaining the same vaunted title, leading to an ever-expanding number of petty states.

Quirini also points out that unlike in more centralized kingdoms, the princes of the realm did not live at court but in their own capitals, where they had their own access to tax revenues. Interestingly, he notes how the poorer among them even engaged in organized crime to raise funds. They sponsored bandits who preyed on travelers, an activity which, of course, further diminished trade and other interaction that might have created more unity among the principalities.

The overall picture Quirini paints is one of strife and social disharmony, leading to an impoverishment of all classes of Germans. Although he reserves what little praise he offers for the merchant-run cities of the realm, he notes that even in those places, there is much conflict between secular and church authorities and between the rule of merchants and the local princes who claimed authority over the cities within their jurisdictions.

1 100 200 300 400 500 600 700 800 900 1000 1100 1200 1300 1400 1500 1600 1700 1800 1900 2000 CE

England
1528

A Brief Rehersall of the Chiefe Conditions and Qualities in a Courtier

TO be well borne and of a good stocke.

To be of a meane stature, rather with the least then to high, and well made to his propotion.

To be portly and amiable in countenance unto whoso beehouldeth him.

Not to be womanish in his sayinges or doinges.

Not to praise himself unshamefully and out of reason.

Not to crake and boast of his actes and good qualities.

To shon Affectation or curiosity above al thing in al things.

To do his feates with a slight, as though they were rather naturally in him, then learned with studye: and use a Reckelesness to cover art, without minding greatly what he hath in hand, to a mans seeminge.

Not to carie about tales and triflinge newis.

Not to be overseene in speaking wordes otherwile that may offende where he ment it not.

Not to be stubborne, wilful nor full of contention: nor to contrary and overthwart men after a spiteful sort.

Not to be a babbler, brauler, or chatter, nor lavish of his tunge.

Not to be given to vanitie and lightnesse, not to have a fantasticall head.

No lyer.

No fonde flatterer.

Source: Castiglione, Baldassare. *The Book of the Courtier from the Italian of Count Baldassare Castiglione*. Translated by Sir Thomas Hoby. Edited by W. E. Henley. London: David Nutt, 1900, pp. 368–369.

What You Need to Know

This passage is from *The Book of the Courtier*, written by Baldassare Castiglione and published in 1561. Castiglione was an Italian diplomat serving at the court of England's King Henry VIII.

One of the hallmarks of the Renaissance was a renewed interest in the individual as an agent of his or her own destiny. During the earlier Middle Ages, such an idea had been tinged with sacrilege because it was seen to draw the individual away from spiritual to earthly affairs. In the Middle Ages, for example, artists rarely signed their work; in the Renaissance, this became the norm.

Politically, Renaissance ideas about individualism were evinced in the growing power and authority of monarchs, who made it their mission to build stronger institutions to exert their will over their subjects. It also led to war as monarchs competed to expand their realms. But before they could do any of this, they had to assert their authority over local aristocrats, who fought to maintain their political and economic autonomy. One of the ways monarchs did this was by establishing elaborate courts and requiring the nobility to be in attendance there, where the monarch could keep an eye on them.

A Closer Look

King Henry VIII, who ruled England from 1509 to 1547, personified the Renaissance monarch, most notably in his decision to pull England out of the Church of Rome and place himself as the secular authority over the newly established Church of England. Henry's royal court reflected his ambitions. Court life was a lavish affair, meant to display Henry's wealth and power. The aim was to impress aristocratic members of the court and any visiting foreign diplomats with the idea that challenges to Henry's power were futile. To show himself in the best light, Henry made his court a center of learning and culture, bringing in artists and musicians to celebrate his reign.

Henry also filled his courts with aristocrats from around England. The men were known as courtiers, French for "members of the court," and the women, courtesans. (There was no sexual connotation to the latter term then.) Courtiers were expected to spend most of the year at the various courts of Henry VIII, returning to their own estates when necessary. Courtiers, who were typically paid from the royal household budget, could serve as personal attendants to the king, as well as political and economic advisors. They ranged in their duties and ambitions. Some simply hoped to keep their comfortable positions at court and so simply did what members of the royal family asked of them—errands, providing companionship, and doing intimate servant duties, such as personal grooming. Higher ranking and more ambitious courtiers often tried to influence royal decisions, usually on matters that would benefit the courtier's own family, who often lived at court as well but maintained estates in other places. Courtiers were also expected to maintain a certain decorum and dignity, as this excerpt from the Italian-born diplomat and courtier at Henry's court Baldassare Castiglione reveals.

1 100 200 300 400 500 600 700 800 900 1000 1100 1200 1300 1400 1500 1600 1700 1800 1900 2000 CE

2.12.3 Italian Medicinal Jar (*Albarello*)

Italy
1530–1540

Credit: DeAgostini/Getty Images

What You Need to Know

This is a medicinal jar, known in Italian as an *albarello*. Made of glazed earthenware and painted with mineral pigments, it comes from Faenza, Italy, and was manufactured between 1530 and 1540. The words across the middle read: "ung biancho," meaning white unguent, or ointment. It probably refers to a topical medicine of some kind.

The distinguished historian of medicine Charles Rosenberg once remarked that, before the late nineteenth century, one's chance of survival stood in inverse ratio to the distance one kept from the nearest doctor. Indeed, medicine in early modern Europe was rudimentary and sometimes even life threatening, doing little good and much harm to patients. Still, a sufferer would seek any help he or she could get.

A patient had four places to go: faith healers, surgeons, physicians, and apothecaries, or those who concocted medicines. The first worked on the principle that evil spirits caused disease and so their exorcism would cure the patient. Unaware of the germ theory of illness, surgeons performed their operations without any effort to keep out infection and without any anesthetics. Physicians still operated under ancient Greek ideas about the humors of the body being out of balance. Among their most common procedures was bloodletting to bring the humors back into balance. Apothecaries, meanwhile, not only made drugs but diagnosed patients.

A Closer Look

As noted, apothecaries, or pharmacists, often times acted like physicians in sixteenth-century Europe, diagnosing and treating diseases as well as concocting medicines. Like physicians, they subscribed to the idea that an ill person suffered from an imbalance of the four humors: bile, blood, phlegm, and choler, or yellow bile. To bring these back into balance, the patient had to be bled, usually a task for physicians, or purged. Apothecaries specialized in the latter. Their concoctions were often extremely complex, sometimes involving more than 100 ingredients, and quite expensive. There was little science in any of this. With so many components, apothecaries were unable to isolate the effective ingredient, if indeed there were any, in the medicine. This made it impossible to note cause and effect if a patient was cured. Moreover, no two apothecaries followed the same recipes or had access to the same quality of ingredients.

Still, some of these purgatives could be effective. Strong laxatives, for example, might relieve gastrointestinal illnesses. But most were quite dangerous, often causing the patient more harm than the original ailment.

1 100 200 300 400 500 600 700 800 900 1000 1100 1200 1300 1400 1500 1600 1700 1800 1900 2000 CE

CHAPTER XIV

The Manner of Proceeding Against Clerics who Keep Concubines is Prescribed

How shameful a thing, and how unworthy it is of the name of clerics who have devoted themselves to the service of God, to live in the filth of impurity, and unclean bondage, the thing itself doth testify, in the common scandal of all the faithful, and the extreme disgrace entailed on the clerical order. To the end, therefore, that the ministers of the Church may be recalled to that continency and integrity of life which becomes them; and that the people may hence learn to reverence them the more, that they know them to be more pure of life: the holy Synod forbids all clerics whatsoever to dare to keep concubines, or any other woman of whom any suspicion can exist, either in their own houses, or elsewhere, or to presume to have any intercourse with them: otherwise they shall be punished with the penalties imposed by the sacred canons, or by the statutes of the (several) churches. But if, after being admonished by their superiors, they shall not abstain from these women, they shall be ipso facto deprived of the third part of the fruits, rents, and proceeds of all their benefices whatsoever, and pensions; which third part shall be applied to the fabric of the church, or to some other pious place, at the discretion of the bishop. If, however, persisting in the same crime, with the same or some other woman, they shall not even yet have obeyed upon a second admonition, not only shall they thereupon forfeit all the fruits and proceeds of their benefices and pensions, which shall be applied to the places aforesaid, but they shall also be suspended from the administration of the benefices themselves, for as long a period as shall seem fit to the Ordinary, even as the delegate of the Apostolic See. And if, having been thus suspended, they nevertheless shall not put away those women, or, even if they shall have intercourse with them, then shall they be for ever deprived of their ecclesiastical benefices, portions, offices, and pensions of whatsoever kind, and be rendered thenceforth incapable and unworthy of any manner of honours, dignities, benefices and offices, until, after a manifest amendment of life, it shall seem good to their superiors, for a cause, to grant them a dispensation. But if, after having once put them away, they shall have dared to renew the interrupted connexion, or to take to themselves other scandalous women of this sort, they shall, in addition to the penalties aforesaid, be smitten with the sword of excommunication. Nor shall any appeal, or exemption, hinder or suspend the execution of the aforesaid; and the cognizance of all the matters above-named shall not belong to archdeacons, or deans, or other inferiors, but to the bishops themselves, who may proceed without the noise and the formalities of justice, and by the sole investigation of the truth of the fact.

Source: The Council of Trent. *The Canons and Decrees of the Sacred and Oecumenical Council of Trent*. Translated and edited by J. Waterworth. London: Dolman, 1848, pp. 270–271.

What You Need to Know

This document comes from the Council of Trent. Convened by the Catholic Church for eighteen years from 1545 to 1563, the Council, named after the Italian city (Trento) where it began, was a response to the Protestant Reformation and Protestant criticisms about corrupt practices within the Catholic Church. This particular excerpt condemns, and outlines punishments for, carnal relations between priests and women.

Issues concerning the sexuality of priests—their celibacy, prohibitions on marriage, and indulgence in unacceptable carnal activity—are not unique to our own time. Indeed, one of the complaints of Protestant reformers in the sixteenth century was the failure of priests and high church officials to live up to the church's proscriptions on sexual activity among the clergy.

Celibacy for the clergy was not part of the early church's teachings. Indeed, some of the apostles were married. But by around the turn of the second millennium, the Catholic clergy was expected to remain unmarried and celibate. Some historians of religion maintain this was to ensure that the property of priests would not be passed on to heirs but to the church itself. In any case, unable to marry, and unwilling to give up sex, many priests and church officials kept concubines, outraging not only reformers but many ordinary people, particularly in northern Europe.

A Closer Look

Most Catholic priests at the time of the Protestant Reformation lived in farming villages, as that was where the vast majority of the European population lived. There, they performed many duties, including the daily masses, hearing confessions, and officiating at any number of ceremonies, from baptisms to weddings to burials.

While hardly rich, local priests did relatively well for themselves, as peasants paid tithes, or 10 percent of their crops, to the church. Most of this went to local church activities, such as helping the poor, and some was sent to Rome, but enough was collected for the priest to eat a more balanced diet, live in a larger home, and wear more luxurious clothes than most of his neighbors.

While forbidden by church doctrine to marry, many kept common law wives. Usually the community was aware of this arrangement, although to keep up appearances, and prevent investigations by officials in the church, priests would often maintain the pretense that the women they were living with were their housekeepers, often said to be widows to explain the children that were running around the premises.

1 100 200 300 400 500 600 700 800 900 1000 1100 1200 1300 1400 1500 1600 1700 1800 1900 2000 CE

2.12.5 John Calvin's *Ordinances for the Regulation of the Churches*

Switzerland
1547

Concerning the Time of Assembling at Church.

That the temples be closed for the rest of the time, in order that no one shall enter therein out of hours, impelled thereto by superstition; and if anyone be found engaged in any special act of devotion therein or nearby he shall be admonished for it: if it be found to be of a superstitious nature for which simple correction is inadequate, then he shall be chastised.

Blasphemy.

Whoever shall have blasphemed, swearing by the body or by the blood of our Lord, or in similar manner, he shall be made to kiss the earth for the first offence; for the second to pay 5 sous, and for the third 6 sous, and for the last offence be put in the pillory for one hour.

Drunkenness.

That no one shall invite another to drink under penalty of 3 sous.

That taverns shall be closed during the sermon, under penalty that the tavern-keeper shall pay 3 sous, and whoever may be found therein shall pay the same amount.

If anyone be found intoxicated he shall pay for the first offence 3 sous and shall be remanded to the consistory; for the second offence he shall be held to pay the sum of 6 sous, and for the third 10 sous and be put in prison.

That no one shall make roiaumes [great feasts] under penalty of 10 sous.

Songs and Dances.

If anyone sings immoral, dissolute or outrageous songs, or dance the virollet or other dance, he shall be put in prison for three days and then sent to the consistory.

Usury.

That no one shall take upon interest or profit more than five percent, upon penalty of confiscation of the principal and of being condemned to make restitution as the case may demand.

Games.

That no one shall play at any dissolute game or at any game whatsoever it may be, neither for gold nor silver nor for any excessive stake, upon penalty of 5 sous and forfeiture of stake played for.

Source: Calvin, John. Excerpt from *Ordinances for the Regulation of the Churches Dependent upon the Signory of Geneva, 1547*. In *Translations and Reprints from the Original Sources of European History*. Vol. III, no. 3. ch. II, "The Genevan Reformation." Edited by Merrick Whitcomb. Philadelphia: Department of History at the University of Pennsylvania, 1897, pp. 10–11.

TIMELINE   2000 1900 1800 1700 1600 1500 1400 1300 1200 1100 1000 900 800 700 600 500 400 300 200 100 1 BCE

What You Need to Know

This excerpt is from the *Ordinances* of John Calvin, a Protestant religious reformer of sixteenth-century Geneva, Switzerland. In it, and in other works, Calvin set out principles that transformed the Christian faith.

For the first thousand years following the widespread adoption of Christianity in Europe, the Catholic Church was the sole institution of faith. Religion for the typical European of the early sixteenth century was an all encompassing thing, providing both an explanation for the nature of the universe and man's place in it as well as a consolation for the many miseries suffered in an age before modern agriculture, science, and medicine. Organized religion was administered by the parish, or local, priest. While some were selfless and dedicated to their mission, others were anything but. Corruption, absenteeism, and immorality were rife, which higher church officials frequently ignored when they were not participating in such things themselves. Priests sold indulgences—forgiveness for sins—drank to excess, gambled, surrounded themselves with luxuries, and strayed far from the Catholic ideal of clergy celibacy. Such behavior undermined the authority of the church with both ordinary believers and educated theologians. Among the latter was a German friar named Martin Luther, who in 1517 posted his criticisms on the church door in Wittenberg, Saxony (in modern-day Germany), which led to the Reformation and the beginnings of Protestant Christianity. But while Luther was interested in reforming the church as an institution, Calvin went further, attempting to rid society itself of corrupting practices.

A Closer Look

The anchoring idea behind Calvin's theology was the omnipotence of God, whom, he said, mere mortals could not influence through either prayer or good works. Thus, one's spiritual fate was predestined. At first glance, this might seem an invitation to sensual indulgence, for no matter what one did, it had no effect on being saved or damned. But Calvin argued that living a righteous life showed that one was among the "elect," those chosen by God for salvation.

In 1541, Calvin was invited by the authorities in Geneva to administer the reformation there. Calvin insisted that the people of Geneva live up to the highest moral standards. He also insisted that the local government should do all in its power to help and, if necessary, compel citizens through punitive legislation to live up to those standards. In this excerpt, Calvin imposed penalties on blasphemers, drunks, gamblers, singers of "immoral, dissolute, or outrageous songs," and usurers—that is, those charging excessive rates of interest, then considered an immoral act.

Under Calvin's rule the divide between secular and religious authority was effectively done away with. As the document notes, people are to be fined or imprisoned by the government for violating moral principles and engaging in what Calvin considered immoral practices, such as dancing or encouraging others to drink.

2.12.6 Commentary on English Women's Fashions

England
1550

What should we think of the women
   that in London we see?
For more wanton looks
I dare boldly say,
Were never in Jewish whores
than in London wives this day.
And if gait and garments
do show anything,
Our wives do pass their hours . . .
The cap on her head
   is like a sow's maw: . . .
Then fine gear on the forehead
   settle after the new trick.
If their hair will not take color,
then must they be new;
And lay it out in tussocks:
   this thing is too true.
At each side a tussock
   as big as a ball.
A very fair sight
   for a fornicator bestial.
Her face fair painted
   to make it shine bright,
And her bosom all bare
   and most whorelike dight . . .
Upon her white fingers
many rings of gold
With such manner stones
as are most dearly sold. . . .
I have told them but truth,
   let them say what they will;
I have said they be whorelike,
   and so I say still.

Source: Crowley, Robert. "Of Nice Rogues." In *One and Thyrtye Epigrammes*. Reprinted in *Harrison's Description of England in Shakspere's Youth*. Edited by Frederick Furnivall. London: N. Trübner and Co., 1877, pp. 170–171.

TIMELINE   2000 1900 1800 1700 1600 1500 1400 1300 1200 1100 1000 900 800 700 600 500 400 300 200 100 1 BCE

What You Need to Know

In this poem, Robert Crowley criticizes the sumptuous and often sexually provocative dress and cosmetics worn by London women during the Renaissance.

The Puritans faced great countervailing forces in their effort to end corruption and indulgence in the English society of their day. For the country was experiencing great economic growth, change, and turmoil in the mid-sixteenth century. In the countryside, the Enclosure Movement, in which landlords usurped tenant farms and communal pasturage, for the raising of their own flocks of sheep—English wool was much in demand on the Continent—forced large numbers of peasants to flock to cities. Those who remained were gouged for ever higher rents, part of a general European inflationary trend triggered by the flood of precious metals coming into the continent from the Spanish conquest of the Americas. For those who could invest their funds in lands or exports, it was a time of great wealth, even as the poor suffered. Wool was making many members of the English aristocracy rich, even as growing trade led to an expanded middle class, particularly in London. The city was also becoming a center of finance, as European banking shifted from the city-states of Italy to trading hubs in the northern half of the continent.

A Closer Look

A printer by trade, as well as a poet, Crowley was also a Puritan, who, as the name implies, sought to "purify" the Church of England of both excess ritual and corruption. But, as this 1550 poem reveals, it was not just the church that was the target of the wrath of Puritans.

Adopting the principles of Swiss theologian John Calvin, the Puritans stressed the need to live a godly life, which to them meant hard work, thrift, and a will to succeed in secular life. Indeed, worldly success, they said, was a sign that God had chosen someone to be among the "elect," who would achieve salvation. To succeed meant postponing pleasure, or abstaining from it altogether—no drinking to excess, no fornication, not even indulgence in pastimes, such as dancing, music, and theater. If one read, it should not be for pleasure but to uplift oneself. Indulgence in any of this was sinful, and a sign that a person was *not* among the "elect." Women in fancy clothes, Crowley and other Puritans believed, were guilty of pride, one of the seven mortal sins. Indeed, the Puritans held sin and even poverty itself as a sign that someone was not in control of their passions and that their soul was morally corrupt.

1   100 200 300   400   500   600   700   800   900   1000 1100 1200 1300   1400   1500   1600   1700 1800 1900 2000 CE

2.12.7 A Description of Dutch Town Life

Netherlands
1557

The Netherlands comprise thirteen provinces, to wit, three lordships, four duchies, and six counties. The atmosphere is heavy and the sky almost always overcast. Owing to the frequent changes in the wind, one has warm weather and cold several times in the same day. Flanders abounds in various commodities, but produces no wine. Artois raises more grain than all the rest of the country together. Holland enjoys an income of eight hundred thousand crowns yearly from its butter and cheese. The number of towns, larger, medium, and small, amount to some hundred and forty. The largest have from six thousand to twenty-five thousand families. The population of the whole country is estimated at three millions.

The houses are not conveniently disposed and the architecture is not fine. They are for the most part of wood and earth, but the public buildings constructed of stone make a fine appearance. The churches and the open places are remarkable. The streets are wide and adorned with numerous superb fountains, but they are badly paved and might be cleaner.

These provinces swarm with men who practice all the useful arts. The greater number of them are weavers. In Holland alone eight hundred thousand crowns' worth of linens are produced. The manufacture of wall hangings, which goes on in several regions, amounts to nearly as much, and the export of cloths of all kinds is much more considerable still.

The people of the Netherlands excel all other nations in their painting of landscapes and animals. They seem born for music, and produce composers of eminence.

As for attendance upon divine service, nowhere does one find more devotion. Almsgiving and processions take place almost every Sunday in their churches. Nevertheless there are many Lutherans and Anabaptists among them. Gelderland is completely infected with them. There are many in Brabant and especially in Antwerp, but they are more numerous still in Holland and Artois. They are condemned to be burned for this heresy, but they may escape this penalty by retracting, when they lose their heads instead. It is a notable thing that, although the cold climate makes the inhabitants timorous, when condemned to death they face their fate with rare courage.

Source: "A Venetian Ambassador's Description of the Netherlands in 1557." In *Readings in European History*. Vol. II. Edited by James Harvey Robinson. Boston: Ginn and Company, 1906, pp. 171–172.

What You Need to Know

This passage is from the writings of a Venetian ambassador stationed in the Netherlands in the mid-sixteenth century.

The Netherlands was ideally situated for trade, as a number of rivers, most notably the Rhine, flowed into the North Sea on its territory. This meant that the manufactured products of north-western Europe flowed through its ports, where they were traded for raw materials from nearby England and as far away as Russia and the Mediterranean. Several major cities had emerged by the time Charles V took power. These included Ghent, Brussels, Arras, Amsterdam, and Antwerp. The latter was the largest port and most important financial center in Europe, the latter a status it had inherited from the decline of Venice and other Italian city-states, victims of war and a shift in trade from the Mediterranean to the Atlantic following the voyages of Columbus and other Spanish and Portuguese-sponsored navigators.

In addition, like the city-states of northern Italy, the provinces of the Netherlands had a history of self-government. They could impose their own taxes and make their own laws. But unlike Italy, they were politically united under the Holy Roman Empire so did not suffer internecine warfare. Indeed, leaders of the various provinces met from time to time in an Estates-General to address regional issues, though all decisions had to be approved by the various provincial governments. In short, the Netherlands in the sixteenth century was a loose federation under the ultimate control of Charles V, the Hapsburg emperor.

A Closer Look

Although not as rich as it would become in its so-called golden age in the following century, the Netherlands, also known as Holland, after its largest province, was already thriving economically. The Dutch-speaking north excelled in fishing, trade, and international finance while the French-speaking towns of the south, which included territory now part of Belgium, manufactured linens and woolens of the highest quality.

The success of the Netherlands textile industry depended in large part on effective labor organization, although not in factories. Instead, most textile merchants outsourced production to the villages that dotted the Dutch landscape, where many homes featured looms and other equipment for the spinning of thread and the weaving of cloth. Many villages specialized in a certain kind of textile and all were organized into an elaborate economic network that provided financing, transport and trade connections.

The textile trade, as well as finance, made for many mercantile fortunes, which was often spent on art and architecture. Thus, unlike many other European countries, where art and architecture were largely sponsored by the church or landed aristocracy, in Holland, merchants' tastes dictated artistic production. Being practical men focused on this world rather than the next, they preferred art that reflected the real world, such as paintings of landscapes and animals.

England
ca. 1560

Credit: DeAgostini/Getty Images

What You Need to Know

Pictured here is a full-body suit of armor produced in England sometime around the year 1560.

By the sixteenth century, armor had reached its highest level of development. Thick iron plate was able to deflect most any sword or lance. Even the first primitive guns, known as arquebuses, did not have the firepower to penetrate well-made armor, unless discharged at very close range. Plus, they were very inaccurate even at short range. Moreover, these so-called hand-cannons were too heavy and awkward to be held in the arms alone, requiring the use of a one-legged stand for support. Loading the arquebus with gunpowder and a projectile, and then setting up the stand, required a great deal of time, rendering them ineffective in most close-quarter combat.

By the end of the century, however, improvements in small firearms, particularly the introduction of the lighter, more accurate, and more powerful matchlock muskets had diminished the effectiveness of armor, which soon took on a more ceremonial role, even as the knights who wore such outfits were increasingly replaced by masses of infantrymen led by lightly protected but more mobile cavalrymen.

A Closer Look

As armor was becoming increasingly anachronistic on the battlefield, it became relegated to more ceremonial uses, particularly in knights' tournaments. Dating back to the Middle Ages, such tournaments featured highly stylized bouts between knights in armor. These included both individual and team events. The most popular of the former were jousts, in which two knights on horseback would ride at each other bearing lances. They would then clash, attempting to score points by knocking the other from his mount. Team events, also known as melees, would feature several knights battling each other with various weapons, either on foot or horseback. As with jousting, success was measured not by causing actual injury—the weapons were typically blunted in tournaments to prevent bloodletting—but by knocking the opponent to the ground. Still, it is estimated that roughly 10 percent of participants in tournaments were injured badly enough to end their participation before the contest was over. Knights engaged in such tournaments both for glory and money. Indeed, the purses presented to the winner could be substantial, enough to support a knight and his family for as long as a year at a time.

1 100 200 300 400 500 600 700 800 900 1000 1100 1200 1300 1400 1500 1600 1700 1800 1900 2000 CE

2.12.9 Italian Gunpowder Flask

Italy
ca. 1570

Credit: DeAgostini/Getty Images

What You Need to Know

This flask was for holding gunpowder and made in Italy around the year 1570.

While other realms of continental Europe, such as France and Spain, began to coalesce into centrally administered nation-states in the fifteenth and sixteenth centuries, Italy remained divided into competing city-states, along with the Papal States around Rome and the Kingdom of Naples in the south.

This led to a power vacuum on the peninsula, which led both the French and Spanish monarchies to invade, sometimes invited by one of the local powers to gain advantage over another. Such was the cause of the French invasion of the late fifteenth century and the Spanish one of the early sixteenth. Italy became a battleground for competing monarchies and their armies, causing much destruction and preventing the peninsula from achieving political unity until the late nineteenth century.

The continual warfare on the Italian Peninsula led to innovations in weaponry, including the increasingly widespread use of firearms and gunpowder.

A Closer Look

Gunpowder, a chemical compound of sulfur, charcoal, and potassium nitrate (saltpeter) that can cause destruction or propel objects through its explosive power was invented in Tang dynasty China around the ninth century. The first weapons to use gunpowder were also a Chinese invention of around the thirteenth century. Gun technology spread to the Islamic world and on to Europe in a relatively short period, probably by the end of that same century.

Various developments in the fourteenth and fifteenth centuries made gunpowder safer both to manufacture and to use, as well as more powerful. By the late sixteenth century, all of the major armies of Europe were using arquebuses, primitive firearms, in which a burning match set off a gunpowder explosion, propelling a projectile out of the barrel. But, to be effective, the gunpowder had to be kept very dry, hence the need for gunpowder flasks, such as this Italian flask from around 1570. Made of ivory, it features classical images of a water nymph and a horse.

As in other parts of Europe, firearms were coming into increasing use in Italy by 1570. Indeed, one of the first large scale uses of archebuses was in the so-called Italian wars, described above, of the first half of the sixteenth century.

1 100 200 300 400 500 600 700 800 900 1000 1100 1200 1300 1400 1500 1600 1700 1800 1900 2000 CE

2.12.10 A Renaissance Education in England

England
1573

The way is this: after the three concordances learned, as I touched before, let the Master read unto him the Epistles of Cicero, gathered together, and chosen out by Sturmius, for the capacity of children.

First, let him teach the child, cheerfully and plainly, the cause, and matter of the letter. Then, let him construe it into English, so oft, as the child may easily carry away the understanding of it. Lastly parse it over perfectly. This done thus, let the child, by and by, both construe and parse it over again, so, that it may appear, that the child doubteth in nothing, that his master taught him before. After this, the child must take a paper book, and sitting in some place, where no man shall prompt him, by himself, let him translate into English his former lesson. Then, showing it to his master, let the master take from him his Latin book, and pausing an hour, at the least, then let the child translate his own English into Latin again, in another paper book. When the child bringeth it, turned into Latin, the Master must compare it with Tulliesbook, and lay them both together, and where the child doth well, either in chosing, or true placing of Tully's book, let the master praise him, and say, here you do well. For I assure you, there is no such whetstone to sharpen a good wit and encourage a will to learning, as is praise.

But if the child miss, either in forgetting a word, or in changing a good with a worse, or misordering the sentence, I would not have the master either frown or chide with him, if the child have done his diligence, and used no truantship therein. For I know by good experience, that a child that take more profit of two faults gently warned of, then of four things rightly hit. For then the master shall have good occasion to say unto him: "A, Tullie would have used such a word, not this; Tullie would have placed this word here, not there; would have used this case, this number, this person, this degree, this gender; he would have used this mood, this tense, this simple, rather than this compound; this adverb here not there; he would have ended the sentence with this verb, not with that noun or participle, etc." . . .

Let your Scholar be never afraid to ask you any doubt, but use discretely the best allurements ye can to encourage him to the same, lest, his overmuch fearing of you, drive him to seek some misorderly shift, as to seek to be helped by some other book, or to be prompted by some other Scholar, and to go about to beguile you much, and himself more.

With this way of good understanding the matter, plain construing, diligent parsing, daily translating, cheerfull admonishing, and heedfull amending of faults, never leaving behind just praise for well doing, I would have the scholar brought up withal, till he had read and translated over the first book of Epistles chosen out by Sturmius, with a good piece of a Comedy of Terence also.

Source: Ascham, Roger. *The Scholemaster or Plaine and Perfite Way of Teaching Children to Understand, Write, and Speake the Latin Tong but Specially Purposed for the Private Bringing Up of Youth in Ientlemen and Noble Mens Houses, and Commodious Also for All Such as Have Forgot the Latin Tonge.* Aldersgate, England: John Day, 1573, pp. 1–3. Slightly adapted by Lawrence Morris.

TIMELINE   2000 1900 1800 1700 1600 1500 1400 1300 1200 1100 1000 900 800 700 600 500 400 300 200 100 1 BCE

What You Need to Know

This passage from Roger Ascham's *The Scholemaster or Plaine and Perfite Way of Teaching Children to Understand, Write, and Speake the Latin Tong [Tongue]* was published in 1573. Ascham was an English scholar of the mid-sixteenth century and is best known for being the tutor of Queen Elizabeth in her youth and for his writings on education.

Historians apply the term *Renaissance* to a period in Europe history, stretching from the latter years of the thirteenth century to the latter years of the sixteenth. The dates of its commencement vary, reflecting its gradual spread from its roots in the city-states of northern Italy to Northern Europe.

The name means "rebirth" in French and is meant to convey the sense of a renewal of humanistic art and culture after the long hiatus of the Middle Ages, when religion was the dominant filter through which people tried to understand themselves and their place in the universe. This simple definition, however, should be taken with a grain of salt, as the Renaissance, too, was marked by an intense religiosity.

Several elements characterized Renaissance thinking. These included a renewed emphasis on the individual; a revival of interest in the learning of ancient times; and an emphasis on humanistic and secular concerns as opposed to purely spiritual ones.

A Closer Look

Latin was the language of learning, government, and the church through the Middle Ages of European history, a legacy of the Roman Empire. As such, it was a living language, even if it was only read, spoken, and understood by an elite minority, who received their education in it from tutors and at school. Because it was in everyday use, it continued to evolve. But for purists, such as Roger Ascham, living Latin was a vulgar language.

Ascham was somewhat conservative for his time. In both English public schools of his day—public referring not to their funding but to the fact that they were open to all classes of boys (girls were excluded)—and among many private tutors there was a new emphasis in the Renaissance on humanistic teaching. As opposed to the largely theological subject matter of the Middle Ages, education in Renaissance England emphasized humanistic learning, that is, the teaching of the pre-Christian classics of ancient Greece and Rome. Teaching such classics was a way of introducing new subject matter as well, including history, science, and secular philosophy. In this excerpt from his *Scholemaster* (Schoolmaster), Ascham recommends that students go back to the true and pure Latin of ancient orators, such as Cicero. Only in this way could they truly appreciate the accomplishments of the ancient world.

1 100 200 300 400 500 600 700 800 900 1000 1100 1200 1300 1400 1500 1600 1700 1800 1900 2000 CE

2.12.11 Hunting Wild Boar

England
1576

Having described the hunting of an Hart, and all other deer according to my simple skill, I have thought good to set down here a little treatise of the hunting at the wild boar, and of his properties, although he ought not to be counted amongst the beasts of venerie [the hunt] which are chasable with hounds, for he is the proper pray of a mastiff and such-like dogs, for as much as he is a heavy beast, and of great force, trusting and affying himself in his tusks and his strength, and therefore will not lightly flee nor make chase before hounds, so that you cannot (by hunting of the boar) know that goodness or swiftness of them, and therewithal to confess a truth, I think it great pity to hunt (with a good kennel of hounds) at such chases, and that for such reasons and considerations as follow.

First, he is the only beast which can dispatch a hound at one blow, for though other beasts do bite, snatch, tear, or rend your hounds, yet there is hope of remedy if they be well attended; but if a boar do once strike your hound and light between the four quarters of him, you shall hardly see him escape, and therewithal this subtilty he hath, that if he be run with a good kennel of hounds, which he perceiveth hold in round and follow him hard, he will flee into the strongest thicket that he can find, to the end he may kill them at leisure one after another. . . .

You must set relays also, but that must be of the staunchest and best old hounds of the kennel, for if you should make your relays with young hounds, and such as are swift and rash, then when a boar is any thing before the rest of the hounds in chase, he might easily kill them in their fury, at their first coming in to him. . . . [T]he huntsmen must ride in unto him as secretly as they can without much noise, and when they be near him, let them cast round about the place where he standeth, and run upon him all at once, and it shall be hard if they give him not one scoth with a sword, or some wound with a boar-spear; and let them not strike low, for then they shall commonly hit him on the snout, because he watcheth to take all blows upon his tusks or thereabouts. But let them lift up their hands high, and strike right down, and let them beware that they strike not towards their horses, but that other way, for on that side that a boar feeleth himself hurt, he turneth head straightways whereby he might the sooner hurt or kill their horses, if they stroke towards them. And if they be in the plain, then let cast a cloak about their horses, and they may the better ride about the boar, and strike at him as they pass: but stay not long in a place. It is a certain thing experimented and found true, that if you hang bells upon collars and your hounds necks, a boar will not so soon strike at them, but flee endways before them, and seldom stand at Bay.

Source: Turberville, George. *The Noble Arte of Venerie or Hunting* (1576). Oxford: Clarendon Press, 1908, pp. 148–49, 157–59.

What You Need to Know

The accompanying excerpt comes from a 1576 guide titled *The Noble Arte of Venerie or Hunting,* written by English poet and hunting enthusiast George Turberville.

Hunting was the premier sport of aristocrats in the Middle Ages and early modern era of European history. But it was no mere pastime. Although the meat obtained would be a welcome addition to a feast, the prime purpose of boar hunting was to hone the martial skills and values the landed aristocracy so prized and depended on. These included horsemanship, the keeping of dogs, weapons handling, close-quarter combat, and personal courage.

So important was hunting to the aristocracy's larders and sense of themselves that they typically reserved large swathes of forest for their own personal use. As the population of Europe grew in the late Middle Ages and early modern era, big game such as boar became increasingly scarce outside of these reserves. Any peasant caught poaching on these lands met with severe punishment. This was particularly true for hunting boar, as such a formidable animal was seen as an adversary for nobles alone to kill. Among European game, it was the only game animal that could effectively fight back against its pursuers, sometimes to deadly effect.

A Closer Look

Although the boar is a progenitor and relative of the domesticated pig, it bears little resemblance to the docile farm animal. The wild boar (*Sus scrofa*), common across Europe in the Middle Ages and Renaissance and still found in more remote parts of the continent, could stretch up to six feet in length, stand nearly four feet high, and weigh upward of 600 pounds. With a mouth full of sharp teeth and four-inch tusks on its snout, boars could readily kill the dogs and even horses used to hunt them. They were even known to bring down men. Indeed, King Philip IV of France was killed in 1314 when his horse was charged by a boar.

Before the advent of portable and reliable firearms, boar hunting required close engagement with the dangerous animal, as this excerpt reveals. Boar hunting, as with most medieval pursuits, was a communal venture, as lords and their servants led teams of dogs in pursuit. Turberville advises much caution, particularly in the use of dogs. Since boar cannot run as fast as other game and, indeed, often stand their ground rather than flee, dogs are likely to gain their scent easily and come upon them quickly. But the dogs, unless of the large mastiff breed, were no match for a boar, which could singularly dispatch several of these highly trained and prized animals in a single encounter. As already mentioned, boars could also threaten the horses that carried the human hunters. To prevent this from occurring, Turberville advises participants to remain in constant motion to minimize the danger of a direct attack.

1   100   200   300   400   500   600   700   800   900   1000   1100   1200   1300   1400   1500   1600   1700   1800   1900   2000 CE

2.12.12 William Harrison's Description of England

England
1577

[T]here things . . . are grown to be very grevious unto them [copyholders], to wit: the enhancing of rents . . . ; the daily oppression of copyholders, whose lords seek to bring their poor tenants almost to plain servitude and misery, daily devising new means and seeking up all the old how to cut them shorter and shorter, doubling, trebling and now and then seven times increasing their fines, driving them also for every trifle to lose and forfeit their tenures (by whom the greatest part of the realm does stand and is maintained) to the end they may fleece them yet more, which is a lamentable hearing. The third thing they talk of is usury, a trade brought in by the Jews, now perfectly practiced almost by every Christian and so commonly that he is accounted but for a fool that does lend his money for nothing. . . .

[T]he inhabitants of many places of our country are devoured and eaten up and their houses either altogether pulled down or suffered to decay little by little, although sometimes a poor man peradventure does dwell in one of them, who, not being able to repair it, suffers it to fall down and thereto thinks himself very friendly dealt withal, if he may have an acre of ground assigned unto him whereon to keep a cow or wherein to set cabbages, radishes, parsnips, carrots, melons, pumpkins, or suchlike stuff, by which he and his poor household live as by their principal food, since they can do no better. And as for wheat bread, they eat it when they can reach unto the price of it, contenting themselves in the meantime with bread made of oats or barley: a poor estate, God wot!

Source: Harrison, William. *Harrison's Description of England in Shakspere's Youth*. Part I. Edited by Frederick Furnivall. London: N. Trübner and Co., 1877, pp. 241–242, 258–259.

What You Need to Know

The accompanying document is from William Harrison's *Description of England*, published in 1577, during the beginning of the Enclosure Movement, which would last into the eighteenth century. Harrison was a London-born, Cambridge-educated clergyman and antiquarian who spent years collecting documents and interviewing historians about life in Elizabethan England. In this excerpt, Harrison describes the misery associated with the Enclosure Movement.

During the long medieval era in English history, most rural peasants lived on lands owned by wealthy landlords. Some of these people were bound to the land as serfs and required to pay the landlord in kind or in labor. Others were free peasants who paid rents. By the fifteenth century, however, serfdom had largely disappeared in England.

Meanwhile, burgeoning trade across Europe meant an increasing demand for high-quality English wool, which went to feed the growing textile industries of northwestern continental Europe. In response, English landlords began to convert the lands farmed by peasants into pasturage for sheep. In addition, common pasturage lands were legally converted to private property for the feeding of the landlord's own flocks. This process was known as the Enclosure Movement because it enclosed lands once used communally.

The result was the displacement of thousands upon thousands of small farmers who were turned into landless peasants or forced to migrate to growing urban areas to look for work.

A Closer Look

After centuries of stagnation, England's population began to grow again in the sixteenth century, a result of rising prosperity and better agricultural techniques. At the same time, however, this growing population produced a demand for land, a demand exacerbated by the accelerating Enclosure Movement. The result was an inevitable rise in rents for so-called "copyholders," the descendants of medieval serfs who now rented their ever smaller plots of land from wealthy landholders. Harrision denounces the latter not only for raising rents but for using any "trifle" to drive copyholders from the land and for practicing usury, or the charging of excessive interest rates. This, he says, likens them to Jews, a despised group in Elizabethan England who, because of landowning and occupational restrictions, often had to make their living by lending out money. Barely able to survive, he says, tenant farmers were forced to live in houses that were falling down around them. Indeed, he says, lucky was he who was put out of his misery if his house fell down upon him.

1 100 200 300 400 500 600 700 800 900 1000 1100 1200 1300 1400 1500 1600 1700 1800 1900 2000 CE

2.12.13 Stephen Gosson's *The School of Abuse*

England
1579

In our assemblies at plays in London, you shall see such heaving, and shoving, such itching and shouldering to sit by women: such care for their garments, that they not be trod on: such eyes to their laps, that no chips light in them: such pillows to their backs, that they take no hurt: such masking in their ears, I know not what: such giving them pippins to pass the time: such playing at footsaunt [footsie] without cards: such tickling, such toying, such smiling, such winking, and such manning them home, when the sports are ended, that it is a right comedy to mark their behavior, to watch their conceits, as the cat for the mouse, and as good as a course at the game itself, to dog them a little, or follow aloof by the print of their feet, and so discover by slot where the deer takes soil. If this were as well noted as ill seen, or as openly punished as secretly practiced, I have no doubt but the cause would be seared to dry up the effect, and these pretty rabbits very cunningly ferreted from their burrows. For they that lack customers all the week, either because their haunt is unknown or the constables and officers of their parish watch them so narrowly that they dare not quetch, to celebrate the Sabbath flock to theaters, and there keep a general market of bawdry. Not that any filthiness indeed is committed within the compass of that ground, as was done in Rome but that every wanton and his paramour, every man and his mistress, every John and his Joan, every knave and his queen, are there first acquainted and cheapen the merchandise in that place, which they pay for elsewhere as they can agree.

Source: Gosson, Stephen. *The School of Abuse, 1579, and A Short Apologie of The School of Abuse, 1579*. Edited by Edward Arber. London: Alex Murray and Son, 1868, pp. 35–36.

What You Need to Know

This document comes Stephen Gosson's pamphlet *The School of Abuse*, published in 1579, roughly 10 years before Shakespeare wrote his first play, *Two Gentlemen of Verona*. Gosson himself was a playwright and actor; this dual role was typical of Elizabethan dramatists.

Many students of literature argue that the Elizabethan and Jacobean Age of the late sixteenth and early seventeenth centuries represented the pinnacle of dramatic arts in the English language. Dramatists writing and performing their work at the time included not only Shakespeare but Christopher Marlow, Francis Beaumont, John Fletcher, Thomas Middleton, and Thomas Kyd.

London and its immediate environs were dotted with more than two dozen performance venues, serving a population of just 200,000. Some of these venues were small, located in the courtyards of inns. Indeed, such courtyards represented the origins of theaters in late medieval and early modern England. But roughly half were great outdoor amphitheaters, of which Shakespeare's The Globe is the most famous, seating upward of 3,000 persons.

Dramas were *the* popular art form of the day, drawing people from all classes of society. One penny could buy standing room in the pit, while three pence bought a seat.

A Closer Look

To say that theater audiences in Elizabethan England were rowdy is an understatement. Unlike our own time, drama was not considered a high art, although the artistry of Elizabethan dramatists was second to none, but a popular form of entertainment, much like the movies today, except that nobody expected audiences to remain quiet. Indeed, performances were marked by catcalls and thrown objects, if the story or the actors, who were always men, did not live up to audience expectations. On the other hand, a particularly well-delivered soliloquy or sword fight would bring out shouts of "encore," which actors would indulge by reperforming the scene. The sheer cacophony and bedlam produced by an Elizabethan audience is captured in this excerpt.

On one level, *The School of Abuse* is simple satire, as Gosson likens audience members and their behavior to animals, a not surprising description for a playwright and actor whose own efforts may have not received the respect he felt they were due. But the pamphlet is also meant as chastisement. Gosson reflects the growing influence of Puritan religious ideas, when he chides his fellow Londoners who "celebrate the Sabbath" by "flock[ing] to theaters." Gosson would convert to Puritanism in the early 1580s and denounce sinful theater. When the Puritans gained political ascendance in the 1640s, they banned theater outright.

1 100 200 300 400 500 600 700 800 900 1000 1100 1200 1300 1400 1500 1600 1700 1800 1900 2000 CE

2.12.14 The Scottish Diet, Past and Present

Scotland
1580

In sleep they were competent, in meat and drink sober, and contented with such food as was ready at hand and prepared with little cost. Their bread consisted of such stuff as grew most readily on the ground, without all manner of sifting and boldting, whereby to please the palate; but baked up as it came from the mill without any curiosity, which is a great abasing of the force thereof unto our daily nourishment. The flesh whereon they chiefly fed, was either such as they got by hunting, wherein they took great delight, and which increased not a little their strength and nimbleness, or else cattle as they bred at home, whereof beef was accounted the principal, as it is yet in our days, though after another manner and far discrepant from the use and custom of other countries. . . . The common meat of our elders was fish, howbeit not only or so much for the plentie thereof, as for that our lands lay often waste and untilled, because of the great warres which they commonly had in hand. They brake also their fast early in the morning with some slander repast, and so continued without any other diet until suppertime, in which they had but one dish, whereby it came to pass, that their stomachs were never overcharged, nor their bones desirous of rest through the fullness of their bellies.

But how far we in these present days are swerved from the virtues and temperance of our elders, I believe there is no man so eloquent, nor indued with such utterance, as that he is able sufficiently to express. For whereas they gave their minds to doughtiness, we apply our selues to drunkenness; they had plenty with sufficiency, we have inordinate excess with superfluity; they were temperate, we effeminate; and so is the case now altered with us, that he which can devour and drink most, is the noblest man and most honest companion, and thereto hath no peer if he can once find the vein, though with his great travel to purvey himself of the plentifullest number of new fine and delicate dishes, and best provoke his stomach to receive the greatest quantity of them, though he never make due digestion of it.

Being thus drowned in our delicate gluttony, it is a world to see how we stuff ourselves both day and night, never ceasing to engorge and pour in, till our bellies be so full that we must needs depart. Certes it is not supposed meet that we should now content ourselves with breakfast and supper only, as our elders have done before, nor enough that we have added our dinners unto their aforesaid meals, but we must have thereto our beverages and rare suppers, so that small time is spared wherein to occupy ourselves in any godly exercise, sith almost the whole day and night do scarcely suffice for the filling of our paunches. . . .

In like sort they gad over all the world for sweet and pleasant spices, and drugs (provokers unto all lust and licentiousness of behaviour) as men that adventure their own lives to bring home poison and destruction unto their countrymen, as if the mind were not already sufficiently bereft of her image of the divinity, but must yet more be clogged and overladen with such a franked case.

Source: Boetius, Hector. "The Description of Scotland." In *Holinshed's Chronicles of England, Scotland, and Ireland*. Vol. V: Scotland. Ch. XIII. Translated by Raphael Holinshed. London: Johnson, 1808, pp. 22, 26.

What You Need to Know

This selection comes from a book titled *Historia Gentis Scotorum*, or *History of the Scottish People*, written by Scottish historian and philosopher Hector Boetius and published in 1527; Boetius was the Latinized version of Boyce—sometimes rendered Boise—the author's family name. Born in Dundee in 1465, Boetius was educated in Paris. During the Renaissance, there was a strong Scottish affinity with France and French culture.

Scotland, which comprises the northern third of the island of Britain, has been inhabited since the Paleolithic era. By the time of the Romans, who never fully conquered it, the land was home to various tribes who spoke early versions of Gaelic and other Celtic languages. Much of its medieval history was marked by conflicts among the landed nobles for supremacy and a long struggle to maintain their independence from English invaders from the south.

The Renaissance, or rediscovery of ancient learning and a new emphasis on humanism, came to Scotland late, but it deeply influenced both the intellectual and social life of the people. Among its effects was a rising sense of Scottish nationalism, as embodied by the Stewart monarchy. Marriage to the Tudor house, which had taken control of the English monarchy in the late fifteenth century, put the Stewarts on a path to inherit a unified crown for England and Scotland, but that never came to be. When the two countries were finally united in the early eighteenth century, it was under English tutelage.

A Closer Look

In this excerpt, Boetius compares the diet of the Scottish people past and present. Like the writings of many premodern historians, Boetius was not particularly effective in reconstructing the past. For the modern reader, his writing offers a clearer glimpse into his own time. Boetius was writing at a time when Scottish culture, at least among the elite, was becoming increasingly influenced by the sophisticated and, to some like Boetius, the indulgent customs and habits of continental gentry. Boetius is quite critical of the current luxuriousness of Scottish high society comparing it to the more austere but noble habits of the country's past.

Food provides him with the evidence he needs for this unflattering comparison. He describes the simple diet of his forbearers compared with the elaborate preparations, featuring all kinds of exotic spices, of his contemporaries. He also notes the prevalence of gluttony in his own time, as opposed to the "slander [slender] repast[s]" of the past, which has led to obesity and licentiousness, he argues.

1 100 200 300 400 500 600 700 800 900 1000 1100 1200 1300 1400 1500 1600 1700 1800 1900 2000 CE

2.12.15 In Defense of Drinking Irish Whiskey

Ireland
1584

The soil is low and waterish, including diverse little Islands, environed with lakes and marsh. Highest hills have standing pools on their tops. Inhabitants especially new come, are subject to distillations, rheums, and fluxes. For remedie whereof, they use an ordinary drink of *Aqua vitae*, being so qualified in the making, that it drieth more, and also inflameth less than other hot confections do. One Theoricus wrote a proper treatise of *Aqua vitae*, wherein he praiseth it unto the ninth degree. He distinguisheth three sorts thereof, *Simplex, Composita*, and *Perfectissima*. He declareth the simples and ingredients thereto belonging. He wisheth it to be taken as well before meat as after. It drieth up the breaking out of hands, and killeth the flesh worms, if you wash your hands therewith. It scoureth all scurf and scalds from the head, being therewith daily washed before meals. Being moderately taken (sayeth he) it sloweth age, in strengtheneth youth, it helpeth digestion, it cutteth phlegm, it abandoneth melancholie, it relisheth the heart, it lighteneth the mind, it quickeneth the spirits, it cureth the hydropsie, it healeth the strangurie, it pounceth the stone, it expelleth gravel, it puffeth away ventositie, it keepeth and preserveth the head from whirling, the eyes from dazzling, the tongue from lisping, the mouth from maffling, the teeth from chattering, and the throat from rattling; it keepeth the weasan from stifling, the stomach from wambling, and the heart from swelling, the belly from wirtching, the guts from rumbling, the hands from shivering, and the sinews from shrinking, the veins from crumpling, the bones from aching, and the marrow from soaking. Ulstadius also ascribeth thereto a singular praise, and would have it to burn being kindled, which he taketh to be a token to know the goodness thereof. And truly it is a sovereign liquor, if it be orderly taken.

Source: Stanihurst, Richard. "A Treatise Conteining a Plaine and Perfect Description of Ireland." In *Holinshed's Chronicles of England, Scotland, and Ireland*. Vol. VI: Ireland. Ch. II. London: Johnson, 1808, p. 8.

TIMELINE   2000 1900 1800 1700 1600 1500 1400 1300 1200 1100 1000 900 800 700 600 500 400 300 200 100 1 BCE

What You Need to Know

The accompanying document comes from *De Rebus in Hibernia Gestis*, or *Great Deeds in Ireland*, published in Antwerp in 1584. Its author is Richard Stanihurst. The son of a high official in the English-dominated Irish Parliament, the Anglo-Irish Stanihurst, though English-educated, was a long time defender of both Catholicism and the Catholic Irish.

The history of Ireland since the late Middle Ages has been defined, in part, by its relations to its dominant neighbor, England. Since the Norman invasion of the late twelfth century, the Irish have struggled against English hegemony, which took the form of English landlords occupying Irish lands and making Irish peasants work for—and pay rent to—them. The Reformation of the sixteenth century made things worse as English King Henry VIII attempted to impose his new Church of England on the island's devoutly Catholic population. In 1536, the Irish Parliament, which represented the island's English aristocracy, approved Henry VIII's decision to sever ties with Rome and give the king power over all ecclesiastical affairs. Catholic property was seized and the profits repatriated to England. The Catholic priesthood of Ireland then went underground, serving as the nucleus of not only religious dissent but also political opposition to English rule.

A Closer Look

In this excerpt, Stanihurst defends the use of Irish whiskey—the name comes from the Gaelic word *uisce beatha*, itself a bastardization of the Latin word for distilled liquor, *aqua vita*, or "water of life"—as a cure-all and a tonic, drunk to ward off the ills associated with Ireland's cold and wet climate.

But to ask an educated or upper-class Englishman in the sixteenth century his opinion of the Irish was to get an earful. The Irish, as far as they were concerned, were barbarians. There was even talk of exterminating them, although it was never acted on, partly because the cost to do so would have been too high.

One of the chief ways the English defined the Irish as inferior was in the latter's drinking habits. While the English imbibed beer and wine—and saw themselves as indulging moderately in the stuff—the Irish drank the much stronger whiskey and were seen as a nation of sots. Whiskey became a symbol of Ireland to the English. This view of the Irish would persist for centuries and was carried in the cultural baggage English immigrants brought to America.

1 100 200 300 400 500 600 700 800 900 1000 1100 1200 1300 1400 1500 1600 1700 1800 1900 2000 CE

2.12.16 Prescriptions for Treating and Preventing the Plague

England
1596

Plague and Pestilence

Herein are contained diverse and sundry good rules and easy Medicines, which are made with little charge, for the poorer sort of people, as well for the preservation of all people from the Plague before infection, as for the curing and ordering of them after such time as they shall be infected.

A Preservative by Correcting the Air in All Houses

Take *Rosemary* dryed, *Juniper, Bay-leaves*, or *Frankincense*, and cast the same upon the coals in a chafing-dish, and receive the fume or smoke thereof into your head. If you will, put a little *Lavender* or *Sage* that is dryed, into the fire with the rest; it will do much good. . . .

A Preservative Against the Plague

Take a handfull of *Herb-grace*, otherwise called *Rue*, a handful of *Elder-leaves*, a handful of red *Sage*, and a handful of red *Bramble-leaves*, and stamp them well together, and strain them through a fine linen cloth, with a quart of white *Wine*, then take a quantity of *Case Ginger*, and mingle it with them, and drink a good draught thereof both morning and evening for the space of nine days together, and by God's grace it will preserve you.

An Excellent Good Drink to be Taken Every Morning for a Preservative Against the Plague, and for to Avoid Infection

Take a handful of *Winter-Savery*, and boil the same in a quart of good *wine-Vinegar*, with a spoonful of *Grains* being very fine beaten, and put into the same, then put into it a quantity of fine *Sugar*, and so drink a good draught thereof every morning fasting.

A Special Preservative Against the Plague

Take five spoonfuls of *wine-Vinegar*, three spoonfuls of fair *running-Water*, half a spoonful of *Treacle of Jene*, and of *Bole armeniac* as much as a small nut, being beaten to powder, and drink this every morning and every evening. *Proved by M. Knight of Andover*.

Take vi leaves of *Sorrel*, and wash them with *Water* and *Vinegar*, and let them lie to steep in the said *Water* and *Vinegar* a good while, then eat them fasting and keep in your mouth and chew now or then either *Stewall*, or the root of *Angelica*, or a little *Cinnamon*, for any of these is marvellous good.

Medicines to Be Used After Infection Taken

Forasmuch as the greatest cause of the Plague doth stand rather in poison, than in any putrefaction of humors, as other Agues do, the chiefest way is to move much sweating, and to defend the hart by some cordial thing.

Source: A. T. *A Rich Storehouse or Treasury for the Diseased*. London: Thomas Purfoot and Ralph Blower, 1596.

What You Need to Know

This excerpt comes from a 1596 book titled *A Rich Storehouse or Treasurey for the Diseased*, penned by an author whom we only know by the initials "A.T."

In the mid-fourteenth century, the bubonic plague struck Europe with a vengeance, killing off roughly one-third of the population or more, causing untold unsuffering and forever changing the course of the continent's history. But while that epidemic quickly died out, the Plague continued to return to Europe, although in far less virulent forms, well into the modern era, including a major outbreak that spread from Spain to much of Europe in the 1590s. One Elizabethan era archivist recorded 10,675 deaths from the plague in London alone from December 1592 to December 1593, or roughly five percent of the population.

As in its earlier manifestation, the plague of the 1590s was a gruesome illness, which caused high fever, delirium, and painful swelling of the armpits, legs, neck, and groin. Its swelling of the lymph nodes often caused subcutaneous bleeding, which resulted in a darkening of skin color, hence the disease's popular name, the Black Death.

A Closer Look

In the section on the plague, A.T. recommends the burning of strong smelling plants such as bay leaf and lavender and the consumption of liquids infused with herbs. Notably, the author has much more to say on preventative measures. As for "medicines to be used after infection taken," his recommendations are vague. A.T. seems to have understood the limited efficacy of his own medical understanding, and that of his era's.

Since the late nineteenth century, scientists have understood that the Plague is a bacterial disease, carried by the fleas living on rats. Increased sea and land trade in the late Middle Ages and Renaissance allowed the infection to spread rapidly to—and around—Europe. Once it arrived, it could also be spread directly from human to human.

But the people of the time had no idea of any of this because the germ theory of disease would not be discovered until centuries later. Instead, they believed that epidemic diseases, such as the plague, were caused by a "vicious property in the air," which could be recognized by its smell. Not surprisingly, many of the preventative measures against the plague involved replacing bad odors with sweet ones. This was not an entirely useless measure, although its positive effect on stopping the spread of the disease was unintentional. Replacing bad odors with good ones often meant removing garbage, a natural home to rats and the infected fleas they carried.

1 100 200 300 400 500 600 700 800 900 1000 1100 1200 1300 1400 1500 1600 1700 1800 1900 2000 CE

2.12.17 English Pocket Watch

London, England
Seventeenth Century

Credit: DeAgostini/Getty Images

What You Need to Know

This pocket watch was manufactured by the firm of Knotford of London, sometime in the seventeenth century.

European intellectual thought in the seventeenth century was marked by a fundamental contradiction. On the one hand, the century witnessed a great struggle over theological issues and the role of the state in religious affairs. On the other, it was marked by great strides in the field of science. Indeed, historians refer to the achievements of the era as the "scientific revolution," that is, the systematic attempt to explain the natural world through hypothesis, experimentation, and documentation.

England was central to this new approach to understanding the universe, and no one was more crucial to this progress than Isaac Newton, whose laws of physics are still used to explain much about gravity and light. But Newton and others could not have achieved their breakthroughs without improvements in instrumentation, of which accurate timepieces were among the most important.

A Closer Look

Until the spread of the wristwatch in the early twentieth century, most people who carried timepieces carried pocket watches. In addition, one should note the fact that this timepiece only has an hour hand; due to the complicated mechanics involved, minute hands were not added to watches until near the end of the seventeenth century.

Perhaps the most important breakthrough in timekeeping before the development of electronic instrumentation in the twentieth century, was the invention of mechanical timepieces. Pendulum-operated clocks date back to fourteenth-century Europe. But these were, by necessity, bulky things. It was not until the fifteenth century invention of the mainspring—that is, a spiral torsion spring which stores the energy generated by turning a knob and then releases that energy slowly by turning gears, which then turn hands—that it was possible to miniaturize timepieces to a size that could be carried on one's person.

The widespread use of timepieces changed the way people perceived time and made the need for knowing the exact time and time's passage ever more crucial. In the commercial economy that was England in the seventeenth century, time became a commodity as, increasingly, labor was paid by a set unit of time. A growing transportation infrastructure of roads and coach routes increased the need for scheduling. Meanwhile, the contemporary scientific revolution required ever more precise ways to measure time for experimentation and astronomical observation. In short, the old and imprecise ways of measuring time, based on the sun or primitive implements, such as hourglasses, suitable for the slow rhythms of a prescientific, agricultural age were no longer sufficient.

1 100 200 300 400 500 600 700 800 900 1000 1100 1200 1300 1400 1500 1600 1700 1800 1900 2000 CE

2.12.18 Wine or Beer Mug from England

Staffordshire, England
Seventeenth Century

Credit: DeAgostini/Getty Images

What You Need to Know

The ceramic drinking mug shown here, edged in metal, was manufactured in Staffordshire, England, sometime in the seventeenth century. It is not made of anything precious—the metal is probably pewter, an alloy then made of tin and lead—nor does it feature any great artistry. Thus, it was probably used by peasants or middle-class drinkers, perhaps at home or in a public house, or pub.

English men and women of the seventeenth century drank an enormous amount of alcohol. Sailors in the English navy, for instance, were given a ration of one gallon of beer daily, although it should be remembered that the alcoholic content of beer in those days was but a fraction of what it is today. There was little stigma around social drinking. Even the Puritans, who were sharply critical of sensual indulgences of all kinds, were avid drinkers. Not only was drinking considered a normal part of social life—even young persons indulged in it—but it was considered good for the health, which indeed it could be. Liquids with alcoholic content were naturally lower in bacteria than water from polluted sources.

Most ordinary English men and women drank beer. The distillation process for whisky had not yet been perfected so the drink had a harsh tone to it. While wine, having to be imported from continental Europe, was more expensive, increased trade brought its price down significantly over the course of the century.

A Closer Look

Along with consuming of large quantities of alcoholic beverages, English people of means of the seventeenth century also indulged their palates with a growing variety of foods, many of them imports from the mainland Europe. Of particular popularity were foods and methods of food preparation from France, including new kinds of cheeses, sausages, and cured items, such as capers and olives. Fancy French recipes for coulis, roux, ragouts and fricassés—such dishes were known as "kickshaws," after the French word *quelquechose*, literally, "something"—were prepared for ever more demanding diners by chefs imported from the Continent by wealthier merchant and aristocratic families. Continental chefs and visitors, as well as visits by English persons to the mainland, eased old English taboos against eating fresh fruit and vegetables, which had previously been considered unhealthy.

1 100 200 300 400 500 600 700 800 900 1000 1100 1200 1300 1400 1500 1600 1700 1800 1900 2000 CE

2.12.19 Dancing in Elizabethan England

England
1600

Taking advantage of my 3 miles that I had danced the day before, this Wednesday morning I tripped it to Sudbury; whither came to see a very kind Gentleman, Master Foskew, that had before traveled on foot from London to Berwick, who giving me good counsel to observe temperate diet for my health, and other advise to be careful of my company, besides his liberal entertainment, departed, leaving me much indebted to his love.

In this town of Sudbury, there came a lusty tall fellow, a butcher by his profession, that would in a Morris keep me company to Bury: I being glad of his friendly offer, gave him thanks, and forward we did set: but ere we had measured half a mile of our way, he gave me over in the plain field, protesting, that if he might get a 100 pound, he would not hold out with me; for indeed my pace in dancing is not ordinary.

As he and I were parting, a lusty Country lass being among the people, called him faint hearted lout: saying, "if I had begun to dance, I would have held out one mile though it had cost my life." At which words many laughed. "Nay," said she, "if the Dancer will lend me a leash of his bells, I'll venture to tread one mile with him myself." I looked upon her, saw mirth in her eyes, heard boldness in her words, and beheld her ready to tuck up her russet petticoat, I fitted her with bells: which she merrily taking, garnished her thick short legs, and with a smooth brow bade the Taberer begin. The Drum struck, forward marched I with my merry Maid Marian: who shook her fat sides: and footed it merrily to Melford, being a long mile. There parting with her, I gave her (besides her skinfull of drink) an English crown to buy more drink, for good wench she was in a piteous heat: my kindness she requited with dropping some dozen of short curtsies, and bidding God bless the Dancer, I bad her adieu: and to give her her due, she had a good ear, danced truly, and we parted friendly. But ere I part with her, a good fellow my friend, having writ an odd Rime of her, I will make bold to set it down.

A Country Lasse browne as a berry,
Blith of blee in heart as merry,
Cheekes well fed and sides well larded,
Euery bone with fat flesh guarded,
Meeting merry Kemp by chaunce,
Was Marrian in his Morrice daunce.
Her stump legs with bels were garnisht,
Her browne browes with sweating varnish[t];
Her browne hips when she was lag,
To win her ground, went swig a swag,
Which to see all that came after,
Were repleate with mirthfull laughter.
Yet she thumped it on her way,
With a sportly hey de gay,
At a mile her daunce she ended,
Kindly paide and well commended.

Source: Kempe, William. *Kempe's Nine Daies Wonder: Performed in a Daunce from London to Norwich*. Edited by Alexander Dyce. London: Printed for the Camden Society by John Bowyer Nichols, 1840, pp. 9–11.

What You Need to Know

This excerpt comes from popular actor William Kempe's account of a dancing journey, titled *Nine Daies [Days] Wonder*, he took across southern England in 1600.

English popular culture at the beginning of the seventeenth century was vibrant and diverse. A new world of exotic lands and ideas was opening up to Englishmen, as literacy spread from the gentry and merchant classes to more and more of the working classes and better off peasantry. Attending theater was among the most popular pastimes of urban life in the Elizabethan Age, but so were other spectator events, such as boat and horse racing as well as activities modern readers would find unnecessarily cruel. These included cockfighting and bull and bear baiting, in which these animals would be tied to poles and then attacked by dogs trained to the task. Participatory sports included bowling, tennis, shuttlecock (badminton), and pale maille, a game much like modern croquet. Also indulged in were cards and board games, such as chess, draughts (checkers), and a now archaic game named fox and goose.

A Closer Look

It is indeed an amusing account, capturing all of the bawdiness and ribaldry that was Elizabethan popular culture. At one point, he writes of meeting a "lusty Country lass" whom he buys a drink for.

Folk dancing was yet another popular pastime in Elizabethan England. Among the most popular of these dance forms was the Morris dance, typically performed in groups who executed rhythmic steps punctuated by the ringing of the bells tied to pads around their legs. The dance dates from the mid-fifteenth century and was considered unusual when first introduced in England, hence the name Morris, a derivative of Moorish. Living in faraway North Africa and Spain, Moors were seen as very exotic by the English. Originally, Morris dances were performed in courtly settings but, by the mid-1500s, were popular among ordinary folk.

Kempe's marathon dance, which lasted nine days, took him from London to Norwich, a town near the eastern coast of England. Kempe was a popular clown and actor of the 1590s, who performed comic roles in many of Shakespeare's plays. Indeed, it is said that the bard wrote some of these roles, such as Dogberry in *Much Ado about Nothing* and Bottom in *Midsummer Night's Dream*, specifically for Kempe, who was also famous for his humorous song-and-dance sketches, known as jigs.

1 100 200 300 400 500 600 700 800 900 1000 1100 1200 1300 1400 1500 1600 1700 1800 1900 2000 CE

2.12.20 English Act for the Relief of the Poor

London, England
1601

Be it enacted by the authority of this present parliament that the churchwardens of every parish, and four, three or two substantial householders there as shall be thought meet, having respect to the apportion and greatness of the same parish or parishes, to be nominated yearly in Easter week or within one month after Easter, under the hand and seal of two or more justices of the peace in the same county, whereof one to be of the quorum, dwelling in or near the same parish or division where the same parish doth lie, shall be called overseers of the poor of the same parish: and they or the greater part of them shall take order from time to time, by and with the consent of two or more such justices of peace as is aforesaid, for setting to work of the children of all such whose parents shall not by the said churchwardens and overseers or the greater part of them be thought able to keep and maintain their children; and also for setting to work all such persons married or unmarried having no means to maintain them, [or] use no ordinary and daily trade of life to get their living by; and also to raise weekly or otherwise, by taxation of every inhabitant parson, vicar and other, and of every occupier of lands, houses, tithes impropriate or propriations of tithes, coal mines or saleable underwoods, in the said parish, in such competent sum and sums of money as they shall think fit, a convenient stock of flax, hemp, wool, thread, iron and other necessary ware and stuff to set the poor on work, and also competent sums of money for and towards the necessary relief of the lame, impotent, old, blind and such other among them being poor and not able to work, and also for the putting out of such children to be apprentices, to be gathered out of the same parish according to the ability of the same parish; and to do and execute all other things as well for the disposing of the said stock as otherwise concerning the premises as to them shall seem convenient: which said churchwardens and overseers so to be nominated, or such of them as shall not be let by sickness or other just excuse to be allowed by two such justices of peace or more as aforesaid, shall meet together at the least once every month in the church of the said parish, upon the Sunday in the afternoon after Divine Service, there to consider of some good course to be taken and of some meet order to be set down in the premises, and shall within four days after the end of their year and after other overseers nominated as aforesaid, make and yield up to such two justices of peace as is aforesaid a true and perfect account of all sums of money by them received, or rated and assessed and not received, and also of such stock as shall be in their hands or in the hands of any of the poor to work, and of all other things concerning their said office; and such sum or sums of money as shall be in their hands shall pay and deliver over to the said churchwardens and overseers newly nominated and appointed as aforesaid. . . .

Source: Bland, A. E., P. A. Brown, and R. H. Tawney, eds. *English Economic History: Select Documents*. New York: Macmillan Company, 1919, pp. 380–381.

TIMELINE   2000 1900 1800 1700 1600 1500 1400 1300 1200 1100 1000 900 800 700 600 500 400 300 200 100 1 BCE

What You Need to Know

This selection comes from the Act for the Relief of the Poor, passed by Parliament in 1601.

England in the Tudor Era, from 1485 through 1603, was a country undergoing tumultuous and disruptive economic change, both in the cities and the countryside. While England ultimately emerged from these years a more prosperous nation, the growth had its victims—peasants driven from the land and forced to wander the countryside and cities in search of housing, sustenance, and work. There were a host of factors causing this problem. Population growth in the countryside was exacerbated by landlords displacing peasants from the land to raise sheep; pasturage required far less labor than the raising of crops. In addition, the old feudal system, in which lords took care of the peasantry in exchange for a portion of the latter's crop and labor, was breaking down. Precious metals flooding into Europe from the recent Spanish conquest of the Americas was driving up prices and rents.

A Closer Look

The Act calls for the raising of taxes at the local level, which would be used by a committee of church wardens and "substantial householders," that is, property owners, to put poor people, including children, to work. Specifically, the committees were enjoined to purchase various raw materials—including flax, hemp, wool, and irons—as well as tools, to be used in the making of various saleable goods. At the same time, the law called for direct monetary relief to those unable to work, including the "lame, impotent, old, and such other among them [the landless] being poor and not able to work."

The growth in impoverished and landless tenants alarmed authorities and better off members of English society. Social order, they felt, was threatened by the large numbers of "masterless" persons, who were no longer subject to the authority of their social superiors. And, being virtually propertyless, they had little to lose by engaging in crime and social unrest. The security of the nation, many felt, was in grave danger.

Parliament responded to this situation by passing a number of so-called poor laws over the course of the fifteenth and early sixteenth centuries. The purpose of the laws was twofold: to provide aid to the poor but also to keep them under a modicum of state control. Indeed, the poor laws represented a major shift in social policy. Before these laws were instituted, charity was largely the purview of the church; now it was a state affair as well.

1 100 200 300 400 500 600 700 800 900 1000 1100 1200 1300 1400 1500 1600 1700 1800 1900 2000 CE

Credit: DeAgostini/Getty Images

What You Need to Know

This baroque-era guitar from 1624 comes from the workshop of an Italian *liutaio*, or lutemaker, named Mango Longo.

In creating a chronology for European cultural history, scholars generally refer to the early seventeenth century as marking the transition from the Renaissance to the baroque era. Originally a derogatory term, derived from the word for a misshapen pearl in various Romantic languages, baroque was first used to describe the highly ornate architectural style of the era, which detractors compared unfavorably to the strict adherence to classical forms of Renaissance builders.

Elaborate ornamentation, as well as expressive dissonance, was also characteristic of baroque music, as best exemplified by the German composer Johann Sebastian Bach. Bach was in the employ of a prince, as were many lesser composers of his time. The princes and monarchs of the era competed to have the most glorious courts, and musicians were critical to this. The baroque era is also notable for its musical innovation. The opera was invented during this period, while the instrumental concerto first achieved its place as the dominant orchestral composition.

A Closer Look

Guitars are stringed instruments, consisting of a hollow sound box and a long, fretted neck. Strings, held by keys at the top of the neck, descend to near the base of the sound box, where they are held in place by a bar. While similar instruments have existed in the West since ancient times, the origins of the modern guitar go back to fifteenth-century Spain. At the time, the country was divided between a Christian north and a Moorish south, with much cultural interaction between the two. The guitar probably derived from an Arabic instrument known as an *oud*, itself a variation on Indian instruments. Indeed, the word *tar* in Sanskrit means "string," and may be the origin of the term "guitar."

Early guitars typically featured four or five strings; the one shown here has five. By the end of the seventeenth century, however, most guitars featured the modern configuration of six strings. Nevertheless, Baroque era guitars differed significantly in two ways from the guitars we know today: they were both smaller and produced a quieter and more delicate sound. As such, contemporaries considered them ideal for female musicians.

Although popular in Spain, the guitar remained incidental to most European popular and sacred music through the Renaissance and baroque eras. The plucked, stringed instrument of choice was the lute, with its shorter neck and angled head. Both guitars and lutes were often to be found in the homes of middle- and upper-class families and were often played by girls and women. They were considered more appropriate for feminine physiques and manners than keyboard, wind, and string instruments played with bows. Much of the music written for them was also of a more feminine nature, as understood at the time, with love ballads figuring prominently in the repertoire.

1 100 200 300 400 500 600 700 800 900 1000 1100 1200 1300 1400 1500 1600 1700 1800 1900 2000 CE

2.12.22 Sinful Clothes Worn by English Women

England
1631

First, when any one weareth *Apparel* above their degree, exceeding their estate in precious attire. Whence it is that *Gregory* sayeth, "There be some who are of opinion, that the wearing of precious or sumptuous *Apparel* is no sin, which, if it were no fault, the divine Word would never have so punctually expressed, nor historically related, how the *Rich man*, who was tormented in hell, was clothed with Purple and Silk. . . ."

The second point reprehensible is, *Softness* or *Delicacy* of *Apparel:* Soft Clothes introduce soft minds. Delicacy in the *habit*, begets an *effeminacy* in the *heart. John the Baptist*, who was sanctified in his mother's womb, wore sharp and rough garments. Whence we are taught, that the true servant of God is not to wear garments for beauty or delight, but to cover his nakedness; not for State or Curiosity, but necessity and convenience. . . .

The third thing reproveable is, *foreign Fashions:* When we desire nothing more than to bring in some Outlandish habit different from our own, in which respect (so Apishly-antic is man) it becomes more affected than our own. Against such the Lord threatneth, "I will visit the Princes and the Kings' children, and all such as are clothed with strange Apparel." Which "strange Apparell" is after diverse fashions and inventions, wholly unknown to our Ancestors. Which may appear sufficiently to such, who within this 30, or 40, or 60 years never saw such cutting, carving, nor indenting as they now see. . . .

The fourth thing reproveable is, *Superfluity of Apparell*, expressed in these three particulars: first, in those who have diverse changes and suits of Clothes; who had rather have their garments eaten by moths, than they should cover the poor members of Christ. The naked cry, the needy cry, and shriekingly complain unto us, how they miserably labour and languish of hunger and cold. What avails it them that we have such changes of raiments neatly plaited and folded; rather than we will supply them, they must be starved? How do such rich Moth-worms observe the Doctrine of Christ, when hesayeth in his Gospel, *"He that hath two Coats let him give one to him that hath none"*?

Secondly, we are to consider the *Superfluity* of such who will have long garments, purposely to seem greater: yet, which of these can add one cubit to his stature? This puts me in remembrance of a conceited story which I have sometimes heard, of a diminutive Gentleman, who demanding of his Tailor, what yards of Satin would make him a Suit, being answered far short in number of what he expected: with great indignation replied,

"Such an one of the *Guard* to my knowledge had thrice as much for a Suite, and I will second him." Which his Tailor with small importunacy condescended to, making a *Gargantuan's Suite* for this *Ounce of man's flesh*, reserving to himself a large portion of shreds, purposely to form a fitter proportion for his *Ganymede* shape.

Source: Brathwaite, Richard. *The English Gentlewoman, Drawn Out to the Full Body: Expressing What Habilliments Doe Best Attire Her, What Ornaments Doe Best Adorn Her, What Complements Doe Best Accomplish Her*. London: B. Alsop and T. Fawcet, 1631, pp. 13–16.

TIMELINE   2000 1900 1800 1700 1600 1500 1400 1300 1200 1100 1000 900 800 700 600 500 400 300 200 100 1 BCE

What You Need to Know

Excerpted here is *The English Gentlewoman*, a treatise on self-presentation by the poet Richard Braithwaite, published in 1631. In it, the social critic has a lot to say—almost all negative—about the way the English of his day dressed.

The old expression "clothes make the man" meaning, in part, that others see us in the way we dress ourselves, applied even more to early modern England that it does to us today; although outward appearances still speak of inner character to us, this was even more the case then. People were judged by their class and their ranking within the social hierarchy, and clothes reflected that.

Through the Middle Ages, the sheer poverty of the vast majority of Englishmen, as well as the tininess of the mercantile and professional middle class, meant that only the aristocracy were able to wear fancy clothes. Thus, it was simple to tell who belonged to what class by their dress. But with burgeoning trade, prosperity, and a growing middle-class population, that association of dress to social position was no longer so easy to discern, creating much anxiety among the ruling classes of England. And that is Brathwaite's chief criticism—the new tendency of people to dress above their "degree" or station in life.

A Closer Look

The accelerating pace of life, growing urbanization, and new prosperity produced a more rapidly changing fashion scene in seventeenth-century England than had ever been the case before. Much of this reflected increased contact with countries of the European mainland and their fashions. Indeed, Brathwaite is highly critical of "outlandish" clothes, using the term in its original sense of being outside the land, or foreign, presumably because they undermine supposedly stolid English values of restraint and modesty.

Changing fashion tastes evinced themselves not so much in the basic clothes people wore; those remained largely the same—doublets (short, close-fitting jackets), breeches (short pants) and hose for men; long gowns for women. But it was in the way those clothes were styled. There was an increasing tendency toward softer and more comfortable fabrics. Indeed, one of his chief criticisms is directed to the wearing of "soft" and "delicate" clothing, which he sees as evidence of the decadence of contemporaries against the virtue and dignity of the people of the past. Soft clothing, he says, makes for "soft minds" and "effeminacy in the heart," in other words a weak will associated with the inferior gender.

There was also a new appreciation for ease of movement, and clothes reflected that. Padding was removed and waistlines for bodices and doublets raised. Constrictive ruffs around the neck disappeared, and sleeves were shortened. Despite such changes, Brathwaite nevertheless criticizes his fellow countrymen and women for wearing excesses of cloth.

1 100 200 300 400 500 600 700 800 900 1000 1100 1200 1300 1400 1500 1600 1700 1800 1900 2000 CE

2.12.23 Accusation of Heresy during the Spanish Inquisition

Spain
1635

I, Doctor Francisco Gregorio, Fiscal of this Holy Office, appear before your Excellency, and accuse criminally, Pedro Ginesta, brazier, a native of the village of Orliach, bishopric of St. Flor, in Ubernia, in the kingdom of France, resident in the principality, attached to the secret prison of the Inquisition, and now present—stating that the said person, being a baptized and confirmed Christian, and enjoying the graces and benefits which such persons do and ought to enjoy, not having the fear of God before his eyes, but regardless of his own conscience and the justice administered by your Excellency, has committed offenses against our Holy Faith, by saying and performing things which savor of the heretic Luther, in the manner following.

The said prisoner being in a certain part of the village of Semiana in the bishopric of Urgel on the fast of St. Bartholomew last, in company with another certain person, did cause to be cooked a dish of bacon and onions; and, being reminded to take heed, for it was a fast, and such food was forbidden, replied by ordering the meat to be cooked, and in fact when the said meat was cooked, did proceed to eat the same, in company with the other person mentioned, and notwithstanding he was informed by another person while eating, that it was St. Bartholomew's day, and a fast, at which time it was not allowed to each such food, the said prisoner continued to eat the remainder of the said bacon.

Furthermore, the said prisoner being of a nation infected with heresy, it is presumed that he has on many other occasions eaten flesh on forbidden days, after the manner of the sect of Luther, and committed many other offenses against our Holy Faith, besides knowing that others have committed the same offenses, and the said prisoner having been admonished by your Excellency to declare the truth, has not done it, but has perjured himself.

For which reasons I entreat your Excellency that full evidence being given to my accusation, or to such a part of the same as shall suffice for the ends of justice in the decision of the present case, your Excellency will declare my accusation proved, and the said Pedro Ginesta guilty of the above offenses, imposing upon him the heaviest punishments fixed by statute upon the said offenses, and ordering them to be executed upon his person and goods, as a penalty to himself and an example to others; and that the prisoner, if it be found necessary, be put to the torture, and that the same be repeated till he confess the whole truth both of himself and others.

And I formally swear that I do not bring this accusation out of malice, but solely to accomplish the ends of justice, which I now request at your hands.

Source: Inquisidor General de España. *Records of the Spanish Inquisition*. Translated by Samuel Kettell. Edited by Andrew Dickson White. Boston: Samuel G. Goodrich, 1828, pp. 26–28.

TIMELINE   2000 1900 1800 1700 1600 1500 1400 1300 1200 1100 1000 900 800 700 600 500 400 300 200 100 1 BCE

What You Need to Know

This accusation was leveled by an official of the Inquisition in 1635 against a man accused of violating Catholic rules against eating pork on fast days.

Christian Spain in the fifteenth, sixteenth, and seventeenth centuries was not a religiously tolerant place. Pogroms, or officially sanctioned massacres of Jews, had led many of the latter to convert to Catholicism. While some of these so-called *conversos* achieved high government office or commercial success, they remained under suspicion. In 1492, the same year that the Christian monarchs of Spain conquered the last Moorish outpost at Granada, the remaining Jews who refused to convert were ordered out of the kingdom. In the sixteenth century, the conquered Muslim Moors still living in Spain were also ordered to convert or leave.

Although many of the former Jewish *conversos* in Christian Spain accepted their new faith, others were suspected of having secretly returned to their old one. To root out these backsliders, the profoundly pious Ferdinand and Isabella asked—and received—permission from Pope Sixtus IV to reestablish the Inquisition in 1478, a medieval era judicial procedure for punishing heretics.

Technically, the Inquisition was a religious institution, but in fact it was controlled by the Spanish monarchy, who often used it to root out opposition to the government, which, in this deeply pious time, often took the form of religious dissent. Although at first largely aimed at formerly Jewish *conversos*, some of whom served in high government office, the Inquisition soon directed its efforts toward Muslim *conversos*, and after the Reformation of the sixteenth century, Protestant "heretics" as well.

A Closer Look

The inquisition, whose mission was to root out heresy, was a response to the Protestant Reformation sweeping Northern Europe. At first glance, the man's "crime" seems rather insignificant until one remembers that Protestants typically did not feel obliged to obey church-mandated fasting days. Also notable is the fact that the accused hailed from France, where there was a significant minority of Protestants known as Huguenots.

After charges were leveled by Inquisitions officials, often on the basis of anonymous accusations from neighbors and acquaintances, the case was studied by *calificadores*, or qualifiers, to see if heresy had in fact been committed. Meanwhile, the accused was placed in prison until his or her trial could be heard. This could be a matter of weeks or could last years, and often served as a form of preventive detention—that is, an informal sentence of imprisonment.

The trial itself was more of an interrogation than an objective search for the truth. Although the defendant was given counsel, that person was usually a member of Inquisition judiciary who would typically advise the accused to confess. Both before and during, torture might be employed to exact a confession of heresy. Finally, the whole process was shrouded in secrecy; so as to better exact admissions of guilt, the accused was kept isolated and was not allowed to attend mass or receive the sacraments.

1 100 200 300 400 500 600 700 800 900 1000 1100 1200 1300 1400 1500 1600 1700 1800 1900 2000 CE

2.12.24 Pastimes of the English Aristocracy

England
1656

Their practice was, when they met together, to exercise themselves with fencing, wrestling, shooting, and such like exercises, for I observed they did seldom hawk or hunt, and very seldom or never dance, or play music, saying it was too effeminate for masculine spirits; neither had they skill, or did use to play, for ought I could hear, at cards or dice, or the like games, nor given to any vice, as I did know, unless to love a mistress were a crime, not that I know any they had, but what report did say, and usually reports are false, at least exceed the truth.

As for the pastimes of my sisters when they are in the country, it was to read, work, walk, and discourse with each other; for though two of my three brothers were married, my brother the Lord Lucas to a virtuous and beautiful lady, daughter to Sir Christopher Nevile, son of the Lord Abergavenny, and my brother Sir Thomas Lucas to a virtuous lady of an ancient family, one Sir John Byron's daughter; likewise, three of my four sisters, one married Sir Peter Killegrew, the other Sir William Walter, the third Sir Edmund Pye, the fourth as yet unmarried, yet most of them lived with my mother, especially when she was at her country-house, living most commonly at London half the year, which is the Metropolitan city of England: but when they were at London, they were dispersed into several houses of their own, yet for the most part they met every day, feasting each other like Job's children. But this unnatural war came like a whirlwind, which felled down their houses, where some in the wars were crushed to death, as my youngest brother Sir Charles Lucas, and my brother Sir Thomas Lucas; and though my brother Sir Thomas Lucas died not immediately of his wounds, yet a wound he received on his head in Ireland shortened his life.

But to rehearse their recreations. Their customs were in winter time to go sometimes to plays, or to ride in their coaches about the streets to see the concourse and recourse of people; and in the spring time to visit the Spring-garden, Hyde-park, and the like places; and sometimes they would have music, and sup in barges upon the water; these harmless recreations they would pass their time away with; for I observed, they did seldom make visits, nor never went abroad with strangers in their company, but only themselves in a flock together agreeing so well, that there seemed but one mind amongst them: and not only my own brothers and sisters agreed so, but my brothers and sisters in law, and their children, although but young, had the like agreeable natures and affectionable dispositions: for to my best remembrance I do not know that ever they did fall out, or had any angry or unkind disputes. Likewise, I did observe, that my sisters were so far from mingling themselves with any other company, that they had no familiar conversation or intimate acquaintance with the families to which each other were linked to by marriage, the family of the one being as great strangers to the rest of my brothers and sisters, as the family of the other.

Source: Cavendish, Margaret, Duchess of Newcastle. *A True Relation of the Birth, Breeding, and Life of Margaret Cavendish, Duchess of Newcastle*. Edited by Sir Egerton Brydges. Kent, Eng.: Johnson and Warwick, 1814, pp. 7–10.

What You Need to Know

The accompanying passage comes from the 1656 autobiography of Margaret Cavendish, *A True Relation of My Birth, Breeding, and Life.*

Early modern England of the seventeenth century was, like most cultures of its day, a highly patriarchal one. Men not only took care of public affairs but stood at the top of a household hierarchy, making decisions for their wives and children and for their servants, if they were wealthy enough to have them. This, virtually all members of society accepted, was the God-given order of things.

Women were expected to be obedient to men, reserved in temperament, modest in wants and self-presentation, and above all, chaste. Numerous publications of the time, most of them penned by men and aimed at an upper-class readership, underlined these attributes, suggesting that women who fell afoul of social taboos against immodesty and assertiveness were somehow not entirely feminine. Still, not all women accepted or lived by these standards. Indeed, some historians speak of the seventeenth century as a time in which the idea of women's rights first asserts itself in English and continental European society. Among these challengers to male patriarchy, although always a reserved one, was Margaret Cavendish.

A Closer Look

Cavendish was born into the English aristocracy as Margaret Lucas in 1623. Her family, although not wealthy, had an impeccable lineage. She later married William Cavendish, the Marquis of Newcastle. When her husband received the title of duke, she became the Duchess of Newcastle-upon-Tyne. Educated by tutors, she wrote on philosophy and science, as well as penning romantic fiction. Her book *The Blazing World* is considered one of the earliest works of science fiction. At the time, such writing and study was considered inappropriate for the gentle and weak nature of women, as it might lead to their mental and even physical breakdown.

Of all her writings, Cavendish is perhaps best known today for her revealing autobiography. The book is appreciated for its finely rendered descriptions of aristocratic life. In the accompanying excerpt, Cavendish describes her family recreating while at their country estate. The activities engaged in by her brothers and sisters does much to capture the gender-defined roles of the day. Her brothers, she notes, took up their time in exercises of a martial type—fencing, wrestling, and shooting. This offered them a preparation for war, a frequent fact of life for the aristocracy of the day. Indeed, two of Cavendish's brothers would die in combat. She and her sisters, meanwhile, preferred to read, talk, and walk the grounds, all appropriate activities for the gentler sex.

1 100 200 300   400   500   600   700   800   900   1000 1100 1200 1300   1400   1500   1600 1700 1800 1900 2000 CE

2.12.25 Marriage Customs in Different European Countries

Europe
1687

Polygamy, or the use of many Women together, is very usual amongst the Infidels, but it is generally forbidden amongst Christians, who are forbidden, upon pain of death, marrying more than one Woman together; and further she must be married in the Church before the Parson of the Parish. All other Marriages contracted otherwise are declared void and clandestine, the Children born in such are reputed Bastards, and consequently incapable of Succession, and of challenging their Parents' inheritance.

The Ceremonies of Marriages amongst Roman Catholics are prescribed by the Councils. The Council of Trent, for to prevent all abuses in Marriages, declareth and pronounceth all Marriages invalid and void, which have not been celebrated before the Parson of the Parish of the one or the other contracting parties. Wherefore according to the decrees of the Romish Church, as soon as the contracting Parties are agreed, the Parsons of their respective Parishes are bound to proclaim three Banns on three Sundays, or three Holy days consecutively, to the end that if any of the Parishoners know any lawful cause why they may not be joined together, they may reveal it to the Parson of the parish. And in case no body can allege any lawful impediment, then both the parties are conducted by their parents into the Parochial Church of the Woman, where they are betrothed by the Parson of the said parish, who examines them whether they be well contented to be betrothed one to the other, and whether they be not already engaged by promise of Marriage to any other person or persons. . . .

The *Sicilians* did formerly betroth the Man and the Woman at home, and very often were not married till the Hour of Death, or at the extremity of the one, or of the other Parties: But this was forbidden by the order of the Council of *Trent*. The espoused woman did also use to ride through the City with a great Company and Pomp, on horse-back; But that is now quite left off, since the Invention of Coaches. But notwithstanding the Prohibition of the foresaid Council even to this day, as soon as the Articles of the Contract are signed, the man enjoys his Spouse with all liberty, and reaps the sweet Fruits of Marriage many years sometimes before the celebration of it.

In *Poland*, but chiefly in the Country, Of *Prussia* and *Lithuania*, Maids seldom marry under four and twenty Years of Age; and not so neither till they have first wrought, with their own hands, as much stuff, as is sufficient to cloth every one, who must accompany their Bridegroom to Church. Amongst them when any Father seeks a Wife for his Son, he neither regards her Beauty nor Wealth, but only her good Morality, ripeness of Age, and strong constitution of Body. The Women are never married till two of their future Bridegrooms near Relations have had a deep finger in their Pies, and then they use to crave their Father's good consent; those People do still retain many Dregs of the old Superstition of the Heathens: For when the Solemnity of Matrimony is celebrated, the Bride is led three times about a Fire, then they make her sit down, they wash her feet, and with that same water they besprinkle the Nuptial Bed, and all the Utensils of the House. This done, they anoint her Mouth with Honey.

Source: de Gaya, Louis. *Matrimonial Customs, or, The Various Ceremonies and Divers Ways of Celebrating Weddings Practiced amongst All the Nations in the Whole World Done Out of French*. London: A.S., 1687, pp. 14–28.

TIMELINE 2000 1900 1800 1700 1600 1500 1400 1300 1200 1100 1000 900 800 700 600 500 400 300 200 100 1 BCE

What You Need to Know

These excerpts are from Louis de Gaya's 1687 book *Matrimonial Customs*, a *tour d'horizon*, or survey, of the marriage practices of various nationalities around the European continent.

Since its early days, the Christian church had asserted its authority over matrimony, insisting that a legitimate marriage had to have the sanction of the church. But through most of the Middle Ages, marriage, at least among the common folk, was a more informal affair, involving little ceremony and no church approval. The couple, whose betrothal was sometimes arranged for them by their parents, would give their mutual consent to marry, declare themselves married, and then consummate the union. Sometimes a priest and witnesses would be in attendance at the second stage of the process, but oftentimes not.

Under the Council of Trent, an ecclesiastical conference called by the pope to draw up institutional and social reforms in the face of the Protestant Reformation of the sixteenth century, the Catholic Church became much more involved in marriage, requiring the presence of clergy to officiate at weddings and the registering of marriages with the church.

A Closer Look

The Renaissance reawakened scholars' interest in foreign peoples, and de Gaya's book fits into that tradition. Little is known of its author, other than that he was an officer in the French military under King Louis XIV and also wrote extensively about weaponry.

De Gaya begins by noting the most important feature distinguishing Christian marriage from that of infidels—the prohibition on polygamy. He also notes the reforms of the Council of Trent, establishing church authority over marriage. But the most interesting part of the book, at least to modern readers, is his observations on the diverse forms the process of getting married took in different Christian lands.

Of special note are the marriage customs of Sicily and Poland. In the former, he notes the persistence of pre-Council of Trent customs, whereby people went directly from declaring their intention to marry to consummation of the marriage, without ceremony or the involvement of the clergy. In the latter, he observes a number of customs—the bride's circling of a fire three times, the anointing of her mouth with honey, and her kicking the door of her new husband's house—which he attributes to "the Dregs of the Old Superstition of the Heathens," that is, pagans customs that had continued into the Christian age.

1 100 200 300 400 500 600 700 800 900 1000 1100 1200 1300 1400 1500 1600 1700 1800 1900 2000 CE

Part 13:
The World beyond Europe

Sixteenth–Eighteenth Centuries CE

2.13.1 Ottoman Astronomers in the Galata Tower

Istanbul
Sixteenth Century

Credit: DeAgostini/Getty Images

What You Need to Know

This sixteenth-century Ottoman miniature painting is of scholars and astronomers studying at the observatory Suleiman established in the Galata Tower in Istanbul. (The tower itself was built two centuries earlier by Genoese masons living in Christian, Byzantine-controlled Constantinople—the former name for Istanbul—before its fall to Muslim conquerors in 1453.)

The Ottomans were a Turkish-speaking people who, under their eponymous first emperor, Osman, who ruled in the early fourteenth century, expanded out of their kingdom in western Anatolia to ultimately control the Middle East, North Africa, and much of the Balkan Peninsula in Europe by the sixteenth century.

Under the reign of their greatest emperor Suleiman I, also known as the Suleiman the Magnificent, the Ottoman Empire achieved a cultural flowering unparalleled in its history. Suleiman inaugurated vast public building projects across his realm, most notably in the capital Istanbul, and made of his government a great patron of the arts and sciences. He established medical schools and hospitals, indeed, turning one of his own palaces into a research institute. He also contributed to the study of astronomy by establishing what may have been the greatest observatory of its time in the Western world, where astronomers and scholars from across his realm and from as far away as England and China came to study.

A Closer Look

The scientists at the observatory in the Galata Tower were part of a great Islamic tradition in astronomy. Building on the work of ancient world scholars, as well as the knowledge accumulated in the realms that fell under Islamic sway during the medieval era, Islamic astronomers did much to measure and calculate the movement of the planets and the positions of the stars. Much of this inquiry was motivated by religion. Muslims are required to pray five times daily in the direction of Mecca, the holiest city of Islam, which required astronomical measurement to determine. During the month of Ramadan, they were expected to fast from sunrise to sunset, the determination of which also required a study of the heavens.

But like all medieval astronomers, Islamic ones were limited to observations made with the naked eye, as the telescope was yet to be invented. The illustration shows the use of several of these nontelescopic instruments. These include a sector, the long pointed instrument held up by the astronomer on the upper left, several quadrants hanging on the wall (triangular instruments with bowed sides at the bottom), and an astrolabe, the globe-like instrument used by a standing red-clad figure at the bottom. All of these instruments were used to make differing measurements of the positions of the stars.

1 100 200 300 400 500 600 700 800 900 1000 1100 1200 1300 1400 1500 1600 1700 1800 1900 2000 CE

2.13.2 The Markets in the Aztec Capital of Tenochtitlan

Tenochtitlan (Mexico City)
1521

The place where the artists principally resided was named Escapuzalco, and was at the distance of about a league from the city. Here were the shops and manufactories of all their gold and silver smiths, whose works in these metals, and in jewelry, when they were brought to Spain, surprised our ablest artists. . . . Their fine manufactures of cotton and feathers, were principally brought from the province of Costitlan. The women of the family of the great Montezuma also, of all ranks, were extremely ingenious in these works, and constantly employed; as was a certain description of females who lived together in the manner of nuns. . . .

Cortes at the head of his cavalry, and the principal part of our soldiers under arms, marched to the grand square, attended by many noblemen of the court. When we arrived there, we were astonished at the crowds of people, and the regularity which prevailed, as well as at the vast quantities of merchandise, which those who attended us were assiduous in pointing out. Each kind had its particular place, which was distinguished by a sign. The articles consisted of gold, silver, jewels, feathers, mantles, chocolate, skins dressed and undressed, sandals, and other manufactures of the roots and fibres of nequen, and great numbers of male and female slaves, some of whom were fastened by the neck, in collars, to long poles. The meat market was stocked with fowls, game, and dogs. Vegetables, fruits, articles of food ready dressed, salt, bread, honey, and sweet pastry made in various ways were also sold here. Other places in the square were appointed to the sale of earthen ware, wooden household furniture such as tables and benches, firewood, paper, sweet canes filled with tobacco mixed with liquid amber, copper axes and working tools, and wooden vessels highly painted. Numbers of women sold fish, and little loaves made of a certain mud which they find in the lake, and which resembles cheese. The makers of stone blades were busily employed shaping them out of the rough material, and the merchants who dealt in gold, had the metal in grains as it came from the mines, in transparent tubes, so that they could be reckoned, and the gold was valued at so many mantles, or so many xiquipils of cocoa, according to the size of the quills. The entire square was enclosed in piazzas, under which great quantities of grain were stored, and where were also shops for various kinds of goods. I must apologize for adding, that boat loads of human ordure were on the borders of the adjoining canals, for the purpose of tanning leather, which they said could not be done without it. Some may laugh at this but I assert the fact is as I have stated it, and moreover, upon all the public roads, places for passengers to resort to, were built of canes, and thatch with straw or grass, in order to collect this material.

The courts of justice, where three judges sat, occupied a part of the square, their under-officers going in the market, inspecting the merchandise.

Source: Díaz del Castillo, Bernal. *The True History of the Conquest of Mexico*. Translated by Maurice Keatinge. London: J. Wright, 1800, pp. 142–144.

TIMELINE   2000 1900 1800 1700 1600 1500 1400 1300 1200 1100 1000 900 800 700 600 500 400 300 200 100 1 BCE

What You Need to Know

In this account of Tenochtitlan, Bernal Díaz del Castillo, an officer in Cortés's army, writes about the many things for sale in the Aztec markets.

Located on a large island in the vast and shallow Lake Texcoco of the Valley of Mexico, Tenochtitlan was the capital of the Aztec Empire from the fourteenth through the sixteenth centuries, when it fell to the Spanish Conquistador Hernan de Cortés in 1521. At its peak, at the time of the conquest, it was the largest city in the Americas, covering five square miles and populated by an estimate 200,000 persons, which would have made it one of the top ten biggest cities of the world in the early sixteenth century.

The Aztec metropolis was well designed and administered. It was divided into four zones, known as *campan*, representing the four cardinal directions. Each *campan* was then divided into what 20 local districts the Aztecs called, in their Nahuatl language, *calpulli*, or "great houses," as it was believed each was inhabited by people sharing a common ancestry. Wide streets ran through all of the *campan* to the three causeways that connected the city to the mainland and other nearby islands. According to this account from Bernal Díaz del Castillo, who accompanied Cortés on a tour of the city, the two main features of Tenochtitlan were its vast marketplace and immense temples.

A Closer Look

A militaristic people who had conquered much of central Mexico when the Spanish arrived in the early sixteenth century, the Aztecs also had trading networks extending the length and breadth of Meso-America, and beyond. The wealth produced by their conquests—the Aztecs demanded a steady stream of tribute from subjugated tribes—and their trade was in evidence in the marketplace, notes Díaz. Artisans there turned gold and silver into intricately designed jewelry. There were also the feathers and hides of birds and animals from as far away as the jungles of Central America.

Still, most of the vast Aztec marketplaces were devoted to the needs and wants of ordinary citizens of the metropolis, or those from the countryside who came to the capital to shop. Tailors and seamstresses sold the cloaks and loincloths popular with men and the blouses and long skirts preferred by women. There was also a wide array of food, sold in specialized stalls. Butchers offered turkey, duck, chicken, rabbit, and deer meat, while grocers sold beans, squash, corn, and many kinds of peppers. Of particular note to the Spanish was an exotic substance known to the Aztecs as *chocolatl*, or chocolate, which the Aztecs enjoyed as a spiced, rather than sweet, drink.

1 100 200 300 400 500 600 700 800 900 1000 1100 1200 1300 1400 1500 1600 1700 1800 1900 2000 CE

2.13.3 The Coronado Expedition's Description of Zuni Pueblos

New Mexico
1540

Of the situation and condition of the Seven Cities called the kingdom of Cevola, and the sort of people and their customs, and of the animals which are found there.

It now remains for me to tell about this city and kingdom and province, of which the father provincial gave Your Lordship an account. In brief, I can assure you that in reality he has not told the truth in a single thing that he said, but everything is the reverse of what he said, except the name of the city and the large stone houses. For, although they are not decorated with turquoises, or made of lime nor of good bricks, nevertheless they are very good houses, with three and four and five stories, where there are very good apartments and good rooms with corridors, and some very good rooms underground and paved, which are made for winter, and are something like a sort of hot baths. The ladders which they have for their houses are all movable and portable, which are taken up and placed wherever they please. They are made of two pieces of wood, with rounds like ours.

The Seven Cities are seven little villages, all having the kind of houses I have described. They are all within a radius of five leagues. They are all called the kingdom of Cevola, and each has its own name and no single one is called Cevola, but all together are called Cevola. This one which I have called a city I have named Granada, partly because it has some similarity to it, as well as out of regard for Your Lordship. In this place where I am now lodged there are perhaps 200 houses, all surrounded by a wall, and it seems to me that with the other houses, which are not so surrounded, there might be altogether 500 families. . . .

The people of the towns seem to me to be of ordinary size and intelligent, although I do not think that they have the judgment & intelligence which they ought to have to build these houses in the way in which they have, for most of them are entirely naked except the covering of their privy parts, and they have painted mantles like the one which I send to Your Lordship. They do not raise cotton, because the country is very cold, but they wear mantles, as may be seen by the exhibit which I send. It is also true that some cotton thread was found in their houses. They wear the hair on their heads like the Mexicans. They all have good figures, and are well bred. I think that they have a quantity of turquoises, which they had removed with the rest of their goods, except the corn, when I arrived, because I did not find any women here nor any men under 15 years or over 60, except two or three old men who remained in command of all the other men and the warriors.

Source: Coronado, Francisco Vásquez de. Excerpt from letter to Viceroy Mendoza, August 3, 1540. In *The Coronado Expedition, 1540–1542*. Edited by George Parker Winship. Washington, DC: Government Printing Office, 1896, pp. 558–559.

TIMELINE   2000 1900 1800 1700 1600 1500 1400 1300 1200 1100 1000 900 800 700 600 500 400 300 200 100 1 BCE

What You Need to Know

This excerpt from Francisco Vásquez de Coronado, the governor of the Spanish province of Nueva Galicia (now the northwestern Mexican states of Jalisco, Sinaloa, and Nayarit) describes the Seven Cities of Cibola, in what is now New Mexico. It is taken from his report to the viceroy of New Spain in Mexico City.

Given the great cities and fabulous wealth they encountered among the Aztec of the Valley of Mexico, it is not surprising that the Spanish believed there might be other native civilizations with great troves of precious metals elsewhere in North America. Among the most persistent of such stories were those concerning the so-called Seven Cities of Cibola, also known as the Seven Cities of Gold. In 1540, Francisco Vásquez de Coronado launched an expedition to locate Cibola, after sending out an exploratory party the year before that led him to believe the cities did exist. For two years, Coronado and his party explored the American Southwest and southern Great Plains, becoming the first Europeans to see many of these lands. Ultimately, the seven cities were never discovered. Today, most historians believe that rumors about Cibola related to the elaborate constructions of the Zuni people in what is now the American state of New Mexico.

A Closer Look

The Zuni are one of the so-called Pueblo Indians of the American Southwest; other major Pueblo groups include the Hopi, Acoma, and Taos. The name Pueblo was given to these people by the Spanish. The term means "town" in Spanish and refers to the fact that the Zuni and other Pueblo Indians inhabited small urban conglomerations.

Archaeologists believe that the Zuni have lived in the region since sometime in the second millennium BCE. They practiced irrigation agriculture, raising crops such as beans and corns. Coronado describes one of their habitations as consisting of "large stone houses." In fact, the Pueblo built their dwellings out of adobe bricks, consisting of clay mixed with water. Most of the buildings, which housed numerous families, surrounded central courtyards and could be as high as five stories, usually built in a stepped-back fashion that resembled a pyramid, with the roof of the floor below serving as a terrace for the habitations above. Most of the buildings used their ground floors for storage, while access to the living areas was from openings in the ceiling. As Coronado notes, the natives carried ladders around to get in and out of the buildings.

Although a keen observer of what he saw, Coronado could also be blinded by his prejudices. At one point, he doubts that such a primitive people—"most of them are entirely naked except the covering of their privy parts," he says—could have built such elaborate structures.

1 100 200 300 400 500 600 700 800 900 1000 1100 1200 1300 1400 1500 1600 1700 1800 1900 2000 CE

2.13.4 The Janissaries of the Ottoman Empire

Constantinople
ca. 1554

At Buda I made my first acquaintance with the Janissaries; this is the name by which the Turks call the infantry of the royal guard. The Turkish state has 12,000 of these troops when the corps is at its full strength. They are scattered through every part of the empire, either to garrison the forts against the enemy, or to protect the Christians and Jews from the violence of the mob. There is no district with any considerable amount of population, no borough or city, which has not a detachment of Janissaries to protect the Christians, Jews, and other helpless people from outrage and wrong.

A garrison of Janissaries is always stationed in the citadel of Buda. The dress of these men consists of a robe reaching down to the ankles, while, to cover their heads, they employ a cowl which, by their account, was originally a cloak sleeve, part of which contains the head, while the remainder hangs down and flaps against the neck. On their forehead is placed a silver-gilt cone of considerable height, studded with stones of no great value.

These Janissaries generally came to me in pairs. When they were admitted to my dining room they first made a bow, and then came quickly up to me, all but running, and touched my dress or hand, as if they intended to kiss it. After this they would thrust into my hand a nosegay of the hyacinth or narcissus; then they would run back to the door almost as quickly as they came, taking care not to turn their backs, for this, according to their code, would be a serious breach of etiquette. After reaching the door, they would stand respectfully with their arms crossed, and their eyes bent on the ground, looking more like monks than warriors. On receiving a few small coins (which was what they wanted) they bowed again, thanked me in loud tones, and went off blessing me for my kindness. To tell you the truth, if I had not been told beforehand that they were Janissaries, I should, without hesitation, have taken them for members of some order of Turkish monks, or brethren of some Moslem [Muslim] college. Yet these are the famous Janissaries, whose approach inspires terror everywhere.

Source: Busbecq, Ogier Ghiselin de. Letter I to Nicolas Michault. In *The Life and Letters of Ogier Ghiselin de Busbecq*. Vol. I. Edited by C. T. Forster and F. H. B. Daniel. London: Kegan Paul, 1881, pp. 86–88.

TIMELINE   2000 1900 1800 1700 1600 1500 1400 1300 1200 1100 1000 900 800 700 600 500 400 300 200 100 1 BCE

What You Need to Know

The letter here was written by the Flemish diplomat Ogier Ghiselin de Busbecq, who represented the Holy Roman Emperor Ferdinand I at the court of the Sultan of the Ottoman Empire in Constantinople (now Istanbul). The letter dates to around 1554. In it, de Busbecq describes the Janissaries, the elite corps of Ottoman slave soldiers.

At its height in the sixteenth and seventeenth centuries, the Ottoman Empire was one of the largest empires in the world, stretching from Morocco in northwest Africa to the Arabian Peninsula in the east to what is now Hungary and Romania in the northern Balkan Peninsula of Europe. Its population in 1600 surpassed 30 million people, almost equal to the entire population of Western Europe at the time.

Slavery was widely practiced in the empire, as it was in many civilizations at the time. But it was very different from the commercial and racially based form then being developed by Western European colonizers in the Americas. Slaves served in all kinds of positions, from the lowliest farm laborer to the concubine of the sultan to high officials in the government. All races were represented in the ranks of slaves, and the status of slavery did not carry the same social stigma of being less than human that it soon would in the West.

A Closer Look

Accompanying the Ottoman army as it swept through southeastern Europe in the sixteenth century, reaching as far as the gates of Vienna in the 1620s and 1630s, were agents of the sultan, whose job it was to recruit Christian slaves to serve in the Ottoman civil service, army, and in the case of girls, concubinage in the Sultan's harem. The practice, known as *devshirme*, the Turkish word for "collecting," saw the agents purchase the sons and daughters of Christians from their parents. The latter were often eager to take the money, as such service was seen as a way to social advancement. Indeed, some Christians bribed Ottoman officials to take their children.

The youth were converted to Islam. The brightest were sent to the palace school in Istanbul, to be trained for government administration; the toughest were recruited for the army. There they became known as *janissaries*, "recruits" in Turkish, where they formed elite battalions, whose loyalty to the sultan was considered absolute. According to Busbecq, they were scattered about the empire, including the Hungarian city of Buda (now part of Budapest), with the task of ensuring social peace, as well as protecting "Christians, Jews, and other helpless people from outrage and wrong."

1 100 200 300 400 500 600 700 800 900 1000 1100 1200 1300 1400 1500 1600 1700 1800 1900 2000 CE

Credit: Culture Club/Getty Images

What You Need to Know

An image of St. Francis of Assisi is on the cover of this 1555 Spanish-Nahuatl dictionary—Nahuatl was the language of many of the pre-Columbian peoples of Mexico. The dictionary was used by priests and other officials of the Catholic Church in their efforts to convert the native peoples of Mexico and other "New World" lands conquered by the Spanish in the sixteenth century.

With money from the Spanish monarchy, Catholic missionaries and officials quickly established churches and monasteries across the most heavily populated sections of central Mexico. At first, most of the native peoples resisted; they might attend mass, partly out of curiosity, but they rarely took the sacraments and continued to worship their own deities, despite the fact that their gods had failed to protect them against the Spanish.

In 1531, however, one of the few Indian converts, a man rechristened Juan Diego, claimed to have a transcendent encounter with the Virgin Mary, manifested as a native woman. Word quickly spread, encouraged by the archbishop of Mexico and other Catholic officials, who built a shrine on the site of the supposed miracle. Within a few years, hundreds of thousands of pilgrims were visiting the shrine annually, as the church was flooded with converts.

A Closer Look

Wealth, fame, and power were the primary motivations behind the Spanish conquest of Mexico: wealth and fame for the conquistadores, who did the actual conquest; wealth and power for the monarchy back in Madrid who supported them. But faith mattered, too—specifically, the conversion to Catholicism of the millions of people who came under Spanish rule.

The Spanish monarchy claimed a divine right to rule. Thus, their policies and actions had to be in accordance with divine will, at least as the monarchy determined it to be. The conquistadores themselves were also highly devout Catholics; indeed, many of them were the spiritual successors of the *Reconquista*, the 700-year-long war to oust Islamic Moors from Spain itself, a struggle that had only ended a mere one generation before the conquest of Mexico.

Moreover, Catholicism was then on the defensive in Europe itself; the conquest of Mexico coincided with the first years of the Protestant Reformation, as millions of people across Europe left the church for new Protestant sects. The Spanish monarchy, a bulwark of Catholicism, used a significant portion of the wealth it accrued in the Americas on military campaigns to roll back Protestantism in Europe.

1 100 200 300 400 500 600 700 800 900 1000 1100 1200 1300 1400 1500 1600 1700 1800 1900 2000 CE

2.13.6 Bishop Diego de Landa's Account of the Mistreatment of the Maya

Yucatan Peninsula (Mexico)
ca. 1566

The Indians resented the yoke of slavery, but the Spanish had split them up in various areas. Nevertheless, there were some Indians who revolted against them, to which the Spanish responded with some very cruel measures that caused the population to decrease. Some of the chief men from the district of Kupul were burnt alive and others were hanged. They also prosecuted the people of Yobain, in the district of the Chels: they seized some prominent men, chained them, and placed them in a house to which they then set fire. They were burnt alive with unimaginable cruelty. And Diego de Landa said that he had seen a large tree near this area where a captain had hanged a great number of Indian women, and had hanged small children from the feet of their mothers. In this same area, and in another area called Verey two miles from there, they hanged two Indian women, one a virgin and one recently married for no other reason except that they were beautiful. This happened when there was fear of an uprising in the Spanish camp on account of these women and they decided to kill these women in order to make the Indians believe that the Spanish did not care about their women. The beauty of these two and the cruelty of those who killed them is still much remembered by the Indians and the Spanish.

The Indians of the provinces of Cochuah and Chectemal revolted, and the Spanish put them down in such a manner that these two provinces, which had been the most populous and full of people, became the most desolate in the whole country. The Spanish committed cruelties never before heard of, cutting off noses, hands, arms, legs. They cut off women's breasts and threw the women into deep lakes with gourds attached as weights to their feet, and they stabbed the children because they did not march as quickly as their mothers. And if those who wore the neck-ring fell ill or didn't travel as fast as the others, they cut off their heads in front of the others so as not to stop and lose time in untying them. They used similar methods to drag along a great number of captives, men and women, destined for slavery. But it is confirmed that Don Francisco de Montejo never committed any of these cruelties, and that they were never done in his presence; instead, he always condemned them but was not able to stop them.

The Spanish attempted to defend such barbarity by saying that since there were only few Spanish in the country, they were unable to conquer so many people without subjecting them to terrible punishments, and they cited the example of the Hebrew people when they came to the promised land and how such great cruelties were committed at God's own command. On the other hand, the Indians were right to defend their liberty, and to place their trust in the brave captains among them in the hope of ridding themselves of the Spanish.

Source: Landa, Diego de. *Relation des Choses de Yucatán*. Translated and edited by Jean Genet. Paris: Les Éditions Genet, 1928. Translated into English by Lawrence Morris.

TIMELINE   2000 1900 1800 1700 1600 1500 1400 1300 1200 1100 1000 900 800 700 600 500 400 300 200 100 1 BCE

What You Need to Know

This excerpt on the abuse of the Maya is from the Franciscan friar, and later Catholic bishop, Diego de Landa, who served the Catholic Church on Yucatan Peninsula of Mexico, in the mid-sixteenth century.

In 1549, the Franciscan friar, and later Catholic bishop, Diego de Landa arrived in the Yucatan Peninsula of what is now Mexico. The Franciscan religious order had been granted a monopoly by royal authority over the conversion of the Maya of the region to Catholicism. Like virtually all Europeans of his day, de Landa considered the indigenous religions of the Americas a form of idolatry, to be wiped out by whatever means necessary. De Landa went about his task with zeal, diligence, and to modern sensibilities, barbarity. He burned Maya codices, or manuscript books, and destroyed their religious images. He jailed many of their religious leaders, subjecting them to torture—this despite a royal decree granting Amerindians immunity from the Inquisition, which had been set up in Spain to root out heresy. The crown declared the Indians too ignorant to understand that they were committing heresy. Still, de Landa could be an acute observer not just of Maya life but also, ironically, of the cruelties the Spanish inflicted on the indigenous peoples of the Yucatan, as this excerpt from his 1566 account of his experiences there relates.

A Closer Look

In the wake of their conquest of Mesoamerica in the early sixteenth century, the Spanish established what they called the *encomienda* system. *Encomienda* means "tribute," and the system it described resembled that of European serfdom. The king of Spain granted land to his retainers—that is, the former conquistadors who ruled the new royal possessions in the Americas—and the right to exploit the labor of the Indians who lived on the land. It was not legally slavery but, in reality, bore a great resemblance to it. Indeed, de Landa explicitly calls it "slavery." Indians were worked relentlessly and treated pitilessly, to the point of exhaustion, famine, illness, and death.

Given these conditions, it is not surprising that the native peoples periodically revolted against Spanish rule. As de Landa describes, the Spanish responded with the utmost cruelty in putting down these uprisings, dismembering women, drowning victims, and even stabbing "children because they did not march as quickly as their mothers." As the Franciscan also notes, the Spanish justified such barbarity by noting they were few and the Indians were many. To keep order, they had to inflict "terrible punishments." They grounded their argument in biblical precedent, saying that God had told the Hebrews to use similar methods when subduing the idol-worshipping Canaanites. Such justification was ironic, given the fact that it was in the name of God that the Spanish based their right to rule over the native peoples of the Americas.

2.13.7 Illustration of Aztec Silversmiths from the Florentine Codex

Mexico City
1569

Credit: DEA Picture Library/DeAgostini/Getty Images

What You Need to Know

The scenes of Aztec silversmiths depicted here come from the Florentine Codex, a manuscript book on life in Mexico compiled by the Franciscan Friar Bernardino de Sahagún, who had been assigned to assist in the conversion of the native peoples to Catholicism in 1529.

The Florentine Codex is among the greatest sources of information we have on the life of the Aztecs and other peoples of Mexico in the early years of the conquest. Moreover, it provides a picture of what life was like before that cataclysmic event.

The indigenous population of the Americas declined greatly following the arrival of Europeans in the late fourteenth and early fifteenth centuries. The disaster hit those areas where the native population was heaviest. In the Valley of Mexico, for example, it is estimated that the number of Amerindians fell from roughly 25 million in 1519, when the Spanish conquistador Hernán Cortés arrived, to around 1 million by the early seventeenth century, a drop of more than 95 percent. The main cause were epidemic diseases from Europe, for which the natives had little immunity. But the Spaniards made things worse by concentrating Indians in mining camps, plantations, and missions. Losses at the latter were particularly poignant because missions were established by various Catholic religious orders to help the natives adjust to the new, Spanish-ruled order, as well as to convert them to Christianity.

A Closer Look

The Florentine Codex, named for the Italian city where it has long been housed, is a collection of more than 2,000 illustrations and bilingual texts—in Spanish and the Aztec Nahuatl language—Sahagún compiled over nearly half a century, from 1545 until his death in 1590.

Among the items that most interested the Spanish conquistadores when they arrived in the Aztec capital city of Tenochtitlan in the early sixteenth century was the jewelry they found. Their fascination was not just about the gold and silver it contained, which they highly coveted, but the intricacy and delicacy of the artisans' designs, which spoke to a very high smithing skill level.

While the precise process Aztec artisans used to fashion such jewelry is not exactly known, archaeologists presume they used some variant of the lost wax method, which was known at the time to civilizations around the world. In brief, the method uses wax and various forms of clay to form molds, with the metal then poured into them and the wax melted away.

Beyond the craftsmanship involved in fashioning the jewelry, Aztec silver and goldsmiths incorporated many motifs into their jewelry, some derived from their religion and others from the natural world.

1 100 200 300   400   500   600   700   800   900   1000 1100 1200 1300   1400   1500 1600 1700 1800 1900 2000 CE

2.13.8 William Adams on Conflict with the Mapuche

Patagonia
1599

The first of November we came to the ile of Mocha, lying in the latitude of eight and thirtie degrees. Having much wind, we durst not anchor, but directed our course for Cape Sancta Maria, two leagues by south the iland of Sancta Maria; where, having no knowledge of the people, the second of November our men went on land, and the people of the land fought with our men and hurte eight or nine; but in the end they made a false composition of friendship, which our men did beleeve.

The next day our captaine and three and twentie of our chiefe men went on land, meaning for marchandize to get victualls, having wonderfull hunger. Two or three of the people came straight to our boat in freindly manner, with a kind of wine and rootes, with making tokens to come on land, making signes that there were sheep and oxen. Our captaine, with our men, having great desire to get refreshing for our men, went on land. The people of the country lay intrenched, a thousand and above, and straightway fell upon our men and slew them all, among which was my brother Thomas Adams. By this lossse we had scarse so many men whole as could weigh our anchor. So the third day, in great distresse, we set our course for the island of Santa Maria, where we found our Admirall, whom when we saw, our hearts were somewhat comforted. We went aboord them and found them in as greate distrese as we, having lost their Generall with seven and twentie of their men slaine at the island of Mocha, from whence they departed the day before we came by. Here we tooke counsell what we should doe to get victualls. To goe on land by force we had noe men, for the most part were sicke. There came a Spaniard by composition to see our shippe, and soe the next day he came againe, and we let him depart quietly. The third day came two Spaniards aboord us without pawne, to see if they could betray us. When they had seene our shippe they would have gone on land againe, but we would not let them, shewing that they came without leave and we would not let them goe on land againe without our leave, whereat they were greatly offended. We shewed them that we had extreame neede of victualls, and that if they would give us so many sheepe and so many beeves, they should goe on land. So against their wills they made composition with us, which within the time appointed they did accomplish. Having so much refreshing as we could get, we made all things well againe, our men beeing for the most part recovered of their sicknesse.

Source: Adams, William. Excerpt from Letter II to his wife. In *Letters Written by the English Residents in Japan, 1611–1623*. Edited by Jajiro Murnkami, N. Murakami, and K. Murakawa. Tokyo: The Sankosha, 1900, pp. 19–21.

TIMELINE   2000 1900 1800 1700 1600 1500 1400 1300 1200 1100 1000 900 800 700 600 500 400 300 200 100 1 BCE

What You Need to Know

This passage comes from a letter written by an English sailor named William Adams to his wife in 1605, while he was serving as a Western advisor to the Tokugawa Shogun of Japan. It relates to his encounters with the Mapuche Indians, during his long voyage to East Asia.

The tip of South America was an inaccessible land, full of islands, treacherous channels, and snow-covered peaks which descended to water's edge. But it was not just the landscape and cold and rainy weather that would put off European settlement for centuries, it was also the people who inhabited the region. The Mapuche would engage in intermittent conflict with the Spanish, and after independence came in 1810, their Chilean successors well into the nineteenth century. The determination with which the Mapuche defended their land against encroachers is captured in this letter.

A Closer Look

Before their incorporation into the Chilean nation in the nineteenth century, the Mapuche were not a politically unified people. They were, instead, a collection of independent tribes, sharing similar cultures and speaking related Mapudungan languages, living in what is now Chile and the Patagonian region of southern Argentina. They largely lived in small farm villages, where they grew corn, beans, squash, and other vegetables. They also practiced animal husbandry, keeping guinea pigs for meat and llamas for transport and wool production. Although many Chilean groups were incorporated into the Inca Empire in the fifteenth century, the Mapuche remained fiercely independent, as Adams, sailing on a fleet of Dutch East India merchant vessels bound for the East Indies, learned.

One year into the voyage, in 1599, crew members from one of the ships went on an expedition to seek victuals—food and fresh water—at Cape Santa Maria, just south of the modern-day Chilean port of Concepción. Adams admits they knew little of the local inhabitants but were encouraged by the fact that several of them had approached their vessel in canoes bearing gifts—"a kind of wine and rootes." In fact, the Mapuche may have been laying a trap, for when the captain and some his crew went on shore, they were attacked by more than a 1,000 natives lying in wait for them.

1 100 200 300 400 500 600 700 800 900 1000 1100 1200 1300 1400 1500 1600 1700 1800 1900 2000 CE

2.13.9 Houses and Furnishings in India

North India
Early Seventeenth Century

Now I come to take notice of their buildings; and here I must tell my reader, that this people are not much taken or infected with that plague of building (as the Italians call it) wishing the love of it as a curse to possess the thoughts of them they most hate; and therefore, as the stones in India are not all precious, so the houses there are not at all palaces; the poor there cannot erect for their dwellings fair piles, and the Grandees do not cover their heads under such curious roofs, as many of the Europeans do. The reason, first, because all the great men there live a great part of the year, (in which their months are more temperate, as from the middle of September, to the midst of April) in tents, pavilions, or moveable habitations, which, according to their fancies, changing they remove from place to place, changing their air as often as they please. . . .

For their buildings in cities and towns, there are some of them handsome, others fair, such as are inhabited by merchants, and none of them very despicable. They build their houses low, not above two stories, and many of their tops flat and thick, which keep off the violence of the heat; and those flat tops, supported with strong timber, and coated over with a plaster (like that we call plaster of Paris) keep them dry in the time of the rains. . . .

Those broad terraces, or flat roofs, some of them lofty, are places where many people may stand (and so they often do) early in the morning, and in the evening late, like chameleons, to draw, and drink in fresh air; and they are made after this fashion, for prospect, as well as pleasure.

Those houses of two stories have many of them very large upper rooms, which have many double doors in the sides of them, like those in our balconies, to open and let in fresh air, which is likewise conveyed in unto them, by many lesser lights made in the walls of those rooms, which are always free and open; The use of glass windows, or any other shuttings, being not known there, nor in any other very hot countries.

Neither have they any chimneys in their buildings, because they never make any use of fire but to dress their food, which fire they make against firm wall, or without their tents against some bank of earth, as remote as may be from the places where they use to keep, that they may receive no annoyance from the heat thereof.

It is their manner in many places, to plant about, and amongst their buildings, trees which grow high and broad, the shadow whereof keeps their houses by far more cool; this I observed in a special manner when we were ready to enter Amadavar; for it appeared to us, as if we had been entering a wood, rather than a city. Amadavar is a very large and populous city, entered by many fair gates girt about with an high and thick wall of brick, which mounts above the tops of their houses, without which wall there are no suburbs.

Source: Terry, Edward. Excerpt from *A Voyage to East-India*. London: J. Wilkie, 1777, pp. 175–179.

TIMELINE   2000 1900 1800 1700 1600 1500 1400 1300 1200 1100 1000 900 800 700 600 500 400 300 200 100 1 BCE

What You Need to Know

This excerpt about Indian homes comes from *A Voyage to East-India*, written in 1655 by Edward Terry, the chaplain to Thomas Roe, an English diplomat.

In the early seventeenth century, when Terry and Roe were stationed there, North India was under the rule of the Mughals, a Turkic-speaking people from Central Asia who had invaded the region a century before. The Mughals would maintain their control over the region until replaced by the British in the early nineteenth century. The Mughals produced some of the most spectacular monumental architecture on the Indian subcontinent. Perhaps, the greatest example of this is the Taj Mahal, a tomb built by the Mughal emperor Shah Jehan for his deceased third wife Mumtaz Mahal. Rising to 240 feet, its white marble walls studded with gems, it is widely considered the greatest example of funerary architecture in human history. Still, as spectacular as the monumental architecture of the Mughals was, their private dwellings were quite modest, as this excerpt Terry attests.

A Closer Look

In the excerpt printed here, Terry discusses the local architecture. While the hot and wet climate of North India produces some of the most abundant agricultural outputs in the world, it is not particularly conducive to human comfort. As Terry notes, this affected the habitations of the local people, including those of the wealthy. Everything was constructed to maximize the effect of any breezes that might pass through. Houses featured large terraces, while rooms on the upper stories had large double doors. He points out the lack of chimneys because there was no need for heating and that fires for cooking were kept as far away as possible from the rooms where people dwelled. Finally, he describes the planting of "high and broad" trees around the houses to provide shade.

Such designs were to be expected, but Terry notes another feature of Mughal housing that surprises him—the above-noted modesty of the dwellings. Mughals had a reputation in Europe for extravagance and wealth. An alternative spelling for them in English was "moguls," our source for the word describing rich and powerful persons. "I must tell my Reader," he writes, "that this People [the Mughals] are not much taken or infected with that plague of Building. . . . [T]herefore, as the stones in India are not all precious, so the Houses there are not at all Palaces." Roe explains this lack of architectural pretense in part to Mughal heritage. Before their migration to India, they were once a nomadic people and still spent much of the year traveling about from place to place living in "Tents, Pavillions, or moveable habitations." A permanent dwelling was not of the highest priority to them.

1 100 200 300 400 500 600 700 800 900 1000 1100 1200 1300 1400 1500 1600 1700 1800 1900 2000 CE

2.13.10 Muslim Burial Practices in India

North India
Early Seventeenth Century

For the Mahometans, it is their manner to wash the bodies of their dead before they inter them. An ancient custom as it should seem among the Jews; for it is said of Dorcas, that after she was dead, they washed her body, as a preparative to her burial.

They lay up none of the bodies of their dead in their mosques, or churches, (as before) but in some open place in a grave, which they dig very deep and wide; a Jewish custom, likewise to carry the bodies of their dead to bury them out of their cities and towns.

Their mourning over their dead is most immoderate; for besides that day of general lamentation at the end of their Ramjan, or Lent, (before mentioned) they howl and cry many whole days for their friends departed, immediately after they have left the world; and after that time is passed over many foolish women, so long as they survive, very often in the year, observe set days to renew their mourning for their deceased friends; and as a people without hope, bedew the graves of their husbands, as of other near relations, with abundance of (seemingly) affectionate tears; as if they were like those mourning women mentioned in Jer. 9.17 who seemed to have tears at command, and therefore were hired to mourn and weep in their solemn lamentations.

And when they thus lament over their dead, they will often put this question to their deaf and dead carcasses, why they would die? they having such loving wives, such loving friends, and many other comforts; as if it had been in their power to have rescued themselves from that most impartial wounding hand of death.

Which carriage of theirs deserves nothing but censure and pity; though, if it be not theatrical, we may much wonder at it, and say of it, as it was said of the mourning in the floor of Atad, Gen. 50.11, that it is a grievous mourning; or as the mourning of Hadadrimmon in the valley of Megiddon, Zech. 12.11, if we take those lamentations only in a literal sense.

Source: Terry, Edward. Excerpt from *A Voyage to East-India*. London: J. Wilkie, 1777, pp. 287–289.

TIMELINE   2000 1900 1800 1700 1600 1500 1400 1300 1200 1100 1000 900 800 700 600 500 400 300 200 100 1 BCE

What You Need to Know

This passage on Muslim funeral practices in North India comes from *A Voyage to East-India*, written in 1655 by Edward Terry, the chaplain to the English diplomat Thomas Roe.

With some 500 million practitioners, India has the largest Muslim population of any country on Earth, even though the majority of its people follow Hinduism. India is also, arguably, the first country outside of the Middle East and North Africa to have embraced Islam. This fact is not a surprising one given the extensive trading contacts between the two regions, which go back to ancient times. The first mosque in India was erected in what is now the Indian state of Kerala in 629, during the life of the Prophet Muhammad. But it was not until the early eighth century that the Umayyad Caliphate in Damascus, heirs to the Prophet Muhammad, according to Sunni Muslims, made a concerted effort to proselytize in India, dispatching a 6,000-man army to convert the people of India. The soldiers had little use of arms, as they were welcomed by locals seeking relief from oppressive Hindu rulers. The leader of the army promised religious tolerance. Subsequent invasions by Muslim armies from the west and north, the last by the Mughals of Central Asia, had firmly consolidated Islam in North India by the time Edward Terry and Thomas Roe arrived at the Mughal court of the Emperor Jahangir in Agra in the early seventeenth century. There, Terry wrote of what he saw, as in this excerpt on Muslim burial practices.

A Closer Look

All religions have rituals and practices associated with death. Islam, of course, is no exception. As Terry notes, Muslims "wash the bodies of their dead before they inter them." Like any traveler, Terry tries to assimilate what he sees in foreign lands to what he is familiar with at home. In this case, he notes that the Jews of Europe do the same, based on the biblical story of Dorcas, whose burial is described in the book of Acts. Although Terry does not mention it, this similarity to Jewish custom as described in the Bible, reveals that Muslims consider both the Old and New Testament as scripture.

What is perhaps more exotic to Terry is the sheer emotional exuberance of Muslim burials in the time of the Mughals, so different from the staid and somber affairs he was familiar with back in England. Calling their "mourning over their dead . . . most immoderate," he says the attendees "howl and cry many whole days." The bereaved then approach the body, as it awaits burial, and beseech it with question about "why would they die," leaving "such loving wives, such loving friends, and many other comforts" behind. Contributing to the emotional exuberance of the Muslim burials in seventeenth-century India was the use of hired mourners, paid to make extreme displays of grief.

Meanwhile, the real mourners typically engaged themselves in ritualistic prayers, including the *namaz-i-janaza*, or prayer before burial, in which Allah is implored to have mercy on the soul of the deceased and all deceased believers. For the next 40 days, the friends and relatives of the deceased were expected to follow certain purity rituals associated with death; at the end of this period, they then either gave alms to the poor or hosted a feast in which all people were invited to eat.

1 100 200 300 400 500 600 700 800 900 1000 1100 1200 1300 1400 1500 1600 1700 1800 1900 2000 CE

2.13.11 Muslim Prayer in India

North India
Early Seventeenth Century

The Mahometans [Muslims] have a set form of prayer in the Arabian tongue, not understood by many of the common people, yet repeated by them as well as by the Moolaas [Mullahs]; they likewise rehearse the names of God and of their Mahomet certain times every day upon beads, like the miss-led Papists, who seem to regard more the number, then the weight of prayers. . . .

But for the carriage of that people in their devotions. Before they go into their churches they wash their feet; and entering into them, put off their shoes. As they begin their devotions they stop their ears, and fix their eyes, that nothing may divert their thoughts; then in a soft and still voice they utter their prayers, wherein are many words most significantly expressing the omnipotency, greatness, and eternity, and other attributes of God. Many words likewise that seem to express much humiliation, they confessing in diverse submissive gestures, their own unworthiness, when they pray casting themselves low upon their face sundry times, and then acknowledge that they are burdens to the earth, and poison to the air, and the like, being so confounded and ashamed as that they seem not to dare so much as to lift up their eyes towards Heaven; but after all this, comfort themselves in the mercies of God, through the mediation of Mahomet.

If this people could as well conclude, as they can begin and continue their prayers, in respect of their expressions, and carriages in them, they might find comfort; but the conclusion of their devotions mars all.

Yet this, for their commendation (who doubtless, if they knew better would pray better) that what diversions, and impediments soever they have arising either from pleasure or profit, the Mahometans pray five times a day. The Mogul doth so, who sits on the throne; the shepherd doth so that waits on his flock in the field (where, by the way, they do not follow their flocks; but their flocks, them) all sorts of Mahometans do thus whether fixed in a place or moving in a journey, when their times, or hours of prayer come, which in the morning are at six, nine, and twelve of the clock; and at three and six in the afternoon.

When they pray, it is their manner to set their faces that they may look towards Medina near Mecca in Arabia where their great seducer Mahomet was buried, who promised them after one thousand years, to fetch them all to Heaven; which term, when it was out, and the promise not fulfilled, the Mahometans concluded that their forefathers mistook the time of the promise of his coming; and therefore resolve to wait for the accomplishment of it one thousand years more.

Source: Terry, Edward. Excerpt from *A Voyage to East-India*. London: J. Wilkie, 1777, pp. 253–256.

TIMELINE   2000 1900 1800 1700 1600 1500 1400 1300 1200 1100 1000 900 800 700 600 500 400 300 200 100 1 BCE

What You Need to Know

This document is from *A Voyage to East-India*, written in 1655 by Edward Terry, the chaplain to the English diplomat Thomas Roe. In this passage, Terry discusses the religious practices of the Muslims of North India.

Through trade and conquest, India has long been connected to the lands of the Middle East, birthplace of Islam. It was by these means that the Muslim faith first arrived in the subcontinent in the seventh and eighth centuries. With its emphasis on egalitarianism of believers, Islam appealed to many Indians, especially those who belonged to the lower castes of the Hindu system. Under the Delhi sultanate, which lasted from the thirteenth to the early sixteenth centuries, North India came under the rule of Muslim governments. In the early sixteenth century, the Mughals (sometimes spelled Moguls), a nomadic Turkic-speaking people from Central Asia, invaded and conquered the region, becoming the successors to the Delhi sultanate. It was into this cultural landscape that Edward Terry and Thomas Roe, an English diplomat and writer, arrived at the Mughal court in Agra in 1615.

By the time of their arrival, Christians and Muslims had shared much of the Eurasian landmass for more than 1,000 years, the former largely in Europe and the latter across a wide swath from the Levant in the west to the East Indies in the east. Moreover, Muslim lands held many practitioners of Christianity, a religion that predated Islam by more than 500 years.

A Closer Look

Most Christians of Europe at the time had little knowledge of the Islamic faith; Terry's account of their religious practices might have been his readers' first introduction to them. He is most fascinated by the fervor with which the Muslims of India practiced their faith, as manifested by their devotion to prayer. Islam requires believers to pray five times a day in the direction of Mecca, a fact Terry notes to his readers. He is especially impressed by their intense focus during prayer and the extreme self-abnegation of the worshippers themselves. He says that they "acknowledge that they are burdens to the Earth, and poison to the air" Allah has created.

Terry also notes the millenarianism implicit in their faith. A tenet of other faiths, including Christianity, Millenarianism is the belief that God has promised believers a major and positive transformation of human society sometime in the future. For Muslims, Terry notes, this was 1,000 years after God revealed His word to Muhammad. That deadline having passed by Terry's time, the diplomat notes that Muslims were not dissuaded, assuming instead "that their forefathers mistook the time of the promise . . . and therefore resolve to wait for the accomplishment of it one thousand years more."

1   100   200   300   400   500   600   700   800   900   1000   1100   1200   1300   1400   1500   1600   1700   1800   1900   2000 CE

2.13.12 An English Sailor in Japan

Japan
1605

Loving wife, you shall understand how all things have passed with mee from the time of mine absence from you. We set saile with five ships from the Texel in Holland the foure and twentieth of June 1598, and departed from the coast of England the fift of July. And the one and twentieth of August we came to one of the isles of Capo Verde, called Sant'Iago, where we abode foure and twentie dayes. In which time many of our men fell sicke through the unwholsomenesse of the aire, and our Generall among the rest. Now the reason that we abode so long at these ilands was that one of the captaines of the fleet made our Generall beleeve that at these ilands we should find great store of refreshing, as goats and other things, which was untrue. . . .

The nine and twentieth of December wee set saile to goe on our voyage, and in our way we fell with an island called Illha da Nobon, where we landed all our sicke men, taking the island in by force. Their towne contayned some eightie houses. Having refreshed our men we set saile againe. At which time our Generall commanded that a man, for four dayes, should have but one pound of bread, that was a quarter of a pound a day, with the like proportion of wine and water; which scarcitie of victuals brought such feeblenesse that our men fell into so great weaknesse and sicknesse for hunger that they did eate the calves' skinnes wherewith our ropes were covered.

At last it was resolved to goe for Japan, for by report of one Dirrick Gerritson, which had.been there with the Portugals, woollen cloth was in great estimation in that iland, and we gathered by reason that the Malucos and the most part of the East Indies were hot countreyes, where woolen cloth would not be much accepted. Wherefore we all agreed to goe for Japan. So leaving the coast of Chili from thirtie-six degrees of south latitude the seven and twentieth of November 1599, we tooke our course directly for Japan, and passed the line equinoctiall with a faire wind, which continued good for diverse moneths.

Source: Adams, William. Excerpts from Letter II to his wife. In *Letters Written by the English Residents in Japan, 1611–1623*. Edited by Jajiro Murnkami, N. Murakami, and K. Murakawa. Tokyo: The Sankosha, 1900, pp. 22–24.

TIMELINE   2000 1900 1800 1700 1600 1500 1400 1300 1200 1100 1000 900 800 700 600 500 400 300 200 100 1 BCE

What You Need to Know

In 1600, William Adams, an Englishman, sailed with the first Dutch fleet to Japan. In a 1605 letter, excerpted here, he wrote his wife describing what he found there.

In 1543, the Portuguese, who had developed a near-virtual monopoly over European sea trade with East Asia, arrived in Japan. At the time, Japan was still a politically fractured land, with local lords, known as *daimyo* and backed by armed retainers called samurai, ruling over the country. Over the course of the sixteenth century, however, a powerful *daimyo*, Oda Nobunaga, began to conquer and subdue the lands of other *daimyo*. Under his successors, the process was completed. The result of this process, which historians refer to as the period of "national unification," was the Tokugawa shogunate, a centralized government, in which the emperor was the figurehead leader of the Japanese people but real power lay with the shogun, a general who also served as regent.

Meanwhile, in Europe, merchants in the Netherlands had established the Dutch East India Company to conduct trade with the East. More enterprising and better organized than the Portuguese, they soon usurped much of the latter's trade in the East Indies. In 1609, the Tokugawa shogunate granted them exclusive trading rights in Japan. The key figure behind this arrangement was William Adams.

A Closer Look

While most Dutch ships sailed to India and the East Indies, Adams sailed in the pioneering fleet to Japan, a virtually unknown land to Europeans.

Signing up as a sailor for the Dutch East India Company fleet was not for the fainthearted. Voyages to East Asia and the East Indies typically took 200 days or more. They typically began at the *Koopvaardersrede*, or Merchantman's Roadstead, in Amsterdam. There, the sailor would join about 150 others, usually along with 100 soldiers for defense, and perhaps a dozen or two passengers. The typical Indiaman, as the ships were known, weighed in at about 700 tons. Most of the sailors were Dutch or Scandinavians, with the occasional Englishman like Adams.

The ships usually sailed in convoys and were often escorted by warships until well out into the Atlantic, beyond the reach of foreign privateers, or government-sponsored pirates. Beyond that, the convoys provided protection against regular pirates and multiple ships made sure that people could be rescued should one ship founder in a storm or on a reef. Disease was another danger. In the close confines of the ship, epidemics were frequent occurrences. Indeed, crowded conditions, poor diet, and overworked sailors—some of whom had criminal backgrounds—led to frequent brawls and occasional mutinies. Virtually every Dutch East India Company ship had a chaplain abroad to provide religious consolation and guidance, but when that proved insufficient, harsh discipline was employed, including incarceration, whippings, and even executions.

1 100 200 300 400 500 600 700 800 900 1000 1100 1200 1300 1400 1500 1600 1700 1800 1900 2000 CE

2.13.13 Murder of a Native American Boy at Plymouth Plantation

Plymouth Colony (Massachusetts)
1638

Amongst other enormities that fell out amongst them; this year three men were after due trial executed for robbery and murder which they had committed. Their names were these: Arthur Peach, Thomas Jackson and Richard Stinnings. . . .

This Arthur Peach was the chief of them, and the ringleader of all the rest. He was a lusty and a desperate young man, and had been one of the soldiers in the Pequot War and had done as good service as the most there, and one of the forwardest in any attempt. And being now out of means and loath to work, and falling to idle courses and company, he intended to go to the Dutch plantation; and had allured these three, being other men's servants and apprentices, to go with him. But another cause there was also of his secret going away in this manner. He was not only run into debt, but he had got a maid with child (which was not known till after his death), a man's servant in the town, and fear of punishment made him get away. The other three complotting with him ran away from their masters in the night, and could not be heard of. . . .

At length there came a Narragansett Indian boy, who had been in the Bay a-trading, and had both cloth and beads about him—they had met him the day before, and he was now returning. Peach called him to drink tobacco with them, and he came and sat down with them. Peach told the other he would kill him and take what he had from him, but they were something afraid. But he said, "Hang him, rogue, he had killed many of them." So they let him alone to do as he would. And when he saw his time, he took a rapier and ran him through the body once or twice and took from him five fathom of wampum and three coats of cloth and went their way, leaving him for dead. But he scrambled away when they were gone, and made shift to get home, but died within a few days after. By which means they were discovered. And by subtlety the Indians took them; for they, desiring a canoe to set them over a water, not thinking their fact had been known, by the sachem's command they were carried to Aquidneck Island and there accused of the murder, and were examined and committed upon it by the English there.

The Indians sent for Mr. Williams and made a grievous complaint; his friends and kindred were ready to rise in arms and provoke the rest thereunto, some conceiving they should now find the Pequots' words true, that the English would fall upon them. But Mr. Williams pacified them and told them they should see justice done upon the offenders, and went to the man and took Mr. James, a physician, with him. The man told him who did it, and in what manner it was done; but the physician found his wounds mortal and that he could not live, as he after testified upon oath before the jury in open court. And so he died shortly after, as both Mr. Williams, Mr. James and some Indians testified in court.

Source: Bradford, William. Excerpts from *Of Plymouth Plantation*, Book II. In *Colonial Prose and Poetry*. Edited by William P. Trent and Benjamin W. Wells. New York: Thomas Y. Crowell & Company, 1903, pp. 60–62. Spelling slightly modified.

TIMELINE   2000 1900 1800 1700 1600 1500 1400 1300 1200 1100 1000 900 800 700 600 500 400 300 200 100 1 BCE

What You Need to Know

In this selection from *Of Plymouth Plantation*, a 1638 account of the original Pilgrim colony in New England by its leader William Bradford, Bradford describes the killing of a native Narragansett boy who had come to the colony to trade. The murderers were two Englishmen. When the local sachem, or chief, demanded satisfaction for the killing, the colonists extracted a confession from the two men and then had them executed.

In 1620, a group of English religious dissenters, who had earlier fled persecution at home, landed on the coast of what is now Massachusetts, establishing the colony called Plymouth Plantation. We know them today as the Pilgrims.

The settlement was vulnerable. Established as the harsh New England winter set in, it experienced much suffering and loss of life during its first months. Only with the cooperation of the local Pokanoket Indians were the Pilgrims able to survive. Weakened by diseases brought by European fishermen who wintered in the area before the Pilgrims' arrival, the Pokanokets were also under siege from the more powerful Narragansett people. This is one of the reasons why they allied themselves with the Pilgrims.

For their part, the Pilgrims strived to maintain good relations with all the local natives, not only because they relied on them for trade in needed food but also for self-protection. The martial Narragansett could have easily wiped them out.

A Closer Look

While the Pilgrims famously shared a Thanksgiving feast with the local Wampanoag in 1621, in reality, the native Americans of New England had an uneasy relationship with the spreading colonies of English settlers. As Bradford's story hints, they were familiar enough with one another that a young Indian boy could venture into the Pilgrim's settlement unescorted. There was, in fact, not only a good deal of trade between the two peoples—food and animal skins from the natives in exchange for all types of simple manufactured goods from Europe—but natives often did work for the Pilgrims to earn money to buy things from them. While the Pilgrims learned agricultural and hunting skills from the locals, they in turn taught the latter their own take on various crafts, which the natives were already familiar with, such as basket weaving and the cutting of timber.

But the Indians were less willing to adopt the settlers' way of life, including their religion. At the same time, the settlers grew increasingly disinterested in trying to convert the Indians, making only desultory efforts in that direction. Gradually, as the English settlers, particularly after the establishment of the much bigger Puritan colony at what is now Boston, grew in number and strength, they were less accommodating of the Indians. This was especially so after the so-called King Philip's War of 1637, a brutal struggle between the settlers and various Indian peoples—marked by massacres on both sides—that ultimately resulted in the defeat of the Narragansetts.

1 100 200 300 400 500 600 700 800 900 1000 1100 1200 1300 1400 1500 1600 1700 1800 1900 2000 CE

2.13.14 A Spanish Missionary's Voyage up the Amazon River

Amazon Basin
1641

36. The multitude of tribes, and of different nations. All this new world, if we may call it so, is inhabited by barbarians, in distinct provinces and nations, of which I am enabled to give an account, naming them and pointing out their residences, some from my own observations, and others from information of the Indians. They exceed one hundred and fifty, all with different languages. These nations are so near each other, that from the last villages of one they hear the people of the other at work. But this proximity does not lead to peace; on the contrary, they are engaged in constant wars, in which they kill and take prisoners great numbers of souls every day. This is the drain provided for so great a multitude, without which the whole land would not be large enough to hold them. . . .

37. Arms which the Indians use. Their arms consist of short spears, and darts made of strong wood, well sharpened, and which, thrown with dexterity, easily reach the enemy. Others have *estolicas*, weapons with which the warriors of the Incas of Peru were very dexterous. These *estolicas* are flattened poles, about a yard long, and three fingers broad. In the upper end a bone is fixed, to which an arrow of nine *palmos* is fastened, with the point also of bone or very strong palm wood, which, worked into the shape of a harpoon, remains like a javelin hanging from the person whom it wounds. They hold this in the right hand, with the *estolica* clutched by the lower part, and fixing the weapon in the upper bone, they hurl it with such tremendous force and with so good an aim, that at fifty paces they never miss. They fight with these arms, with them they hunt, and with them they become masters of any fish that are hidden under the waves. What is more wonderful, with these arrows they transfix the turtles, when, from time to time and for a very few moments, they shew their heads above the water. . . .

Some of these nations use bows and arrows, a weapon which, among all the others, is respected for the force and rapidity with which it inflicts wounds. Poisonous herbs are plentiful, of which some tribes make a poison so fatal, that an arrow, stained with it, destroys life the moment that it draws blood.

38. Their means of communication are by water, in canoes. All those who live on the shores of this great river are collected in large villages, and, like the Venetians and Mexicans, their means of communication are by water, in small vessels which they call canoes. These are usually of cedar wood, which the providence of God abundantly supplies, without the labour of cutting it or carrying it from the forest; sending it down with the current of the river. . . .

39. The tools which they use. The tools which they use to make not only their canoes, but also their houses and anything else they require, are hatchets and adzes, not forged in the smithies of Biscay, but manufactured in the forges of their understanding, having, as in other things, necessity for their master.

Source: de Acuña, Cristoval. Excerpts from *New Discovery of the Great River of the Amazons*. In *Expeditions into the Valley of the Amazons, 1539, 1540, 1639*. Translated and edited by Clements R. Markham. London, Hakluyt Society, 1859, pp. 79–82.

What You Need to Know

Published in 1641, *New Discovery of the Great River of the Amazons*, was written by Spanish missionary Cristoval de Acuña, who, with a companion named Pedro Texeira made his way up the Amazon between 1637 and 1639.

When the Spanish and Portuguese settled South America in the sixteenth century, they largely avoided it, kept away by its thick jungle, unforgiving climate, and its poor soil, depleted by the incessant rains and lush growth. A few intrepid explorers, however, made their way up the intricate river system of the region, beginning with the Spaniard Francisco de Orellana in 1542.

The Spanish believed that the region was sparsely inhabited, as settled agriculture was untenable. However, at the time of Columbus the Amazon basin may have been home to as many as five million people who survived by hunting and gathering the plentiful game, fruits, and nuts of the forest. Among the first to realize the full diversity of human societies in the region was Spanish missionary de Acuña.

A Closer Look

According to de Acuña's account, he encountered no less than 150 distinct peoples during the course of his journey, each speaking a distinct language. He also notes the density of the population, saying that villages were literally within earshot of one another. But rather than leading to accommodation among themselves, the proximity triggered constant warfare, the main scourge of the region. Although saying they fled his own expedition, de Acuña is nevertheless impressed by the Amazonians' weapons and their skill in using them, particularly for hunting and fishing. He also points out that they were experts in concocting herbal poisons.

Other evidence of their material culture comes in the form of river vessels and tools. De Acuña observes that the canoes they built were light and easily carried from portage to portage. He also describes their tools, which include stone axes and hatchets. In general, the impression left by de Acuña is of peoples who live in a land of abundance, which they nevertheless war over, pointing out how they do not even need to move cedar logs to the river to make into canoes as thick trees were everywhere. He also admires their ingenuity, noting how, being beyond the pale of European culture in South America, they make for themselves all that they need.

1 100 200 300   400   500   600   700   800   900   1000 1100 1200 1300   1400   1500   1600   1700 1800 1900 2000 CE

2.13.15 Report from the Governor of New Sweden

Delaware River and Bay
1644

Our savages also become very proud here in the river. I have told them the whole year that we shall receive much people with our ships, but three days after the ship arrived and they observed that there was only one ship and no people they fell in between Tinnakungh and Uplandh and murdered a man and a woman on their bed, and they killed a few days afterwards two soldiers and a servant. When their commanders found out that I drew the people together in order to prevent a future and a greater damage, then they feared and came together from all places excusing themselves in the highest manner, and said that this had happened without their knowledge, and asked for peace, which was granted them on the following conditions: that in case they hereafter practised the smallest hostilities against our people then we would not let a soul of them live, upon which they gave their writing and all their sachems signed their names to it and (according to their custom) gave us twenty beavers and some sewant1 and we presented them with a piece of cloth. But yet they do not trust us and we trust them much less.

Nothing would be better than that a couple of hundred soldiers should be sent here and kept here until we broke the necks of all of them in the river, especially since we have no beaver trade with them but only the maize trade. They are a lot of poor rascals. Then each one could be secure here at his work, and feed and nourish himself unmolested without their maize, and also we could take possession of the places (which are the most fruitful) that the savages now possess; and then, when we have not only bought this river but also won it with the sword, then no one whether he be Hollander or Englishman could pretend in any manner to this place either now or in coming times, but we should then have the beaver trade with the black and white Minquas alone, four times as good as we have had it, now or at any past time. And if there is some delay in this matter it must nevertheless in the end come to this and it cannot be a voided; the sooner the better, before they do us more harm. They are not to be trusted, as both example and our own experience show, but if I should receive a couple of hundred good soldiers and in addition necessary means and good officers, then with the help of God not a single savage would be allowed to live in this river. Then one would have a passage free from here unto Manathans, which lies at a distance of three small days' journeys from here across the country, beginning at Zachikans.

Source: Printz, Johan. Excerpt from "Report of Governor Johan Printz, 1644." In *Narratives of Early Pennsylvania, West New Jersey and Delaware, 1630–1707*. Edited by Albert Cook Myers. New York: Charles Scribner's Sons, 1912, pp. 102–104.

TIMELINE   2000 1900 1800 1700 1600 1500 1400 1300 1200 1100 1000 900 800 700 600 500 400 300 200 100 1 BCE

What You Need to Know

This excerpt comes from a 1644 report to the headquarters of the Swedish West India Company by Johan Printz, governor of New Sweden.

Perhaps the least known of the European settlement enterprises on mainland North America was that of New Sweden, a colony of tiny settlements along the lower Delaware River in what is now the states of Delaware, New Jersey, and Pennsylvania. It was founded in 1638 by the royally chartered Swedish West India Company, whose shareholders hoped to make a profit from growing tobacco and trading in beaver and other fur pelts with the native peoples of the region. The company sponsored more than a dozen voyages between the ports of Sweden and the navigable Delaware River, transporting roughly 600 settlers, mostly Swedes and Finns, but also Germans and Dutchmen. The first leader of the settlement was Peter Minuit, the director of the Dutch West India Company, which founded New Amsterdam (later New York City) fourteen years earlier. Minuit tried to negotiate for lands and trading rights with the *sachems*, or chiefs, of the local Susquehannock Indians. As was often the case, there were misunderstandings between the two, leading to disagreements with the Native Americans over what exactly they had ceded to the Swedish West India Company. As Printz, one of Minuit successors notes, those disagreements had come back to haunt the colony.

A Closer Look

New Sweden, between its founding in 1638 and its ultimate absorption by the Dutch colony of New Netherlands in 1655—the latter occurring despite Printz's best efforts to impose strict rules on the colonists, improve agricultural production, and build forts and settlements—was a precarious enterprise. The problem was that few settlers wanted to come. By 1650, the colony had but 200 Europeans living in it and no contact with the Swedish West India Company for years on end.

Even worse for the colony, as Printz notes in the letter, the lack of ships encouraged the Indians to try and retake the lands they had supposedly ceded to Minuit. At one point, Printz begs the company to send a troop of soldiers, for a lack of security was preventing settlers from farming. "A hundred good soldiers," he writes, and "with the help of God not a single savage would be allowed to live in this river [the Delaware]." Such a force would also prevent incursions by other European competitors, such as the English and the Dutch.

The local Algonquian-speaking natives around New Sweden were, in fact, largely sedentary agriculturalists, who typically produced large surpluses of corn, melons, and squash, which, along with fish, venison, and bear meat obtained from surrounding forests and streams, they sold to the colonists, in exchange for what little goods from Europe the latter had. In other words, New Sweden was ill served by the Swedish West India Company, which rarely sent supply ships. Thus, the colonists had little to exchange with the natives and so could not compete with the Dutch and English for the lucrative fur trade.

1 100 200 300 400 500 600 700 800 900 1000 1100 1200 1300 1400 1500 1600 1700 1800 1900 2000 CE

2.13.16 François Bernier on Indian Astrology

Northern India
1663

Next to the garden is the great royal square, faced on one side by the gates of the fortress, and on the opposite side of which terminate the two most considerable streets of the city. . . .

Here too is held a bazar or market for an endless variety of things; which like the Pont-neuf at Paris, is the rendezvous for all sorts of mountebanks and jugglers. Hither, likewise, the astrologers resort, both Mahometan and Gentile. These wise doctors remain seated in the sun, on a dusty piece of carpet, handling some old mathematical instruments, and having open before them a large book which represents the signs of the zodiac.

In this way they attract the attention of the passengers, and impose upon the people, by whom they are considered as so many infallible oracles. They tell a poor person his fortune for a payssa (which is worth about one sol); and after examining the hand and face of the applicant, turning over the leaves of the large book, and pretending to make certain calculations, these impostors decide upon the Sahet or propitious moment of commencing the business he may have in hand. Silly women, wrapping themselves in a white cloth from head to foot, flock to the astrologers, whisper to them all the transactions of their lives, and disclose every secret with no more reserve than is practised by a scrupulous penitent in the presence of her confessor. The ignorant and infatuated people really believe that the stars have an influence which the astrologers can control. . . .

I am speaking only of the poor bazar-astrologers. Those who frequent the court of the grandees are considered by them eminent doctors, and become wealthy. The whole of Asia is degraded by the same superstition. Kings and nobles grant large salaries to these crafty diviners, and never engage in the most trifling transaction without consulting them. They read whatever is written in heaven; fix upon the Sahet, and solve every doubt by opening the Koran.

Source: Bernier, François. Excerpt from letter to Monsieur de la Mothe le Vayer, July 1, 1663. In *Travels in the Mogul Empire, A.D. 1656–1668*. Oxford: Oxford University Press, 1914, pp. 243–245.

TIMELINE   2000 1900 1800 1700 1600 1500 1400 1300 1200 1100 1000 900 800 700 600 500 400 300 200 100 1 BCE

What You Need to Know

In 1655, the French physician François Bernier embarked on a 12-year journey across the Middle East, East Africa, and South Asia. In this excerpt from a 1663 letter, he writes to a fellow French writer during his visit to the north Indian cities of Agra and Delhi.

North India at the time was under the rule of the Mughals, a Turkic-speaking people originally from Central Asia, who ruled the region from the early sixteenth century until they were usurped by British colonialists in the early nineteenth. Initially, the Mughals tried to rule North India themselves. But under Akbar, their greatest ruler, who reigned from 1556 to 1605, they realized that it was more effective to administer this vast and heavily populated land by delegating authority to local Hindu leaders. The Mughals were also quite tolerant on matters of faith, as Bernier's descriptions of the various astrologers in the marketplace of Delhi—"Mahometan [Muslim] and Gentile [Hindu, Jain, Buddhists and peoples of other non-Western faiths]" alike—attests.

A Closer Look

As a physician and scientist—his 1684 book on various types of human beings is considered the first treatise on racial classification in the modern era—Bernier naturally has little tolerance for astrology, viewing those who believe in it to be "ignorant and infatuated people." Nevertheless, his description of its practice reveals much about the importance of astrology in the everyday lives of ordinary Indians in the time of the Mughals.

He describes the astrologers, whom he facetiously calls "doctors," as being seated on carpets, using mathematical instruments and ancient books holding the signs of the zodiac. In fact, while these fortune-tellers were probably not great mathematicians—Bernier all but says they are charlatans—they were nevertheless the heirs to a tradition that informed the greatest achievements in the field in the Middle Ages. Indeed, modern arithmetic and algebra originated in India and were passed to Europe via the Islamic lands of the Middle East.

Bernier also notes that astrology did not just hold a grip on the minds of ordinary market women and merchants of the Delhi bazaar but also on the "kings and nobles" of the land, who based their every decision and transaction on what astrologers said the stars foretold. "The whole of Asia," this student of the Scientific Revolution says, "is degraded by the same superstition." Such attitudes would lead his fellow Europeans to decide in coming centuries that they knew what was best for the Indian people and should thus rule over them.

1 100 200 300 400 500 600 700 800 900 1000 1100 1200 1300 1400 1500 1600 1700 1800 1900 2000 CE

2.13.17 A Dutchman's Description of Colonial Plantation Life

Maryland
1679

As to the present government of Maryland, it remains firm upon the old footing, and is confined within the limits before mentioned. All of Maryland that we have seen, is high land, with few or no meadows, but possessing such a rich and fertile soil, as persons living there assured me that they had raised tobacco off the same piece of land for thirty consecutive years. The inhabitants, who are generally English, are mostly engaged in this production. It is their chief staple, and the money with which they must purchase every thing they require, which is brought to them from other English possessions in Europe, Africa and America. There is, nevertheless, sometimes a great want of these necessaries, owing to the tobacco market being low, or the shipments being prevented by some change of affairs in some quarter, particularly in Europe, or indeed to both causes, as was the case at this time, whereby there sometimes arises a great scarcity of such articles as are most necessary, as we saw when there. So large a quantity of tobacco is raised in Maryland and Virginia, that it is one of the greatest sources of revenue to the crown by reason of the taxes which it yields. Servants and negroes are chiefly employed in the culture of tobacco, who are brought from other places to be sold to the highest bidders, the servants for a term of years only, but the negroes forever, and may be sold by their masters to other planters as many times as their masters choose, that is, the servants until their term is fulfilled, and the negroes for life. These men, one with another, each make, after they are able to work, from 2,500 pounds to 3,000 pounds and even 3,500 pounds of tobacco a year, and some of the masters and their wives who pass their lives here in wretchedness, do the same. The servants and negroes after they have worn themselves down the whole day, and come home to rest, have yet to grind and pound the grain, which is generally maize, for their masters and all their families as well as themselves, and all the negroes, to eat. Tobacco is the only production in which the planters employ themselves, as if there were nothing else in the world to plant but that, and while the land is capable of yielding all the productions that can be raised anywhere, so far as the climate of the place allows.

Source: Danckaerts, Jasper. Excerpt from journal entry for December 15, 1679. In *The Journal of Jasper Danckaerts, 1679–1680*. Edited by Bartlett Burleigh James and J. Franklin Jameson. New York: Charles Scribner's Sons, 1913, p. 133.

What You Need to Know

This passage is from a journal kept by Jasper Danckaerts, a Dutchman who traveled to the colony of Maryland to scout a possible location for a colony of Labadists, a radical French Protestant sect.

The Province of Maryland was founded as a proprietary colony by England's Lord Baltimore in 1632 as a haven for the country's Catholics, then experiencing persecution. A propriety colony was effectively the estate of a single individual, who had been granted the land by the king. Baltimore wanted the colony to be tolerant of all Christian faiths but, in fact, was torn in its early years by the same religious disputes from which England was suffering.

Despite the disputes and the colony's Catholic origins, it was not a particularly religious place, as the Puritan colonies of New England were. In fact, it bore a close resemblance to its older, southern neighbor Virginia. Economic profit, by means of commercial agriculture, was the primary motive of most settlers, who tended not to live in towns and cities but on isolated tobacco plantations. There were two types of laborers on these plantations, as noted by Danckaerts—black slaves and white indentured servants.

A Closer Look

Over the course of the seventeenth century, roughly 130,000 Englishmen migrated to Virginia and Maryland. Of these, approximately 80 percent were indentured servants—three quarters of whom were males between the ages of 15 and 24.

The indentured servant system had a long history in England, although it mostly involved boys being apprenticed to an artisan to learn a trade. In exchange, the servant worked for the artisan for a set period of years—usually seven, although longer if he tried to escape or committed any infractions. The term *indenture* came from the contract the two signed, as two identical halves cut in half along indented lines were given to each party. In British North America, indentured servitude meant something else entirely—a system to exploit the most vulnerable of England's poor, lured to America by the promise of land. In fact, many indentured servants in the early years of settlement died before their seven-year term was up.

Upon arriving in Maryland, as Danckaerts notes, both Englishmen and Africans were bid upon by planters, "the [white] servants until their term is fulfilled and the negroes for life." Aside from this very important distinction, however, their lives were often much the same—endless hard labor. After working the fields all day, he says, and expecting to come to home to rest, they were instead put to work grinding the grain for the entire plantation.

1 100 200 300 400 500 600 700 800 900 1000 1100 1200 1300 1400 1500 1600 1700 1800 1900 2000 CE

2.13.18 A Jesuit Missionary's Expedition to the Sonoran Desert

Sonoran Desert
1699

[O]n February 7 [1699] we began this entry, the Señor Lieutenant Juan Matheo Manke, Father Adamo Gilg, and I, with some servants and more than ninety pack animals. We entered by the northwest to San Marzelo del Sonoidag, where a new ranch was begun, with thirty-six head of cattle which I ordered sent ahead for the fathers of California, if perchance they should go up to the near-by port of Santa Clara. Passing very near it, we entered upon the more than forty leagues of coast and new road between there and the mouth of the Rio Grande and its confluence with the Rio Colorado. By the natives whom we found along this road we were received with all love. We spent the twenty-second of February, the day of the Chair of St. Peter in Antioch, on the Rio Grande, whither more than fifty natives, Pimas, Yumas, Opas, and Cocomaricopas, had gathered; and we named the post and ranchería San Pedro, as another ranchería lower down was named San Pablo.

And because eighty leagues farther to the east, on this same river, close to La Encarnacion and Casa Grande, there was the ranchería of San Andres, afterwards, at the suggestion of Father Adamo, giving other rancherías the names of the other holy apostles, this Rio Grande we named Rio de los Santos Apostoles. To this it may be added that all its inhabitants are fishermen, and have many nets and other tackle with which they fish all the year, sustaining themselves with the abundant fish and with their maize, beans, and calabashes, etc. These people so new, of very different dress, customs, and languages, all received us with the utmost friendship, affection, and pleasure on their part and ours, their chiefs coming out to meet us more than a league's journey, giving us afterward of their eatables, etc. We preached to them the word of God in the Pima language, and, with an interpreter, in the language of the Cocomaricopas, which is that spoken by the Opas and the Yumas. It was well received, and they would have given us many little ones to baptize, but we accepted and baptized only a few sick persons. We informed ourselves in regard to the rancherias and people farther to the north, northeast, and northwest, and of the very populous Rio Colorado near-by, which is even larger than the Rio Grande, and they told us that the Yumas, Cutganes, and Alchedomas came next in order. We dispatched Christian messages and talks in all directions and occasionally some little gifts and gewgaws; and already here in Nuestra Señora de los Dolores I have received very friendly replies, in which they call me to go to treat of their eternal salvation.

Source: Kino, Eusebio. *Kino's Historical Memoir of Pimería Alta: A Contemporary Account of the Beginning of California, Sonora, and Arizona, by Father Eusebio Francisco Kino, S.J. Pioneer Missionary Explorer, Cartographer, and Ranchman 1683–1711.* Vol. I. Edited by Herbert Eugene Bolton. Cleveland: Arthur H. Clark Company, 1919, pp. 193–195.

TIMELINE   2000 1900 1800 1700 1600 1500 1400 1300 1200 1100 1000 900 800 700 600 500 400 300 200 100 1 BCE

What You Need to Know

The accompanying document is an excerpt from the writings of Eusebio Kino, an Italian Jesuit missionary, who spent the last 24 years of his life from 1683 to 1711, founding and administering Catholic missions on the Baja Peninsula of Mexico and in what is now southern Arizona.

The Indians he encountered in these regions lived largely along the various rivers, including the Colorado and what he refers to as the Rio Grande or the Rio de los Santos Apostoles (known today as the Gila). He notes that the natives existed on fishing and the raising of crops, the latter made possible by an elaborate system of irrigation.

Kino notes the warm welcome the missionaries received, with the Indians sharing their food with the newcomers. Curiosity also played a factor: the missionary notes that Indian chiefs, who typically stayed close to their home villages, traveled many miles to see them.

A Closer Look

Conversion of the native peoples of the Americas to Catholicism was one of the main purposes of Spanish exploration and conquest in the Western Hemisphere from the late fifteenth-century voyages of Columbus on, even if the humanitarian principles on which the faith rested were often ignored in the rush to exploit the people and resources of these newly encountered lands.

But the various religious orders—the Franciscans, Dominicans, and the Jesuits—took seriously their mission to convert the Indians to Catholicism and what they considered a more civilized way of life. As Kino describes, one of the first things he and his expedition did upon arriving in a new place was to spread the gospel. The Jesuits made a major effort to learn the native languages and, as Kino notes, were able to preach in Pima, a major language of the American Southwest, although they required an interpreter for the less commonly spoken tongue of the Cocomaricopas. Kino claims the Indians were eager to hear the word of God and that the message "was well received." At the same time, missionaries such as Kino were not above doling out "some small gifts and gewgaws" to lure the Indians in the first place.

1 100 200 300 400 500 600 700 800 900 1000 1100 1200 1300 1400 1500 1600 1700 1800 1900 2000 CE

2.13.19 Letter from a Tobacco Planter on the Worth of His Plantation

Virginia
1686

The plantation where I now live contains a thousand acres, at least 700 acres of it being rich thicket, the remainder good hearty plantable land, without any waste either by marshes or great swamps. The commodiousness, conveniency, and pleasantness yourself well knows. Upon it there is three quarters well furnished with all necessary houses, grounds, and fencing, together with a choice crew of negroes at each plantation, most of them this country born, the remainder as likely as most in Virginia, there being twenty-nine in all, with stocks of cattle and hogs at each quarter. Upon the same land is my own dwelling house furnished with all accommodations for a comfortable and genteel living, as a very good dwelling house with rooms in it, four of the best of them hung [with tapestry] and nine of them plentifully furnished with all things necessary and convenient, and all houses for use furnished with brick chimneys; four good cellars, a dairy, dove-cote, stable, barn, henhouse, kitchen, and all other conveniences and all in a manner new, a large orchard of about 2500 apple trees, most grafted, well fenced with a locust fence, which is as durable as most brick walls; a garden a hundred foot square, well paled in; a yard wherein is most of the aforesaid necessary houses, pallisadoed in with locust puncheons which is as good as if it were walled in and more lasting than any of our bricks; together with a good stock of cattle, hogs, horses, mares, sheep, etc., and necessary servants belonging to it for the supply and support thereof.

About a mile and half distance a good water grist mill, whose toll I find sufficient to find my own family with wheat and Indian corn for our necessities and occasions. Up the river in this county, three tracts of land more; one of them contains 21,996 acres, another 500 acres, and one other 1000 acres, all good, convenient, and commodious seats, and which in few years will yield a considerable annual income.

Source: Fitzhugh, William. Excerpt from letter to Dr. Ralph Smith, April 22, 1686. In "Letters of William Fitzhugh," *Virginia Magazine of History and Biography*. Vol. I. Richmond: The Virginia Historical Society, 1893, p. 395.

TIMELINE   2000 1900 1800 1700 1600 1500 1400 1300 1200 1100 1000 900 800 700 600 500 400 300 200 100 1 BCE

What You Need to Know

This excerpt of a letter written by Virginia tobacco planter William Fitzhugh in 1686 is an assessment of his estate.

Jamestown, the first permanent English settlement on the North American mainland, established in 1607, proved a disaster in its early years. It had been set up by a chartered company, which lured settlers with promises of precious metals and a life of leisure ruling over the natives. Stories of the wealth and ease of Spanish life in Mexico were rife in Europe at the time.

Conditions proved anything but luxurious or leisurely. Disease and starvation gripped the colony, made worse by the settler's unwillingness to do much productive work. Instead, they sought to feed themselves by robbing the local natives, organized into a confederation by chief Powhatan, of their crops and food stores. This, of course, produced conflict and further suffering for all concerned. While surviving, the colony hardly lived up to its promise as a base for the English settlement of North America—not until the late 1610s, when it was discovered that tobacco, which was growing increasingly popular in Europe, grew there exceptionally well.

A Closer Look

By the 1630s, tobacco plantations lined the many rivers surrounding the Chesapeake region of Delaware and Tidewater of Maryland and Virginia. Unlike New England, where people lived in small villages and towns, the planters of the Chesapeake lived on isolated farms. The rivers were deep enough for oceangoing vessels to navigate so there was little need for ports. They could ship their tobacco to, and import goods directly from, England. Isolated as they were, the farms were largely self-sustaining, as Fitzhugh notes. The goods they imported consisted of a few foods they could not grow themselves, such as sugar and tea, and those manufacturing items they could not make on their own.

Fitzhugh also points out the fact that the main house was "pallisadoed," that is, surrounded with a high palisade fence for protection. How necessary this was in 1686 is questionable. By then, the Indians of the Chesapeake had largely been subdued by English arms or felled by imported European diseases. However, the colony was still recovering from a major rebellion of lower-class Englishmen a decade before. That uprising, known as Bacon's Rebellion, after its leader Nathaniel Bacon, had convinced many Chesapeake planters that indentured English servants were not the most reliable labor force. Instead, tobacco farmers, such as Fitzhugh, increasingly turned to slaves from Africa to work their plantations.

1 100 200 300 400 500 600 700 800 900 1000 1100 1200 1300 1400 1500 1600 1700 1800 1900 2000 CE

2.13.20 Spanish Silver Eight *Real* Coin

Alta Peru (Bolivia)
1688

Credit: Hoberman Collection/Corbis

What You Need to Know

The eight *real* coin pictured here was struck in silver at the Potosí colonial mint, in what is now Bolivia, in 1688. A real, meaning "royal" in Spanish, had become a key medium of exchange in the expanding international economy of the late seventeenth century.

Much of wealth dug from the ground at Potosí and other Spanish-controlled mines in the Americas ended up transported to the royal treasury in Seville on the Guadalquivir River, where ships from across the Atlantic docked upon their arrival in Spain.

The precious metal proved a mixed blessing for the Spanish nation. It brought enormous wealth and power to the monarchy, allowing Spain to have an outsized influence in the politics of Europe. At the same time, however, the influx fed both inflation at home and a high exchange rate for Spanish currency abroad. The latter made goods in Spain uncompetitive, undermining the Spanish manufacturing. Indeed, say economic historians, the flood of wealth from the Americas is one of the prime reasons why the Spanish economy fell behind that of other Western European economies until the late twentieth century.

A Closer Look

Inca legend had it that the silver mine at Potosí Mountain—sometimes called *cerro rico*, or "mountain of riches" in Spanish—was discovered by the Inca emperor Huayna Capac, some 70 years before Pizarro's arrival. Visiting other mines in the region, he is said to have looked at the mountain and declared, "its heart is full of silver."

Indeed, it was. But it would be the Spanish conquerors of the Andes who would reap its full potential. Between the mid-sixteenth century and the late eighteenth, they would dig up 45,000 tons of pure silver from the mine. Or, rather, it was their indigenous Amerindian workers who dug it up. The Spanish adopted the *mita* labor system originally developed by the Incas. But while under the Incas, the *mita* system was a contract labor system used for public works construction, usually in the vicinity of the laborers' villages, under the Spanish it was commercialized and expanded. Every village and town was required to send a seventh of its male labor force to work for the Spanish, many in the mines around distant Potosí. Conditions were horrendous. Freezing weather, a lack of food and potable water, and close living conditions led to famine and epidemic that killed off tens of thousands of workers, many of whom could not leave because of the debts they had accrued to the mine owners.

1 100 200 300 400 500 600 700 800 900 1000 1100 1200 1300 1400 1500 1600 1700 1800 1900 2000 CE

2.13.21 Scene from the Qing Dynasty Play *The Peach Blossom Fan*

China
1699

Scene 23: The Message on the Fan

1644, eleventh month

[Fragrant Princess enters, looking pale and wan.]

Fragrant Princess [sings]:
The cold wind pierces my thin gown,
I am too weary to burn incense.
A streak of bright blood still glistens on my eyebrow.
My languid soul floats over my lone shadow;
My life is spring gossamer in this frosty moonlit tower.
The night seems endless:
When dawn appears, the same grief lingers on.

[Speaks]: In a moment of despair, I tore my flesh to defend my virtue. Alone, I peek and pine
   in my empty room. I have lost my sole companion.

[Sings]: Long Bridge is wrapped in cloud and frozen snow,
My tower is closed and visitors are few.
Beyond the balustrade, a line of wild geese;
Outside the curtain, icicles are dripping.
The brazier is burnt out, all perfume faded.
I shrink and shiver in the biting wind.

[Speaks]: Though I live in a pleasure resort, the flowers and moon have ceased to bring me
   joy. I have done with worldly vanities.

[Sings]: My 'broidered window curtain is forlorn,
Though the parrot's foolish voice cries "Serving tea,"
And the white cat sleeps serenely on its cushion.
So loose my skirt, it flaps about my waist;
So tired my feet, their phoenix-patterned shoes
Feel tossed upon the crests of boisterous waves.
Excess of grief breeds sickness. Love and joy
Have fled this chamber never to return.

[Speaks]: I never cease thinking of my beloved lord. Since his flight I have had no news of
   him, but I shall preserve my chastity for his sake.

Source: Shangren, Kong. Excerpt from *T'ao-hua- shan*. In *The Peach Blossom Fan*. Translated by Chen Shih-hsiang and Harold
Acton. Berkeley: University of California Press, 1976, pp. 168–169.

TIMELINE   2000 1900 1800 1700 1600 1500 1400 1300 1200 1100 1000 900 800 700 600 500 400 300 200 100 1 BCE

What You Need to Know

Born in 1648, a distant descendent of the philosopher Confucius, Kong Shangren wrote a number of poems and plays but is best remembered for *The Peach Blossom Fan*. The historical drama, which incorporated music and dance, depicts the events leading to the downfall of the Ming dynasty through the love story of its two protagonists, a young scholar named Hou Fangyu and the courtesan Li Xiangjun, the "fragrant princess."

Over the course of the fourteenth century, a series of natural and man-made calamities led to the downfall of the Mongol Yuan dynasty of China. In the midst of the turmoil caused by this decline arose a rebel leader named Zhu Yuanzhang, who ultimately united the country under the Ming dynasty, the first to be founded and led by people from the south of China. The Ming dynasty, although not particularly successful militarily, nevertheless marked a cultural pinnacle of Chinese history, producing some of the most beautiful paintings, porcelain, and literature ever produced in China.

But continuing military pressure from the north, combined with government mismanagement of the economy, undermined Ming authority, leading to their decline and eventual replacement by the Qing dynasty in 1644. The Qing would be the last dynasty in Chinese history, replaced by a republican government in 1912. The Qing were not ethnic Chinese but, rather, people from Manchuria and many Chinese resented their rule, longing for the return of the Ming. Such nostalgia was reflected by poets and writers, like the playwright Kong Shangren in his masterwork *The Peach Blossom Fan*, written in 1699.

A Closer Look

Theater in the Qing dynasty was extremely popular. Virtually every Chinese town had a theater, while larger cities might boast dozens of them, some quite large. Indeed, many wealthy families had large rooms in their palaces, with fixed stages built into them, devoted to performances by professional actors. Typically, public theaters did double duty. The ground floor often had tables laid perpendicular to the stage so that when there was no performance, they could be used as restaurants and teahouses.

The bigger theaters were equipped with stage lighting, usually oil lamps or candles, but smaller theaters might rely on natural light only, meaning they could only host daytime performances.

The stages were relatively small, as Chinese theater of the era used few props beyond chairs, tables, and few portable items, such as a teapot or sword. Playwrights wrote with this in mind, so that descriptions of surroundings were often mouthed by the characters or the chorus.

1 100 200 300 400 500 600 700 800 900 1000 1100 1200 1300 1400 1500 1600 1700 1800 1900 2000 CE

2.13.22 Edo-Period Painting of Men Drinking Tea

Japan
Early Eighteenth Century

Credit: DeAgostini/Getty Images

What You Need to Know

This early eighteenth-century painting by the artist Kaigetsudo Ando depicts three men drinking tea and engaging in conversation.

Over the course of the sixteenth century, Japan underwent a dramatic political, cultural, and social reorganization. Government was centralized under a shogunate, a kind of military regency, which effectively stripped the old aristocracy, the *daimyo*, and their armed retainers, the samurai, of most of their political power and much of their economic wealth.

This left the noble class with little to do and much time on their hands, as any kind of work or commerce was believed to be beneath their dignity. Instead, they spent most of their time indulging in consumption of luxury goods and pleasurable pursuits. Japan's burgeoning cities were filled with institutions that catered to the whims of the aristocracy, particularly its male component, including theaters, restaurants, brothels, and teahouses.

A Closer Look

All classes of Japanese men typically drank their tea in one of two settings. The first were rooms in private houses devoted to the activity, known as *chashitsu*, or "tea rooms." In such rooms, indulging in tea was about more than simply boiling some water, steeping tea leaves, and drinking the brew. By the eighteenth century, the preparation, serving, and drinking of tea involved elaborate rituals and ceremony, based on philosophical principles. Every aspect of the activity became formalized, from the architecture of the room to the types of tea prepared and the implements used to prepare and serve it. The movements of both the servers and the drinkers were also carefully choreographed.

By the Edo period from 1603 to 1867, named for the capital of the Tokugawa Shogunate at the time (Edo was renamed Tokyo in 1868), tea was often drunk in public teahouses. Here, ritual was much less important. Indeed, even the tea itself was merely an amenity to the real purposes of the places—romantic dalliance and sexual indulgence. Such teahouses were filled with private rooms. Some of these were hired for trysts between men and their mistresses; others were used by young couples seeking an escape from parental control. In still others, men were served the tea by geishas, whose services included anything from cultured conversation to musical performance to sexual favors.

2.13.23 Colonial Tombstone Epitaphs

Massachusetts
Eighteenth Century

[Cherub's Head]

Memento Mori

Here lies the body of Joseph Davis, son of Mr. Benjn. Davis & Mrs. Sarah his wife

He died Febr. 13th 1761 inn ye sixteenth year of his age

Likeways Elizabeth there daughter died Febr. 27th 1762 in ye 12 month of her age.

. . .

Memento Mori

[Cherub's Head]

Here lies the body of Mr. Josiah Boyden, who departed this Life Octr. seventeenth 1772 in ye 72d year of his age. Also 8 of his Children 5 sons & 3 daughters all lyeing near this place

. . .

Here lies the body of Joseph Stone son of Mr. Nathaniel Stone & Mrs. Sybel his wife who died Novr. 10th 1772. Aged 2 years.

. . .

Memento mori

[Cherub]

Here lies Buried ye body of Mrs. Prudence Warren, wife of Mr. Abijah Warren; she departed this Life Febr. 1st 1773. Aged 23 years. Likeways a little babe still born 10 days before she died.

. . .

Blessed are the dead who dye in the Lord. Here also lies the Body of Mrs. Susanna Lawrence, Relict of the above named Colln. William Lawrence. She was a woman of Piety and good Sense, an industrious, Prudent wife; and indulgent parent, a good Neighbour, a faithfull Friend, a hater of Hypocrisy and Guile; a lover of hospitality, Patiet under Affliction and Resigned to the will of Heaven in death by which she was called out of the world to Receive the Rewards of a faithfull Servant on the 10th of Sept. & in the 80th year of her Age. ad: 1771.

Source: Green, Samuel A., ed. *Epitaphs from the Old Burying Ground in Groton, Massachusetts*. Boston: Little, Brown, & Company, 1878, pp. 39, 42, 56–57.

TIMELINE   2000 1900 1800 1700 1600 1500 1400 1300 1200 1100 1000 900 800 700 600 500 400 300 200 100 1 BCE

514

What You Need to Know

The selection of epitaphs is from eighteenth-century tombstones of the Puritan town of Groton, Massachusetts.

In the decades following King Henry VIII's break from the Roman Catholic Church and the establishment of the Anglican Church, England was riven by religious controversy and conflict. While some preferred a return to Catholicism, others wanted to further purify the Anglican Church of Catholic style ritual and belief. The latter were known, appropriately enough, as Puritans.

Influenced by the teachings of the Franco-Swiss theologian John Calvin, the Puritans believed that God had preordained the destiny of all men and women, selecting some for salvation and others for damnation. Nobody could influence an omnipotent God but they could obtain signs that they were among the so-called elect by righteous living. It was an unforgiving spiritual outlook, which required them not only to police themselves against various sins but others in their community as well. Moreover, it spared not even children, who themselves might end up in Hell. Such views made death an often terrifying event for Puritans. And, as these epitaphs reveal, death was a common occurrence for the young as well as the old.

A Closer Look

New England was among the most salubrious environments anywhere in the world in which to live in the eighteenth century. There were both natural and man-made factors involved. The long, cold winters and relatively cool summers kept infectious diseases somewhat at bay. Strong, religiously based communities of like-minded believers meant that people watched out for one another. Good government ensured that basic public health measures, as they were understood in that time, were enacted in law and those laws enforced.

Still, disease struck often and hard. Today, we are accustomed to seeing the highest mortality rates among the elderly. But in the eighteenth century, two other contingents were well represented among the deceased—young children and women of childbearing age. With their weaker immune systems, children under the age of five were especially susceptible to infectious diseases. Women meanwhile experienced what, in modern times, would seem frightfully high rates of mortality in childbirth, often reaching as high as one in five.

The epitaphs here, memorializing the dead, are notable for two things. The large presence of the young and aspects of deceased's lives the Puritans chose to remember. In memorializing Susanna Lawrence, for example, the epitaph writer chose to focus on her "Piety and good Sense," as well as her industriousness, all Puritan virtues.

2.13.24 Edo-Period Japanese Kimono

Japan
Eighteenth Century

Credit: Universal History Archive/Getty Images

What You Need to Know

This image is of an Edo-period Japanese kimono, or traditional robe worn primarily by women. Literally meaning, "a thing to wear," the kimono was a straight-lined garment hanging from neck to feet, and usually bound by a sash, known as an *obi*.

By the eighteenth century, Japan had been unified politically under the Tokugawa shogunate. A shogunate was essentially a military-controlled regency, in which the emperor served as the semi-divine symbol of national unity but where real power rested in the hands of a shogun, or chief general. The shogunate had replaced the old medieval order in which local nobles, known as *daimyo*, asserted political autonomy by means of armed retainers, or *samurai*. Under the Tokugawa, the *daimyo* and *samurai* had little power but the former, in particular, retained much wealth. They largely spent their time decorating their palaces, commissioning art, engaging in romantic intrigues, and adorning themselves for an endless series of festivals and parties, for which they dressed up in elaborate costumes, such as this richly embroidered kimono with a dragon motif from the eighteenth century. Although sometimes worn by men, the kimono is primarily a women's robe. Simple ones were worn for everyday use, but ones like that featured here were for special occasions.

A Closer Look

In the eighteenth century, Japanese women were almost entirely subordinated to the men in their lives. This was especially true of upper-class women, like those who might have worn this kimono. Their marriages were arranged for them, usually to advance the economic interests of their families. Once wed, they had little life outside of their homes. Indeed, it was considered scandalous for a young women to leave her house unchaperoned by a relative, either male or elderly female. A different but equally subordinate role awaited some poor women. If of exceptional beauty, they might be sold by their parents to houses of prostitution catering to upper-class customers. There, they would become geishas, or "accomplished persons," trained in the arts of conversation and entertaining, along with sex.

But there was also change afoot for some women, particularly of the working and middle classes. Growing commercial enterprise in Tokugawa Japan provided employment opportunities in textile manufacturing, although usually the women were not allowed to keep control of their earnings, turning them over to either their fathers or their husbands. Still, employment meant they could leave the home and gave them a certain sense of autonomy, as they contributed to their household's financial well-being.

1 100 200 300 400 500 600 700 800 900 1000 1100 1200 1300 1400 1500 1600 1700 1800 1900 2000 CE

2.13.25 Qing Dynasty Pewter Altar Set

China
Eighteenth Century

Credit: DeAgostini/Getty Images

What You Need to Know

This set of three altar pieces, rendered from pewter, which at the time was an alloy of tin and lead, was used either in a eighteenth-century Buddhist temple in Qing dynasty China or in the household shrine of a wealthy family. They were made during the rule of the longest serving of Qing emperors, Kangxi, who ruled from 1662 to 1722.

In the mid-seventeenth century, the only dynasty to emerge out of southern China—the Ming—began to experience a decline, a result of economic woes and military setbacks. In 1644, the Ming capital of Beijing fell to invaders from Manchuria, in what is now northwest China. The Manchu, who established the Qing dynasty, were the last royal dynasty in Chinese history, finally falling to a republican revolution in 1911–1912. Other than the Yuan dynasty of the Mongols in the thirteenth and fourteenth centuries, the Qing were the only non-Chinese dynasty to rule the country.

To govern a country with more than 200 million people—then as now the largest in the world—the vastly outnumbered Manchu co-opted the intellectual and political elite of China by offering them positions in the new government. Qing dynasty rulers were also careful to maintain older Chinese systems of governance, beliefs, and social practices, including that of Buddhism, as indicated by this set of altar pieces rendered from pewter during the reign of the longest-serving Qing emperors.

A Closer Look

Kangxi was an exceptional ruler, and not just for the length of his reign. Freed from the precedents of earlier dynasties, he enacted many bureaucratic reforms and economic measures, often times after making long investigative tours of his realm. But Kangxi is best remembered for his contributions to Chinese arts, learning, and religion. He invited scholars to his court and subsidized a vast encyclopedia of Chinese literature.

Kangxi promoted the Gelugpa School of Buddhism. Originating in Tibet, the Gelugpa School, emphasizes ethics and the rigorous analysis of Buddhist teachings through monastic discipline. Gelugpa Buddhism also preaches a simplicity of faith, as reflected in this rather unadorned altar set rendered out of simple pewter, an alloy then composed of tin and led. The pieces on either side are candleholders, while the item in the middle holds incense sticks, both essential to Buddhist worship.

The altar set shown here might have been used in a temple or in the household shrine of a wealthier family because Buddhists do not believe in the necessity of worshipping at temple. Worshippers would light candles as offerings to their ancestors, usually when requesting the latter to protect them from evil or harmful spiritual forces. The incense was used to purify both the worshipper and the altar space, so as to draw the ancestors near.

1 100 200 300 400 500 600 700 800 900 1000 1100 1200 1300 1400 1500 1600 1700 1800 1900 2000 CE

2.13.26 Turkish Shadow Puppets

Ottoman Empire
ca. Eighteenth Century

Credit: Culture Club/Getty Images

What You Need to Know

The shadow puppets shown here are from the Ottoman Empire of the eighteenth century.

The Ottomans, named after an early ruler named Osman, began as a small Turkic-speaking people in Western Anatolia (now modern-day Turkey), situated between the Christian Byzantine Empire and Islamic lands of the Middle East. Their situation required an openness to and tolerance of other cultures, as was evident when they captured the once impregnable Byzantine capital of Constantinople (the name of which they later changed to Istanbul) in 1453. Over the next century and a half, Ottoman armies would capture much of the Middle East, North Africa, and southeastern Europe, where they would rule over a conglomerate of ethnicities, races, and religions. The empire, although whittled down, would last until its defeat in World War I. One of the reasons for its endurance was not just tolerance but an effective administrative structure, which gave great leeway to local rulers, as long as they paid taxes and owed allegiance to the sultan in Istanbul.

A Closer Look

Shadow plays, in which puppet masters manipulate cutout figures placed between a source of light and a screen, thereby casting shadows, is an art form known across many cultures, from China to Europe. The Ottoman Empire had its own version, known as Karagöz and Hacivat, in which a single puppet maker manipulated and voiced all of the characters, usually accompanied by a tambourine or other instrument. The exact origins of the plays are unknown but they probably date back to the seventeenth century.

The name for these plays comes from the two main characters who figure in all of them: Karagöz, which means "black eye" in Turkish and Hacivaz, or the "pilgrim Ivaz." They are stock characters—Karagöz, the illiterate peasant with native wit and Hacivaz, the educated elite who, nevertheless, lacks what we would call street smarts. Many of the plays featured a plot revolving around Hacivat trying to get something for nothing and Karagöz warning against it, even though he almost always goes along with the scheme. Ultimately, Karagöz's plans end up in disaster, providing much merriment for the typically working-class and peasant audiences of the performances. The plays also featured all kinds of characters representing the diversity of Ottoman life. Alongside the Kurd and African in this collection are—from top left—a circus performer, a Dervish sufi ascetic, Hacivat's wife, and a hashish smoker. The two ships are also of note. The one on the bottom left represents a ship used on the Black Sea, the other a Mediterranean vessel. In the seventeenth century, both bodies of water were largely or partly under Ottoman control.

The geographic extent of the empire and its cosmopolitan nature are reflected in this collection, which includes a Kurd (center figure) and a North African guitar player (top right).

1 100 200 300 400 500 600 700 800 900 1000 1100 1200 1300 1400 1500 1600 1700 1800 1900 2000 CE

2.13.27 Newspaper Advertisement for Slave Auction in Boston

Boston, Massachusetts
ca. 1700

TO BE SOLD on board the Ship *Bance-Island*, on tuesday the 6th of *May* next, at *Ashley-Ferry*; a choice cargo of about 250 fine healthy NEGROES, juft arrived from the Windward & Rice Coaft. —The utmoft care has already been taken, and fhall be continued, to keep them free from the leaft danger of being infected with the SMALL-POX, no boat having been on board, and all other communication with people from *Charles-Town* prevented.

Auftin, Laurens, & Appleby.

N. B. Full one Half of the above Negroes have had the SMALL-POX in their own Country.

Credit: MPI/Getty Images

What You Need to Know

This Boston newspaper advertisement from around 1700 announces the sale of 250 "fine healthy Negroes."

Nobody knows—or ultimately can know—how many Africans were transported to the Americas as part of the trans-Atlantic slave trade, which began in the early sixteenth century and continued through the late nineteenth. The consensus range is between 10 and 20 million, with perhaps another 10 million dying between the time they were captured and the time they landed in the Americas. The height of the trade was the eighteenth century, when the growth of the plantation culture in Brazil, the Caribbean, and the southern United States reached its peak and before the British and U.S. governments banned the trans-Atlantic trade in the first decade of the nineteenth century. It continued after that, of course, but in the form of smuggling. As this Boston advertisement for 250 "fine healthy Negroes" from around 1700 reveals, slavery existed in all British North American colonies, not just the southern ones, before the Revolution.

A Closer Look

While the emphasis on the clean health of imported slaves—as well as their freedom from small pox, a dreaded communicable disease of the time—was not unusual for advertisements of this type, there are a couple of things about the notice that attract our attention. One is the origin of the slaves. The Windward and Rice Coasts, largely corresponding to modern-day Sierra Leone and Liberia—ironically, one a colony and the other a country later founded as havens for freed slaves, from Britain and America, respectively—were not a major source of slaves. Most came from points north (modern-day Senegal), east (Nigeria), and south (Angola). The other is the destination of the slaves. Of the millions of slaves brought directly from Africa to the America, as opposed to those being move about within the Americas—only a small percentage, perhaps 1 out of 20—landed in Britain's North American colonies, and only a tiny fraction of those went to those north of the Chesapeake. The reasons for this, at least at first, were purely economic. The shorter growing season made slavery less profitable in the North, as did the types of crops grown. Grains only need a large labor force at harvest, making it more economical to hire labor when needed rather than having to support it all year. Most likely, these slaves would have been destined to live individually or in small groups on farms, where they performed all kinds of tasks, or as servants in urban households.

1   100 200 300   400   500   600   700   800   900   1000 1100 1200 1300   1400   1500   1600   1700 1800 1900 2000 CE

2.13.28 A Slaver's Description of the Middle Passage

West Africa
1732

It has been observed before, that some slaves fancy they are carried to be eaten, which makes them desperate; and others are so on account of their captivity: so that if care be not taken, they will mutiny and destroy the ship's crew in hopes to get away.

To prevent such misfortunes, we use [*sic*] to visit them daily, narrowly searching every corner between decks, to see whether they have not found means, to gather any pieces of iron, or wood, or knives, about the ship, notwithstanding the great care we take not to leave any tools or nails, or other things in the way: which, however, cannot be always so exactly observed, where so many people are in the narrow compass of a ship.

We cause as many of our men as is convenient to lie in the quarter-deck and gunroom, and our principal officers in the great cabin, where we keep all our small arms in a readiness, with sentinels constantly at the door and avenues to it; being thus ready to disappoint any attempts our slaves might make on a sudden.

These precautions contribute very much to keep them in awe; and if all those who carry slaves duly observed them, we should not hear of so many revolts as have happened. Where I was concerned, we always kept our slaves in such order, that we did not perceive the least inclination in any of them to revolt, or mutiny, and lost very few of our number in the voyage.

Source: Macintyre, Donald. *The Adventures of Sail, 1520–1914*. London, Elek, 1970, pp. 117–119.

What You Need to Know

This excerpt is from *Descriptions of the Coast of North and South Guinea*, written by the French slaver John Barbot, and published in 1732. "Guinea" is an archaic name for the coastal region of western, central and southern Africa, from roughly modern-day Angola to the Gambia River.

Between the early sixteenth century and the late nineteenth, European and American slavers transported somewhere between 10 and 30 million African slaves to the Western Hemisphere. This slave trade was one component of a vast trans-Atlantic trading network, known as the Triangle Trade, after its three legs. The first leg involved transporting European manufactured goods to Africa, where they were used to obtain slaves who were brought to the Americas. The sugar and other crops they raised were then shipped to Europe, completing the triangle. (In fact, the system was more complicated than this, involving trade in various directions.) Because the trip from Africa to the Americas was the second leg of the triangle, it was referred to as the "Middle Passage." Despite the claims of some of the slavers, including Barbot, conditions on the Middle Passage were extraordinarily brutal. This excerpt, however, ignores Barbot's claims of humane treatment of slaves, focusing instead on the terrors of the slaves themselves.

A Closer Look

Most Africans destined for slavery in the Americas were not directly acquired by European slavers, who rightfully kept their distance from the interior of the continent, fearing disease and hostile peoples there. Instead, they relied on African intermediaries to bring slaves to the coast. These slaves had little idea what they were being driven there for. As Barbot notes, many thought the Europeans were buying them to eat them.

Even those who did not hold such beliefs still had much to fear, not knowing what fate lay in store for them on European slaves ships or the destinations they were being sent to. Many of course were also extremely angry at being abducted and recognized that, once at sea, they had little chance of escape. Such fears and anger led to frequent conspiracies. European slavers recognized the dangers and took measures to avoid them. As Barbot describes, they conducted regular searches of the ship's holds to find any weapons or materials that could be used as weapons. The slavers also maintained small armories on board. Such measures Barbot said effectively kept the slaves in line. Historians have also noted, however, that the sheer disorientation of the enslavement process, as well as the weakness of many of the slaves after forced marches to the coast and lengthy internment in seaside barracoons, or prisons set up to hold slaves for sale, also played a part in keeping slaves pacified.

1 100 200 300   400   500   600   700   800   900   1000 1100 1200 1300   1400   1500 1600 1700 1800 1900 2000 CE

2.13.29 Race and Class in Colonial Lima

Lima, Peru
1748

The inhabitants of Lima [Peru] are composed of whites, or Spaniards, Negroes, Indians, Mestizos, and other casts, proceeding from the mixture of all three.

The Spanish families are very numerous; Lima according to the lowest computation, containing 16 or 18 thousand whites, Among these are reckoned a third or fourth part of the most distinguished nobility of Peru; and many of these dignified with the stile of ancient or modern Castilians, among which are no less than 45 counts and marquises. The number of knights belonging to the several military orders is also very considerable. Besides these are many families no less respectable and living in equal splendor; particularly 24 gentlemen of large estates, but without titles, though most of them have ancient seats, a proof of the antiquity of their families.

All those families live in a manner becoming their rank, having estates equal to their generous dispositions, keeping a great number of slaves and other domestics, and those who affect making the greatest figure, have coaches, while others content themselves with calashes or chaises, which are here so common, that no family of any substance is without one. It must be owned that these carriages are more necessary here than in other cities, on account of the numberless droves of mules which continually pass thro' Lima, and cover the streets with their dung, which being soon dried by the sun and the wind, turns to a nauseous dust, scarce supportable to those who walk on foot.

The Negroes, Mulattoes, and their descendants, form the greater number of the inhabitants; and of these are the greatest part of the mechanics; though here the Europeans also follow the same occupations, which are not at Lima reckoned disgraceful to them, as they are at Quito; for gain being here the universal passion, the inhabitants pursue it by means of any trade, without regard to its being followed by Mulattoes, interest here preponderating against any other consideration.

The third, and last class of inhabitants are the Indians and Mestizos, but these are very small in proportion to the largeness of the city, and the multitudes of the second class. They are employed in agriculture, in making earthen ware, and bringing all kinds of provisions to market, domestic services being performed by Negroes and Mulattoes, either slaves or free, though generally by the former.

The usual dress of the men differs very little from that worn in Spain, nor is the distinction between the several classes very great; for the use of all sorts of cloth being allowed, every one wears what he can purchase. So that it is not uncommon to see a Mulatto, or any other mechanic dressed in a tissue, equal to any thing that can be worn by a more opulent person.

Source: Juan, Don George, and Don Antonio de Ulloa. *A Voyage to South America: Describing at Large the Spanish Cities, Towns, Provinces, etc. on that Extensive Continent: Undertaken, by Command of the King of Spain, by Don George Juan, and Don Antonio de Ulloa, Captains of the Spanish Navy*. Vol. II. Book VII. Translated by John Adams. London: John Stockdale, 1806, pp. 53–56.

TIMELINE   2000 1900 1800 1700 1600 1500 1400 1300 1200 1100 1000 900 800 700 600 500 400 300 200 100 1 BCE

What You Need to Know

This selection comes from *A Voyage to South America*, penned by George Juan and Antonio de Ulloa, two Spanish astronomers dispatched by the French Academy of Sciences to measure the Equator. The excerpt printed here is an account of their time in Lima.

In the mid-eighteenth century, the Spanish Empire in the Americas was a vast thing, stretching from the temperate forests of what is now the Upper Midwest of the United States to the rain forest of Central America to the windswept pampas of southern Argentina. Its population was as diverse as its environment—Europeans, divided between administrators from Spain and so-called Creoles, or whites native to the Americas; Native Americans; Mestizos or persons of mixed European and Indian heritage; Africans, and Mulattoes, or persons of mixed European and African heritage. The mélange of peoples was most evident in the colonial cities, such as Lima, capital of the vast Vice-Royalty of Peru, which then encompassed all of the modern-day states of Peru and Ecuador, as well as parts of Bolivia and Chile. Lima was also divided by class, as noted by Juan and de Ulloa.

A Closer Look

As the capital of Peru, Lima was home to the largest population of Europeans and European descendants in all of South America, who numbered, according to Juan and de Ulloa, between 16,000 and 18,000. These were the elite of the city, they note, who "live in a manner becoming their rank." Owners of great estates, they had servants and slaves to cater to their every need and went about in fancy carriages. Juan and de Ulloa note that such vehicles were especially necessary because city streets were covered in the dung left by the herds of mules that passed through.

But elite Lima also included mestizos. One family in particularly, the Ampuero, the two observers remark were descendants of the Inca, a term that then usually applied to the rulers of the pre-Columbian empire of the same name, and the Spanish commanders who conquered them in the mid-sixteenth century.

Beneath these elite whites and Mestizos were those Juan and de Ulloa refer to as the "Negroes, Mulattoes, and their descendants." These represented the largest portion of the city's population, many of them working as "mechanics," that is, skilled workers. At the bottom of the social hierarchy were the Indians and poor mestizos, who made up the smallest population of the city, working in agriculture on nearby farms and performing unskilled work.

What all these classes shared, when they could afford it, the two observers note, is a penchant for fancy dress, as there were no legal restrictions on what people of different status were allowed to wear. "It is not uncommon," Juan and de Ulloa write, "to see a Mulatto, or any other mechanic dressed in a tissue [fabric], equal to any thing that can be worn by a more opulent person."

1 100 200 300 400 500 600 700 800 900 1000 1100 1200 1300 1400 1500 1600 1700 1800 1900 2000 CE

2.13.30 Description of Colonial Philadelphia

Philadelphia, Pennsylvania
1759

Philadelphia, if we consider that not eighty years ago the place where it now stands was a wild and uncultivated desert, inhabited by nothing but ravenous beasts, and a savage people, must certainly be the object of every one's wonder and admiration. It is situated upon a tongue of land, a few miles above the confluence of the Delaware and Schuylkill; and contains about 3,000 houses, and 18 or 20,000 inhabitants. It is built north and south upon the banks of the Delaware; and is nearly two miles in length, and three quarters of one in breadth. The streets are laid out with great regularity in parallel lines, intersected by others at right angles, and are handsomely built: on each side there is a pavement of broad stones for foot passengers; and in most of them a causeway in the middle for carriages. Upon dark nights it is well lighted, and watched by a patrol: there are many fair houses, and public edifices in it. The stadt-house is a large, handsome, though heavy building; in this are held the councils, the assemblies, and supreme courts; there are apartments in it also for the accommodation of Indian chiefs or sachems; likewise two libraries, one belonging to the province, the other to a society, which was incorporated about ten years ago, and consists of sixty members. Each member upon admission, subscribed forty shillings; and afterward annually ten. They can alienate their shares, by will or deed, to any person approved by the society. They have a small collection of medals and medallions, and a few other curiosities, such as the skin of a rattle-snake killed at Surinam twelve feet long; and several Northern Indian habits made of furs and skins. At a small distance from the stadt-house, there is another fine library, consisting of a very valuable and chosen collection of books, left by a Mr. Logan; they are chiefly in the learned languages. Near this there is also a noble hospital for lunatics, and other sick persons. Besides these buildings, there are spacious barracks for 17 or 1800 men; a good assembly-room belonging to the society of Free Masons; and eight or ten places of religious worship; viz. two churches, three Quaker meeting-houses, two Presbyterian ditto, one Lutheran church, one Dutch Calvinist ditto, one Swedish ditto, one Romish chapel, one Anabaptist meeting-house, one Moravian ditto: there is also an academy or college, originally built for a tabernacle for Mr. Whitefield. At the south end of the town, upon the river, there is a battery mounting thirty guns, but it is in a state of decay. It was designed to be a check upon privateers. These, with a few alms-houses, and a school-house belonging to the Quakers, are the chief public buildings in Philadelphia. The city is in a very flourishing state, and inhabited by merchants, artists, tradesmen, and persons of all occupations.

Source: Burnaby, Andrew. *Travels through North America*. Reprinted in Rufus Rockwell Wilson, ed., *Burnaby's Travels through North America*. New York: A. Wessels Company, 1904, pp. 88–90.

What You Need to Know

This passage comes from *Travels through North America*, penned by Andrew Burnaby, an English clergyman and travel writer, and published in 1775, although it describes Philadelphia at the time of his visit in 1759.

England in the seventeenth century was a nation in the midst of religious ferment, with all kinds of radical new doctrines and sects gaining adherents. It was also a nation torn by religious conflict.

The English Civil War of the 1640s and 1650s produced much religious dissent from the Church of England. Among those seeking a purer and more direct path to God was George Fox, founder of the Religious Society of Friends, better known as the Quakers. The term *Quaker* was applied to practitioners whose intense religious fervor caused them to "quake." The Quakers, well known for their pacifism, also believed in simplicity of living and worship.

The Quakers' radical egalitarianism—noted for the absence of clergy at their services and for allowing women as well as men to speak about their faith in church—quickly attracted many progressive Englishmen. Among them was a wealthy real estate speculator named William Penn. In 1681, King Charles I granted Penn a vast estate in Britain's North American possessions to pay a debt owed to Penn's father. The tract became known as Pennsylvania, Latin for "Penn's Woods." Its commercial and political hub was Philadelphia, described here by Andrew Burnaby, who visited it 16 years earlier.

A Closer Look

Like many visitors to the city—the largest in British North America in the years leading up to the American Revolution—Burnaby was impressed by the fine planning behind the city, as manifested in its neat north grid of streets, an unusual sight for an Englishmen used to the maze of streets typical of towns back home. Making the orderliness even more impressive, he remarks, with typical Eurocentric contempt for the native peoples of North America, is the fact that "not eighty years ago the place where it now stands was a wild and uncultivated desert [that is, wilderness], inhabited by nothing but ravenous beasts, and a savage people."

Burnaby's contempt for Native Americans was not, however, entirely shared by Penn and the other Quaker leaders of Pennsylvania. The English writer notes that the "stadt-house," or state-house, incorporated "apartments for accommodation of Indian chiefs, or sachems," brought to the capital to discuss governance issues that affected them.

Burnaby also takes note of two other features of Quaker life on display in Philadelphia. One was a love of learning, as manifested in two public libraries and a museum of scientific "curiosities." The second is the tolerance they showed for people of other faiths. He lists churches belonging to Lutherans, Dutch Calvinists, Anabaptists, Moravians, and Romish [Catholics], as well as an assembly room for Free Masons, a fraternal order that embraced Deism, a faith that rejected the idea of a God that intervened in the affairs of men.

1 100 200 300 400 500 600 700 800 900 1000 1100 1200 1300 1400 1500 1600 1700 1800 1900 2000 CE

2.13.31 Marriage Negotiations in Colonial Virginia

Virginia
1764

Dear Sir:

My son, Mr. John Walker, having informed me of this intention to pay his addresses to your daughter Elizabeth, if he should (be) agreeable to yourself, lady and daughter, it may not be amiss to inform you what I feel myself able to afford for their support, in case of an union. My affairs are in an uncertain state, but I will promise one thousand pounds, to be paid in 1766, and the furth sum of two thousand pounds I promise to give him; but the uncertainty of my present affairs prevents my fixing on a time of payment. The above sums are all to be in money or lands and other effects, at the option of my son, John Walker.

And the reply:

Dear Sir:

Your son, Mr. John Walker, applied to me for leave to make his addresses to my daughter, Elizabeth. I gave him leave, and told him at the same time that my affairs were in such a state it was not in my power to pay him all the money this year that I intended to give my daughter, provided he succeeded; but I would give him five hundred pounds more as soon after as I could raise or get the money, which sums you may depend I will most punctually pay to him.

Source: Walker, Thomas. Letter to Bernard Moore, May 27, 1764; Moore, Bernard. Letter to Thomas Walker, May 28, 1764. In Mary Newton Stanard, *Colonial Virginia: Its People and Customs*. Philadelphia: J. B. Lippincott Company, 1917, pp. 172–173.

What You Need to Know

These letters exchanged between Virginia planter Thomas Walker and Bernard Moore in 1764, concern the possible marriage of their children. Both wanted to make sure that their offspring made socially proper matches.

By the late colonial period in the mid-eighteenth century, Virginia had left behind its primitive frontier roots. The gentry of the colony, most rural planters, had grown wealthy off the raising, production, and sale of tobacco and other commercial crops to Europe, Asia, and other parts of the Americas. They built large houses for themselves on their great estates, modeled after English country manors, where they indulged in all kinds of recreation and entertainment—dancing, card playing, horse racing and other pursuits. They traveled about in elegant carriages and dressed in the latest fashions from Europe. They cultivated refined manners in themselves and their children, using stylized forms of address and adhering to strict rules of polite behavior.

A Closer Look

Such elegance, leisure activities, and high-society behavior rested of course on the profits these planters derived from their extensive lands and their workforces of African-American slaves. And although quite profitable, the raising of tobacco and other commercial crops could also be financially precarious. Planters were not always the best businessmen, spending more than they took in and borrowing the difference. Even those who were not particularly indulgent still suffered from the common financial plight of agriculturalists, having to borrow heavily against future crops to ensure enough money to see them through until the harvest. This problem can be noted in these letters, where the fathers of both the groom-to-be and bride-to-be complain of experiencing "uncertain" and unsettled financial affairs. While each assured the other that they would have the money—the groom's father to set the new couple up on an estate of their own and the bride's father to provide an adequate dowry—they admitted they could not provide it until some future date.

As in upper-class England, marriages among the colonial Virginia gentry were arranged by the parents, in large part to secure the financial future of the two families involved. At the same time, as these letters attest, the potential betrothed had a say in matters as well. In his letter to Bernard Moore, Thomas Walker notes that his son would like "to pay his addresses to your daughter . . . if he should [be] agreeable to yourself, lady [Moore's wife], and daughter."

2.13.32 An Account of Tahitian Navigation

Tahiti
1774

There are many sailing-masters among the people, the term for whom is in their language *fatere*. They are competent to make long voyages like that from Otahiti [Tahiti] to Oriayatea [Ra'iatea], which counts 40 or 50 leagues [one league = 30 nautical miles], and others farther afield. One of them named Puhoro came to Lima on this occasion in the frigate; and from him and others I was able to find out the method by which they navigate on the high seas: which is the following.

They have no mariner's compass, but divide the horizon into 16 parts, taking for the cardinal points those at which the sun rises and sets. . . .

When setting out from port the helmsman reckons with the horizon. Thus partitioned counting from E, or the point where the sun rises; he knows the direction in which his destination bears: he sees, also, whether he has the wind aft, or on one or other beam, or on the quarter, or is close-hauled: he knows, further, whether there is a following sea, a head sea, a beam sea, or if it is on the bow or the quarter.

He proceeds out of port with a knowledge of these [conditions], heads his vessel according to his calculation, and aided by the signs the sea and wind afford him, does his best to keep steadily on his course. This task becomes more difficult if the day be cloudy, because of having no mark to count from for dividing out the horizon. Should the night be cloudy as well, they regulate their course by the same signs; and, since the wind is apt to vary in direction more than the swell does, they have their pennants, [made] of feathers and palmetto bark, to watch its changes by and trim sail, always taking their cue for a knowledge of the course from the indication the sea affords them.

When the night is a clear one they steer by the stars; and this is the easiest navigation for them because, these being many [in number], not only do they note by them the bearings on which the several islands with which they are in touch lie, but also the harbors in them, so that they make straight for the entrance by following the rhumb of the particular star that rises or sets over it; and they hit it off with as much precision as the most expert navigator of civilized nations could achieve.

They distinguish the planets from the fixed stars, by their movements; and give them separate names. To the stars they make use of in going from one island to another, they attach the name of the island, so that the one which serves for sailing from Otahiti [Tahiti] to Oriayatea [Ra'iatea] has those same names, and the same occurs with those that serve them for making the harbors in those islands.

What took me most in two Indians whom I carried from Otahiti [Tahiti] to Oriayatea [Ra'iatea] was that every evening or night, they told me, or prognosticated, the weather we should experience on the following day, as to wind, calms, rainfall, sunshine, sea, and other points, about which they never turned out to be wrong: a foreknowledge worthy to be envied, for, in spite of all that our navigators and cosmographers have observed and written about the subject, they have not mastered this accomplishment.

Source: Andia y Varela, Don José. "The Journal of Don José de Andía y Varela." In *The Quest and Occupation of Tahiti by Emissaries of Spain during the Years 1772–76.* Vol. II. Translated and edited by Bolton Glanvill Corney. London: Hakluyt Society, 1915, pp. 284–287.

TIMELINE   2000 1900 1800 1700 1600 1500 1400 1300 1200 1100 1000 900 800 700 600 500 400 300 200 100 1 BCE

What You Need to Know

In this excerpt, Spanish mariner Don José Andia y Varela describes Tahitian navigation skills in a journal he kept while on the Polynesian island in 1774.

The Pacific basin south of the Tropic of Cancer is a region of almost incomprehensible vastness, measuring roughly 50 million square miles, or equivalent to roughly the entire land mass of the planet. Scattered across this emptiness are the dozens of island groups—with the exception of the North and South Island of New Zealand, all no larger than 4,100 square miles—the Polynesians call home. It is no wonder that the Pacific basin was the last major region on Earth to be settled by humans, other than Antarctica.

While the exact origins of the various Polynesian peoples is unknown, DNA evidence suggests that they came from mainland Southeast Asia. Sometime in the second millennium BCE, it is believed, they began taking to the islands closest to the Southeast Asian Mainland, then moving across the tropical and South Pacific, until attaining their farthest reaches of Hawaii and New Zealand, around the years 300 to 800 CE and 900 to 1200 CE, respectively. Some archaeologists argue that they may have even reached the west coast of South America. Their ability to find these lands in that watery realm makes them, arguably, the greatest navigators in history until the modern era.

A Closer Look

As with all great oceangoing navigators, the Polynesians, who lacked knowledge of the compass and the sextant for measuring the altitude of stars from the horizon, were experts at reading the skies nonetheless, as Andia y Varela notes. What he fails to mention is that sailing south of the equator, they lacked the fixed Polaris, or North Star, which helped guide mariners in northern waters. Instead, he says, they divided the horizon into 16 parts, measured from the rising and setting sun. He also relates how the Polynesians were well versed in reading the winds and the ocean currents to determine how fast they were traveling and whether they were drifting off course. This allowed them to travel between islands they knew about with near unerring accuracy. How they found the islands in the first place, however, is open to conjecture, although most scholars agree it was probably by accident, either driven there by storms or in search of pelagic fish. They did all this with relatively simple tools; their canoes were made from wood hewn with stone adzes, bone, and coral, and tied together with coconut fiber. Yet these vessels weathered storms and long distances in salt water.

1 100 200 300   400   500   600   700   800   900   1000 1100 1200 1300   1400   1500   1600   1700   1800 1900 2000 CE

2.13.33 Captain Cook on the Food of the Nootka People of North America

British Columbia and Pacific Northwest
1778

It seems that the herrings also supply them with another grand resource for food, namely a vast quantity of roe, very curiously prepared. It is strewed upon, or, as it were, incrustated about, small branches of the Canadian pine. They also prepare it upon a long narrow sea-grass, which grows plentifully upon the rooks, under water. This caviare, if it may be so called, is kept in baskets or bags of mat, and used occasionally, being first dipped in water. It may be considered as the winter bread of these people, and has no disagreeable taste.

Of the sea-animals, the most common that we saw in use amongst them, as food, is the porpoise; the fat, or rind of which, as well as the flesh, they cut in large pieces, and having dried them, as they do the herrings, eat them without any farther preparation. . . .

It may also be presumed that they feed upon other sea animals, such as seals, sea-otters, and whales; not only from the skins of the two first being frequent amongst them, but from the great number of implements, of all sorts, intended to destroy these different animals; which clearly points out their dependence upon them; though, perhaps, they do not catch them in great plenty at all seasons; which seemed to be the case while we lay there, as no great number of fresh skins, or pieces of flesh, were seen. The same might be said of the land-animals, which, though doubtless the natives sometimes kill them, appeared to be scarce at this time; as we did not see a single piece of flesh belonging to any of them; and though their skins be in tolerable plenty, it is probable that many of these are procured by traffic from other tribes.

As the Canadian pine-branches and sea-grass, on which the fish roe is strewed, may be considered as their only winter vegetables; so, as the spring advances, they make use of several others, as they come in season. The most common of these, which we observed, were two sorts of liliaceous roots, one simply tunicated, the other granulated upon its surface, called mahkatte and koohquoppa, which have a mild sweetish taste, and are mucilaginous, and eaten raw. The next, which they have in great quantities, is a root called aheita, resembling, in taste, our liquorice; and another fern root, whose leaves were not yet disclosed. They also eat raw another small, sweetish, insipid root about the thickness of sarsaparilla; but we were ignorant of the plant to which it belongs; and also of another root, which is very large and palmated, which we saw them dig up near the village, and afterwards eat it. It is also probable that, as the season advances, they have many which we did not see; for though there be no appearance of cultivation amongst them, there are great quantities of alder, gooseberry, and currant bushes, whose fruits they may eat in their natural state, as we have seen them eat the leaves of the last, and of the lilies, just as they were plucked from the plant.

Source: Cook, James. *The Voyages of Captain James Cook around the World: Comprehending a History of the South Sea Islands*. Vol. III. London: Jaques and Wright, 1825, pp. 55–58.

TIMELINE   2000 1900 1800 1700 1600 1500 1400 1300 1200 1100 1000 900 800 700 600 500 400 300 200 100 1 BCE

What You Need to Know

This passage comes from *The Voyages of Captain James Cook around the World*, which was published after the 1779 death of the famed explorer and navigator. The excerpt printed here describes the food gathering practices of the Nootka people of Vancouver Island, in what is now the Canadian province of British Columbia.

The name *Nootka* is a misnomer. British captain James Cook, who visited Vancouver Island in British Columbia and the Olympic Peninsula of Washington State, mistakenly thought he was in Nootka Sound and so gave this name to the people he encountered there. In fact, the so-called Nootka referred to themselves as the Nuu-Chah-nulth. Today, we use the term *Nootka* to refer to all speakers of the Wakashan family of languages, which includes many tribes with very different customs and social orders.

The region they inhabit is one of the most fertile on the North American continent. A temperate climate and abundant rainfall nurture thick forests, which the Nootka used to build their immense communal houses and seagoing canoes. And, indeed, the Nootka spent much of their time on water, fishing and gathering seafood from the abundant rivers and coastal waters, as attested by this excerpt from Cook's book.

A Closer Look

The Nootka did not just fish in open boats, they also built elaborate weirs in the mouths of the numerous rivers that ran through their rainy environment. These were used to trap salmon during their annual upriver runs to spawn. Cook makes special note of a particular Nootka delicacy he likens to "caviare." It was made by spreading the roe of herring onto pine branches or sea grass and allowing it to dry. It was then placed in baskets and remoistened for eating. It was, the captain notes, the "winter break of these people." In addition, the Nootka smoked and dried their fish catches for later consumption.

Cook also points out the Nootka were hunters of porpoises. Left barely mentioned is their whale hunting. The Nootka took to the sea in the early spring, as whales made their way up the coast from breeding grounds off Mexico to feed in the fish-rich waters of the North Pacific. While Cook notes that the Nootka relied largely on fish for their diet, they also gathered roots, berries, and other edible plants from the thick forests surrounding their villages.

But the Nootka apparently were not avid hunters, as Cook says he saw virtually no land animal flesh in and around their habitations, despite the fact that the forests were filled with game of all kinds. Then again, with coastal waters and rivers as thick with sea life as they were, there was little need to go after other sources of animal protein.

1 100 200 300 400 500 600 700 800 900 1000 1100 1200 1300 1400 1500 1600 1700 1800 1900 2000 CE

2.13.34 Material Culture of the Sandwich Islands

Hawaii
1778–1779

They fabricate a great many white mats, which are strong, with many red stripes, rhombuses, and other figures interwoven on one side; and often pretty large. These probably make a part of their dress occasionally; for they put them on their backs when they offered them for sale. But they make others coarser, plain and strong, which they spread over their floors to sleep upon.

They stain their gourd-shells prettily with undulated lines, triangles, and other figures of a black colour; instances of which, We saw practiced at New Zealand. And they seem to possess the art of varnishing; for some of these stained gourd-shells arc covered with a kind of lacker; and on other occasions, they use a strong size, or gluey substance, to fasten their things together. Their wooden dishes and bowls, out of which they drink their ava, are of the etooa-tree or cordia, as neat as if made in our turning-lathe, and perhaps better polished. And amongst their articles of handicraft, may be reckoned small square fans of mat or wicker-work, with handles tapering from them of the same, or of wood; which are neatly wrought with small cords of hair, and fibres of the cocoa-nut core intermixed. The great variety of fishing-hooks are ingeniously made; some of bone, others of wood pointed with bone, and many of pearl shell. Of the last, some are like a sort that we saw at Tongataboo; and others simply carved, as the common sort at Otaheite, as well as the wooden ones. The bones are mostly small, and composed of two pieces; and all the different sorts have a barb, either on the inside, like ours, or on the outside, opposite the same part; but others have both, the outer one being farthest from the point. Of this last sort, one was procured, nine inches long, of a single piece of bone, which doubtless belonged to some large fish. The elegant form and polish of this could not certainly be outdone by any European artist, even if he should add all his knowledge in design to the number and convenience of his tools. They polish their stones by constant friction, with pumice-stone in water; and such of their working instruments or tools, as I saw, resembled those of the Southern Islands. Their hatchets, or rather adzes, were exactly of the same pattern, and either made of the same sort of blackish stone, or of a clay-coloured one. They have also little instruments made of a single shark's tooth, some of which are fixed to the forepart of a dogs jaw-bone, and others to a thin wooden handle of the same shape; and at the other end there is a bit of string fastened through a small perforation. These serve as knives occasionally, and are perhaps used in carving.

Source: Cook, James. *The Voyages of Captain James Cook around the World: Comprehending a History of the South Sea Islands.* Vol. III. London: Jaques and Wright, 1825, pp. 15–16.

TIMELINE   2000 1900 1800 1700 1600 1500 1400 1300 1200 1100 1000 900 800 700 600 500 400 300 200 100 1 BCE

What You Need to Know

In this selection from *The Voyages of Captain James Cook around the World*, Cook describes the material culture of the Polynesian people of the islands, who are believed to have reached the archipelago sometime between 300 and 500 CE.

The Hawaiian Islands are the most isolated major island group in the world; the nearest large landmass, North America, is 2,500 miles away. Archaeologists and historians posit two theories for how the Hawaiians got to the islands and settled—a single settlement by people from the Marquesas Island group some 3,000 miles to the south or multiple migrations over the course of a 1,000 years by the Marquesans and later the Tahitians. In either case, finding the Hawaiian archipelago in the vastness of the Pacific Ocean speaks to the Polynesians extraordinary navigation skills and seamanship, in that they achieved this migration in open, double-hulled canoes, propelled by oars and sails. In early 1778, Captain James Cook of the British Royal Navy and his crew became the first Europeans to set eyes on the Hawaiian Islands, which they named the Sandwich Islands, after the Earl of Sandwich, then the First Lord of the Admiralty. While Cook would be killed by Hawaiians the following year, the journals of his three exploratory voyages around the Pacific would be published as *The Voyages of Captain James Cook around the World*, in 1825.

A Closer Look

By the time they reached the islands, the Polynesians had perfected the settlement of new lands, bringing with them the domesticated plants and animals they would need to survive in their new environment, including dogs, pigs, chickens, taro, yams, banana, and sugarcane. They also brought with them, and no doubt further developed, the skills to turn raw materials into useful and decorative artifacts. Indeed, in this passage, Cook remarks on the similarities in the decoration on "gourd-shells" between the Hawaiians and the Maori of New Zealand whom he encountered on earlier voyages, or early on this voyage.

Cook is impressed by what he sees of the skill and artisanship of the Hawaiians. He notes "ingeniously made" fishhooks of bone, wood, and shell, and he says that the wooden bowls and dishes they produced were so smooth and even they looked as though they had been turned on a lathe, though the Hawaiians did not have such a tool. Those bowls, he adds, were used to drink what he refers to as "ava." In fact, the drink is called kava and was made from the roots of a certain kind of pepper plant, known to the Hawaiians at the time as the "etooa-tree." Kava has mild psychoactive properties that gently sedate and anesthetize drinkers. Polynesians, then and now, use it to relax, often drinking it in social situations.

1 100 200 300   400   500   600   700   800   900   1000 1100 1200 1300   1400   1500   1600   1700 1800 1900 2000 CE

2.13.35 Olaudah Equiano on the African Slave Trade

Nigeria
1789

The first object which saluted my eyes when I arrived on the coast was the sea, and a slave-ship, which was then riding at anchor, and waiting for its cargo. These filled me with astonishment, which was soon converted into terror, which I am yet at a loss to describe, nor the then feelings of my mind. . . . I was now persuaded that I had gotten into a world of bad spirits, and that they were going to kill me. Their complexions, too, differing so much from ours, their long hair, and the language they spoke, which was very different from any I had ever heard, united to confirm me in this belief. Indeed, such were the horrors of my views and fears at the moment, that, if ten thousand worlds had been my own, I would have freely parted with them all to have exchanged my condition with that of the meanest slave in my own country.

In a little time after, amongst the poor chained men, I found some of my own nation, which in a small degree gave ease to my mind. I inquired of these what was to be done with us? They gave me to understand we were to be carried to these white people's country to work for them. I then was a little revived, and thought, if it were no worse than working, my situation was not so desperate: but still I feared I should be put to death, the white people looked and acted, as I thought, in so savage a manner; for I had never seen among any people such instances of brutal cruelty; and this not only shewn towards us blacks, but also to some of the whites themselves. One white man in particular I saw, when we were permitted to be on deck, flogged so unmercifully with a large rope near the foremast, that he died in consequence of it; and they tossed him over the side as they would have done a brute. This made me fear these people the more; and I expected nothing less than to be treated in the same manner. I could not help expressing my fears and apprehensions to some of my countrymen: I asked them if these people had no country, but lived in this hollow place the ship? They told me they did not, but came from a distant one. "Then," said I, "How comes it in all our country we never heard of them?" They told me, because they lived so very far off. I then asked where were their women? Had they any like themselves! I was told they had: "And why," said I, "do we not see them?" They answered, because they were left behind. I asked how the vessel could go? They told me they could not tell; but that there were cloths put upon the masts by the help of the ropes I saw, and then the vessel went on; and the white men had some spell or magic they put in the water when they liked in order to stop the vessel. I was exceedingly amazed at this account, and really thought they were spirits.

Source: Equiano, Olaudah. *The Interesting Narrative of the Life of Olaudah Equiano, or Gustavus Vassa, the African, Written by Himself*. London: published by the author, 1794, pp. 46, 48–50.

TIMELINE   2000 1900 1800 1700 1600 1500 1400 1300 1200 1100 1000 900 800 700 600 500 400 300 200 100 1 BCE

What You Need to Know

This excerpt comes from *The Interesting Narrative of the Life of Olaudah Equiano, or Gustavus Vassa, the African*, published in 1789.

By the early seventeenth century, Europe, Africa, and the Americas were bound together by an elaborate trans-Atlantic trading system that saw manufactured European goods shipped overseas, Africans transported as slaves to the Americans, and the products of plantations and mines in the Americas brought back to Europe. It was known as the Triangle Trade, although that simple geometry belies the system's complexity, and its second leg—the shipping of Africans to the Americas—as the Middle Passage.

The slave trade was a high-risk venture but also one that brought large returns. To achieve these, slavers had to make a decision. They could minimize costs, by packing as many slaves into their holds as possible, which brought higher mortality rates and thus lost profits or taking fewer slaves and getting a higher percentage of them to the Americas alive. But even on those ships where captains went with the latter option, the conditions of passage were awful, as this excerpt from *The Interesting Narrative of the Life of Olaudah Equiano, or Gustavus Vassa, the Africa*, published in 1789, makes clear.

A Closer Look

Historians are only as good as their sources. One of the most intractable problems they face in reconstructing the past is that most of the documentation is both by and about elites. That is why Equiano's account is so useful. Not only does it provide a glimpse into what slaves experienced on the Middle Passage—tales that can be had from the accounts of a number of slaver sources, as well—but it does so from the eyes of one of the slaves. A member of the Igbo ethnic group of what is now southeastern Nigeria and the son of a local nobleman, Equiano, who would later also go by the European name Gustavo Vassa, was kidnapped by fellow Africans while still a boy and marched to a British slaving fort on the coast. The excerpt here relates what happened next.

Equiano, like most other captives, was both disoriented and terrified by his experience. Expressing the beliefs he had grown up with, he became convinced he had been brought to "a world of bad spirits," a view supported in his mind by the strangeness of the white people he encountered at the fort. Things become even stranger and more horrifying once he was on the slaving ship. He was shocked to see one white man flogging another so brutally that the victim died and was tossed overboard. He uses the word *savage* to describe it. It is an ironic comment. For by the time Equiano wrote his narrative—years after he had been freed and assimilated to British life—he was surely aware that the term was used by Europeans to describe his own people.

1 100 200 300 400 500 600 700 800 900 1000 1100 1200 1300 1400 1500 1600 1700 1800 1900 2000 CE

Part 14:
The Age of Reason

Eighteenth and Early Nineteenth Centuries

2.14.1 French Coffee Grinder

France
Eighteenth Century

Credit: DeAgostini/Getty Images

What You Need to Know

This wooden coffee grinder, with a metal mechanism, is from eighteenth-century France.

No one knows exactly when and where coffee was first discovered, and so stories of its origins abound. The most widely repeated concerns a ninth-century Ethiopian goatherd noticing his animals frolicking after eating the bright red beans of a particular bush. He gave the beans to a local monk, who made a drink of it and liked how it kept him up all night for prayer.

What we do know for sure is that by the fifteenth century, coffee—probably from the Arabic word *qahhwat al-bun*, or "wine of the bean"—was under cultivation on the Arabian Peninsula. European travelers to the Middle East brought back stories of the drink. At first, Arab growers and merchants tried to monopolize the trade. But in the latter half of the seventeenth century, the Dutch got hold of some seedlings, which they planted successfully in their colonies in the East Indies. France followed suit in the Caribbean and, by the eighteenth century, coffee had become one of Europe's favorite beverages.

A Closer Look

With its caffeine content producing a mild stimulating effect, coffee was the ideal social drink, fostering both alertness and conversation. This aspect of the drink led to the creation of the coffeehouse, also known by the French word "café," in many continental countries.

The first was opened in Vienna in the middle of the seventeenth century, as that city was the closest major Western European metropolis to the Ottoman Empire, which controlled Arabia in the seventeenth century. By the latter part of the century, there were literally thousands of coffeehouses across Europe.

In eighteenth-century Paris, as in many other metropolises, the coffeehouse became a popular meeting places for writers, intellectuals, politicians, and businessmen to discuss the issues of the day or negotiate deals. For example, the Café Procope, which opened in 1686—and remains open to this day—was a popular meeting spot for Enlightenment thinkers and may have been where Denis Diderot first developed his idea for the *Encyclopédie*, the great mid-eighteenth-century book that attempted to compile and present the latest thinking on all matters religious, social, political, and scientific. Still, coffeehouses' role in the development of progressive political thought had one major limitation: in some European countries, including France, they were off-limits to women.

2.14.2 Italian Ophthalmologist's Surgical Instruments
Rome, Italy
Eighteenth Century

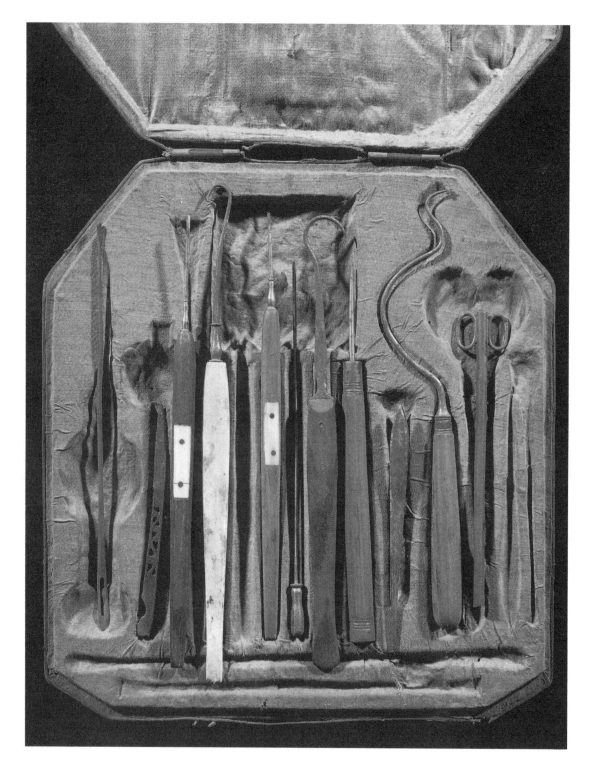

Credit: DeAgostini/Getty Images

What You Need to Know

The accompanying image shows the surgical instruments used in one branch of medicine, ophthalmology, in the eighteenth century. These particular examples come from Rome.

The *Scientific Revolution* is a term used by historians to describe a new way of looking at nature embraced by European thinkers beginning in the sixteenth century. Rather than attributing forces of nature to the unknowable doings of God, or relying on the writings of classical philosophers to explain them, European scientists began to observe nature directly. Through rational thought and experimentation, they sought to understand elemental laws that would explain the universe.

Great breakthroughs were made as a result of this new way of thinking—Antonie van Leeuwenhoek's discovery of microorganisms, for example, or William Harvey's explanation for how blood circulated through the body. Still, despite such discoveries, medicine remained a rather rudimentary science, of little benefit to patients.

A Closer Look

Ophthalmology is the branch of medicine that researches, diagnoses, and treats maladies of the eye. The earliest writings on ophthalmology date back to India in the first millennium BCE. Ancient Greek philosophers and scientists, most notably Rufus of Ephesus of the first century CE, were among the first to examine the eye via dissection to discover its various components. Medieval Arab scientists built on this work and added research of their own. In particular, they sought practical applications for the science, improving surgical methods for treating cataracts.

Great European breakthroughs awaited the development of the microscope, which allowed anatomical structures, including the eye, to be examined in detail beyond the reach of the human eye. Using these instruments, scientists began to discover some of the processes by which the eye worked. Still, surgery on the eye remained rudimentary through the eighteenth century, with methods for treating cataracts, the most obvious of eye diseases, often worse than the disease itself. Unaware of asepsis, the need for keeping germs out of exposed tissue, and not having any atropine solutions, which are used to dilate the pupil, ophthalmological surgery often caused infection even as the blunt instruments, such as those shown here, could produce damaging inflammation that made cataracts worse.

2.14.3 European Snuff Box

Germany
Eighteenth Century

Credit: DEA/A. Dagli Orti/DeAgostini/Getty Images

What You Need to Know

Among the favorite consumables of eighteenth-century aristocrats was snuff, a form of tobacco, often infused with various scents, that is inhaled into the nose. An eighteenth-century box for holding it is shown here.

The eighteenth century—at least until the outbreak of the French Revolution in 1789—was the golden age of the European aristocracy. Political security, economic wealth, and scientific progress had made their lives one of ease and comfort. Nowhere was this more evident than in what they consumed.

While the poor were lucky to enjoy meat on special occasions, the rich—both of the old landed variety and the new mercantile classes—indulged in it often and to great excess. A typical supper might include several meat courses, along with various kinds of fish, cheese, fruits, and vegetables. The wealthy also consumed much alcohol, partly because it was often safer than tainted water supplies. Meals, which might last through most of the evening, were filled with wines from across Europe, a bounty made possible by new transportation systems and commercial viniculture. After the meal was over, the men would then retire to a separate room where they would indulge in snuff.

A Closer Look

Tobacco, of course, is a crop native to the Americas, and so it was indigenous South Americans who were the first to use snuff. The early Spanish conquistadores and missionaries of the sixteenth century noted the practice and brought it back to Europe.

Producing snuff is a complicated process, which makes it a more expensive way to consume tobacco than by simply chewing or smoking it. In short, snuff was a luxury product and, by the eighteenth century, it was widely used among the European aristocracy, partly as a way to demonstrate their superior social status.

Snuff has to be consumed carefully. A gentle inhalation is all that is needed to get it to the lining of the nostrils, where the nicotine is absorbed into the bloodstream. Too strong a whiff, and it enters the nostrils, causing sneezing. Thus, taking snuff was a delicate act, befitting aristocratic men (as well as a few women willing to flout social convention).

Snuff was taken on the hand itself, and thus no implements for its use were needed. But the boxes that contained it were often of luxurious quality. The box here is made of Meissen porcelain, from what is now Germany, the finest porcelain produced in Europe at that time. The image is typical of the frilly rococo style favored by the wealthy of the eighteenth century and shows a typically upper-class scene of well-dressed, courting lovers.

1 100 200 300 400 500 600 700 800 900 1000 1100 1200 1300 1400 1500 1600 1700 1800 1900 2000 CE

2.14.4 Front Page of *The Daily Courant*

London, England
March 12, 1702

Numb. 2.

The Daily Courant.

Thursday, March 12. 1702.

From the Vienna Journal, Dated March 1. 1702.

Vienna, March 1.

THE Regiment of Huffars commanded by Major General Colonitz, confifting of 1000 Men, is on its March from Hungary towards Bohemia and the Empire; and feveral other Imperial Regiments are marching this way. Our new Levies are carry'd on with great Succefs, and Recruits are continually fending away to their refpective Regiments. We have Advice from Adrianople that the Sultan is in that City, and that my Lord Pagett, Embaffadour from England, is alfo arriv'd there from Conftantinople, and preparing to fet out for this Place in a few days. Count Teckely lives in fo Poor a Condition at Ifmid, otherwife call'd Nicomedia in Afia, the place to which he is banifh'd, that his Wife is reduc'd to Sell her Jewels for their Subfiftance; the Port having taken from them all their Eftate.

Copenhagen, Feb. 11. The French Embaffador is preparing for his Departure from hence, and feems very much diffatisfy'd with the Succefs of all his Negotiations at this Court: but chiefly, becaufe Seven new Regiments are raifing for the Service of the States General. There is a Report that the King intends in a fhort time to take a Journey to Holftein, and from thence to Norway.

From the Vienna Journal, Dated March 4. 1702.

Vienna, March 4. Our Forces defign'd for Italy continue their March thither with all Expedition, and our Army there will be much more Numerous this Year than it was the laft. The Levy-Money is diftributed to the Officers of the new Regiments of Huffars that are now raifing; and fome of them are to Serve in Italy, the others on the Rhine. Proveditore General Vorftern has laid up great Magazines of Provifions in the Countrey of Friuli; and having agreed with feveral Undertakers for the tranfporting of it from thence by the way of the Gulf of Venice towards the River Po; he has already fent into Italy by that means, about 60000 Bufhels of Oats, and 20000 of Wheat; fo that we do not in the leaft apprehend that our Army there can be in any Want of Provifions the next Campaign.

Warfaw, Feb. 19. We are fully convinc'd by two Letters which the King of Sweden has written to the Cardinal Primate, That that Prince is not in the leaft inclin'd to come to an Accommodation with us; which makes us fear that the Unfortunate breaking up of the Diet will foon be follow'd by a General Sedition. The hopes we were in that the Mufcovites would have given the Swedes fomeDiverfion on the other Side of Narva, are vanifh'd; nor will Oginski's Party be able to hinder them from taking Poffeffion of Birfa. And tho' the Affairs of Lithuania are Adjufted, it caufes but little Joy among us, fince we evidently fee that neither Party have yet laid afide their Animofities.

From the Harlem Courant, Dated March 18.

Bruxelles, March 15. The King has made the following Promotion of General Officers, who are to Serve in his Army in Flanders the next Campaign. Don Andrea Benites, heretofore Colonel of the Guards of his Electoral Highnefs of Bavaria, and the Count D' Autel, Governor of Luxemburg, are made Lieutenant Generals: The Counts of Grebendonk and Toulongeon, the Barons of Winterfelt and Noiremont, Don John de Ydiaques, and Don Antonio Amenzaga, Brigadiers, and the Sieur Verboom Engineer General. Orders are given for the fpeedy repairing the Caftle of *Ter Veur*, where an Apartment is to be got ready for the Duke of Burgundy, who is coming into this Countrey to Command as Generaliffimo this Campaign. On Friday laft the Marquifs of Bedmar went to Ghent, where he is to receive on Sunday next, the Homage from the States of Flanders in the Name of His Catholick Majefty.

From the Amfterdam Gazette, Dated March 16.

Vienna, March 1. The Emperour has refolved to difpofe of the Confifcated Eftates of the Hungarian Rebels, and apply the Produce of them to the Charge of the War; They are valued at three Millions of Crowns.

Francfort, March 8. The French Envoy in his Speech to the Deputies of the Circle of Franconia, in the Diet held at Nuremberg, having rudely tax'd the Emperour with infringing the Peace, they broke up without admitting him again into their Affembly.

Harwich, March 10. At Six a Clock in the Evening Yefterday, fail'd the Eagle Pacquet-Boat with a Meffenger and an Exprefs for Holland: And this Morning a hired Smack fail'd with a Second Exprefs for Holland.

London, March 12. The Right Honourable the Earl of Marlborough is declared Captain General of the Forces in England and Holland.

When the King's Body was laid out, there was found a Bracelet about his Right Arm, with His Queen's Wedding Ring on it. He was open'd on Tuefday Morning, his Brain was in very good order, but there was hardly any Blood left in the Body, and his Lungs were very bad.

ADVERTISEMENT.

IT will be found from the Foreign Prints, which from time to time, as Occafion offers, will be mention'd in this Paper, that the Author has taken Care to be duly furnifh'd with all that comes fromAbroad in any Language. And for an Affurance that he will not, under Pretence of having Private Intelligence, impofe any Additions of feign'd Circumftances to an Action, but give his Extracts fairly and Impartially; at the beginning of each Article he will quote the Foreign Paper from whence 'tis taken, that the Publick, feeing from what Country a piece of News comes with the Allowance of that Government, may be better able to Judge of the Credibility and Fairnefs of the Relation: Nor will he take upon him to give any Comments or Conjectures of his own, but will relate only Matter of Fact; fuppofing other People to have Senfe enough to make Reflections for themfelves.

This Courant (as the Title fhews) will be Publifh'd Daily: being defign'd to give all the Material News as foon as every Poft arrives: and is confin'd to half the Compafs, to fave the Publick at leaft half the Impertinences, of ordinary News-Papers.

LONDON. Sold by E. Mallet, next Door to the *King's-Arms* Tavern at *Fleet-Bridge.*

Credit: Fox Photos/Getty Images

What You Need to Know

The first daily English newspaper, printed in England, was *The Daily Courant*, the front page of the second edition of which, from March 12, 1702, is reprinted here.

The origin of newspapers is based in government pronouncements. Regular notices of government announcements began in Venice in the sixteenth century, which issued one monthly that could be purchased by individuals. Around the same time, merchants began issuing handwritten news broadsheets to one another, for which they would charge a fee.

The first real commercial newspapers—with regular print runs, a broad array of news, and purchasable by anyone—dates to seventeenth-century Germany. In fact, the very first English language paper was printed in Amsterdam in 1620, largely because of English government restrictions on the private distribution of news. Within a quarter century of *The Courant*'s debut there were more than 30 newspapers being issued in England, the expansion a result of rising literacy rates and the spread of printing presses.

A Closer Look

As noted, the English government in the early eighteenth century practiced prior censorship, that is, they blocked certain kinds of news—usually of a domestic nature—from being printed in the first place. Thus, the lead story from this edition focuses on the War of the Spanish Succession, a pan-European conflict to determine who would accede to the throne following the death of Spain's King Charles II.

Like many governments to come, that of England's King William III and Queen Anne, who ruled the country in the early eighteenth century, viewed newspapers with suspicion. In 1711, Parliament passed a law taxing all newspapers in the hope that it would drive them out of business or else force them to raise their prices and thereby put the cost of a newspaper out of reach of ordinary persons. In fact, the tax did little to drive newspapers out of business or even to reduce the demand for them. This was for good reason. The newspapers contained a broad array of news, including items on social, economic, and other matters of interest to a broad array of readers, even if they could not discuss the doings of Parliament and the crown.

At a penny or two a copy, the papers were not inordinately expensive. Still, the target audience for these early newspapers was primarily merchants, who needed the information they contained to make business decisions. Most people either read the newspapers at home, delivered to subscribers by young boys, or in coffeehouses, which also served as places for doing business. In England, the London papers had a national reach, as they were delivered by coach to coffeehouses and taverns throughout the country, although often weeks after they had been printed.

2.14.5 Building a New Russian Capital

St. Petersburg, Russia
1703

A description of the city of St. Petersbourg, with several observations relating to it.

I am now going to relate many Particulars not yet mentioned, of a City which may be called a Wonder of the World, was it only in consideration of the few Years that have been employed in the raising of it.

His Czarish Majesty from his younger Years shewed a particular Inclination for Shipping and Sea-affairs . . . when Fortune seconded his Arms so far that in the Year 1702 he took Notebourg And the Year following Nie-Schantz, a trading Town, having observed that about a German Mile further down, the River Neva forms several Islands, the conveniency of the Situation inspired him with Thoughts of building a Town there, in order to get footing in the Baltick [Sea]. The Czar being more and more pleased with the Situation of the neighboring Country, which actually is one of the most agreeable to be found in those Parts, resolved not only to build a Fortress on the River Neva, as he designed at first, but also to make his chief Dock there for building large Men of War [war-ships]. . . . The resolution was no sooner taken, but Orders were forthwith issued, that next Spring a great number of Men, Russians, Tartars, Cosacks, Calmucks, Finlandish and Ingrian Peasants, should be at the place to execute the Czar's Design. . . .

At the same time that they were going on with the Fortress, the City itself also by degrees began to be built, and to this End Numbers of People both of the Nobility and the trading Part of the Nation were ordered to come from Russia to settle at Petersbourg and to build Houses there, all which was executed with such Forwardness, that in a short time the Place swarmed with Inhabitants. The Boyars and others of the Nobility brought with them numerous Retinues and many Servants. The Merchants and Shop-keepers found their Account at this new Place, where everything was excessive dear. Many Swedes, Finlanders, and Livonians, [and] . . . All sorts of Artificers, Mechanicks, and Seamen with their Families were drawn to Petersbourg, in order to encourage Shipping and settle a Commerce by Sea. Many Labourers being Russians, Tartars, and Calmucks, having served the Time prefixed by their Sovereign, and being unwilling to return so far home, engaged with the Boyars who were building Houses every Day, and got sufficient Work to get their Bread by; some thousands of them even built houses for themselves, and settled at Petersbourg. . . . All those Circumstances together very much contributed to the sudden peopling of Petersbourg, which now hardly yields to any in Germany as to the number of Houses and Inhabitants: For there are reckoned at this time sixty odd thousand Houses in that City.

Source: Weber, Christian. *The Present State of Russia in Two Volumes . . . with a Description of Petersbourg and Cronslot, And Several Other Pieces Relating to the Affairs of Russia.* London: W. Taylor, W. and J. Innys, and J. Osborn, 1723, 297–302.

TIMELINE   2000 1900 1800 1700 1600 1500 1400 1300 1200 1100 1000 900 800 700 600 500 400 300 200 100 1 BCE

What You Need to Know

This passage comes from an account by Friedrich Christian Weber, a Dutch-born diplomat from the German-speaking state of Hanover. It describes St. Petersburg, the new capital of Russia built by Czar Peter I.

Peter I, also known as Peter the Great, ruled Russia from 1682, inheriting the throne at age 10, until his death in 1725. The nation he inherited was torn by religious, social, and political conflict, prey to invading forces from east and west. Upon reaching maturity, Peter made it his mission to reassert the power of the monarchy, in the name of modernizing and rationalizing the Russian government and Russian society. He developed a civil service-based bureaucracy to administer his vast realm and built a great army, to crush his international rivals and expand the Russian state. The cost of the latter was borne by the peasantry, many of whose youth were drafted into the military for lifetime service under frequently awful conditions. Nothing epitomized Peter's efforts to modernize the Russian state at any cost than the building of St. Petersburg, his new capital for the country.

A Closer Look

Peter believed that Russia's future lay with Europe. In making this decision, Peter contributed to a long struggle, being fought within the country to this day, about whether Russia belongs culturally and socially to Europe or is a realm distinctly its own. Both in its location and its layout, St. Petersburg was to be a modern metropolis, although unlike any in Europe of its day.

Typically, the great cities of Europe, as elsewhere, had emerged in places with practical advantages—a natural harbor, river, or trading junction. St. Petersburg was built on a frozen marsh not far from the Arctic Circle. Its only advantage was that it faced the Baltic and hence Europe. Because the city was planned from the beginning, there would be no maze of streets and no haphazard scattering of squares and marketplaces. Streets would be on a grid and public spaces distributed rationally around the city.

Peter even dictated who would live there. His government was filled with foreign experts, who would comprise the core of the city's middle class. And, as Weber describes, he ordered the landed aristocrats of Russia, known as boyars, to situate their urban residences there. The fact that so many did so attests to Peter's absolute authority.

St. Petersburg would serve as Russia's capital until the Bolshevik Revolution of the early twentieth century. The communist leaders decided to relocate the capital to Moscow for the inverse of Peter's decision to move to build St. Petersburg, to distance themselves from Europe and potential invasion.

1 100 200 300 400 500 600 700 800 900 1000 1100 1200 1300 1400 1500 1600 1700 1800 1900 2000 CE

2.14.6 Voltaire on Inoculation

France
1733

It is inadvertently affirmed in the Christian countries of Europe that the English are fools and mad-men. Fools, because they give their children the small-pox to prevent their catching it; and mad-men, because they wantonly communicate a certain and dreadful distemper to their children, merely to prevent an uncertain evil. The English, on the other side, call the rest of the Europeans cowardly and unnatural. Cowardly, because they are afraid of putting their children to a little pain; unnatural, because they expose them to die one time or other of the small-pox. But that the reader may be able to judge whether the English or those who differ from them in opinion are in the right, here follows the history of the famed inoculation, which is mentioned with so much dread in France.

The Circassian women have, from time immemorial, communicated the small-pox to their children when not above six months old by making an incision in the arm, and by putting into this incision a pustule, taken carefully from the body of another child. This pustule produces the same effect in the arm it is laid in as yeast in a piece of dough; it ferments, and diffuses through the whole mass of blood the qualities with which it is impregnated. The pustules of the child in whom the artificial small-pox has been thus inoculated are employed to communicate the same distemper to others. There is an almost perpetual circulation of it in Circassia; and when unhappily the small-pox has quite left the country, the inhabitants of it are in as great trouble and perplexity as other nations when their harvest has fallen short. . . .

Some pretend that the Circassians borrowed this custom anciently from the Arabians; but we shall leave the clearing up of this point of history to some learned Benedictine, who will not fail to compile a great many folios on this subject, with the several proofs or authorities. All I have to say upon it is that, in the beginning of the reign of King George I, the Lady Wortley Montague, a woman of as fine a genius, and endued with as great a strength of mind, as any of her sex in the British Kingdoms, being with her husband, who was ambassador at the Porte, made no scruple to communicate the small-pox to an infant of which she was delivered in Constantinople.

The chaplain represented to his lady, but to no purpose, that this was an un-Christian operation, and therefore that it could succeed with none but infidels. However, it had the most happy effect upon the son of the Lady Wortley Montague, who, at her return to England, communicated the experiment to the Princess of Wales, now Queen of England. It must be confessed that this princess, abstracted from her crown and titles, was born to encourage the whole circle of arts, and to do good to mankind. She appears as an amiable philosopher on the throne, having never let slip one opportunity of improving the great talents she received from Nature, nor of exerting her beneficence.

Source: Voltaire. Excerpts from Letter XI, "On Inoculation." In *Letters Concerning the English Nation*. Translated by John Lockman. London: C. Davis and A. Lyon, 1773. Reprinted in *French and English Philosophers: Descartes, Rousseau, Voltaire, Hobbes*. Edited by Charles W. Eliot. New York: P. F. Collier, 1889, pp. 93–96.

TIMELINE   2000 1900 1800 1700 1600 1500 1400 1300 1200 1100 1000 900 800 700 600 500 400 300 200 100 1 BCE

What You Need to Know

In this excerpt from his 1733 *Letters on the English*, the French Enlightenment thinker Voltaire satirizes his countrymen's reluctance to inoculate against small pox.

Although major medical breakthroughs were made in the eighteenth century, the daily practice of medicine remained largely unchanged from medieval times. There were four classes of healers: faith healers; pharmacists, who often diagnosed and treated illnesses as well as concocting medicines; surgeons, who largely dealt with traumatic injuries; and physicians.

The latter were typically apprenticed to other physicians when in their teens and then completed their education with a few university courses and an internship at a hospital. At the time, hospitals were ghastly places, where patients, bedded indiscriminately regardless of illness were barely cared for by ill-trained and often drunken nurses. Fresh air was considered harmful, so there was little circulation, and infection was rampant.

While some physicians sought to apply the latest medical techniques, most clung to old practices dating to ancient times, including the practice of bleeding patients to remove bad "humors" within them. France was particularly notorious for these kinds of practices, including, as Voltaire notes, resistance to the latest discoveries in inoculation against small pox.

A Closer Look

Born François-Marie Arouet, the man known to much of Europe by his nom de plume Voltaire, was a French Enlightenment thinker of the early and mid-eighteenth century, highly regarded for his acerbic wit. As a member of the Enlightenment, a European intellectual movement of the time that sought to replace a blind acceptance of faith, with reason and a scientific approach to an understanding of nature and human society, Voltarie had little respect for tradition, including his countryman's reluctance to inoculate people against small pox.

Using his legendary gift of satire, he points out that the English are called "fools and madmen" for inoculating their children, by which he meant the true fools were the critics of the English. In a more serious vein, he points out that the practice of small pox inoculation was widespread among the Circassians, an impoverished people of the Ottoman Empire, then considered culturally backward by educated Europeans. In fact, inoculation against small pox was practiced throughout the vast Ottoman Empire. The famed travel writer Mary Montagu brought news of the process back to England in the early eighteenth century, where it soon came into widespread use. From there it spread to other European countries. The French, among the last to adopt the practice, did so only after an epidemic in the 1750s that killed thousands, afflicting but ultimately sparing the heir to the French throne.

1 100 200 300 400 500 600 700 800 900 1000 1100 1200 1300 1400 1500 1600 1700 1800 1900 2000 CE

2.14.7 Benjamin Franklin's *Poor Richard's Almanack*

British North America
1736

Loving Readers,

Your kind Acceptance of my former Labours, has encouraged me to continue writing, tho' the general Approbation you have been so good as to favour me with, has excited the Envy of some, and drawn upon me the Malice of others. These Ill-willers of mine, despited at the great Reputation I gain'd by exactly predicting another Man's Death, have endeavour'd to deprive me of it all at once in the most effectual Manner, by reporting that I my self was never alive. They say in short, That there is no such a Man as I am; and have spread this Notion so thoroughly in the Country, that I have been frequently told it to my Face by those that don't know me. This is not civil Treatment, to endeavour to deprive me of my very Being, and reduce me to a Non-entity in the Opinion of the publick. But so long as I know my self to walk about, eat, drink and sleep, I am satisfied that there is really such a Man as I am, whatever they may say to the contrary: And the World may be satisfied likewise; for if there were no such Man as I am, how is it possible I should appear publickly to hundreds of People, as I have done for several Years past, in print? I need not, indeed, have taken any Notice of so idle a Report, if it had not been for the sake of my Printer, to whom my Enemies are pleased to ascribe my Productions; and who it seems is as unwilling to father my Offspring, as I am to lose the Credit of it: Therefore to clear him entirely, as well as to vindicate my own Honour, I make this publick and serious Declaration, which I desire may be believed, to wit, That what I have written heretofore, and do now write, neither was nor is written by any other Man or Men, Person or Persons whatsoever. Those who are not satisfied with this, must needs be very unreasonable.

R. SAUNDERS . . .

Fish & Visitors stink in 3 days . . .

There's more old Drunkards than old Doctors . . .

He that takes a wife, takes care . . .

Source: Franklin, Benjamin. "Preface to *Poor Richard*, 1736." In *The Writings of Benjamin Franklin*. Vol II. Edited by Albert Henry Smyth. New York: Macmillan, 1905, pp. 208–209; Franklin, Benjamin. Aphorisms in *Poor Richard's Almanack*. Waterloo, IA: U.S.C. Publishing Co., 1914, pp. 21, 51, 28.

TIMELINE   2000 1900 1800 1700 1600 1500 1400 1300 1200 1100 1000 900 800 700 600 500 400 300 200 100 1 BCE

What You Need to Know

This is a 1736 excerpt from Benjamin Franklin's *Poor Richard's Almanack*, a popular annual compendium of humorous writings and practical information.

Historians have often referred to Benjamin Franklin as the "first American." By that, they mean his rise from poverty and obscurity to wealth and international renown provided a template for the so-called American dream, although that term was not coined until the early twentieth century. Franklin's family in Boston tried to give him a good education, but expenses got in the way. So he was put to work in his half brother's print shop and educated himself in the works of the Enlightenment thinkers of Europe, who insisted that reason and scientific thought could not only explain the workings of nature but improve human society as well.

Printers, by definition, were often among the more literate and educated of laborers, and so it was that Franklin turned to writing, again along very American lines. While his essays were infused with both the Calvinist ethics of his youth, which advocated plain living and hard work, as well as the Enlightenment teachings of Europe, they were written in a humorous and accessible style that the common man and woman could understand. Nowhere was this combination of ethics, book learning, and plain common sense more in evidence than *Poor Richard's Almanack*, a yearly compendium of useful information Franklin launched in 1732.

A Closer Look

The "Poor Richard" in the almanac's title referred to "Richard Saunders," a pseudonym of Franklin's. From the beginning, Franklin's publication was a huge success throughout Britain's North American colonies, with print runs as high as 10,000, an extraordinary number given that the population of the colonies in the 1730s was less than 900,000, of which roughly a fifth were illiterate African-American slaves. While the almanac included information on farming, history, and household tips, most read it for its humor and folk wisdom. Even in his own time, people frequently quoted his adages: "haste makes waste," "a penny saved is a penny earned," and "early to bed, early to rise, makes a man healthy, wealthy, and wise."

Poor Richard's Almanack made Franklin rich and famous, the latter fact providing the grist for the humorous excerpt reprinted here. In it, Franklin insists that he is, in fact, the author of the almanac, despite the "Ill-willers of mine . . . reporting that I my self was never alive." Like many eighteenth-century essayists, Franklin preferred to write under a pseudonym. In many cases, readers were fully aware of the writers' true identities. And never was that more the case than with *Poor Richard's Almanack*. Franklin's trademark humor, and often earthy language, is also notable in the selections of adages printed here.

1 100 200 300 400 500 600 700 800 900 1000 1100 1200 1300 1400 1500 1600 1700 1800 1900 2000 CE

2.14.8 French Encyclopedia Article on Chocolate

France
1750s

Chocolate, a type of cake or bar prepared with different ingredients but whose basic element is cocoa. . . . The beverage made from this bar retains the same name; the cocoa nut originates from the Americas: Spanish travelers established that it was much used in Mexico, when they conquered it around 1520. . . .

Spaniards, who learned about this beverage from the Mexicans and were convinced, through their own experience that this beverage, though unrefined, was good for the health, set out to correct its defaults by adding sugar, some ingredients from the Orient, and several local drugs that it is unnecessary to list here, as we only know their name and as, from all these extras, only the vanilla leaf traveled to our regions (similarly, cinnamon was the only ingredient that was universally approved) and proved to resist time as part of the composition of chocolate.

The sweet scent and potent taste it imparts to chocolate have made it highly recommended for it; but time has shown that it could potentially upset one's stomach, and its use has decreased; some people who favor the care of their health to the pleasure of their senses, have stopped using it completely. In Spain and in Italy, chocolate prepared without vanilla has been termed the healthy chocolate; and in our French islands in the Americas, where vanilla is neither rare nor expensive, as it can be in Europe, it is never used, when the consumption of chocolate is as high as in any other part of the world. . . .

When the cocoa paste has been well shredded on the stone (see Article Cocoa), sugar can be added once it has been filtered through a silk-cloth sifter; the secret to the true proportion of cocoa and sugar is to put equal quantity of both: one could in fact subtract one quarter out of the dosage of sugar, as it might dry up the paste too much, or render it too sensitive to changes in the air, or endanger it even more to the apparition of worms. But that suppressed quarter of sugar must be used when chocolate, the beverage, is being prepared.

Once sugar is well mixed with the cocoa paste, a very thin powder can be added, made with vanilla seeds and cinnamon sticks finely cut and sifted together; this new mixture shall be mixed on the stone; once every ingredient is well incorporated, the mixture shall be poured into chocolatière pots, the shape of which it will take, and where it will harden. When one loves scents, one could add some amber essence into the pots.

Source: Venel, Gabriel. "Chocolate." In *Encyclopédie*. Vol. III. Edited by Denis Diderot and Jean le Rond d'Alembert. Paris: André Le Breton, 1751–1777, pp. 359–360. Translated by and courtesy of Philippe Bonin.

What You Need to Know

This article on chocolate, written by Gabriel Venel for the *Encyclopédie*, was a compendium of information published in France in the 1750s.

Christopher Columbus famously sailed across the Atlantic in 1492 to pioneer a new all-oceanic route to the East Indies, to bring back the tropical spices Europeans so craved. Columbus, of course, was ultimately thwarted in his efforts by landing in the Americas. Nevertheless, Columbus's voyage inaugurated an even greater revolution in European cuisine than anything he could have imagined when he first set out.

It was part of what historians called the Columbian Exchange, a movement of new crops and foodstuffs from the New World to the Old. The exchange, of course, also went in the opposite direction. Some of the new foods would utterly transform not just cuisine but the very social order of countries. The potato, for example, highly productive in cold and damp climates, caused a population explosion in Ireland and parts of Eastern Europe. Less fundamental, but no less ubiquitous, was the introduction of chocolate.

A Closer Look

Archaeologists have discovered evidence of cacao consumption dating back to Central America of the mid-second millennium BCE. The beans inside the pods of the cacao tree are the raw material of chocolate. By the time of the Aztecs nearly 3,000 years later, chocolate had become so popular and widespread that the beans were used as a form of currency.

The Spanish conquistadors were the first Europeans to encounter chocolate, but they did not like it, probably because the Aztecs preferred to consume it in its original bitter form, unsweetened. One Spaniard called it a "drink for pigs." But sweetened, it appealed not only to the conquistadores but much of Europe. By the seventeenth century, it was being drunk across the continent. So many resources were dedicated to its production and trade that it was widely available almost everywhere and affordable by all classes. In addition, chocolate was appreciated not just as a treat but for its supposed nutritional, medicinal, and even aphrodisiacal properties. It is no wonder that when European taxonomists gave it its Latin nomenclature, they chose for its genus name *theobroma*, that is, "food of the gods."

As Venel relates, by the mid-eighteenth century, chocolate was no longer consumed as just a beverage but matched with all kinds of ingredients and incorporated into any number of recipes, typically of a dessert variety.

1 100 200 300 400 500 600 700 800 900 1000 1100 1200 1300 1400 1500 1600 1700 1800 1900 2000 CE

What You Need to Know

In the preradio age, ships communicated with each other using correspondence signals, which in this plate from the 1750s, could be in the form of cannon shots and flags.

The eighteenth century was a time of rapidly expanding overseas trade but, as part of an economic system, bore only a passing resemblance to modern free trade. Mercantilism, or mercantile capitalism, was a highly regulated system of trade, welding private profit to national power. Government regulations were written to both enhance the trading opportunities of private individuals and joint stock companies, precursors of corporations, and to make sure those enterprises served the larger national interests.

The most obvious manifestation of mercantilism was empire. European countries, particularly Britain, but also France, the Netherlands, Spain, and Portugal, sought to expand—or defend—their empires to make sure that the profits from colonial economic enterprise would redound to the national treasury. Nations also tried to enhance their economic standing, and hence their national power, by closing off their colonial markets to competitors. Many had regulations requiring that all goods traded between colonies and mother countries be transported on ships owned my merchants from that country. The mercantile system was successful in its day, leading to a vast expansion in shipping, which required the defense of ever-larger navies. Coordinating the activities of these navies required better communication.

A Closer Look

The use of flags to communicate between ships was nothing new in the eighteenth century. Indeed, the ancient Greeks used them in their internecine fighting and in the naval battles they fought against invading Persians. But the flags could only communicate simple messages. It was the Dutch, during their Golden Age of trade and imperial expansion in the seventeenth century, who perfected the art of nautical flag communications, requiring every captain in both the naval and mercantile fleets to understand what different flags meant. Experience with the Dutch in battle demonstrated to the English, who over the course of the eighteenth century would come to possess the greatest naval and mercantile fleet in history to that time, the value of nautical communication.

At first, the British Navy reserved the use of flags for the ship in an armada where the admiral resided, hence, the term "flag ship," meaning the lead, or directing, ship. Eventually, all ships were given flags and the communication became two way, as illustrated in this plate from French philosopher Denis Diderot et al.'s *Encyclopédie* of the 1750s.

1 100 200 300 400 500 600 700 800 900 1000 1100 1200 1300 1400 1500 1600 1700 1800 1900 2000 CE

2.14.10 Frederick the Great's Regulations for Public Schools

Prussia
1763

General School Regulations, August 12, 1763.

We Frederick, *by the grace of God, King, etc.:*

Whereas, to our great displeasure, we have perceived that schools and the instruction of youth in the country have come to be greatly neglected, and that by the inexperience of many sacristans and schoolmasters, the young people grow up in stupidity and ignorance, it is our well considered and serious pleasure, that instruction in the country, throughout all our provinces, should be placed on a better footing, and be better organized than heretofore. For, as we earnestly strive for the true welfare of our country, and of all classes of people; now that quiet and general peace have been restored, we find it necessary and wholesome to have a good foundation laid in the schools by a rational and Christian education of the young for the fear of God and other useful ends. Therefore, by the power of our own highest motive, of our care and paternal disposition for the best good of all our subjects, we command hereby, all governors, consistories and other collegiates of our country; that they shall, on their part, contribute all they can, with affection and zeal, to maintain the following General School Regulations, and in future to arrange all things in accordance with the law to the end that ignorance, so injurious and unbecoming to Christianity, may be prevented and lessened, and the coming time may train and educate in the schools more enlightened and virtuous subjects.

Section 1. First, it is our pleasure that all our subjects, parents, guardians or masters, whose duty it is to educate the young, shall send their children to school, and those confided to their care, boys and girls, if not sooner, certainly when they reach the age of five years; and shall continue regularly to do so, and require them to go to school until they are thirteen or fourteen years old, and know not only what is necessary of Christianity, fluent reading and writing, but can give answer in everything which they learn from the school books, prescribed and approved by our consistory.

2. Masters to whom children in Prussia, by custom are bound to render work for certain years, are seriously advised not to withdraw such children from school until they can read well, and have laid a good foundation in Christian knowledge; also made a beginning in writing, and can present a certificate from the minister and school master to this effect to the school-visitors. Parents and guardians ought much more to consider it their bounden duty that their children and wards receive sufficient instruction in the necessary branches.

Source: Frederick II. Excerpt from General School Regulations (1763). In *Memoirs of Eminent Teachers and Educators with Contributions to the History of Education in Germany*. Edited by Henry Barnard. Rev. ed. Hartford, CT: Brown & Gross, 1878, p. 593.

TIMELINE   2000 1900 1800 1700 1600 1500 1400 1300 1200 1100 1000 900 800 700 600 500 400 300 200 100 1 BCE

What You Need to Know

This is an excerpt of regulations establishing a public school system in Prussia in 1763. The regulations were largely the work of Prussia's king Frederick II.

Frederick II, also known as Frederick the Great, ruled as king of Prussia from 1740 to 1786. Prussia, in the eighteenth century, was the most powerful of the kingdoms and principalities of German-speaking Central Europe, thanks in part to the innovations Frederick brought to the nation's military.

A philosopher by nature, Frederick argued for an enlightened absolutism, that is, a political system in which all authority rested in a heredity monarch but a monarch who ruled rationally with an eye to social, economic, and technological progress for his people. Many of Frederick's reforms, both in the military and domestic arena, would be adopted by the German state, after it was unified in the latter half of the nineteenth century. Central to Frederick's plans for a progressive Prussian state was the development of public schools.

A Closer Look

Traditionally in Prussia, as in virtually all of Europe, education was not for everyone. The youth of the landed aristocracy and, increasingly, the mercantile classes were educated in the home by private tutors or in private academies that were very costly and very exclusive about who they accepted. Meanwhile, a few particularly talented youth from the lower classes might receive an education in a school affiliated with a church. It was simply taken for granted that literacy and learning was the preserve of the upper classes.

The Enlightenment of the eighteenth century began to alter such attitudes. The Enlightenment was an intellectual movement that sought to use reason and science to discover universal laws that explained nature and man's place in it. Reason, Enlightenment thinkers also believed, could reform human society as well. Frederick was a disciple of the Enlightenment, but he also came to believe that a well-educated populace was a source of state power, in that literate people would make better workers, soldiers, and participants in civil life.

With his regulations of 1763, Frederick established the first national public education system in history. As the first part of the regulation reveals, school attendance was not exactly compulsory but was highly encouraged for children from age five to thirteen or fourteen. At the very least, Frederick declared, no child should leave school until he or she (schools were to be for both sexes, another breakthrough) had "a good foundation in Christian knowledge; [and] also made a beginning in writing."

1 100 200 300 400 500 600 700 800 900 1000 1100 1200 1300 1400 1500 1600 1700 1800 1900 2000 CE

2.14.11 Newspaper Notices for Runaway Servants and Apprentices

British North America
1770–1771

Trenton Goal, December 28, 1769.

This is to give notice, there was committed to my custody, by William Clayton, Esq., as a run-away apprentice on the 24th day of October last, THOMAS SANDAMAN. This is to inform his master or sheriff that he run away from, that they come and pay charges and take him away, *or he will be sold* to pay cost and charges, on Saturday the 20th day of January, 1770, by me

PETER HANKINSON, *Goaler.*

—The Pennsylvania Journal, No. 1413, January 4, 1770.

Three Pounds Reward

Run-away on Friday the 12th Inst. from the Subscriber at Hunterdon County, in New-Jersey, an Apprentice, named David Cox, about Twenty Years of Age, a Carpenter and Joiner by Trade, but its likely he may pass for a Mill-Wright, as he has two Brothers of that Trade, that works near Albany. He is about 5 Feet 10 Inches high, large boned, knock kneed, of a dark Complexion, down Look, black Eyes, black Hair, and wears it tied. Had on when he went away, a grey coloured Coat and Jacket, pretty much worn, with Horn Buttons on them, new Leather Breeches, with black Horn Buttons, Russia Shirt, black Yarn Stockings, new Shoes, also a rusty Castor Hat, wears it cocked: It is also suspected he has stole his Indentures, and will very likely show them for a Pass, as he is near of Age. Whoever apprehends said Apprentice, and secures him in any Goal, so that his Master may have Notice thereof, shall have the above Reward, paid by me.

JAMES TAYLOR.

N. B. Perhaps he may change his Cloaths, that he may not be discovered.

—The N. Y. Gazette, or Weekly Post Boy, No. 1412, January 22, 1770.

New Jersey, November 24, 1769.

Run-away the 22d September, from the Subscriber, living in Monmouth County, in the Township of Shrewsbury, in the Province of East New-Jersey; an indented Servant Man, named Walter Clark, born *in the Jerseys*, about Twenty-four Years of Age, a Black-Smith by trade, and understands farming Business; he is about six Feet high, has black curled Hair, and keeps his Mouth much open: He took several Suits of Apparel with him, all of a brownish Colour, some Broad Cloth, and some thin Stuff; also one striped double-breasted Jacket. Whoever takes up the above said Servant and delivers him to me the Subscriber, shall have Three Pounds Reward, and reasonable Charges paid, by me.

BENJAMIN JACKSON.

Source: Newspaper extracts, 1770–1771, in *New Jersey Archives*, First Series, XXVII. Reprinted in *A Source Book in American History to 1787*. Edited by Willis Mason West. Boston: Allyn and Bacon, 1913, pp. 366–368.

TIMELINE   2000 1900 1800 1700 1600 1500 1400 1300 1200 1100 1000 900 800 700 600 500 400 300 200 100 1 BCE

What You Need to Know

These are notices from colonial American newspapers in 1770 and 1771, placed there by masters seeking the return of runaway indentured servants and apprentices.

Historically in America, free labor has been defined as an employer-employee relationship in which the employee agrees to work for an employer, with the two sides negotiating the terms of employment as legal equals. The employee agrees to provide labor in exchange for wages, and both are free at any time to sever the relationship for almost any reason. Free labor is, of course, the dominant style of employment in America today.

But this was not always the case in colonial America. Aside from the roughly 20 percent of the population that was enslaved at the time of Revolution, many white Americans were bound by working contracts that bore little resemblance to free labor values. These people were primarily indentured servants and apprentices. The former, who represented almost half of all European immigrants to the American colonies, usually had their ship passage paid by a broker. When the immigrant arrived, the broker sold him or her to the highest bidder; the servant was then required to labor for the purchaser of the contract for a number of years—usually seven. For this labor, they received nothing more than room, board, the lifting of their financial obligation to the broker, and usually, a small stipend at the end of their service to get them started as free laborers. Apprentices were typically teenage boys, sometimes younger, and occasionally girls, whose parents contracted with a craftsman to have them learn a trade in return for labor. As with indentured servants, the apprentices were not free to sever the contract at will, as these runaway notices reveal.

A Closer Look

There were more than mere legal differences between the servants and apprentices of colonial times and modern employees. Today, an employee typically has a strictly financial relationship with his or her employer, which is often a large bureaucratic corporation. When work is done, the employee goes home to live life as he or she pleases. The lives of servants and apprentices, by contrast, were intricately intertwined with their masters, whom they typically lived with, ate with, and sometimes socialized with. But, of course, they were not equals. The power differential, combined with the ordinary emotions and passions inherent in all intimate human relationships, often led to discontent among servants and apprentices. Not having the right to freely vacate their contracts, many chose instead to run away. Indeed, so common were runaways that the advertisements by masters seeking their return represented an important source of revenue for colonial newspapers. The ads contained information one would expect them to—from where and whom the servant had runaway, a description of the runaway, and the reward for his or her return. What they do not mention is the punishment such servants were likely to get upon being returned—typically, several dozen lashes of whip and an extension of their contract's term.

1 100 200 300 400 500 600 700 800 900 1000 1100 1200 1300 1400 1500 1600 1700 1800 1900 2000 CE

2.14.12 An Account of a Public Execution in London

London, England
1774

Saturday, July 2nd.

Early in the morning [yesterday] the prisoners [who were to be executed] employed themselves in singing psalms and other acts of devotion. Exactly at seven o'clock they were brought from the cells into the Press-yard, in order to the taking off their irons.—Jones trembled as if his frame was dissolving, while Hawke appeared, if not with unconcern, with a fortitude very unusual. While the irons were taking off, an acquaintance of Hawke accosted him with a "How d'ye, Billy?"—which the other replied to with cheerfulness, and enquired after an old acquaintance whom he had heard was indisposed. From Newgate to the place of execution Hawke behaved with much calm resignation, while Jones prayed and wept incessantly. When they came within 200 yards of Oxford Street Turnpike, Hawke looked round him, as if he rather wished than feared the journey at an end. When they arrived at the place of execution about 20 minutes were spent in devotion, and then they were tied up. A number of pigeons were now thrown into the air, as were others at stated periods during the melancholy ceremony. About a minute before they were turned off Hawke kicked off his shoes with great violence, and at the instant the cart moved he drew up his knees to his breast, so as to fall with a violent jerk, which almost instantly deprived him of life. There was a hearse in waiting, with a handsome black coffin with yellow nails, on which was the following inscription:

MR. WILLIAM HAWKE,

Died July 1st, 1774, Aged 24

Hawke has desired that a tombstone may be erected to his memory, with an epitaph from a stone in Stepney Churchyard, beginning thus:

"Adieu, vain world! I've had enough of thee!"

Just as the unhappy men were turned off, a young fellow, a shoe-maker by trade, was detected picking a gentleman's pocket of a gold watch, and consigned to the care of the constables, who carried him before a magistrate.

Much has been said with great humanity and truth on the dreadful frequency of executions at Tyburn, and nothing is more evident than that they have very little effect in restraining men from committing depredations on the public. A reformation in our criminal laws has been long and loudly called for: In the opinion of the celebrated H. Fielding Esq., the lives of those executed are thrown away. It is not so much the severity as the certainty of punishment which deters men of bad morals. He who is about to commit a robbery estimates the numbers whom the jury will not convict from a proper reluctance to hang men for a petty act of pilfering, those who escape, because no evidence but the most certain will convict for a capital offence, with the numbers who are pardoned at the report, where it is become a kind of maxim to hang none but those who have been guilty of repeated offences, and laughs at the danger when there are so many chances of escaping. The beneficial effects of the severities of Pope Sextus the Fifth must convince every man that legal severity is real mercy. Our Laws should be carefully reviewed and the number of capital offences greatly lessened; but when that is done, the sentence of the law should be the voice of fate.

Source: Hampden, John. *An Eighteenth Century Journal: Being a Record of the Years 1774–1776*. London: MacMillan & Co., 1940, pp. 181–182.

What You Need to Know

The accompanying text comes from an account of a 1774 execution in London; the guilty party had been convicted of pick-pocketing a gold watch.

In 1965, the British Parliament abolished the death penalty (1973 in Northern Ireland), ending a long and bloody history of capital punishment in the United Kingdom. As in virtually all human societies, Britain from the time of its formation in 1706—and England long before that—had used the death penalty as a means to punish the guilty, deter crime, and assert the power of the state. Unlike in the United States today, however, capital punishment was used promiscuously, for a variety of crimes that today would be punished by terms in prison or even community service.

In the late seventeenth century, there were roughly fifty statutory offenses for which the death penalty applied. By the latter part of the next century, there were more than 220. Grand larceny was one, although the "grand" meant anything worth more than 12 pence, around $30 or $40 in today's money. So notorious were the laws that called for such punishment that they were cumulatively referred to in popular speech as the "bloody code."

A Closer Look

In an age when law enforcement was sporadic and the ability to track down criminals limited, the law was made to be terrible. That is, it was written to be so draconian that it would prevent crime from occurring in the first place. As one seventeenth-century parliamentarian famously remarked, "Men are not hanged for stealing horses, but that horses may not be stolen." To have the maximum deterrent effect, the condemned were hanged in public for all to see. "If they [public executions] don't draw spectators," the famed eighteenth-century essayist Samuel Johnson once noted, "they don't answer their purpose."

From the twelfth century onward, the primary site for public executions was the so-called Tyburn Tree, a row of elms alongside a similarly named stream, situated in the heart of London, not far from Buckingham Palace, the London residency of the royal family. But as Hampden remarks, the executions seemed to have little effect, as the very crime of pick-pocketing for which the criminal he observed was being executed was committed in the crowd that was watching it. Ultimately, such thinking about the limits of capital punishment as a deterrent to crime won out. By the early nineteenth century, reforms were passed limiting the number of capital crimes. New types of sentencing were introduced as well, among them transport to distant Australia.

1 100 200 300   400   500   600   700   800   900   1000 1100 1200 1300   1400   1500   1600   1700 1800 1900 2000 CE

2.14.13 Colonial Minutemen Agreement

British North America
1775

We whose names are hereunto subscribed do voluntarily enlist ourselves as minute men, to be ready for military operation upon the shortest notice. And we hereby promise and engage that we will immediately, each of us, provide for and equip himself with an effective fire-arm bayonet pouch, knapsack, and round of cartridges ready made. And that we may obtain the skill of complete soldiers, we promise to convene for exercise in the art military, at least twice every week; and oftener if our officers shall think necessary, And as soon as such a number shall be enlisted as the present captain, lieutenant and ensign of the company of militia shall think necessary, we will proceed to choose such officers as shall appear to them and to the company to be necessary; the officers to be chosen by a majority of the votes of the enlisted company. And when the officers are duly chosen, we hereby promise and engage that we will punctually render all that obedience to them respectively as is required by the laws of this province or practised by any well regulated troops. And if any officer or soldier shall neglect to attend the time and place of exercise, he shall forfeit and pay the sum of two shillings lawful money for the use of the company unless he can offer such an excuse to the officers of the company as to them shall appear sufficient.

Source: Ipswich minutemen contract. In *Essex Institute Historical Collections*. Vol. XIV, no. 4. Salem, MA: Essex Institute, 1878, pp. 237–238.

What You Need to Know

This is a January 1775 commitment contract for a "minute company," in Ipswich, Massachusetts; minute companies were elite forces with colonial militias, ready to fight "at a minute's notice."

Civilian militias had a long history in Britain's North American colonies, especially those in New England. With the British Army far away and hostile Native Americans, not to mention rival French and Dutch colonists, close by, the need for self-defense was obvious. Beginning with the Massachusetts Bay Colony, founded in 1630, various colonies and settlements established and required all able bodied adult men to be members of the militia, bringing their own arms and being subject to periodic training camps.

Some settlements that were particularly vulnerable to attack established elite corps within the militias, known as "minute companies." Because they were well trained, they could be ready for combat in very short order, hence the name, derived from the slogan "at a minute's notice." When the British Army itself became the foe, the "minute companies" were expanded, through commitment contracts, like the one here. A number of these "minute companies" would provide the colonial firepower in the April 1775 battles of Concord and Lexington, which would begin the American Revolution.

A Closer Look

The British military, although not the largest in the world by any means, was nevertheless one of the most effective, highly disciplined and well armed, its officers fully trained in the latest tactics in European warfare. It is no wonder that Lord Dartmouth, London's secretary of state for America, dismissed the growing resistance to British rule as a "rude rabble without plan," in a January 1775 letter to the head of forces in Boston, General Thomas Gage. Dartmouth had a point.

The minutemen differed from the regular militia in that they were an elite force, chosen by officers from the ranks of the militia for their enthusiasm, reliability, and physical endurance. Most of them were relatively young, under 25 years of age, and often unmarried. Age aside, they represented a solid cross section of colonial society, with officers from among the more well-to-do and the soldiers themselves typically coming from the families of landholding farmers and artisans.

When Gage, following up on Dartmouth's orders, sent his troops to seize illegal patriot armories in Concord and Lexington, they were met by withering fire from patriot militias who, unfamiliar with classical European warfare, fired from behind trees rather than in neat formations. Ultimately, the British were forced to retreat, ceding the first field of battle to the minute men.

1 100 200 300 400 500 600 700 800 900 1000 1100 1200 1300 1400 1500 1600 1700 1800 1900 2000 CE

2.14.14 Abigail Adams to John Adams: "Remember the Ladies"

British North America
1776

I long to hear that you have declared an independency. And, by the way, in the new code of laws which I suppose it will be necessary for you to make, I desire you would remember the ladies and be more generous and favorable to them than your ancestors. Do not put such unlimited power into the hands of the husbands. Remember, all men would be tyrants if they could. If particular care and attention is not paid to the ladies, we are determined to foment a rebellion, and will not hold ourselves bound by any laws in which we have no voice or representation.

That your sex are naturally tyrannical is a truth so thoroughly established as to admit of no dispute; but such of you as wish to be happy willingly give up the harsh title of master for the more tender and endearing one of friend. Why, then, not put it out of the power of the vicious and the lawless to use us with cruelty and indignity with impunity? Men of sense in all ages abhor those customs which treat us only as the vassals of your sex; regard us then as beings placed by Providence under your protection, and in imitation of the Supreme Being make use of that power only for our happiness.

Source: Adams, Abigail. Excerpt of letter in *Familiar Letters of John Adams and His Wife Abigail Adams during the Revolution with a Memoir of Mrs. Adams*. Edited by Charles Francis Adams. New York: Hurd and Houghton, 1875, p. 150.

TIMELINE 2000 1900 1800 1700 1600 1500 1400 1300 1200 1100 1000 900 800 700 600 500 400 300 200 100 1 BCE

What You Need to Know

In this excerpt from a letter dated March 1776, Abigail Adams writes from her home in Massachusetts to her husband. At the time, John Adams served as a delegate to the Second Continental Congress, an assembly then contemplating declaring independence from Britain.

As in many political upheavals, the American revolutionaries began their struggle with modest enough demands. They had a number of grievances with the British government, concerning taxation, restrictions on western settlement, government monopolies, and, overlying these specific complaints, their lack of representation in Parliament. Most had no desire to break their ties with London. In the early 1770s, the vast majority of colonists were not only loyal subjects of King George III but proud Englishmen.

But Britain's tone-deaf, heavy-handed response to their complaints ultimately pushed many over the edge into demanding a full break. In March 1775, delegates from the colonies met in Philadelphia, initially to coordinate their response to British repression. Sixteen months later, however, open warfare between the British military and colonial militias and armies, along with the publication of a fiery pamphlet by a radical printer named Tom Paine, led them to declare independence. Paine and other patriots based their stand for independence on the argument that "all men are created equal" and deserving of a voice in government. Of course, by "all men," the founders meant white men, some limiting that to those with property. But, as this letter attests, demands for equality once unleashed were not so easily circumscribed.

A Closer Look

In the most famous of the letters exchanged between the two, which is excerpted here, Abigail argues "all men would be tyrants if they could." Before mentioning this, she asks that John, in considering laws for any nation to be declared independent, "remember the ladies and be more generous and favorable to them than your ancestors." By using the word *tyrants*, Abigail was appropriating a term the patriots themselves used to describe the British government. In doing so, she extended the meaning of the struggle against Britain to encompass more radical ideals, such as more freedom for women.

The Revolutionary War, like many wars, helped to elevated the status of women. In colonial society, a women's sphere was restricted. She was delegated the tasks of running household affairs, managing the servants, and raising young children. Field work and running the business end of the farm were the tasks of men. They had virtually no rights related to property, divorce, or to serve in any public position, even as a juror. But with men off to fight the British, women were left the task of running things on the home front, which lead to a sense of empowerment. Such was the case with Abigail and John Adams during the Revolutionary War, although John, of course, was away politicking rather than soldiering. Nevertheless, Abigail was left in charge of the family's farm back in Massachusetts, a complex business and the main source of the family's income. As historians have noted in many Revolutionary War era letters from wives to absent husbands, Abigail initially spoke of "your" farm, later switching to the possessive "our," a telling change.

1 100 200 300 400 500 600 700 800 900 1000 1100 1200 1300 1400 1500 1600 1700 1800 1900 2000 CE

2.14.15 Diagram of British Slave Ship

England
1780s

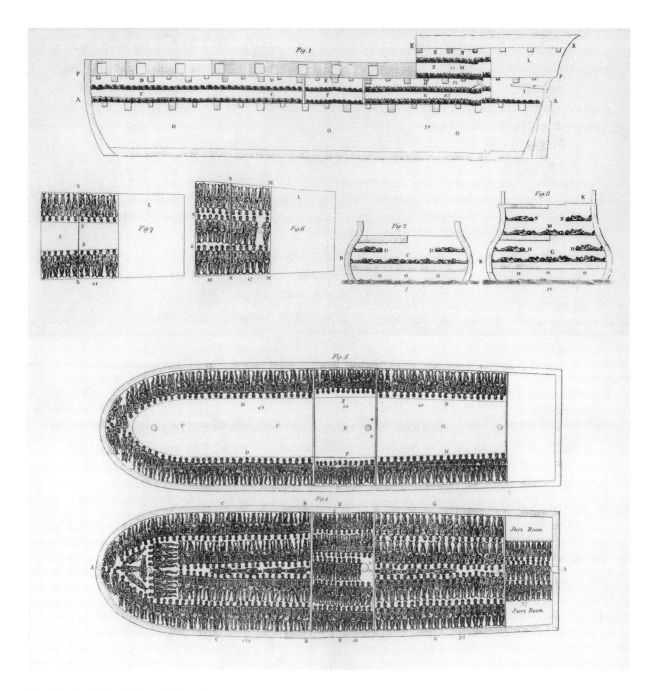

Credit: The Print Collector/Getty Images

What You Need to Know

A diagram of a British slave ship *Brooks*, active in the 1780s, is shown here.

The statistics of the trans-Atlantic slave trade are staggering. They enumerate what, to modern thinking, may be the greatest violation of human rights in history. Between the late fifteenth century, when it began, largely to bring small numbers of Africans to Europe and the sugar islands of the Atlantic, and the time it ended as a largely illegal operation in the late nineteenth, the slave trade brought an estimated 10 to 12 million people across the sea. In their new homes, they served as domestic servants, miners, farmhands, urban workers, and, most of all, laborers on the great sugar, tobacco, rice, cotton, and other commercial crop plantations of the Americas.

Virtually all were brought in the holds of slave ships, so packed together that more than one in ten died en route, their bodies tossed to the waves without any pretence of ceremony.

A Closer Look

Of those 10 to 30 million slaves brought to the Americas, more than half were transported in the eighteenth century. The leading country in this enterprise, as in so many other aspects of the period's trade, was Britain. The ship shown here, the *Brooks*, was based out of Liverpool, the epicenter of the nation's trafficking in human beings. Two things about the image strike the viewer. First are the words "regulated slave trade" at the top of the document. Responding to the outcry of antislave trade advocates, Parliament passed the Slave Trade Act of 1788, which regulated the number of slaves that could be carried on a given size ship. But the act hardly made for a humane crossing, as the illustration reveals.

In fact, the diagram was drawn and published by a leading antislaver William Elford and the Plymouth chapter of the Society for Effecting the Abolition of the Slave Trade. It became the most effective propaganda tool that those seeking an end to the trade possessed, as it showed just how meaningless the 1788 act really was. It notes that the *Brooks* could legally carry 454 slaves, two-thirds of whom were stowed in the bottom of the hold and the other third on a shelf above. This allowed roughly six square feet of room for adults and five for children, and this for a voyage that could last from two to four months, not to mention the time sitting off the coast of Africa waiting for a full load.

1 100 200 300 400 500 600 700 800 900 1000 1100 1200 1300 1400 1500 1600 1700 1800 1900 2000 CE

2.14.16 Thomas Jefferson on American Education

United States
1785

But why send an American youth to Europe for education? What are the objects of a useful American education? Classical knowledge; modern languages, chiefly French, Spanish, and Italian; mathematics; natural philosophy; natural history; civil history; and ethics. In natural philosophy, I mean to include chemistry and agriculture, and in natural history, to include botany, as well as the other branches of those departments. It is true that the habit of speaking the modern languages cannot be so well acquired in America; but every other article can be as well acquired at William and Mary College as at any place in Europe. When college education is done with and a young man is to prepare himself for public life, he must cast his eyes (for America) either on law or physic [medicine]. For the former, where can he apply so advantageously as to Mr. Wythe? For the latter, he must come to Europe. The medical class of students, therefore, is the only one which need come to Europe. . . .

Let us view the disadvantages of sending a youth to Europe. To enumerate them all would require a volume. I will select a few. If he goes to England, he learns drinking, horse racing, and boxing. These are the peculiarities of English education. The following circumstances are common to education in that and the other countries of Europe. He acquires a fondness for European luxury and dissipation, and a contempt for the simplicity of his own country; he is fascinated with the privileges of the European aristocrats, and sees with abhorrence the lovely equality which the poor enjoy with the rich in his own country; he contracts a partiality for aristocracy or monarchy; he forms foreign friendships which will never be useful to him, and loses the seasons of life for forming in his own country those friendships which, of all others, are the most faithful and permanent. . . .

He returns to his own country a foreigner, unacquainted with the practices of domestic economy necessary to preserve him from ruin, speaking and writing his native tongue as a foreigner, and therefore unqualified to obtain those distinctions which eloquence of the pen and tongue insures in a free country. . . .

It appears to me, then, that an American coming to Europe for education loses in his knowledge, in his morals, in his health, in his habits, and in his happiness. I had entertained only doubts on this head before I came to Europe; what I see and hear since I came here proves more than I had even suspected. Cast your eye over America. Who are the men of most learning, of most eloquence, most beloved by their countrymen and most trusted and promoted by them? They are those who have been educated among them, and whose manners, morals, and habits are perfectly homogeneous with those of the country.

Source: Jefferson, Thomas. Excerpts from letter to J. Banister, Junior (October 15, 1785). In *Memoirs, Correspondence, and Private Papers of Thomas Jefferson, Late President of the United States*. Edited by Thomas Jefferson Randolph. London: Henry Colburn and Richard Bentley, 1829, pp. 345–347.

TIMELINE   2000 1900 1800 1700 1600 1500 1400 1300 1200 1100 1000 900 800 700 600 500 400 300 200 100 1 BCE

What You Need to Know

On October 15, 1785, Thomas Jefferson wrote to his friend John Banister, a lawyer and former revolutionary war officer, about the merits of an American versus a European education.

Society in colonial British North America, particularly among the upper classes, was highly imitative of the mother country's, a fact much lamented by proto-American nationalists, such as the writer and statesman Benjamin Franklin. Part of this deference to English ways had to do with prosperity. More money and better trading contacts with Britain allowed the upper classes to display their social superiority to the poor and middling classes through consumption and leisure activities. Upper-class colonists adopted the stylized forms of behavior that they read about in British books or encountered on visits to the home country.

There were, of course, more serious borrowings. Many educated colonists were followers of Europe's Great Enlightenment figures, who sought to replace blind faith and adherence to ancient customs with reason and a search for a more rational social order. Indeed, it was Enlightenment thought that helped inspire the Revolution that severed political ties with Britain. But as this excerpt from Jefferson's letter to Banister reveals, some Americans still clung to the idea of a superior European culture.

A Closer Look

Jefferson always insisted that one of the greatest accomplishments of his extraordinarily productive life was his role in the founding of the University of Virginia. So he may be forgiven his bias in favor of American education. But he does make a number of effective and, to the modern reader, illuminating points about how educated Americans viewed their new republic.

He begins by praising America's institutions of higher learning, most notably his own alma mater William and Mary College. (The University of Virginia was not founded until 1819.) Other than for the study of medicine, he says, they provide as good an education as anything available in Europe, a patriotic stance worthy of the writer of the Declaration of Independence. But he also advises against a British education because of the social values it might inculcate in the young, particularly a fondness for luxury, dissipation, and monarchical government. The American Revolution, for Jefferson and other patriots, was not just about republican government but small "r" republican values—frugality, self-sacrifice, a lack of deference to class distinctions, and a belief that all white men (women, as well as most black men, were still seen as ineligible for participation in public life), regardless of birth or social standing, had the ability and the right to participate in their own governance.

1 100 200 300 400 500 600 700 800 900 1000 1100 1200 1300 1400 1500 1600 1700 1800 1900 2000 CE

2.14.17 Poverty in the French Countryside

France
1787–1789

The 22d. Poverty and poor crops in Amiens; women are now ploughing with a pair of horses to sow barley. The difference of the customs of the two nations [England and France] is in nothing more striking than in the labours of the sex; in England, it is very little that they will do in the fields except to glean and make hay; the first is a party of pilfering, and the second of pleasure: in France, they plough and fill the dung-cart. Lombardy poplars seem to have been introduced here about the same time as in England. . . .

The 10th. Cross the Dordonne by a ferry . . . Pass Payrac, and meet many beggars, which we had not done before. All that country, girls and women, are without shoes and stockings; and ploughmen at their work have neither sabots nor feet to their stockings. This is a poverty, that strikes at the root of national prosperity; a large consumption among the poor being of more consequence than among the rich: the wealth of a nation lies in its circulation and consumption; and the case of poor people abstaining from the use of manufactures of leather and wool ought to be considered as an evil of the first magnitude. It reminded me of the misery of Ireland. Pass Pont-de-Rondez and come to high land . . . Pass by several cottages, exceedingly well built, of stone and slate or tiles, yet without any glass to the windows; can a country be likely to thrive where the great object is to spare manufactures? Women picking weeds in their aprons for their cows, another sign of poverty I observed, during the whole way from Calais. . . .

The 12th. Walking up a long hill, to ease my mare, I was joined by a poor woman, who complained of the times, and that it was a sad country; demanding her reasons, she said her husband had but a morsel of land, one cow, and poor little horse, yet they had a franchar (42 lb.) of wheat, and three chickens, to pay as quit-rent to one Seigneur; and four francharof oats, one chicken and 1 livre [French royal currency equal to about $5.50 U.S. in 1790] to pay to another, besides heavy tailles [real estate taxes] and other taxes. She had seven children, and the cow's milk helped make soup. But why, instead of a horse, do not you keep another cow? Oh, her husband could not carry his produce so well without a horse; and asses are little used in that country. It was said, at present, that something was to be done by some great folks for such poor ones, but she did not know who not how, but God send us better, car les tailles & les droits nous ecrasent [because the taxes and feudal levies are crushing us]. This woman, at no great distance, might have been taken for sixty or seventy, her figure was so bent, and face so furrowed and hardened by labour, but she said she was only twenty-eight. An Englishman who has not travelled, cannot imagine the figure made by infinitely the greater part of the countrywomen in France; it speaks, at first sight, hard and severe labour: I am inclined to think, that they work harder than the men, and this, united with more miserable labour of bringing a new race of slaves into the world, destroys absolutely all symmetry of person and every feminine appearance. To what are we to attribute this difference in the manners of the lower people in these two kingdoms? To Government.

Source: Young, Arthur. *Travels in France during the Years 1787, 1788 and 1789: With an Introduction, Biographical Sketch, and Notes*. London: George Bell and Sons, 1892, 8–9; 27–29; 197–198.

TIMELINE   2000 1900 1800 1700 1600 1500 1400 1300 1200 1100 1000 900 800 700 600 500 400 300 200 100 1 BCE

What You Need to Know

The desperate condition of the French peasantry on the eve of that country's 1789 revolution is depicted in Englishman Arthur Young's *Travels in France during the Years 1787, 1788 and 1789*, published in 1792, parts of which are excerpted here.

Historians cite any number of causes for the French Revolution—hostility to aristocratic privilege, a reaction to ancient customs and practices, new ideas about the right of ordinary people to participate in government. But the most immediate and compelling reasons for the bloody uprising of 1789 were simpler: hunger and poverty.

For centuries the ordinary people of France had relied on grain as the basis of their diet. But a series of poor harvests in the middle and late 1780s had led to shortages and rising prices. People were forced to spend more of their income on bread, undermining demand for other manufactured goods. France was plunged into an economic depression that gripped both city and countryside. In Paris, this led to the assault on the Bastille Prison and Armory, the opening shot of the Revolution. The uprising in Paris reverberated across rural France, leading to peasant uprisings against local landlords and merchants.

A Closer Look

Young was one of Britain's leading experts on agricultural economics, as well as an advocate for the rights of farm laborers. His visit to France on the eve of that country's revolution revealed to him that while Britain's rural poor had problems of their own, conditions were far worse across the Channel.

In this excerpt, Young begins by noting just how poorly clad French peasants were, a very bad sign for the economy as it showed, as noted earlier, that few were purchasing the country's manufactures. He also remarked on the poor harvests, noting that he saw women picking weeds to feed their cows, rather than relying on harvests of hay.

But his most trenchant observations concerned the role of government in the countryside, specifically the onerous taxes the peasants were forced to pay. Indeed, the French system of taxation before the Revolution was a scandal. Seeking to fill its coffers, drained in part by expenses relating to France's military aid to American revolutionaries, the government was extremely rigorous in its tax collection, a process that was often farmed out to private contractors who received a portion of the revenues. On top of that, there were still feudal era levies to local aristocrats. Thus, even as harvests declined and unemployment spread, the tax burden did not ease. At one point, comparing the relative prosperity of the English countryside to the poverty of the French, Young asks, "To what are we to attribute this difference?"

"Government" is his one word answer.

2.14.18 Cavalry Officer's Sabretache

Vicenza, Italy
1797

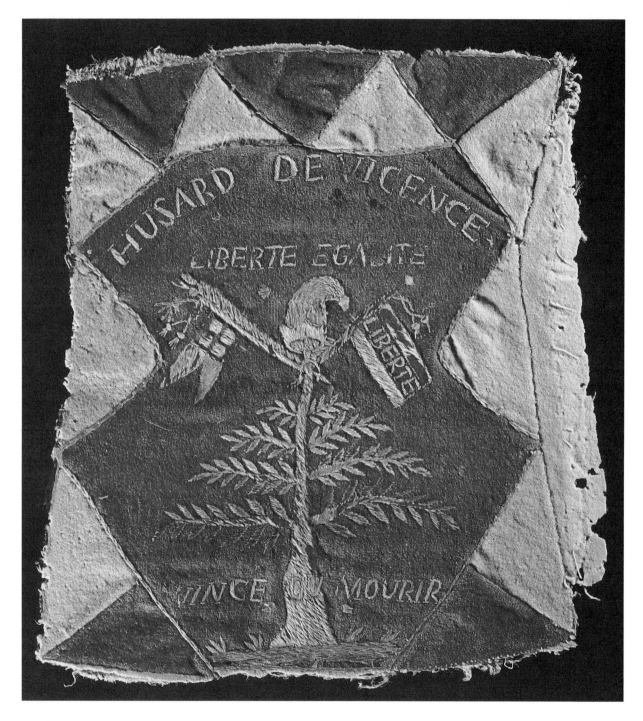

Credit: DeAgostini/Getty Images

What You Need to Know

The slogan adopted by the French revolutionaries—*liberté, égalité, fraternité*, or "freedom, equality, and brotherhood"—became the rallying cry of revolutionaries across Europe, as attested to by this 1797 *sabretache*, French for "flat bag," worn by a cavalry officer of the Guard Hussars of Vicenza, Italy. The bag features both the slogan of "freedom, equality, and brotherhood" and the words "vince ou mourir," French for "victory or death," indicating the military turn the revolution took from its early years.

On July 14, 1789, a crowd of commoners in Paris, frustrated by high bread prices and unemployment, stormed the Bastille, a medieval era prison in the heart of the city that was also used to store gunpowder. So began the French Revolution, whose effects would reverberate across Europe and around the world, down to this very day.

While the initial causes of the mob's attack on the Bastille were empty guts and pocketbooks, the French Revolution soon became a more radical and all-encompassing event, in which participants called for a complete transformation of government, law, religion, the social order, and economics. No longer would aristocrats enjoy special legal privileges because of their birth; no longer would the government be the private preserve of the king.

A Closer Look

Those who took up the revolutionary banner in France and other countries were a disparate lot. Some were members of bourgeoisie, the rising middle class that, by 1789, numbered several millions, of a total population of 25 million in France. While a minority of the population, they occupied key positions in the revolutionary movement, including serving in the officer corps of the French revolutionary armies. Many of the rising bourgeoisie were angry at the existing feudal order in France, which granted nobles legal monopolies over certain businesses, such as bread making and wine production.

The urban poor and peasants, who would make up the bulk of the revolutionaries and the revolutionary armies that spread the new political order across Europe, also had their grievances against the nobles, particularly their right to tax the poor for their own profit.

Notably, even elements of the nobility joined the cause. Many had liberal proclivities themselves, especially those wealthier middle class, who through government service or purchase of titles, had become members of the nobility but had not given up their convictions that the old order of noble privilege was antiquated and holding back political and economic progress.

1 100 200 300 400 500 600 700 800 900 1000 1100 1200 1300 1400 1500 1600 1700 1800 1900 2000 CE

2.14.19 French *Assignats*

France
Late Eighteenth–Early Nineteenth Centuries

Credit: DeAgostini/Getty Images

What You Need to Know

Among the first acts of the French National Assembly formed shortly before the Revolution was expansion of the money supply, so as to bring economic relief to the masses. More money in circulation lowered the cost of money, thereby reducing debt burdens. That expansion took the form of *assignats*, or paper money, some examples of which are shown here.

The origins of the French Revolution, which ultimately led to the overthrow of monarchies and principalities across Europe and the spread of republican forms of government, lay, in part, in monetary matters. When King Louis XVI tried to raise taxes to support the revolutionaries in America, fighting France's rival, Britain, for their independence, he was thwarted by the aristocrat-controlled Parlement. This forced him to borrow heavily to meet the government's obligations, which included continuing expansion of the vast palace complex at Versailles.

To pay the loans, he once again had to seek new taxes but this would also require the approval of Parliament. When he was again turned down, he dissolved Parliament and issued new taxes by decree, both of which Parliament declared "null and void." Frustrated, the king was forced to call for elections to a new and more representative kind of national assembly, with much greater powers. The age of absolute monarchy in France had come to an end, a fact made even more apparent by the popular attack on the Bastille, a royal prison and armory in Paris, on July 14, 1789, an act that inaugurated the French Revolution.

A Closer Look

The attack on the Bastille did not end the economic suffering of the French people, although the seizure of church property in 1790 relieved some of the financial constraints on the government. Many of the first *assignats* were backed by these government-seized assets and were accepted by both domestic and foreign creditors. But the revolutionary government soon racked up huge bills of its own, both in the form of subsidies to the poor and in a series of wars meant to defend and then spread the revolution across Europe. To meet these expenses, it began to expand the money supply with little concern about what this would do to prices. In fact, these issues did what even an economist in the dawning days of that field of study would have understood they would do; they caused hyperinflation, rapidly rising prices and the erosion of people's savings, by disrupting the economy and causing food shortages, which, in turn led to bread riot. The chaos produced a conservative backlash that helped see an end to the more radical phases of the revolution, ultimately leading to the rise of Napoleon, who finally solved France's monetary problems with his issuance of a new franc, backed by precious metals, in 1803.

1 100 200 300 400 500 600 700 800 900 1000 1100 1200 1300 1400 1500 1600 1700 1800 1900 2000 CE

2.14.20 Ottoman Prayer Rug

Turkey
Nineteenth Century

Credit: DeAgostini/Getty Images

What You Need to Know

The Ottoman Empire was an Islamic state, as illustrated by this prayer rug from the nineteenth century.

The Ottoman Empire began in the early fourteenth century, when a Turkic-speaking people in the southwestern part of the Anatolian Peninsula began to expand their holdings, ultimately conquering Constantinople, capital of the thousand-year-old Byzantine Empire, in 1453. Under a series of highly effective sultans in the sixteenth century, the empire reached its greatest expanse, encompassing most of the Middle East, North Africa, and southeastern Europe.

By the eighteenth century, however, the empire was in terminal decline, although it would take World War I to finally finish it off. There were a number of reasons—external and internal—for the Ottoman's ebbing power. Europe's expansion overseas led to economic isolation. A lack of clear succession rules produced much infighting among elites whenever a sultan died. Third, as in much of Europe, a population explosion put much pressure on the land. But unlike in Western Europe, there was little in the way of economic progress to absorb the ever-growing number of laborers. Finally, the Ottoman Empire chose to cut itself off from Europe and its new scientific thinking. As an Islamic state, it viewed Europeans as infidels.

A Closer Look

Prayer rugs, like the one pictured here, were a critical part of daily life. According to Islamic scripture, Muslims are to pray five times a day, no matter where they are. The Koran also says that the person undertaking prayer ritually cleanse himself. The prayer rug provided a protective barrier against the filth of the ground or floor. Because prayer rugs were essential to the practice of the Islamic faith, they were manufactured in great numbers in the Ottoman Empire, both in artisanal shops and large factories. By the late nineteenth century, the mechanical looms, first introduced in the British industrial revolution of the late eighteenth century had spread to the major cities of the Ottoman Empire. Such mass-produced rugs, however, could not reproduce the detail or elegance of handmade rugs, like this one, which was no doubt in the possession of a wealthy individual.

1 100 200 300 400 500 600 700 800 900 1000 1100 1200 1300 1400 1500 1600 1700 1800 1900 2000 CE

2.14.21 Napoleon's Retreat from Moscow

France and Russia
1812

But when the rear portion of the army began to defile before them, another impression was produced. A great confusion ensued. All those in the Marshal's army who recognized any of their companions left their ranks and ran toward them, offering bread and clothes; they were frightened by the voracity with which these wretches ate; many embraced each other weeping. One of the brave and kindly officers of the Marshal took off his own uniform to give it to a poor soldier whose ragged garments exposed him naked to the cold, putting on his own back a tattered old infantry coat, because he was more capable of resisting the rigors of the weather. If excessive misery withers the soul, on the other hand it sometimes expands it to the highest point, as one may see. Many of the most wretched blew their brains out in despair. In that act, the last which nature indicates to put an end to wretchedness, there was a resignation and coolness that made one shudder. Those who thus assailed their own lives were not seeking death so much as a term to insupportable sufferings, and in this disastrous campaign I saw what vanities are physical force and human courage where that moral force which is born of a determined will is non-existent. . . .

By five o'clock in the evening of the 25th some trestles had been fixed above the stream, constructed of wooden beams taken from Polish cabins. It was rumored in the army that the bridge would be finished during the night. The Emperor was much annoyed when the army deceived itself in this way, because he knew that people grow much more quickly discouraged when they have indulged in vain hopes; for this reason he took great care to have the rear of the army made acquainted with the slightest incidents, so as never to leave the soldiers under so cruel an illusion. The trestles gave way at a little past five o'clock. They were not strong enough. It was necessary to wait until the next day, and the army relapsed into its dismal conjectures. It was plain that next day it would have to sustain the enemy's fire; but there was no room for choice. At the end of that night of anguish and sufferings of every sort, the first trestles were driven down into the river. People do not comprehend that the soldiers had stood up to their lips in water full of floating ice, summoning every force with which nature had endowed them, and all the remaining courage born of energy and devotion in order to drive piles several feet deep in to a miry river bed; struggling against the most horrible fatigues; pushing away with their hands enormous masses of ice which would have knocked them down and submerged them by their weight; fighting, in a word, and fighting unto death with cold, the greatest enemy of life. Well, that is what our French pontonniers did. Several of them were either dragged down by the currents or suffocated by the cold. That is a glory, it seems to me, which outweighs many another.

Source: Wairy, Louis Constant. *Memoirs of Constant, First Valet de Chambre of the Emperor, on the Private Life of Napoleon, His Family and His Court*. Vol. 4. Translated by Elizabeth Gilbert Martin. New York: C. Scribner's Sons, 1895, 2–10.

TIMELINE   2000 1900 1800 1700 1600 1500 1400 1300 1200 1100 1000 900 800 700 600 500 400 300 200 100 1 BCE

What You Need to Know

This account of the disastrous retreat from Moscow of Napoleon Bonaparte's army in 1812 was written by his valet Louis Constant Wairy.

From early on, the leaders of the French Revolution had universalist aspirations. The principles they fought for—an end to aristocratic privilege, the participation of all of the citizenry in public life, freedom from the oppressive customs and laws of the past—*liberté, égalité, fraternité* (freedom, equality, brotherhood)—were the principles by which all of humankind should live, they believed. Indeed, when they wrote up the defining document of the revolution in 1789, they called it *The Declaration of the Rights of Man and of the Citizen*, not the declaration of the rights of Frenchmen.

Such aspirations terrified the established political order across Europe, which declared war on the revolutionary government. Mobilizing every element of French society and the French economy—a first in the history of European warfare—the revolutionaries not only turned back the forces of reaction but launched a series of wars to defend the revolution and spread its principles across Europe. Under Napoleon Bonaparte, the authoritarian heir to the revolution, the crusade was taken even farther afield to the Middle East and Russia, although his campaign in the latter met with a devastating setback, as described in Wairy's account.

A Closer Look

The vast Grand Armée of 600,000 that invaded Russia in June of 1812 was an amalgam of nationalities. While a minority of the soldiers were French, roughly two-thirds came from other nations that were either under governments established by Napoleon or were simply allied to France. Most of the men in the army were peasants or the urban poor, though the officer corps came from the educated elite of various countries. Whatever class they came from, they were highly motivated, believing that the revolutionary gains they had made—more political participation and an end to economically unfair advantages for the nobility—could only be secured by defeating those reactionary forces, such as that of the Tsarist government of Russia—that sought to reverse the tide of revolution.

At first, the army made great advances into the vast plains of western Russia, reaching the gates of Moscow by December. But from the beginning, the army was plagued by logistical problems. Most had not been issued the coats needed to survive Russia's brutal winter. Supply wagons were held back by the lack of decent roads and heavy snows. Foraging for food was difficult in such a sparsely populated country. These problems led to starvation and disease. Thus, of the 600,000 soldiers who began the invasion in June just 125,000 were left alive when Napoleon departed Russia in December.

1 100 200 300 400 500 600 700 800 900 1000 1100 1200 1300 1400 1500 1600 1700 1800 1900 2000 CE

2.14.22 Description of Slave Conditions in Brazil

Brazil
1820s

There is no town on Itaparica; but there is a villa, or village, with a fort on the Punto de Itaparica, which commands the passage between it and the main land, and also the mouth of the river, on which stands Nazareth da Farinha, so called from the abundance of that article which it produces. There are also a great many fazendas, which, with their establishment of slaves and cattle, may be considered as so many hamlets. Each sugar farm, or ingenho, as the fazendas are oftener called here, has its little community of slaves around it; and in their huts something like the blessings of freedom are enjoyed, in the family ties and charities they are not forbidden to enjoy. I went into several of the huts, and found them cleaner and more comfortable than I expected; each contains four or five rooms, and each room appeared to hold a family. These out-of-door slaves, belonging to the great ingenhos, in general are better off than the slaves of masters whose condition is nearer to their own, because, "The more the master is removed from us, in place and rank, the greater the liberty we enjoy; the less our actions are inspected and controuled; and the fainter that cruel comparison becomes betwixt our own subjection, and the freedom, or even dominion of another."

But, at best, the comforts of slaves must be precarious. Here it is not uncommon to give a slave his freedom, when he is too old or too infirm to work; that is, to turn him out of doors to beg or starve. A few days ago, as a party of gentlemen were returning from a *picnic*, they found a poor negro woman lying in a dying state, by the side of the road. The English gentlemen applied to their Portuguese companions to speak to her, and comfort her, as thinking she would understand them better; but they said, "Oh, 'tis only a black: let us ride on," and so they did without further notice. The poor creature, who was a dismissed slave, was carried to the English hospital, where she died in two days. Her diseases were age and hunger. The slaves I saw here working in the distillery, appear thin, and I should say over-worked; but, I am told, that it is only in the distilling months that they appear so, and that at other seasons they are as fat and cheerful as those in the city, which is saying a great deal. They have a little church and burying-ground here, and as they see their little lot the lot of all, are more contented than I thought a slave could be.

Source: Callcott, Lady Maria. *Journal of a Voyage to Brazil: And Residence There, during Part of the Years 1821, 1822, 1823.* London: Longman, Hurst, Rees, Orme, Brown, and Green, 1824, 144–145.

TIMELINE 2000 1900 1800 1700 1600 1500 1400 1300 1200 1100 1000 900 800 700 600 500 400 300 200 100 1 BCE

What You Need to Know

In 1824, Lady Maria Callcott published her *Journal of a Voyage to Brazil: And Residence There, during Part of the Years 1821, 1822, 1823* describing life in that South American nation. In this excerpt she describes life on the country's sugar plantations.

No place in the Americas imported more slaves than Brazil, a colony of Portugal first founded in 1500. Over the course of nearly four centuries of the trans-Atlantic slave trade, roughly four million African slaves were landed in Brazil, or about 40 percent of all slaves brought to the Americas. (That percentage is based on a total import figure of 10 million, accepted by most historians, though on the lower end of the total spectrum of slave trade estimates.) In 1822, when Brazil achieved a semi-independent status from Portugal, slaves represented about a third of the total population of 3.6 million. The fact that 4 million were imported and only 1.2 million survived speaks to the tragically high death rates among Brazilian slaves.

A Closer Look

In this excerpt from *Journal of a Voyage to Brazil*, which was published in 1824, Lady Callcott begins by describing the *fazenda*, or plantation, system prevalent on the Ilha, or Island, of Itaparica, just off the coast of Salvador. Northern Brazil, where the island is located, was the main plantation district in the country in the early 1820s, where the country's abundant sugar crop was grown. Plantations in the region were also called *ingenhos*, from the Portuguese word for "engine," signifying the presence of sugar mills.

Indeed, as Callcott reports, the vast size of the *ingenhos* redounded in the slave's favor. As they themselves noted to her, "the more the master is removed from us, in place and rank, the greater liberty they enjoy." In fact, Callcott notes that the slaves did enjoy a certain sense of liberty in their own communities.

Still, the brutality of the system was never far away. Callcott notes coming across an old black woman dying by the side of the road and her desire to succor her dismissed by her elite Brazilian companions on the grounds that the woman "'tis only a black." As Callcott remarks, Brazilian planters were in the practice of freeing slaves who were too aged or infirm to work, saving themselves the expense of supporting a nonproductive laborer but condemning that person to die in abject poverty.

1 100 200 300 400 500 600 700 800 900 1000 1100 1200 1300 1400 1500 1600 1700 1800 1900 2000 CE

2.14.23 Brazilian Slave Music

Brazil
1820s

I heard the sounds of music . . . the voice of the slaves on this their night of holiday, beguiling their cares with . . . airs, played on . . . African instruments. Taking one of my ship-mates with me, I immediately went to the huts of the married slaves, where all merrymakings are held; and found parties playing, singing, and dancing to the moonlight. A superstitious veneration for that beautiful planet is said to be pretty general in . . . Africa, as that for the Pleiades was among the Indians of Brazil; and probably the slaves, though baptized, dance to the moon in memory of their homes.

As for the instruments, they are the most inartificial things that ever gave out musical sounds; yet they have not an unpleasing effect. One is simply composed of a crooked stick, a small hollow gourd, and a single string of brass wire. The mouth of the gourd must be placed on the naked skin of the side; so that the ribs of the player form the soundingboard, and the string is struck with a short stick. A second has more the appearance of a guitar: the hollow gourd is covered with skin; it has a bridge, and there are two strings; it is played with the finger. Another of the same class is played with a bow; it has but one string, but is fretted with the fingers. All these are called Gourmis. There were, besides, drums made of the hollow trunks of trees, four or five feet long, closed at one end with wood, and covered with skin at the other. In playing these, the drummer lays his instrument on the ground and gets astride on it, when he beats time with his hands to his own songs, or the tunes of the gourmis. The small marimba has a very sweet tone. On a flat piece of sonorous wood a little bridge is fastened; and to this small slips of iron, of different lengths, are attached, so as that both ends vibrate on the board, one end being broader and more elevated than the other. This broad end is played with the thumbs, the instrument being held with both hands. All these are tuned in a peculiar manner, and with great nicety, especially the marimba; but, as I am no musician, I cannot explain their methods.

Source: Callcott, Lady Maria. *Journal of a Voyage to Brazil: And Residence There, during Part of the Years 1821, 1822, 1823*. London: Longman, Hurst, Rees, Orme, Brown, and Green, 1824, 198–199.

What You Need to Know

In the accompanying account, British travel writer Lady Maria Callcott describes slave music in Brazil; the excerpts come from her 1824 *Journal of a Voyage to Brazil: And Residence There, during Part of the Years 1821, 1822, 1823*.

Unlike in the British Caribbean and the southern United States, Brazil continued to import large numbers of slaves through much of the nineteenth century. Indeed, Brazil was the last country in the global West to outlaw the importation of slaves and slavery itself. This meant that there was a steady inflow of African cultural customs into the country. In addition, Brazil was home to large *quilombos*, or communities of maroons (that is, runaway slaves) who maintained African cultural customs.

Calcott mentions dance and music as part of the legacy, but there was much more to it. African slaves brought their culinary traditions with them, particularly the taste for palm oil in cooking and the making of sauces. In the spiritual sphere, African religious traditions melded with the Catholicism of local inhabitants to produce syncretic faiths, such as *candomblé*, which incorporated the various gods of the Yoruba people of what is now Nigeria.

A Closer Look

From Samba to Forro to Bossa Nova, Brazil has one of the richest traditions of folk and popular music of any country on Earth. The main source of this musical wealth lies in the diversity of the country's population—indigenous, European, and perhaps most importantly, African—and the inevitable cross-fertilization of styles that comes from such diversity.

In this excerpt from her book, about a visit to plantations around the city of Salvador, in northern Brazil, Callcott begins by describing how African beliefs lived on in the country. She notes that the African custom of "veneration" for the moon was an important part of slave celebrations, although Callcott had never actually been to Africa. She is on solider ground when describing the instruments being played. She notes a number of simple stringed instruments, drums, and the marimba, all of which had African origins. The marimba she mentions, for example, a percussion instrument, in which wooden bars of varying length and tonal quality are struck with a small mallet, is a direct descendant of the various kinds of xylophones played in West and Central Africa, the source region of many of the slaves transported to Brazil.

1 100 200 300 400 500 600 700 800 900 1000 1100 1200 1300 1400 1500 1600 1700 1800 1900 2000 CE

2.14.24 Haitian Rural Law Code

Haiti
1826

Art. 2. Citizens whose employment is agriculture, shall not be taken from their labours, excepting in the cases provided for by the law.

Art. 3. It being the duty of every Citizen to aid in sustaining the State, either by his active services, or by his industry, those who are not employed in the civil service, or called upon for the military service; those who do not exercise a licensed profession; those who are not working artisans, or employed as servants; those who are not employed in felling timber for exportation; in fine, those who cannot justify their means of existence, shall cultivate the soil.

Art. 4. Citizens whose employment is agriculture, shall not be permitted to quit the country to inhabit the towns and villages, without a permission from the Justice of Peace of the commune they desire to quit, and of the commune in which they desire to establish themselves. The Justice of Peace shall give this permission *only* after having ascertained that the person asking it, is of good morals, that his conduct has been regular in the canton he is about to quit, and that he possesses the means of existence in the town he desires to inhabit. All those who do not conform to these regulations, shall be considered as vagabonds, and treated as such. . . .

Art. 183. Field-labour shall commence on Monday morning, and shall never cease until Friday evening, (legal holidays excepted); and in extraordinary cases, when the interest of the cultivator, as well as of the proprietor, appears to require it, work shall be continued until Saturday evening.

And be it further enacted by the authority aforesaid, That from and after the commencement of this Act, the slaves belonging to, and employed on any plantation, shall, over and above the holidays hereinafter to be mentioned, be allowed one day in every fortnight, to cultivate their own provision-grounds, exclusive of Sundays . . . under the penalty of twenty pounds; to be recovered against the overseer, or person having the care of such slaves. Provided always, that the number of days so allowed to the slaves for the cultivation of their grounds, shall be at least twenty-six in the year.

Source: *The Rural Code of Haiti*. London: J. Ridgway, 1827, 2–4; 89–92.

What You Need to Know

Even after the successful revolution in the 1790s and early 1800s won Haiti independence and its slave population their freedom, economic inequality persisted between the elite and the peasantry. In 1826, the country passed the *Code Rural*, or Rural Law Code, to try to force free peasants back on to the plantations they had fled.

Haiti, the country that now encompasses the western half of the island of Hispaniola, has a proud history of both popular rebellion and official oppression. The name comes from the native Arawak word for "land of mountains" and the inaccessible region served as pirate's lair in the seventeenth century. In the eighteenth century, however, French settlers established plantations there and imported hundreds of thousands of African slaves to work them. By the latter part of the century, Saint Domingue, as it was known, was France's wealthiest colony and the world's leading producer of both sugar and coffee. The French also established a rigid social hierarchy in the colony, with themselves at the top, followed by Creoles, or native-born whites, mixed race persons, or mulattoes, freed slaves, and finally slaves.

When France was rocked by revolution in 1789, Saint Domingue's lower classes, notably the mullatoes and freed slaves, revolted against Creole rule. Under the leadership of a freed slave named Toussaint L'Ouverture, the rebellious forces drove the French and most of the Creoles out of the colony in 1801, emancipated the slaves, and declared a republic three years later.

A Closer Look

For slaves, life on a Haitian plantation was brutal, and typically short. Roughly half of the two million slaves imported onto the island during the eighteenth century died within a few years of arrival. The high mortality rate was due to overwork and lack of food, which led to frequent epidemics. Most slaves worked 12 hour days, six days a week, sowing, tending, reaping, and processing the tobacco, coffee, and (primarily) sugar crops. Because virtually all arable land was devoted to commercial crops for export, food had to be imported, which made it more expensive. For many planters, it was simply cheaper to import new workers than to adequately feed those already in country. Moreover, most planters were absentee, and thus they did not see the suffering they caused, which made it easier to practice this slow form of genocide.

At the same time, Haiti's mountainous interior encouraged runaways, and the colony was home to a number of maroon, or fugitive slave, communities. To prevent this from happening, slave owners and their overseer surrogates maintained order through systematic torture. Even slaves caught nibbling on sugar cane in the fields might have their mouths muzzled in iron masks.

1 100 200 300   400   500   600   700   800   900   1000 1100 1200 1300   1400   1500   1600   1700 1800 1900 2000 CE

2.14.25 The Mexican Caste System in the Nineteenth Century

Mexico
1827

Before the revolution, this population was divided into seven distinct castes. 1. The old Spaniards, designated as Gachupines, in the history of the civil wars. 2. The Creoles, or Whites of pure European race, born in America, and regarded by the old Spaniards as natives. 3. The Indians, or Indigenous copper-coloured race. 4. The Mestizos, or mixed breed of Whites and Indians, gradually merging into Creoles, as the cross with the Indian race became more remote. 5. The Mulattoes, or descendants of Whites and Negroes. 6. The Zambos, or Chinos, descendants of Negroes and Indians. And, 7. The African Negroes, either manumitted, or slaves.

Of these Castes, the three first, and the last, were pure, and gave rise, in their various combinations, to the others; which again, were sub-divided, *ad infinitum*, by names expressing the relation borne by each generation of its descendants to the White, (Quarteroons, Quinteroons, &c.) to which, as the ruling colour, any approximation was desirable. The principal seat of the white population of Mexico is the Table-land, towards the centre of which the Indian race is likewise concentrated, (in the intendancies of La Puebla, Mexico, Guanajuato, Oaxaca, and Valladolid;) while the Northern frontier is inhabited almost entirely by Whites, and descendants of Whites, before whom it is supposed that the Indian population must have retired, at the time of the conquest. In Durango, New Mexico, and the Provincias Internas, the pure Indian breed is almost unknown; in Sonora it is again found, because the conquerors there overtook the last tribes of the original inhabitants, who had not yet placed the River Gila (lat. 33 N.) between themselves and the Spanish arms. The coasts are inhabited, both to the East and West, by Mulattoes and Zambos, or, at least, by a race in which a mixture of African blood prevails. It was in these unhealthy regions that the slaves formerly imported into Mexico were principally employed, the natives of the Table-land being unable to resist the extreme heat of the climate.

They have multiplied there in an extraordinary manner, by intermarriages with the Indian race, and now form a mixed breed, admirably adapted to the *Tierra caliente*, but not possessing, in appearance, the characteristics either of the New World, or of the Old.

The Mestizos (descendants of Natives and Indians) are found in every part of the country; indeed, from the very small number of Spanish women who at first visited the New World, the great mass of the population has some mixture of Indian blood. Few of the middling classes (the lawyers, the Curas, or parochial clergy, the artizans, the smaller landed proprietors, and the soldiers,) could prove themselves exempt from it; and now that a connexion with the Aborigines has ceased to be disadvantageous, few attempt to deny it. In my sketch of the revolution, I always include this class under the denomination of *Creoles*; as sharing with the Whites of pure Spanish descent the disadvantages of that privation of political rights, to which all *Natives* were condemned, and feeling, in common with them, that enmity to the Gachupines, (or old Spaniards,) which the preference constantly accorded to them could not fail to excite.

Source: Ward, Henry George. *Mexico in 1827*. Vol. 1. London: Colburn, 1828, 28–31.

What You Need to Know

This passage from English diplomat Henry George Ward's *Mexico in 1827* describes the various social and racial castes of the country six years after it had won independence from Spain in 1821.

When the Spanish conquistadores arrived in the Valley of Mexico in the early sixteenth century, they encountered one of the largest concentrations of native peoples in all of the Americas, perhaps as many as 10 million. For what is now the entire country of Mexico, population estimates run to 20 million. Ultimately, diseases introduced from Europe, for which the indigenous population had little immunity, would reduce those numbers by as much as 90 percent within a century.

Still, enough Amerindians survived to form a major part of the country's population upon independence in 1821. Of Mexico's roughly seven-million-strong population then, roughly half were Amerindian. The other half was largely composed of mixed-race persons, primarily mestizos, or European-Indian mixes, and Afro-mestizos. Those of pure European descent—either born immigrants or native-born, represented a tiny minority of perhaps one or two percent.

A Closer Look

Mexican ideas about race in the nineteenth century were complicated. Whereas in the United States, race was seen as binary—that is, black and white—Mexicans recognized a large number of different racial classifications. For example, Ward mentions mulattoes (mixed white and black), zambos (mixed African and Amerindian), and mestizos, along with those of pure Spanish or European descent. *Creole* was a more fluid term. It could mean those who were predominantly of European descent—in both culture and color—but who had some African or Amerindian heritage, or simply those whites born in the country and who adhered to a Mexican culture distinct from that of Spain.

Race in nineteenth-century Mexico also implied caste distinctions. As Ward points out, the various racial classifications recognized by Mexican custom often defined what class one belonged to, and even the occupation a person pursued or would be allowed to pursue, although after the Revolution and independence all laws enforcing such customs were done away with.

Indeed, because white elites fighting Spanish rule had to recruit those of mixed race castes to successfully achieve independence, there developed in Mexico after the revolution a new attitude toward what it meant to be Mexican. Thus, to appeal to the nonwhites of the country, and especially the Mestizo minority, elites became to laud the country's pre-Columbian peoples and culture. As Ward notes of Mexico six years after independence was achieved, "a connexion with the Aborigines has ceased to be disadvantageous, few attempt to deny it." Moreover, he says, it was the Mestizoes who shared with Creoles—that is, native-born persons of European descent—a common enmity toward *Gachupines*, or the old Spanish aristocracy.

1 100 200 300 400 500 600 700 800 900 1000 1100 1200 1300 1400 1500 1600 1700 1800 1900 2000 CE

Part 15:
The Rise of Nationalism

Late Eighteenth–Early Twentieth Centuries

2.15.1 Pioneering Lands in Brazil

Brazil
1779

That [Campos dos Goitacezes] district is a highly important one, and worthy of the particular attention of your Excellency; its immense plains are extremely fertile, and the sugar-cane and all kinds of vegetables flourish there. It has also much excellent timber, admirable balsams, oils, and gums, and many other precious drugs, with all of which commerce might be increased. It also possesses excellent mines of gold, which may be of great utility to the State when His majesty shall be informed of their situation, and permit them to be worked by the people. It has many navigable rivers in which even now a good commerce is carried on. For many years it was the general asylum of all malefactors, thieves, and assassins, who sought refuge there, and were allowed so much liberty that they felt no actual subjection; but lived in idleness, cultivating no more than was necessary for their subsistence. It has been extremely difficult to reduce them to order. I found, however, that this had been facilitated by the Viceroys, my predecessors, and by following in their steps both commerce and agriculture have increased under my government, as your Excellency will see from the annexed relation of the Colonel of Militia; but as these people have had such a bad education, it is necessary for the present to avoid giving them any power or authority, which may fill them with vanity, and lead to disastrous consequences.

I have followed the system of conceding many grants of land to people of this Capital who go to settle there,—I have sent for many of the inhabitants here, that I might speak to them,—I have retained them here for some time, in order that they might be witnesses of a people living in a state of subjection, and that they might observe what respect and obedience is paid to the magistrates, and other individuals in authority; and during all the time that they have remained here I have made them feel their dependence as much as possible. Finally, when I have again sent them away, I have always rendered them some benefit, and they have thus been gradually civilized in such a manner that those horrible disorders, which were once a daily source of disquietude to the Governors of this Captaincy, have no longer existence.

The greatest care ought to be taken that no attorneys, public writers, or other people of unquiet spirits, go to establish themselves there, since as the people have had a bad education, no sooner do they hear any turbulent individuals flattering them, and inciting them to insolence, than they immediately forget their duty, and range themselves under his banners.

Source: Armitage, John. *The History of Brazil: From the Period of the Arrival of the Braganza Family in 1808, to the Abdication of Don Pedro the First in 1831*. Vol. II. London: Smith, Elder and Company, 1836, pp. 179–181.

What You Need to Know

This excerpt is from a 1779 report by Marques de Lavradio, the Portuguese governor for Brazil, then a colony of Lisbon, addressed to his successor. In it, de Lavradio discusses his efforts to entice residents of the capital, then Rio de Janeiro, to settle rural lands in the Campos dos Goitacezes in the northern part of Rio de Janeiro state.

With its population of roughly 100,000 in the late eighteenth century, Rio was the largest city in Brazil. Its geography—hemmed in by steep hills in various directions and bays and the Atlantic Ocean in others—made for crowded living conditions. Even then, its people displayed the racial diversity for which it remains famous today—whites, blacks, and a variety of mixed-race persons.

It was also where many of Brazil's vast numbers of imported slaves disembarked after their journey across the Atlantic. Around the docks were a number of marketplaces for slaves, including the infamous "fattening houses," where slaves, emaciated by the long journey across the Atlantic, were plumped up on beans, rice, and fatty meat so as to increase their value. Still, there were so many of them that slave traders lacked facilities to hold them, allowing them to roam the streets of the city, barely clothed, if not entirely naked, and suffering from a host of diseases picked up in the crowded holds of slave ships. Thousands died before they could be purchased and shipped to plantations in the countryside, their corpses rotting amid the garbage and sewage of the streets.

De Lavradio's solution, never effectively realized, was to immediately remove newly arrived slaves to a district on the edge of the city, where buyers could examine them before shipping them to their plantations in other parts of the colony.

A Closer Look

When European settlers began to exploit the lands and mines of Brazil in the early sixteenth century, they first sought to enslave the colony's indigenous peoples. But this proved difficult. Many died of European diseases for which they had no immunity; others ran away back to their villages. By the middle and latter years of the century, Brazilian plantation and mine owners had switched to African slaves. Over the next three centuries, they would make Brazil the number one destination of African slaves in the Americas—some 3.5 million out of a total of 12 to 15 million.

While disembarking at Rio and other coastal cities, most were destined in the seventeenth and eighteenth centuries for the sugar plantations in the rural areas surrounding Rio and Sao Paulo. Conditions there were bleak for slaves, some of the worst in the Americas. Most received inadequate food, little clothing, no medical care. They were forced to work up to 18 hours a day during harvest season and were brutally punished for the slightest infractions of plantation rules.

But the slaves did have some advantages. The Catholic Church ensured that they were given numerous religious holidays off and, during slack seasons, they were allowed to work for themselves, some of them earning the money to buy their freedom.

1 100 200 300 400 500 600 700 800 900 1000 1100 1200 1300 1400 1500 1600 1700 1800 1900 2000 CE

2.15.2 The Role of Women in Islamic West Africa

West Africa
Late Eighteenth–Early Nineteenth Centuries

Most of our educated men leave their wives, their daughters . . . morally abandoned, like beasts, without teaching them what God prescribes should be taught them, and without instructing them in the articles of the Law which concern them. Thus, they leave them ignorant of the rules regarding ablutions, prayer, fasting, business dealings, and other duties which they have to fulfill, and which God commands that they should be taught.

Men treat these beings like household implements which become broken after long use and which are then thrown out on the dung-heap. This is an abominable crime! Alas! How can they thus shut up their wives, their daughters . . . in the darkness of ignorance, while daily they impart knowledge to their students? In truth, they act out of egoism, and if they devote themselves to their pupils, that is nothing but hypocrisy and vain ostentation on their part.

Their conduct is blameworthy, for to instruct one's wives, daughters, and captives is a positive duty, while to impart knowledge to students is only a work over and above what is expected, and there is no doubt but that the one takes precedence over the other.

Muslim women—Do not listen to the speech of those who are misguided and who sow the seed of error in the heart of another; they deceive you when they stress obedience to God and to his Messenger (May God show him bounty and grant him salvation), and when they say that the woman finds her happiness in obedience to her husband.

They seek only their own satisfaction, and that is why they impose upon you tasks which the Law of God and that of his Prophet have never especially assigned to you. Such are—the preparation of food-stuffs, the washing of clothes, and other duties which they like to impose upon you, while they neglect to teach you what God and the Prophet have prescribed for you.

Yes, the woman owes submission to her husband, publicly as well as in intimacy, even if he is one of the humble people of the world, and to disobey him is a crime, at least so long as he does not command what God condemns; in that case she must refuse, since it is wrong of a human creature to disobey the Creator.

Source: dan Fodio, Usman. *Light of the Intellects*, 1812. Reprinted in *The Human Record, Sources of Global History, Vol. II: Since 1500*. Edited by Alfred J. Andrea and James H. Overfield. New York: Houghton Mifflin Company, 2001.

TIMELINE   2000 1900 1800 1700 1600 1500 1400 1300 1200 1100 1000 900 800 700 600 500 400 300 200 100 1 BCE

What You Need to Know

This excerpt on Muslim women comes from the writings of Usman dan Fodio, who lived from 1754 to 1817. A Fulani from what is today northern Nigeria, dan Fodio was the founder of the Sokoto Caliphate, a vast state that stretched from Lake Chad to Senegal.

In the late eighteenth and early nineteenth centuries, much of interior West Africa was convulsed by a series of Islamic revival movements, of which dan Fodio's was the most significant. Sparked by scholars and reform-minded religious leaders, these revival movements sought to purify the faith in order to create societies that lived along traditional Muslim principles of justice and equality among believers. They proselytized among nonbelievers and worked to purge animist ideas and practices from West African Islam. But they also turned against Islamic states ruled over by traditional leaders, who they saw as corrupt.

By the mid-nineteenth century, they had founded a series of highly organized states across the Sahel region. When European colonial administrators arrived in force in the latter years of the century, however, they saw such states as a threat to their rule, and sent their armies, which including many native soldiers, to destroy them, which they largely succeeded in doing—despite several military setbacks—by 1900.

A Closer Look

As the head of the Sokoto Caliphate, Usman dan Fodio tried to revive Islam from the corruption into which he believed it had fallen by returning the faith to its roots in the era of the Prophet Muhammad. As this excerpt on the role of Muslim women reveals, dan Fodio's efforts were often progressive.

Dan Fodio paints a picture of extreme repression—women kept isolated in the home, not given a proper education, and forced to perform tasks of drudgery. And all of this treatment justified by appeals to what the Koran and other Sharia, or Islamic law, supposedly dictated. In fact, Muslim women in eighteenth and nineteenth century West Africa had a certain degree of independence, particularly if they were members of the working or lower middle classes. For example, women were the mainstays of the marketplace, buying, selling, and trading handiworks of their own making and food that their families had raised.

Still, as dan Fodio points out, the women received almost no formal education. Instead, at mosque and in the home, they were taught total obedience to the husband and to find satisfaction in purely domestic chores.

1 100 200 300 400 500 600 700 800 900 1000 1100 1200 1300 1400 1500 1600 1700 1800 1900 2000 CE

2.15.3 Account of the Settlement of Port Jackson, Australia

Port Jackson, Australia
1791

If it be recollected how large a body of these people are now congregated, in the settlement of Port Jackson, and at Norfolk Island, it will, I think, not only excite surprize, but afford satisfaction, to learn, that in a period of four years few crimes of a deep rye, or of a hardened nature have been perpetrated: murder and unnatural sins rank not hitherto in the catalogue of their enormities: and one suicide only has been committed. . . .

In so numerous a community many persons of perverted genius, and of mechanical ingenuity, could not but be assembled. Let me produce the following example: Frazer was an iron manufacturer, bred at Sheffield, of whose abilities, as a workman, we had witnessed many proofs. The governor had written to England for a set of locks, to be sent out for the security of the public stores, which were to be so constructed as to be incapable of being picked. On their arrival his excellency sent for Frazer, and bade him examine them; telling him at the same time that they could not be picked. Frazer laughed, and asked for a crooked nail only, to open them all. A nail was brought, and in an instant he verified his assertion. Astonished at his dexterity, a gentleman present determined to put it to farther proof. He was sent for in a hurry, some days after, to this hospital, where a lock of still superior intricacy and expence to the others had been provided. He was told that the key was lost, and that the lock must be immediately picked. He examined it attentively; remarked that it was the production of a workman; and demanded ten minutes to make an instrument *"to speak with it."* Without carrying the lock with him, he went directly to his shop; and at the expiration of his term returned, applied his instrument, and open flew the lock. But it was not only in this part of his business that he excelled: he executed every branch of it in superior style. Had not his villainy been still more notorious than his skill, he would have proved an invaluable possession to a new country. He had passed through innumerable scenes in life, and had played many parts. When too lazy to work at his trade, he had turned thief in fifty different shapes; was a receiver of stolen goods; a soldier; and a traveling conjurer. He once confessed to me, that he had made a set of tools for a gang of coiners, every man of whom was hanged.

Source: Tench, Watkin. *A Complete Account of the Settlement at Port Jackson in New South Wales*. London: Nicol, 1793, pp. 205–207.

TIMELINE   2000 1900 1800 1700 1600 1500 1400 1300 1200 1100 1000 900 800 700 600 500 400 300 200 100 1 BCE

What You Need to Know

In this passage from *A Complete Account of the Settlement at Port Jackson in New South Wales*, British officer Watkin Tench describes some of earliest settlers of Port Jackson, the first British settlement in Australia.

Britain did not invent the idea of exiling criminals when it founded Australia as a penal colony in 1788; both the Greeks and Romans, to name just two civilizations, had used such penalties. Nor was Australia the first penal colony established by the British. They had done so with the colony of Georgia, in North America, decades earlier. But the American Revolution had ended that penal option, which created a crisis in Britain's penal system. The so-called "Bloody Codes" of the 1770s listed more than 200 offenses—most of them minor property crimes—as capital offenses. Both juries and judges hesitated in applying such penalties so the number of prisoners grew rapidly. By the late 1780s, the government was reduced to refitting transport ships as floating prisons.

And so Parliament turned to Australia, the coast of which had been explored by James Cook in the 1770s, as a new place for convict exile. The first fleet of eleven ships, with some 1,000 convicts, left England in May 1787, arriving in Australia the following January. By 1868, when the system was finally abolished, some 161,000 convicts had been sent to Australia. They were joined there by hundreds of thousands of free English and Irish immigrants.

A Closer Look

Life in Port Jackson (later Sydney) Australia was extremely harsh in the years immediately following the first settlement of criminals there in 1788. Most of the convicts were from the slums of London, as this account of a particularly skilled picklock hints. Although set to work on farms, they knew little of agriculture. For their part, the guards who accompanied them saw such work as beneath their dignity. The colony also lacked draft animals. Food was in short supply, and thus expensive. Hunger was rampant.

All of the convicts were put to work, although the same class system prevailing in Britain was reproduced here. Educated criminals were given clerical work; the poor and uneducated labored on government farms and public works projects, at least at first. Above the convicts were colony officials and jailers, most from Britain's middle class. They soon took on the role of the local gentry, buying land and setting up factories and putting the convicts to work for them. The colony was also very much a man's world, with women representing just 20 percent of the population. But their small numbers worked in their favor, as they were able to marry the most educated of the convicts, although some became prostitutes.

Yet for all the roughness and lack of supplies, the colony, the writer notes, was a surprisingly crime-free place. Perhaps this is not surprising. Truly hardened and violent criminals were likely to have been executed in England; largely nonviolent offenders were sent to Australia.

1   100   200   300   400   500   600   700   800   900   1000 1100 1200 1300   1400   1500   1600   1700   1800   1900 2000 CE

2.15.4 Building a Log Barn on the Canadian Frontier

Canada
Nineteenth Century

Would some of my readers like to know how to raise a log barn? I shall try to teach them. For such an undertaking much previous labour and foresight are required. In our case, fortunately, there was a small cedar swamp within a hundred paces of the site we had chosen for our barn, which was picturesquely separated from the house by a ravine some thirty feet deep, with a clear spring of the sweetest and coldest water flowing between steep banks. The barn was to consist of two large bays, each thirty feet square and eight logs high, with a threshing floor twelve feet wide between, the whole combined into one by an upper story or loft, twenty by seventy-two feet, and four logs high, including the roof-plates.

It will be seen, then, that to build such a barn would require sixty-four logs of thirty feet each for the lower story; and sixteen more of the same length, as well as eight of seventy-two feet each, for the loft. Our handy swamp provided all these, not from standing trees only, but from many fallen patriarchs buried four or five feet under the surface in black muck, and perfectly sound. To get them out of the mud required both skill and patience.

All the branches having been cleared off as thoroughly as possible, the entire tree was drawn out by those most patient of all patient drudges, the oxen, and when on solid ground, sawn to the required length. A number of skids were also provided . . . and plenty of handspikes.

Having got these prime essentials ready, the next business was to summon our good neighbours to a "raising bee." On the day named, accordingly, we had about thirty practised axemen on the ground by day-break, all in the best of spirits, and confident in their powers for work. Eight of the heaviest logs, about two feet thick, had been placed in position as sleepers or foundation logs, duly saddled at the corners. Parallel with these at a distance of twenty-feet on either side, were ranged in order all the logs required to complete the building.

Well, now we begin. Eight of the smartest men jump at once on the eight corners. In a few minutes each of the four men in front has his saddle ready that is, he has chopped his end of the first log into an angular shape. . . .

Breakfast and dinner form welcome interludes. Ample stores of provender, meat, bread, potatoes, puddings various, tea and coffee, have been prepared and are thoroughly enjoyed, inasmuch as they are rare luxuries to many of the guests. . . .

Then, and not till then, after supper, a little whiskey was allowed. Teetotalism had not made its way into our backwoods; and we were considered very straightlaced indeed to set our faces as we did against all excess. Our Highland and Irish neighbours looked upon the weak stuff sold in Canada with supreme contempt; and recollecting our Galway experience, we felt no surprise thereat.

Source: Thompson, Samuel. *Reminiscences of a Canadian Pioneer for the Last Fifty Years*. Toronto: Hunter, Rose & Co., 1884, pp. 80–83.

What You Need to Know

The accompanying document comes from Samuel Thompson's *Reminiscences of a Canadian Pioneer for the Last Fifty Years*, published in 1884. Born in England in 1810, Thompson immigrated to Canada in his early 20s, settling on farms in Upper Canada (now Ontario), before becoming a newspaper editor in Toronto and Quebec City.

In many ways, Canada's history parallels that of the United States. With its vast territory, the country was a magnet for European immigrants eager to farm lands of their own, lands opened up by the removal of the native peoples who had inhabited them for tens of thousands of years. Over the course of the nineteenth century, the Canadian frontier slowly moved westward, as first the woodlands of Ontario and then the prairies of Manitoba, Saskatchewan, and Alberta were settled.

As in the United States, Canadian agriculture from the early nineteenth century onward was largely dominated by commercial farming. Grains and oil seeds were raised on large homesteads, granted to pioneers, first by the British government, and after independence in 1867, by the Canadian one. The Great Lakes provided a natural outlet for the produce of Ontario but as the prairie provinces were settled, the government laid plans for a transcontinental railroad, which was completed in 1885.

A Closer Look

In this excerpt, Samuel Thompson describes the construction of a barn on the Canadian frontier. The "raising bee," a British expression, was a collective enterprise, in which members of a local community would come together to help a farmer put up a barn. The farmer would typically supply the material and the community members would contribute tools and labor. It was a purely voluntary activity, the idea being that, when other members of the community needed a barn built, the farmers who had been helped would contribute their labor in turn.

Because farmers could not be expected to leave their own farms for very long, all of the materials would be prepared in advance by the farmer in question along with some hired help. Barn raisings typically lasted two or three days, usually in June or July, months between planting and harvest when time could be spared from farm work.

Barn raisings were also times for socializing, a much needed respite from the loneliness of isolated homesteads. Whole families would descend on a farm and the barn raising would usually be followed by an evening of festivities, before the farm families got back in their wagons and returned to their own farms.

1   100   200   300   400   500   600   700   800   900   1000   1100   1200   1300   1400   1500   1600   1700   1800   1900   2000 CE

2.15.5 Qing Dynasty Opium Pipe

China
Nineteenth Century

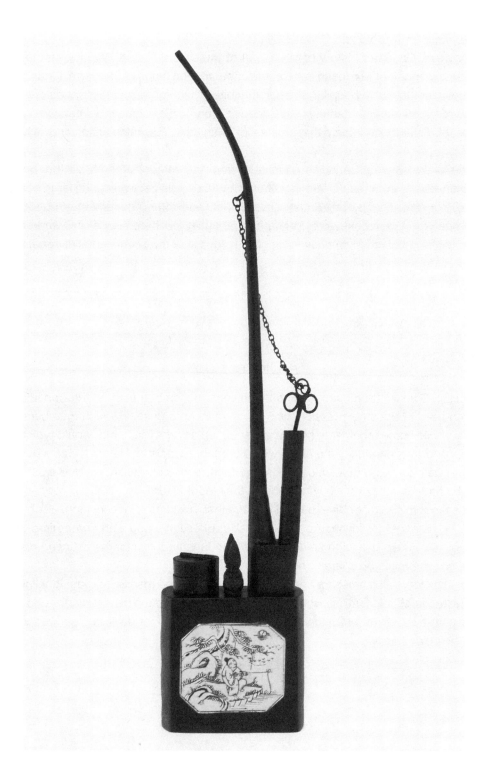

Credit: Shariff Che' Lah | Dreamstime.com

What You Need to Know

Shown here is a pipe for smoking opium, dating to nineteenth-century China.

Largely as the result of British trade policies, the price of opium dropped dramatically in China in the nineteenth century. China had long enjoyed a trade surplus with the West, as its silks, porcelain, and other fine goods were highly coveted there. Thus, the British sought a product they could sell the Chinese that would address this imbalance and make fortunes for merchants. They found it in opium, which was largely grown in British-controlled areas in the Indian subcontinent and Southeast Asia. Clipper ships would transport the drug to heavily guarded barges off Chinese cities, where the stuff would be sold to local traders, who were often members of criminal gangs. By 1900, roughly 10 percent of China's adult population, as well as some of its youth, were regular opium smokers.

The Qing dynasty government of China first protested the trade and made it illegal. But demand was too great and many officials whose job it was to enforce the ban were users themselves or were willing to accept bribes to look the other way to let the drug into the country.

A Closer Look

Opium is a narcotic derived from the opium poppy. Smoking it produces a dreamlike state for the user, who also experiences a sense of physical pleasure and euphoria. Smoking opium required paraphernalia. Balls of yellowish-brown opium first had to be heated to release the flammable residues. Then, the ball was placed in the bowl of a pipe. In this image, the bowl is opposite down and separate from the stem that held it, which is the large cylinder on the right. That cylinder contains a scissors for cutting the wick of oil lamps, where the opium was first heated. The fat cylinder on the left is where extra opium was held and the long stem in the middle was for the user to draw in the smoke.

Originally a drug used by the Chinese elite, it became popular among the masses in the nineteenth century when prices dropped. The wealthy typically smoked their opium in the home, which often had a special room dedicated to the practice. The room would be richly fitted out with tapestries and comfortable couches, as smoking the drug produced lethargy in the user. Ordinary Chinese in urban areas more often visited opium dens, where they obtained the drug and the pipes to smoke it. Such dens lined the streets of poor and reputable neighborhoods alike and could range from filthy storefronts, where smokers laid down on simple wooden palettes, to elaborate smoking parlors, with wealthy trappings.

1 100 200 300 400 500 600 700 800 900 1000 1100 1200 1300 1400 1500 1600 1700 1800 1900 2000 CE

2.15.6 Samoan Love Song

Samoa
Nineteenth Century

There was Tafitofau and Ongafau, and they had two daughters; the one was Sinaleuuna and the other Sinaeteva. The two girls sat and wished they had a brother. Again Ongafau had a child, and it was a boy. The child grew up, but his sisters never saw him. They lived apart from their parents and the boy.

Then Tafitofau and Ongafau said to the boy, who was called Maluafiti: "Go with some food to the ladies." The lad went down, the girls looked and were struck with his beauty. He came with the food and said he was their brother. The sisters rejoiced and gave thanks that their desire was granted; they had now a brother. . . . Then the sisters sat down and filled into a bamboo bottle, the liquid shadow of their brother.

A report came from Fiji of the beautiful lady Sina. . . . The two sisters dressed up and went to tell her all about their handsome brother, but they were slighted and shamefully treated by Sina. Sina did not know they were the sisters of Maluafiti. . . .

The sisters were still ill-treated by Sina; their anger rose. . . . They threw out from the bottle on to the water the shadow of their brother. Sina looked at the shadow and was struck with its beauty: "That is my husband," said she, "wherever I can find him." Then Sinaleuuna wept and uttered in soliloquy: "Oh, Sinaleuuna, Sinaeteva, you are enraged! Where is our brother? 'Tis for him we are here and slighted."

Sina called out to the villagers for all to come. All the beautiful young men to assemble and find out of whom the figure in the water was the image. They sought in vain, they could not find the shadow was bright and beautiful and compared with no one. . . .

But Sina heard not the weeping of the sisters of Maluafiti. Again their song rang out, "Where is our brother? 'Tis for him we are here and slighted." "Oh, Maluafiti! rise up, it is day; your shadow prolongs our ill-treatment. Maluafiti come and talk with her face to face instead of that image in water."

Sina had listened, and now she knew 'twas the shadow of Maluafiti. These are his sisters too, and I've been ill-using them, Sina reproached herself: "Oh! I fear these ladies; I knew not they were seeking a wife for their brother, Maluafiti." "Come, oh come," said Sina, "forgive me, I've done you wrong." Sina begged pardon in vain, the ladies were angry still.

The canoe of Maluafiti arrived. He came to court Lady Sina, and also to fetch his sisters. He came, he heard the tale of his sisters, and then up flew implacable rage. Sina longed to get Maluafiti; he was her heart's desire, and long she had waited for him.

Maluafiti frowned and would return, and off he went with his sisters. Sina cried and screamed, and determined to follow swimming. The sisters pleaded to save and to bring her, Maluafiti relented not, and Sina died in the ocean.

Source: Turner, George. *Samoa: A Hundred Years Ago and Long Before*. London: Macmillan, 1884, pp. 98–101.

What You Need to Know

The lyrics printed here come from a Samoan love song. They were transcribed by a British missionary named George Turner, who served in the islands for nearly two decades in the middle of the nineteenth century.

Song was an essential part of traditional Samoan culture and remains so to this day. Before sustained European contact in the early nineteenth century, Samoans possessed a number of musical instruments, including various forms of drums and pipes, as well as the iconic conch shell. But the human voice is the central form of expression in Samoan music. Vocal music on the island is highly emotional, incorporating musical forms of laughter, weeping, anger, and joy.

Samoans incorporated song into ritual and everyday life. British author Robert Louis Stevenson of *Treasure Island*, who settled in Samoa and died there in the late nineteenth century, noted how islanders were wont to improvise song for every occasion—when out fishing, performing farm chores, traveling to other islands, and courting. At the same time, there were traditional songs performed on religious occasions and milestone ceremonies, such as the birth of a child or a wedding. Not surprisingly, when Christian missionaries arrived in the nineteenth century, Samoans were recruited to the new faith through the singing of hymns.

A Closer Look

This love song relates the story of two sisters who seek a match for their brother in a beautiful woman on the island of Fiji. But they are ill-treated there, and when the brother finds out, he comes to fetch them. Spurning the Fijian woman's love, he sails off. The woman follows him only to drown in the ocean.

The story in the song deviates from traditional Samoan courtship rituals. Typically, a young man interested in a woman would not approach her directly but would go to her family with gifts, asking their permission first before courting the woman. All wooing would be done in the presence of the young woman's family. Given the nature of such courtship, it is not surprising that the wooer and the wooed were not to have any physical contact before marriage. Should the young man fail to adhere to these customs, he was likely to be spurned by the woman's family—if he was lucky, for it was not uncommon that violators of a woman's honor would receive a beating from her brothers or other male relatives.

2.15.7 Burning of Widows in India

British India
1820

ADVOCATE: I alluded . . . to the real reason for our anxiety to persuade widows to follow their husbands, and for our endeavours to burn them pressed down with ropes: viz., that women are by nature of inferior understanding, without resolution, unworthy of trust, subject to passions, And void of virtuous knowledge; they, according to the precepts of the Sastra, are not allowed to marry again after the demise of their husbands, and consequently despair at once of all worldly pleasure; hence it is evident, that death to these unfortunate widows is preferable to existence. . . .

OPPONENT: The reason you have now assigned for burning widows alive is indeed your true motive, as we are well aware; but the faults which you have imputed to women are not planted in their constitution by nature; it would be, therefore, grossly criminal to condemn that sex to death merely from precaution. By ascribing to them all sorts of improper conduct, you have indeed successfully persuaded the Hindu community to look down upon them as contemptible and mischievous creatures, whence they have been subjected to constant miseries. I have, therefore, to offer a few remarks on this head. . . .

At marriage the wife is recognized as half of her husband, but in after-conduct they are treated worse than inferior animals. For the woman is employed to do the work of a slave in the house, such as, in her turn, to clean the place very early in the morning, whether cold or wet, to scour the dishes, to wash the floor, to cook night and day, to prepare and serve food for her husband, father, mother-in-law, sisters-in-law, brothers-in-law, and friends and connections! (for amongst Hindus more than in other tribes relations long reside together, and on this account quarrels are more common amongst brothers respecting their worldly affairs.) If in the preparation or serving up of the victuals they commit the smallest fault, what insult do they not receive from their husband, their mother-in-law, and the younger brothers of their husband? After all the male part of the family have satisfied themselves, the women content themselves with what may be left, whether sufficient in quantity or not.

Source: Roy, Rammohun. *The English Works of Raja Rammohun Roy*. Allahabad, India: The Panini Office, 1906, pp. 359–360, 362.

What You Need to Know

This document comes from the work of Ram Mohan Roy, an Indian social reformer of the early nineteenth century. The excerpt here, from 1820, is part of an imaginary dialogue between an advocate and opponent of *sati* (also spelled *suttee)*, a funerary practice in which widows were burned alongside the bodies of their late husbands.

Scholars are unsure where and why the practice of *sati* began, although one argument is that it grew out of war. When one side lost in a war, they would put their own women to death rather than allow them to be defiled by the victorious enemy.

When the British first began colonizing India in a major way in the eighteenth century, they tolerated *sati*, so as not to antagonize local Hindus and thus jeopardize British political and economic interests on the subcontinent. Gradually, however, under pressure from Christian missionaries, they took a harsher attitude, finally outlawing it in areas under their control in 1829.

A Closer Look

Although fictional, the dialogue captures the very low status of women in early nineteenth-century Indian society, which evinced itself at every stage in a female's life.

Families that could not afford more children practiced female infanticide. Girls received virtually no formal education, even in wealthier households where brothers were tutored. Legally speaking, they were little more than property. Traditionally, a bride—oftentimes still in her early teens—was seen as a "gift" from her father to her new husband, along with a dowry to get the new couple started in life. The new wife then joined the husband's family, where she was put under the authority of the husband's mother or other matriarch of the household.

Widows faced an even worse fate. Without their husbands, they became little more than slaves of their late husband's family. (Notably, this is the argument offered by the advocate of *sati* in Roy's dialogue.) Yet they had few options to improve their lot. Remarriage was virtually taboo, and they were expected to remain in a kind of mourning the rest of their lives—heads shaved, eating bland food, wearing plain garments. Just meeting one in the street was considered a bad omen.

Sati, the Sanskrit word for "chaste," was connected to purity. That is, a widow who chose to immolate herself on her husbands' funeral pyre achieved a purity of soul that would advance her in future reincarnations on the path to enlightenment and freedom from corporeal existence, as per Hindu belief. While some Europeans and Indian reformers spoke of forced *sati*, in fact it was almost always a voluntary act, although pressure might be put on a woman by the husband's family.

2.15.8 Opium Addiction in Nineteenth-Century England

London, England
1821

The next morning, as I need hardly say, I awoke with excruciating rheumatic pains of the head and face, from which I had hardly any respite for about twenty days. On the twenty-first day, I think it was, and on a Sunday, that I went out into the streets; rather to run away, if possible, from my torments, than with any distinct purpose. By accident I met a college acquaintance who recommended opium. Opium! dread agent of unimaginable pleasure and pain! . . .

I saw a druggist's shop. The druggist—unconscious minister of celestial pleasures!—as if in sympathy with the rainy Sunday, looked dull and stupid, just as any mortal druggist might be expected to look on a Sunday; and, when I asked for the tincture of opium, he gave it to me as any other man might do: and furthermore, out of my shilling, returned me what seemed to be real copper halfpence, taken out of a real wooden drawer. Nevertheless, in spite of such indications of humanity, he has ever since existed in my mind as the beatific vision of an immortal druggist, sent down to earth on a special mission to myself.

Arrived at my lodgings, it may be supposed that I lost not a moment in taking the quantity prescribed. I was necessarily ignorant of the whole art and mystery of opium-taking: and, what I took, I took under every disadvantage. But I took it:—and in an hour, oh! Heavens! what a revulsion! what an upheaving, from its lowest depths, of the inner spirit! what an apocalypse of the world within me! That my pains had vanished, was now a trifle in my eyes:—this negative effect was swallowed up in the immensity of those positive effects which had opened before me—in the abyss of divine enjoyment thus suddenly revealed. Here was a panacea—a pharmakon nepenthez for all human woes: here was the secret of happiness, about which philosophers had disputed for so many ages, at once discovered: happiness might now be bought for a penny, and carried in the waistcoat pocket: portable ecstasies might be had corked up in a pint bottle: and peace of mind could be sent down in gallons by the mail coach. But, if I talk in this way, the reader will think I am laughing: and I can assure him, that nobody will laugh long who deals much with opium: its pleasures even are of a grave and solemn complexion; and in his happiest state, the opium-eater cannot present himself in the character of *L'Allegro*: even then, he speaks and thinks as becomes *Il Penseroso*. Nevertheless, I have a very reprehensible way of jesting at times in the midst of my own misery: and, unless when I am checked by some more powerful feelings, I am afraid I shall be guilty of this indecent practice even in these annals of suffering or enjoyment. The reader must allow a little to my infirm nature in this respect: and with a few indulgences of that sort, I shall endeavour to be as grave, if not drowsy, as fits a theme like opium, so anti-mercurial as it really is, and so drowsy as it is falsely reputed.

Source: Quincey, Thomas de. *The Confessions of an Opium-Eater: Being an Extract from the Life of a Scholar*. New York: Macmillan, 1900, pp. 70–73.

What You Need to Know

Thomas de Quincey was a successful British journalist and essayist of the first half of the nineteenth century, who wrote about art, literature, and society. But he is best known for his 1821 autobiographical account of his drug addiction, *Confessions of an Opium-Eater*.

Opium is believed to have first been discovered in Mesopotamia in the fourth millennium BCE. It was known to the ancient Greeks; many scholars believe that the Lotus Eaters episode in Homer's *Odyssey* is really about opium. With long-distance trade cut off, the drug largely disappeared from Europe in the Middle Ages, only to be reintroduced during the age of exploration, first brought back by Portuguese traders in the early sixteenth century.

As Britain expanded into South Asia in the eighteenth century, it became involved in the growing and trading of opium. The country fought two wars with China in the mid-nineteenth century to import the drug there as a means of redressing a trade imbalance. British merchants made great fortunes, but their trade also led to an upsurge in use in Britain itself. In the form of laudanum, it became especially popular among middle- and upper-class women, seeking a means to relieve the boredom of their lives of pampered, homebound boredom. Doctors routinely prescribed it as a means to relieve what was perceived as a "hysteria" epidemic among such women.

A Closer Look

Opium in nineteenth-century Britain was perfectly legal, sold at chemist shops, or pharmacies throughout the country, although it was more readily available in major ports and cities. Britain's imperial expansion into South and Central Asia, where opium originated, produced a steady supply at relatively inexpensive prices. British newspapers routinely listed opium imports in the shipping news.

Although its hallucinogenic powers were well known by de Quincey's time, it was widely consumed as an analgesic. The author's own addiction began when he used it for his neuralgia. Typically, it was taken in a tincture, known as laudanum, which usually contained more alcohol than opium, although de Quincey prefers to eat his straight, despite the nausea this form of ingestion causes.

In the early nineteenth century, opium eating was largely a private activity, the drug taken at home. But the arrival of opium-smoking Chinese sailors in the second half of the nineteenth century saw the introduction of opium dens, where the drug was smoked communally. It was the spread of such dens, which were seen as propagating other vices, such as prostitution and gambling, as well as a growing recognition of the dangers of opium that led to the first restrictions on its sale—although not its criminalization—in 1868.

1 100 200 300 400 500 600 700 800 900 1000 1100 1200 1300 1400 1500 1600 1700 1800 1900 2000 CE

2.15.9 Fishing Laws in the Kingdom of Hawaii

Hawaii
1839

384. All fishing grounds appertaining to any government land, or otherwise belonging to the government, excepting only ponds, shall be, and are hereby forever granted to the people, for the free and equal use of all persons: provided, however, that, for the protection of such fishing grounds, the Minister of the Interior may taboo the taking of fish thereon, at certain seasons of the year.

385. The Minister of the Interior shall give public notice of any such taboo imposed by him; and no such taboo shall be in force until such notice has been given. Every person who shall violate such taboo shall be punished by a fine not exceeding fifteen dollars, and the value of the fish taken.

386. No person residing without the Kingdom shall take any fish within the harbors, streams, reefs, or other waters of the same, for the purpose of carrying them for sale, or otherwise, to any place without the Kingdom, under penalty of a fine not exceeding two hundred dollars, in the discretion of the Court. . . .

388. The konohikis shall be considered in law to hold said private fisheries for the equal use of themselves, and of the tenants on their respective lands; and the tenants shall be at liberty to use the fisheries of their konohikis, subject to the restrictions imposed by law.

389. The konohikis shall have power each year, to set apart for themselves one given species or variety of fish natural to their respective fisheries, giving public notice, by *viva voce* proclamation, and by at least three written or printed notices posted in conspicuous places on the land, to their tenants and others residing on their lands, signifying the kind and description of fish which they have chosen to be set apart for themselves.

390. The specific fish so set apart shall be exclusively for the use of the konohiki, if caught within the bounds of his fishery, and neither his tenants nor others shall be at liberty to appropriate such reserved fish to their private use, but when caught, such reserved fish shall be the property of the konohiki, for which he shall be at liberty to sue and recover the value from any person appropriating the same.

396. The several District Justices shall have power to try and punish all offenses against the provisions of the last preceding section, committed in their respective districts.

Source: *Compiled Laws of the Hawaiian Kingdom*. Honolulu: Hawaiian Gazette Office, 1884, pp. 92–94.

TIMELINE   2000 1900 1800 1700 1600 1500 1400 1300 1200 1100 1000 900 800 700 600 500 400 300 200 100 1 BCE

What You Need to Know

This selection is a list of laws concerning fishing. The laws were first drawn up in 1839 but only set down in print in 1884.

Hawaii was first settled by Polynesians, mostly like from Tahiti or the Marquesas Islands, around the year 1300 CE. In 1778, the British sea captain James Cook and his crew became the first non-Polynesians to set eyes on the islands. The islands soon became a regular provisioning stop for whaling and trading ships from Europe and the United States. The introduction of new diseases decimated the island's population.

But the arrival of Europeans also sparked a sense of unity in the islands, as well as the means to achieve unification politically. Using European-provided weapons, King Kamehameha I established the Kingdom of Hawaii in 1810. His successors, Kamehameha II and Kamehameha III, modernized the state by replacing traditional *kapu* law, which typically involved various spiritual taboos, with a Western-style legal system.

But such efforts were insufficient to ward off outside control. Over the course of the nineteenth century, American businessmen—often the descendants of Christian missionaries—gradually took control of the island's economy, imposing their own constitution in 1887, granting them virtually all power, and finally the dissolution of the kingdom and the annexation of the islands to the United States in the 1890s.

A Closer Look

As an island people, the Hawaiians were expert fishermen, using virtually every method of fishing, including nets, hooks and lines, and spears. Hooks were usually made from shell or bone, animal and human, dangling at the end of lines made from plant fibers. Hawaiians also used lures, either made from brightly colored shells or strips of leaf, and baited their hooks with shrimp or crab.

Traditionally, Hawaiians divided all food into two classes, *ai*, or vegetables, and *i'a*, or seafood, although the latter could also be construed as meat, and so would include chicken, pig, and dog, the three forms of animal meat eaten by Hawaiians before European settlement in the early nineteenth century. Fish catches were often so abundant that Hawaiians used them to feed their domesticated animals, as well as themselves.

Still, there were limits to what could be taken. In 1839, King Kamehameha III codified traditional Hawaiian fishing rights—which were periodically updated, such as with these laws from 1884 by setting aside some fishing grounds for commoners and others for the headmen, also known as *konohikis*. In the former, fishermen, who often fished communally, were entitled to their entire catch. In the latter, they had to given a portion to the *konohiki*.

1 100 200 300 400 500 600 700 800 900 1000 1100 1200 1300 1400 1500 1600 1700 1800 1900 2000 CE

2.15.10 The Indian Caste System

British India
1840

Great attention is paid to ceremony. A person of distinction is met a mile or two before he enters the city; and a visitor is received (according to his rank) at the outer gate of the house, at the door of a room, or by merely rising from the seat. Friends embrace if they have not met for some time. Bramins are saluted by joining the palms, and raising them twice or thrice to the forehead: with others, the salute with one hand is used, so well known by the Mahometan name of salaam. . . . Visitors are seated with strict attention to their rank, which on public occasions it often takes much previous negotiation to settle. Hindus of rank are remarkable for their politeness to inferiors, generally addressing them by some civil or familiar term, and scarcely ever being provoked to abusive or harsh language. The lower classes are courteous in their general manners among themselves, but by no means so scrupulous in their language when irritated. All visits end by the master of the house presenting betel leaf with areca nut, etc., to the guest; it is accompanied by attar of roses or some other perfume put on the handkerchief, and rosewater sprinkled over the person; and this is the sign for taking leave. . . .

Among the most striking of the religious exhibitions is that of the capture of Lanka, in honor of Rama, which is necessarily performed out of doors. Lanka is represented by a spacious castle with towers and battlements, which are assailed by an army dressed like Rama and his followers, with Hanuman and his monkey allies. The combat ends in the destruction of Lanka, amidst a blaze of fireworks which would excite admiration in any part of the world, and in a triumphal procession sometimes conducted in a style of grandeur which might become a more important occasion. . . .

The regular dress of all Hindus is probably that which has been mentioned as used in Bengal, and which is worn by all strict Bramins. It consists of two long pieces of white cotton cloth, one of which is wrapped round the middle and tucked up between the legs, while part hangs down a good deal below the knees; the other is worn over the shoulders, and occasionally stretched over the head, which has no other covering. The head and beard are shaved, but a long tuft of hair is left on the crown. Mustachios are also worn, except perhaps by strict Bramins. Except in Bengal, all Hindus who do not affect strictness now wear the lower piece of cloth smaller and tighter, and over it a white cotton or chintz or silk tunic, a colored muslin sash round the middle, and a scarf of the same material over the shoulders, with a turban; some wear loose drawers like the Mahometans.

Source: Elphinstone, Mountstuart. "Indian Customs and Manners in 1840." Excerpt from *History of India* reprinted in *The World's Story: A History of the World in Story, Song and Art. Vol. II: India, Persia, Mesopotamia, and Palestine.* Edited by Eva March Tappan. Boston: Houghton Mifflin, 1914, pp. 171–173, 176.

TIMELINE   2000 1900 1800 1700 1600 1500 1400 1300 1200 1100 1000 900 800 700 600 500 400 300 200 100 1 BCE

What You Need to Know

This excerpt comes from the writings of Mountstuart Elphinstone, a Scottish official in the British colonial government in India in the early nineteenth century. In the early 1840s, after his return to England, he published the massive *History of India*, from which this excerpt on castes is taken.

The British first arrived in India as traders in the early seventeenth century, establishing "factories," or trading posts, in various parts of the country. After defeating the French for influence in the subcontinent in the 1760s, and then defeating a number of indigenous kingdoms, they effectively achieved control over India by the early nineteenth century, although it would not become an official crown colony until the 1850s.

British colonialists were fascinated by the caste system but they never really understood what it meant and how it worked. Not surprisingly, coming from such a class-bound society, they assumed it was a purely social ranking, a means by which upper-caste Brahmin asserted their authority and social superiority over lower castes. In fact, the term *caste* is not indigenous to India but was applied by early Portuguese explorers and means "lineage" or "breed."

A Closer Look

The traditional caste system in India organized society into hereditary groups. There are four basic castes, from top to bottom: Brahmins, the priestly caste; Kshatriyas, warriors and property owners; Vaishyas, or traders and artisans; and Shudras, unskilled laborers and peasant farmers. Castes also have a nonworldly dimension, in that members of higher castes are seen as more spiritually pure and cleaner than those in lower castes. Thus, members of higher castes often avoided physical contact with those in castes beneath them.

For traditional Indians of the nineteenth century, one's position on the rungs of the caste ladder did not measure economic, social, or political power but progress, achieved over many lifetimes, on the path to enlightenment and freedom from the tribulations of mortal beings. Elphinstone remarks on the harmony between castes and the respect members of higher castes afforded to lower castes in daily life. In effect, Indians accepted their caste position as the fulfillment of their soul's destiny, rather than being the result of larger social or economic forces.

As noted, the British did not really understand the caste system. But that did not stop them from trying to use it to impose their control over a colony vastly larger, in terms of area and population, than their home country. Assuming that Brahmins were akin to their own upper class, the British granted them political and economic power over lower castes. Nineteenth-century British ideas about race played a role as well. The fact that many Brahmins were descended from lighter skinned Central Asians, who had arrived in India thousands of years before, only confirmed to the British that they were cultural and even biological superiors within Indian society. Gradually, such ideas began to influence how Indians themselves saw the caste system, turning what had once been a spiritual concept into a political one.

1   100   200   300   400   500   600   700   800   900   1000   1100   1200   1300   1400   1500   1600   1700   1800   1900   2000 CE

2.15.11 Polynesian Warrior Dress

Tahiti
1840

The dress and ornaments of the warriors of Tahiti and the adjacent islands were singular, and unlike those of most savage nations, being often remarkably cumbersome. Their helmets, though less elegant and imposing than the fine Grecian-formed helmet of the Hawaiians, were adapted to produce considerable effect. Some of the Tahitians wore only a fillet or bandage round the temples, but many had a quantity of cloth bound round, in the form of a high turban, which not only tended to increase their apparent stature, but broke the force of a blow from a club, or a thrust from a spear.

The most elegant head-dresses, however, were those worn by the inhabitants of the Austral Islands, Tubuai, Rurutu, &c. Their helmets were considerably diversified in form, some resembling a tight round cap, fitted closely to the head, with a light plume waving on the summit. Those used by the natives of Tubuai and High Island, resembled an officer's cocked hat, worn with the ends projecting over each shoulder; the front beautifully ornamented with the green and red wing and tail feathers of a species of paroquet. The Rurutuan helmet is graceful in appearance, and useful in the protection it affords to the head of the wearer. It was a cap fitted close to the head, and reaching to the ears, made with thick stuff or native cloth, on a cane of framework. The lower part of the front is ornamented with bunches of beautiful red and green feathers, tastefully arranged; and above these a line of the long slender tail feathers of the tropic or man-of-war bird, is fixed on a wicker frame: the hinder part of the cap is covered with long flowing human hair, of a light-brown or tawny colour, said to be the human beard; this is fastened to a slight network, attached to the crown of the helmet, and being detached from any other part, often floats wildly in the wind, and increases the agitated appearance of the wearer. . . .

Some of the fighting men wore a kind of armour of net-work, formed by small cords, wound round the body and limbs so tight as merely to allow of the exercise of the arms and legs, and not to impede the circulation of the blood, and a kind of wooden armour for the breast, back, and sides, covered with successive folds of thick cloth, bound on with ropes.

Source: *Missionary Records: Tahiti and Society Islands*. Vol. III. London: Religious Tract Society, 1840, pp. 83–85.

What You Need to Know

This excerpt on Tahitian dress comes from *Missionary Records: Tahiti and Society Islands*, which was published in London by the Religious Tract Society in 1840.

Tahiti and the Society Islands were first settled by Polynesian explorers in the latter centuries of the first millennium BCE, reached by outrigger canoes from nearby archipelagos, such as Samoa and Fiji.

Polynesian society in Tahiti, as in many of the other islands they settled, was, as noted, clan based. Each was headed by an *ali'i*, or headman, who was, in turn, advised by the *ari'i*, or nobles. Both the *ali'i* and the *ari'i* claimed descent from the gods and thus their decision to go to war was seen as having the approval of those gods.

With the arrival of Europeans on a sustained basis in the late eighteenth and early nineteenth century, warfare in Tahiti took on a new cast, as chiefs attempted to capture territory to secure more of the provisions that could be traded for coveted manufactured goods from abroad.

A Closer Look

While Christian missionaries could be quite misguided in their understanding of traditional customs and religion of the people they were trying to convert, they often provided excellent accounts of non-European peoples' material culture. The excerpts here describe the various forms of battle dress of Tahitian warriors.

As Europeans came into increased contact with Tahiti in the late eighteenth century, there developed an image of the islands as a peaceful paradise on Earth. In fact, warfare was endemic to the islands of Tahiti before the regular arrival of Europeans. (Tahiti had first been encountered by Europeans in the late sixteenth century, but for the next 200 years, visits were sporadic.)

The warfare grew out of Tahiti's clan-based social organizations, each of which was led by a chief. The chief's power was based more on persuasion than power; he had to win the approval of the nobles before going to war, for instance.

Before European contact, most of the warring was highly ritualized, in which raiders would attempt to capture some of the property and persons of neighboring clans. Many of the battles were, in fact, fought over alleged insults to the chief of the clan. The elaborate dress they wore, and which is described here, had both a pragmatic function—wooden shields and helmets—and a spiritual one: they were said to be invested with *mana*, or the supernatural power of the chiefs and noble warriors who wore them.

1 100 200 300 400 500 600 700 800 900 1000 1100 1200 1300 1400 1500 1600 1700 1800 1900 2000 CE

2.15.12 Solomon Northrup's Description of a Louisiana Slave Auction

New Orleans, Louisiana
1841

In the first place we were required to wash thoroughly, and those with beards to shave. We were then furnished with a new suit each, cheap, but clean. The men had hat, coat, shirt, pants, and shoes; the women frocks of calico, and handkerchief to bind about their heads. We were now conducted into a large room in the front part of the building to which the yard was attached, in order to be properly trained, before the admission of customers. The men were arranged on one side of the room, the women at the other. . . .

Next day many customers called to examine Freeman's "new lot." The latter gentleman was very loquacious, dwelling at much length upon our several good points and qualities. He would make us hold up our heads, walk briskly back and forth, while customers would feel of our hands and arms and bodies, turn us about, ask us what we could do, make us open our mouths and show our teeth, precisely as a jockey examines a horse which he is about to barter for purchase. Sometimes a man or woman was taken back to the small house in the yard, stripped, and inspected more minutely. Scars upon a slave's back were considered evidence of a rebellious or unruly spirit, and hurt his sale. . . .

The same man also purchased Randall. The little fellow was made to jump, and run across the floor, and perform many other feats, exhibiting his activity and condition. All the time the trade was going on, Eliza was crying aloud, and wringing her hands. She besought the man not to buy him, unless he also bought herself and Emily. She promised, in that case, to be the most faithful slave that ever lived. The man answered that he could not afford it, and then Eliza burst into a paroxysm of grief, weeping plaintively. Freeman turned around to her, savagely, with his whip in his uplifted hand, ordering her to stop her noise, or he would flog her. He would not have such work—such sniveling; and unless she ceased that minute, he would take her to the yard and give her a hundred lashes. Yes, he would take the nonsense out of her pretty quick—if he didn't, might he be d—d. Eliza shrunk before him, and tried to wipe away her tears, but it was all in vain. All the frowns and threats of Freeman, could not wholly silence the afflicted mother. She kept on begging and beseeching them, most piteously, not to separate the three. Over and over again she told them how she loved her boy. A great many times she repeated her former promises—how very faithful and obedient she would be; how hard she would labor day and night, to the last moment of her life, if he would only buy them all together. But it was of no avail; the man could not afford it. The bargain was agreed upon, and Randall must go alone. Then Eliza ran to him; embraced him passionately; kissed him again and again; told him to remember her—all the while her tears falling in the boy's face like rain.

Source: Northup, Solomon, and David Wilson. *Twelve Years a Slave: Narrative of Solomon Northup*. New York: Miller, Orton & Mulligan, 1855, pp. 78–82.

TIMELINE   2000 1900 1800 1700 1600 1500 1400 1300 1200 1100 1000 900 800 700 600 500 400 300 200 100 1 BCE

What You Need to Know

In this excerpt from Solomon Northrup's *Twelve Years a Slave*, published in 1855, he describes being sold in a New Orleans slave auction.

In 1808, the United States banned the importation of slaves from outside the country. While a brisk smuggling trade continued, the overall drop in slave imports was dramatic. This left two means for obtaining new slaves. One was natural increase. The other was the internal slave trade. The typical sale was small and local, one master selling a few slaves to a neighbor. But there was also a long-distance trade in slaves, which involved professional slave traders. Much of this involved the sale of large lots of slaves from older regions to newer ones, typically, from the Chesapeake and Upper South to the Deep South. Virginia, which had the largest slave population of any state, was experiencing agricultural decline (caused by tobacco depleting the soil) and a transition to grain production, which required less labor. At the same time, cotton production in the Deep South, from Georgia to East Texas, was booming. These economic factors led to a vibrant long-distance, internal trade in slaves. Historians estimate that roughly 25,000 slaves annually were transported—or marched—across interstate lines between 1830 and the outbreak of the Civil War.

A Closer Look

Solomon Northrup was a free, middle-class African-American from Upstate New York who was kidnapped and sold into slavery. He spent a dozen years on Louisiana plantations until an itinerant Canadian-born carpenter with antislavery proclivities helped to free him. At one point during his captivity, he was sold at a slave auction to a sugar planter.

The slave auction was one of the cruelest aspects of an inhumane system. Often, they followed the breakup of an estate. Slaves would be marched to the auction site, full of all manners of dread. Would they be sold to an especially cruel master or, worse, would they be sold separately from family and friends?

Although Northrup notes that at his auction, the slaves were asked to clean themselves up and put on decent clothing, oftentimes the sale involved humiliation. Northrup relates how his fellow slaves were asked to open their mouths, so buyers could inspect their teeth, as if they were horses. But it was sometimes worse, as slaves were told to strip naked, often in front of the opposite sex, so potential buyers could look over their bodies for injuries or whipping scars, the latter to show if they had a rebellious streak. The slaves were also typically required to perform, so as to attest to their soundness of limb.

1 100 200 300 400 500 600 700 800 900 1000 1100 1200 1300 1400 1500 1600 1700 1800 1900 2000 CE

2.15.13 British Instructions on Negotiating with African Chiefs

West Africa
1844

1. The suppression of the Slave Trade may be materially assisted by obtaining the co-operation of the Native Chiefs of Africa in the object; you are therefore authorized to conclude engagements for this purpose with the African Chiefs; but you must strictly adhere to the regulations herein laid down on the subject.

2. You will procure the fullest and most correct information as to the state of those parts of the coast in which Slave Trade is carried on, so as to enable you to determine, with what Chiefs it may be expedient to enter into negotiations for the conclusion of Engagements.

With this in view, you will endeavor to ascertain the power and influence of the several Chiefs; their personal character, and the habits of the people; the extent and force of the country; the sources, amount, and description of the legitimate trade carried on. . . .

6. Every opportunity is to be taken of impressing the minds of the Native Chiefs and their people with a conviction of the efforts Great Britain has made for their benefit, and of her earnest desire to raise them in the scale of nations. It is most desirable to excite in them an emulation of the habits of the Christian world, and to enable them to make the first practical step towards civilization by the abandonment of the Slave Trade. . . .

12. In case the Slave Trade is actually carried on within the jurisdiction of the Chief at the time the Engagement is concluded, . . . you will then require that all the Slaves held for exportation shall be delivered up to you to be made free at a British colony. You will also demand that all implements of the Slave Trade, such as shackles, bolts, and handcuffs, chains, whips, branding irons, etc., or articles of Slave equipment for fitting up vessels to carry Slaves, shall be given up to you, or destroyed in your presence. You will also insist on the immediate destruction of the barracoons, or buildings exclusively devoted to the reception of Slaves, and, if necessary, you will enforce all these demands. . . .

14. You are not, without the signed consent in writing of a Native Chief, to take any step upon his territory for putting down the Slave Trade by force, excepting when, by Engagement, Great Britain is entitled to adopt coercive measures on shore for that purpose. . . .

16. In the event, however, of ultimate failure of the negotiations you will finally state to the Chief that every civilized Naval Power in the world has declared that it has abandoned the Slave Trade; that most nations have united with Great Britain in endeavors to put it down; that Great Britain will not allow the subjects of the Chief . . . to carry Slaves for sale to or from any places beyond the limits of his own territory, and that Her Majesty's Officers have orders to liberate Slaves when found embarked in boats of his subjects for that purpose.

Source: Admiralty. "Instructions for Negotiating with Chiefs of Africa." In *Instructions for the Guidance of Her Majesty's Naval Officers: Employed in the Suppression of the Slave Trade*. London: T. R. Harrison, 1844, pp. 18–20.

TIMELINE   2000 1900 1800 1700 1600 1500 1400 1300 1200 1100 1000 900 800 700 600 500 400 300 200 100 1 BCE

What You Need to Know

These selection of instructions were given to British military officers in the nineteenth century after Britain abolished slavery. They advised officers on how to negotiate with West African chiefs to stop the slave trade.

Historians note that there were a number of factors that led to Britain's decision to ban the international trade in slaves in 1808. Among these were the changing economics of empire. With the rise of manufacturing, Britain was no longer as reliant on the commercial crops produced by slaves in the colonies for its financial well-being. But there were also nobler reasons. By the early nineteenth century, the British people grew increasingly opposed to the immorality of the slave trade. This was largely the result of a campaign by a determined and effective coalition of abolitionists, who communicated the horrors and injustices of the business through a mass propaganda campaign.

Once Britain committed to ending the trade—and then abolishing slavery itself in the empire in 1833—it took strong measures, particularly at sea, seizing roughly 150,000 slaves in 60 years. But on land, the British had to use a mix of force and persuasion. The instructions here emphasize the importance of winning the goodwill of local authorities. At the same time, they make it clear that should any evidence of slave trading be found on a chief's territory, it must be seized and/or destroyed.

A Closer Look

In 1807, the British banned the international trade in African slaves. Enforcing the ban relied on three measures: seizing slave ships at sea; forcing coastal slaving forts to close down; and, as these instructions to British officers indicate, convincing the African suppliers of slaves to halt their practices.

To achieve the last of these, British military officers were expected to negotiate with local chiefs, the idea being that once the man in authority had agreed to stop dealing in slaves, his people would follow. Even the British recognized this was not always a straightforward task. At one point, the instructions say that the officer should "ascertain the power and influence" of the chiefs. In fact, in most West African communities, the chief had great status but little actual power. He ruled at the behest of other members of his age cohort; indeed, a chief was often chosen for his persuasive powers rather than his strength, as he was more likely to get things done through effective debate than by a show of power. And getting his people to cease something as lucrative as the slave trade would indeed require all of a chief's persuasive powers.

2.15.14 Life on the Pampas of Argentina

Argentina
1846

The whole remaining population inhabit the open country, which, whether wooded or destitute of the larger plants, is generally level, and almost everywhere occupied by pastures, in some places of such abundance and excellence, that the grass of an artificial meadow would not surpass them. Mendoza, and especially San Juan, are exceptions to this general absence of tilled fields, the people here depending chiefly on the products of agriculture. Everywhere else, pasturage being plenty, the means of subsistence of the inhabitants—for we cannot call it their occupation—is stock-raising. Pastoral life reminds us of the Asiatic plains, which imagination covers with Kalmuck, Cossack, or Arab tents. The primitive life of nations—a life essentially barbarous and unprogressive—the life of Abraham, which is that of the Bedouin of to-day, prevails in the Argentine plains, although modified in a peculiar manner by civilization. . . .

Nomad tribes do not exist in the Argentine plains; the stock-raiser is a proprietor, living upon his own land; but this conditions renders association impossible, and tends to scatter separate families over an immense extent of surface. Imagine an expanse of two thousand square leagues, inhabited throughout, but where the dwellings are usually four or even eight leagues apart, and two leagues, at least, separate the nearest neighbors. The production of movable property is not impossible, the enjoyments of luxury are not wholly incompatible with this isolation; wealth can raise a superb edifice in the desert. But the incentive is wanting; no example is near; the inducements for making a great display which exist in a city, are not known in that isolation and solitude. Inevitable privations justify natural indolence; a dearth of all the amenities of life induces all the externals of barbarism. Society has altogether disappeared. There is but the isolated self-concentrated feudal family. Since there is no collected society, no government is possible; there is neither municipal nor executive power, and civil justice has no means of reaching criminals. I doubt if the modern world presents any other form of association so monstrous as this. . . .

Moral progress, and the cultivation of the intellect, are here not only neglected, as in the Arab or Tartar tribe, but impossible. Where can a school be placed for the instruction of children living ten leagues apart in all directions? Thus, consequently, civilization can in no way be brought about. Barbarism is the normal condition, and it is fortunate if domestic customs preserve a small germ of morality. Religion feels the consequences of this want of social organization. The offices of the pastor are nominal, the pulpit has no audience, the priest flees from the deserted chapel, or allows his character to deteriorate in inactivity and solitude. Vice, simony, and the prevalent barbarism penetrate his cell, and change his moral superiority into the means of gratifying his avarice or ambition and he ends by becoming a party leader.

Source: Sarmiento, Domingo F. *Life in the Argentine Republic in the Days of the Tyrants*. New York: Kurd and Houghton, 1868, pp. 14–16, 18.

TIMELINE   2000 1900 1800 1700 1600 1500 1400 1300 1200 1100 1000 900 800 700 600 500 400 300 200 100 1 BCE

What You Need to Know

This passage comes from Domingo Sarmiento's *Life in the Argentine Republic*, published in 1846, and discusses life on the pampas, or grasslands, surrounding the capital, Buenos Aires.

Argentina was not a major center of Spanish colonial life until the eighteenth century. But its environment had been transformed centuries earlier by the runaway livestock of Europeans, herds of which filled the pampas. The indigenous peoples of the region adapted their culture to take advantage of these animals. The arrival of Europeans in the region led to the wholesale slaughter of Indians, and their death by diseases for which they had little immunity.

By the early nineteenth century, the pampas were home to hundreds of *estancias*, or vast ranches, worked by *gauchos*. With nearby markets relatively small, the ranches were largely undeveloped; cattle were allowed to graze on the open grasslands, subject to occasional herding and slaughter. But as transportation links to Europe improved in the middle and later years of the nineteenth century, the Argentine cattle industry modernized, with cattle fed from crops raised on the *estancias*. Railroads began to penetrate pampas, ending the need for long-distance cattle drives. Many of the *gauchos* were forced to abandon life on the range for work on farms and in beef-processing facilities.

A Closer Look

Domingo Sarmiento, who later became president of Argentina, was a journalist and educational reformer in his younger years, when he wrote this survey of his country. The pampas represented ideal pasturage and so there arose vast cattle raising ranches in the region. This, as Sarmiento notes, meant that dwellings were far apart. And because the population was so scattered, there was little government and social infrastructure. Instead, life centered on the households of the cattle ranchers. The male heads of these households, mostly of European descent, were not unlike feudal lords, dispensing justice, providing for the material needs of their workers, and officiating at weddings and other ceremonies.

Most of the people whose lives they controlled were *gauchos*, the Argentine equivalent of American cowboys. Most of the gauchos were mestizos, that is, of mixed European and Indian descent, or immigrants from Southern Europe. They spent much of their lives out in the open, herding cattle on the pampas, or in simple mud huts, floors lined with hides, surrounding the homesteads of ranchers. Several times a year, they would bring cattle to local towns, engaging in drinking, gambling, visiting prostitutes, and singing verses celebrating their riding, fighting, and lovemaking skills.

1 100 200 300 400 500 600 700 800 900 1000 1100 1200 1300 1400 1500 1600 1700 1800 1900 2000 CE

2.15.15 On Ageing Gracefully in Rural America

New York
1849

You can scarce understand, dear Doctor, with what pleasure I find this new spring in my path—the content with which I admit the conviction, that, without effort or self-denial, the mind may slake its thirst, and the heart be satisfied with but the waste of what lies so near us. I have all my life seen men grow old, tranquilly and content, but I did not think it possible that *I* should. I took pleasure only in that which required young blood to follow, and I felt that, to look backward for enjoyment, would be at best a difficult resignation.

Now, let it be no prejudice to the sincerity of my philosophy, if, as a corollary, I beg you to take a farm on the Susquehannah, and let us grow old in company. I should think Fate kinder than she passes for, if I could draw you, and one or two others whom we know and "love with knowledge," to cluster about this—certainly one of the loveliest spots in nature, and, while the river glides by unchangingly, shape ourselves to our changes with a helping sympathy. Think of it, dear Doctor! Meantime, I employ myself in my rides, selecting situations on the river banks which I think would be to yours and our friends' liking; and in the autumn, when it is time to transplant, I intend to suggest to the owners where trees might be wanted in case they ever sold, so that you will not lose even a season in your shrubbery, though you delay your decision. Why should we not renew Arcady? God Bless you. . . .

And I will allow that I can scarce write a letter to you without shaping it to the end of attracting you to the Susquehannah. At least, watch when you begin to grow old, and transplant yourself in time to take root, and then we may do as the trees do—defy the weather until we are separated. . . . Friends are not pebbles, lying in every path, but pearls gathered with great pain, and rare as they are precious. We spend our youth and manhood in search and proof of them, and, when Death has taken his toll, we have too few to scatter—none to throw away. I, for one, will be a miser of mine. I feel the avarice of friendship growing on me with every year—tightening my hold and extending my grasp. Who, at sixty, is rich in friends? The richest are those who have drawn this wealth of angels around them, and spent care and thought on the treasuring. Come, my Doctor! I have chosen a spot on one of the loveliest of our bright rivers. Here is all that goes to make an Arcadia, except the friendly dwellers in its shade. I will choose you a hillside, and plant your grove, that the trees, at least, shall lose no time by your delay. Set a limit to your ambition, achieve it, and come away. It is terrible to grow old amid the jostle and disrespectful hurry of a crowd. The Academy of the philosophers was *out* of Athens. You can not fancy Socrates run against, in the market-place. Respect, which grows wild in the fields, requires watching and management in the cities. Let us have an old man's Arcady.

Source: Willis, Nathaniel Parker. Excerpts from Letters IX and XI. *Rural Letters and Other Records of Thought at Leisure Written in the Intervals of More Hurried Literary Labor*. New York: Baker and Scribner, 1849, pp. 91, 100–101.

TIMELINE   2000 1900 1800 1700 1600 1500 1400 1300 1200 1100 1000 900 800 700 600 500 400 300 200 100 1 BCE

What You Need to Know

This collection of letters was written by Nathan Parker Willis in the 1840s. Willis, originally from Maine, had settled in New York City, where he developed a reputation as one of the city's leading magazine editors and publishers, publishing the work of his friends Henry Wadsworth Longfellow and Edgar Allan Poe. In 1846, at age 40, Willis left the city for semiretirement in a rural spot near where the Susquehanna River joins the Hudson in Upstate New York. In these letters, he is trying to convince a doctor friend to do likewise and join him.

Although the letters praise the peace and beauty of nature, its unspoken message is a condemnation of city life. By the late 1840s, New York City had swollen to nearly half a million people, fed by immigration from abroad and migration from the American countryside. The rapid expansion had outpaced the capacity of government, or private industry, to meet basic infrastructural needs. To name just one particularly rancid problem, the city was awash in garbage and waste, animal and human. Factories and animal rendering plants sent out noxious fumes and polluted local water supplies. Crime was rife, overwhelming the city's informal constable corps. Some wealthier New Yorkers moved to the outskirts of the city, where they built mansions for themselves. But some city residents, particularly literary ones, concluded that the countryside offered both a healthier way of life and artistic inspiration.

A Closer Look

Willis, as noted, was not alone in his decision to abandon urban life for the countryside. In fact, an entire intellectual movement, known as Transcendentalism, which advocated country life, had arisen in the 1830s and 1840s. The Transcendentalists were about more than merely escaping garbage and noxious fumes; they wanted to turn their backs on modernism itself. Urbanization and the competitive market economy, they felt, had blinded men and women to their own higher natures, their place in what Ralph Waldo Emerson, a leading Transcendentalist thinker, called the "Over-soul," that is, man's intimate connection to his fellow man and to nature.

Such a connection could only be reestablished by returning to the traditional communal values of rural life, although some, like Henry David Thoreau, felt that the connection required complete isolation. Utopian communities were established to achieve these ends. And although Willis was not advocating such a radical measure for his friend, he nevertheless felt that he would be better served by turning his back on the city in his aging years.

1 100 200 300 400 500 600 700 800 900 1000 1100 1200 1300 1400 1500 1600 1700 1800 1900 2000 CE

2.15.16 A Non-Muslim's Pilgrimage to Mecca

Arabian Peninsula
1853

There at last it lay, the bourn of my long and weary Pilgrimage, realising the plans and hopes of many and many a year. The mirage medium of Fancy invested the huge catafalque amid its gloomy pall with peculiar charms. . . . I may truly say that, of all the worshippers who clung weeping to the curtain, or who pressed their beating hearts to the stone, none felt for the moment a deeper emotion than did the Haji, from the far north. It was as if the poetical legends of the Arab spoke truth, and that the waving wings of angels, not the sweet breeze of morning, were agitating and swelling the black covering of the shrine. But, to confess humbling truth, theirs was the high feeling of religious enthusiasm, mine was the ecstasy of gratified pride.

Few Moslems contemplate for the first time the Ka'abah, without fear and awe: there is a popular jest against new comers, that they generally inquire the direction of prayer. This being the Kiblah, or fronting place, Moslems pray all around it; a circumstance which of course cannot take place in any spot of Al-Islam but the Harim [Haram—the mosque in Mecca]. The boy Mohammed, therefore, left me for a few minutes to myself; but presently he warned me that it was time to begin. Advancing, we entered through the Bab Beni Shaybah, the "Gate of the Sons of the Shaybah" (old woman). There we raised our hands, repeated the Labbayk, the Takbir, and Tahlil; after which we uttered certain supplications, and drew our hands down our faces. Then we proceeded to the Shafei's place of worship—the open pavement between the Makam Ibrahim and the well ZemZem—where we performed the usual two-bow prayer in honour of the Mosque. This was followed by a cup of holy water and a present to the Sakkas, or carriers, who for the consideration distributed, in my name, a large earthen vaseful to poor pilgrims. . . .

Then commenced the ceremony of Tamif or circumambulation, our route being the Malaf—the low oval of polished granite immediately surrounding the Ka'abah. I repeated, after my Mutawwif, or cicerone [guide], "In the Name of Allah, and Allah is omnipotent! I purpose to circuit seven circuits unto Almighty Allah, glorified and exalted!" This is technically called the Niyat (intention) of Tawaf. . . .

At the conclusion of the Tawaf it was deemed advisable to attempt to kiss the stone. For a time I stood looking in despair at the swarming crowd of Badawi and other pilgrims that besieged it. But the boy Mohammed was equal to the occasion. . . . [He] collected about half a dozen stalwart Meccans, with whose assistance, by sheer strength, we wedged our way into the thin and light-legged crowd. The Badawin turned round upon us like wild-cats, but they had no daggers. The season being autumn, they had not swelled themselves with milk for six months; and they had become such living mummies, that I could have managed single-handed half a dozen of them. After thus reaching the stone, despite popular indignation testified by impatient shouts, we monopolised the use of it for at least ten minutes. Whilst kissing it and rubbing hands and forehead upon it I narrowly observed it, and came away persuaded that it is an aerolite. It is curious that almost all travellers agree upon one point, namely, that the stone is volcanic.

Source: Burton, Richard. *Personal Narrative of a Pilgrimage to El Medinah and Meccah*. Vol. II. London: Longman, Brown, Green, Longmans, and Roberts, 1857, pp. 185–193.

What You Need to Know

This passage comes from Sir Richard Burton's *Personal Narrative of a Pilgrimage to El Medinah and Meccah*, published in 1857. Burton, a British scholar and explorer, traveled throughout Asia, Africa, and the Americas in the nineteenth century.

The nineteenth century represented a golden age of exploration. Unlike the state-sponsored, commercially oriented expeditions of the fifteenth and sixteenth centuries, however, the expeditions of the nineteenth century were often undertaken by individuals—sometimes sponsored by newspapers and magazines—eager for fame and possible fortune. Many, like Burton, wrote best sellers about their exploits.

The nineteenth century saw a great expansion of empire, as various European states exploited technical advances in transportation, medicine, and weaponry to establish colonies across Africa and Asia. The reading public of Europe was curious about these exotic lands and peoples coming under their control.

While the Arabian Peninsula where Mecca is located remained under the administration of the Muslim Ottoman Empire throughout the nineteenth century, Burton's ability to penetrate the holiest sanctum of Islam—at great personal risk to himself—was an act of imperialism in and of itself, a demonstration that the entire world was open to the white man.

A Closer Look

In 1853, Sir Richard Burton disguised himself as a Muslim to undertake the *hajj*, or pilgrimage to Islam's holy cities of Mecca and Medina. The *hajj* is one of the five pillars of Islam or acts of religious faith required of all Muslims. (The *hajj* is only required of those faithful who have the means to undertake the journey, which, in premodern times, could be quite long and arduous.)

Pilgrims from across the Islamic world in the nineteenth century typically made the *hajj* in groups. From India, where Burton served as an officer in the British East India Company, they would have sailed to the port of Jedda on the Red Sea, and then made their way by camel caravan the last 40 miles to Mecca. There, they would sleep where they could. Wealthier pilgrims rented out houses in the city, while most camped out in tent cities on the outskirts.

The *hajj* was a highly choreographed affair, which included a circumambulation of the Kaaba, Islam's holiest site, always in a counterclockwise direction, among other rituals. As Burton notes, even in the nineteenth century, the annual *hajj* attracted vast numbers of pilgrims who evinced their faith with fervor.

1 100 200 300 400 500 600 700 800 900 1000 1100 1200 1300 1400 1500 1600 1700 1800 1900 2000 CE

2.15.17 Account of the Great Sepoy Rebellion in India

British India
1857

Sunday, the 10th of May, dawned in peace and happiness. The early morning service, at the Cantoment Church, saw many assembled together, some never to meet on earth again. The day passed in quiet happiness; no thought of danger disturbed the serenity of that happy home. Alas! how differently closed the Sabbath which dawned so tranquilly. We were on the point of going to the evening service, when the disturbance commenced on the Native Parade ground. Shots and volumes of smoke told of what was going on: our servants begged us not to show ourselves, and urged the necessity of closing our doors, as the mob were approaching. Mr. Greathed, after loading his arms, took me to the terrace on the top of the house. . . .

The increasing tumult, thickening smoke, and fires all around, convinced us of the necessity of making our position as safe as we could; our guard were drawn up below. After dark, a party of insurgents rushed into the grounds, drove off the guard, and broke into the house, and set it on fire. On all sides we could hear them smashing and plundering, and calling loudly for us; it seemed once or twice as though footsteps were on the staircase, but no one came up. We owed much to the fidelity of our servants: had but one proved treacherous, our lives must have been sacrificed.

After some time, the flames got the ascendant, and the smoke became intolerable. Just as the fire threatened our destruction, we heard the voice of one of our servants calling to us to come down. At all risks, we descended. Our faithful servant, Golab Khan, seeing our perilous situation amidst the increasing flames, and that every moment was precious, with his characteristic presence of mind and quickness, had suddenly thought of a plan by which to draw away the mob, who, after having satisfied themselves with all the plunder they could get, were every moment becoming more eager in their search for us. He boldly went up to them, won their confidence by declaring himself of their faith, and willing to give us up into their hands. He assured them it was useless to continue their search in the house; but if they would all follow him, he would lead them to a hay-stack, where we had been concealed.

The plan succeeded. . . . The artillery depot, with its large enclosure, was converted into a fort, and became a home for every one; many families occupied the rooms in the long range of barracks, and the space between was filled with tents. Here we found shelter. . . . Our position was perfectly secure and well guarded, and became every day more strongly intrenched. Active preparations at the same time went on in organising a field force. At length all was in readiness, and the order for the march was hailed with delight; sanguine were our hopes that a fortnight, or at the most three weeks, would see our gallant little army on its victorious return. With many and oft-repeated good wishes and prayers, we saw them depart. On the night of the 27th May they marched away.

Source: Greathed, Elisa. Excerpt from Introduction. In Hervey Harris Greathed, *Letters Written during the Siege of Delhi*. London: Longman, Brown, Green, Longmans, and Roberts, 1858, pp. xiv–xviii, xx–xxi.

TIMELINE   2000 1900 1800 1700 1600 1500 1400 1300 1200 1100 1000 900 800 700 600 500 400 300 200 100 1 BCE

What You Need to Know

The accompanying document describes the first days of the great Indian rebellion of 1857 against the British presence in India. The British referred to it as the "Great Mutiny" or "Great Sepoy Rebellion," as it first arose among the sepoys, or native infantrymen of the British East Indian Company's army. Until the rebellion, the chartered corporation was a power unto itself in India, administering and ruling much of the subcontinent. This account was written by Elisa Greathed, the wife of the company's commissioner in Meerut, a city in northern India where the rebellion began.

Because the British were so few in number in India, they relied on sepoys to keep the peace. These soldiers, typically of the Brahmin class but also Muslims, were recruited in family groups, so that whole battalions consisted of related young men, whose immediate superiors were often more elder and respected members of a clan. The British often turned over the soldiers' pay to one of these noncommissioned officers, who would then purchase goods for his family of men.

This family- and clan-based organization created a strong *esprit de corps* in the ranks and made sepoy battalions extremely cohesive and effective on the battlefield. But, as the British learned to their dismay, this strong sense of unity could prove dangerous if the sepoys turned against their colonial masters, as they did in 1857.

A Closer Look

The immediate cause of the rebellion was a switch the British made to a new form of rifle cartridge, pregreased with animal fat. Because the soldier had to bite the cartridge to release the gunpowder, he would be in fact putting such animal fat to his lips. If the grease came from cattle, it offended Hindus, for whom the cow was sacred. If from pigs, it was *haram*, or prohibited, to Muslims. But, of course, there were larger underlying reasons as well, including decisions to reassign battalions to distance provinces, the removal of certain religious perquisites to Brahmin soldiers, and a general sense of discontent at the disruptions the British presence in India was causing to the families of soldiers, including land seizures, Christian missionary affronts to native religious values, and haughty colonial attitudes toward local peoples.

As Greathed describes, the rebels offered no quarter to British civilians. But, unnoted by the author, were the savage reprisals the British exacted, by means of remaining loyal troops, to the rebellious sepoys and their families and communities. Massacres occurred on both sides, as the rebellion spread across the subcontinent. Historians estimate some 100,000 rebellious sepoys were killed in the uprising, against roughly 1,000 to 1,500 British civilians. But the real cost may have been borne by Indian civilians, which may have numbered in the millions.

The rebellion led the British to reorganize the Indian army and for the British government to take direct control of the subcontinent's administration away from the East India Company and turn India into a crown colony, which it would remain until independence in 1947.

1 100 200 300 400 500 600 700 800 900 1000 1100 1200 1300 1400 1500 1600 1700 1800 1900 2000 CE

2.15.18 Life on the Oregon Trail

American West
1857

Although there is not much to cook, the difficulty and inconvenience in doing it amounts to a great deal—so by the time one has squatted around the fire and cooked bread and bacon, and made several dozen trips to and from the wagon—washed the dishes . . . and gotten things ready for an early breakfast, some of the others already have their night caps on—at any rate it is time to go to bed. In respect to women's work, the days are all very much the same—except when we stop . . . then there is washing to be done and light bread to make and all kinds of odd jobs. Some women have very little help about the camp, being obliged to get the wood and water . . . make camp fires, unpack at night and pack up in the morning—and if they are Missourians they have the milking to do if they are fortunate to have cows. I am lucky in having a Yankee for a husband, so am well waited on. . . .

When the sun was just peeping over the top of the mountain, there was suddenly heard a shot and blood curdling yell, and immediately the Indians we saw yesterday were seen riding at full speed directly toward the horses . . . father put his gun to his shoulder as though to shoot. . . . The Indians kept . . . circling . . . and halooning . . . bullets came whizzing through the camp. None can know the horror of it, who have not been similarly situated . . . [the Indians] did not come directly toward us, but all the time in a circular way, from one side of the road to the other, each time they passed, getting a little nearer, and occasionally firing a shot. . . . Father and Reel could stand it no longer, they must let those Indians see how far their Sharps rifles would carry. Without aiming to hit them, they made the earth fly. . . .

It is now 18 days since we have seen a train . . . [we] found the body of a nude woman on the bank of the slough. . . . A piece of hair rope was around her neck. . . . From appearances it was thought she had been tortured by being drawn back and forth through the slough, by this rope around her neck. The body was given the best burial that was possible, under the circumstances.

Source: Carpenter, Helen M. "On the Oregon Trail." *Overland Journey*. Newberry Microfilm 4–7. Compiled by M. J. Mattes, 1945; transcribed by Louise Ridge- 2/46, p. 2, entry for June 22, 1856. Reprinted in *Our Nation's Archive: The History of the United States in Documents*. Edited by Erik Bruun and Jay Crosby. New York: Black Dog, 1999, pp. 319–320.

TIMELINE   2000 1900 1800 1700 1600 1500 1400 1300 1200 1100 1000 900 800 700 600 500 400 300 200 100 1 BCE

What You Need to Know

This excerpt is from the journal of Helen Carpenter, a newly married woman who accompanied her husband and other pioneers on a wagon train to the Oregon Territory in 1857.

In the early 1800s, President Thomas Jefferson dispatched a scientific and exploratory team to report on the territory he had recently acquired through the Louisiana Purchase. The team went beyond the territory into the Oregon country, an area constituting the modern-day states of Oregon and Washington and the Canadian province of British Columbia, then disputed between Britain and the United States. The accounts of that country were highly positive, noting its rich farmlands, abundant rainfall, and thick stands of timber.

By the 1840s, thousands of pioneers were setting out on what came to be called the Oregon Trail, eventually forcing Washington and London to reach an agreement to divide up the territory. The trail began on the western bank of the Missouri, at Independence, and continued some 1,500 miles to the Willamette Valley of Oregon. Wagon trains averaged about 12 to 15 miles a day, meaning that the journey took more than three months, and as long as six. When gold was discovered in California in 1848, the trail added a fork in western Wyoming, with a southern branch leading across the Sierras to the mining camps.

A Closer Look

For American women in the nineteenth century, daily life was an endless round of domestic chores—cooking, cleaning, sewing, and even manufacturing the basic provisions of life, such as butter, soap, and so on. On the Oregon Trail, the tasks were made that much harder by having to be done out in the open with limited equipment and with the ever-present need to keep moving. There was also, Carpenter notes, the fear of attack by Native American peoples resisting intruders on their land.

Days began early on the trail, with a trumpet blast well before sunrise. Men and boys went out to round up grazing cattle, while the women started fires and cooked up bacon, porridge, and "Johnny Cakes" (pancakes). Cleaning dishes and folding up bedrolls followed, as the men pulled down tents and repacked wagons.

By just after dawn, the wagons were moving again, and would not stop, other than briefly for lunch, until about 5 PM, at which time wagons had to be unloaded, tents pitched, and suppers prepared. Just as full darkness fell, the wagon train went to sleep, except for those scheduled for guard duty.

1 100 200 300 400 500 600 700 800 900 1000 1100 1200 1300 1400 1500 1600 1700 1800 1900 2000 CE

2.15.19 Foraging for Food during the American Civil War

United States
1860s

Here was one other source from which soldiers—at least, some soldiers—replenished their larder, or added to its variety. The means employed to accomplish this end was known as *Foraging*, which is generally understood to mean a seeking after food, whether for man or beast, and appropriating to one's own use whatsoever is found in this line, wheresoever it is found in an enemy's country. It took the army some time to adopt this mode of increasing its stores. This arose from the fact that early in the war many of the prominent government and military officers thought that a display of force with consideration shown the enemy's property would win the South back to her allegiance to the Union; but that if, on the other hand, they devastated property and appropriated personal effects, it would only embitter the enemy, unite them more solidly, and greatly prolong the war; so that for many months after war began, Northern troops were prohibited from seizing fence-rails, poultry, swine, straw, or any similar merchandise in which they might under some circumstances feel a personal interest; and whenever straw-stacks and fences were appropriated by order of commanding officers, certificates to that effect were given the owners, who might expect at some time to be reimbursed. But the Rebellion waxed apace, and outgrew all possibility of certificating everybody whose property was entered upon or absorbed, and furthermore it came to be known that many who had received certificates were in collusion with the enemy, so that the issuance of these receipts gradually grew beautifully less.

Then, there was another obstacle in the way of a general adoption of foraging as an added means of support. It was the presence in the army of a large number of men who had learned the ten commandments, and could not, with their early training and education, look upon this taking to themselves the possessions of others without license as any different from stealing. These soldiers would neither forage nor share in the fruits of foraging. It can be readily imagined, then, that when one of this class commanded a regiment the diversion of foraging was not likely to be very general with his men. But as the war wore on, and it became more evident that such tender regard for Rebel property only strengthened the enemy and weakened the cause of the Union, conscientious scruples stepped to the rear, and the soldier who had them at the end of the war was a curiosity indeed.

Source: Billings, John Davis. *Hardtack and Coffee: Or, The Unwritten Story of Army Life*. Boston: G. M. Smith & Company, 1887, pp. 231–232.

What You Need to Know

The accompanying document comes from an 1887 memoir—*Hardtack and Coffee: Or, The Unwritten Story of Army Life*—written by a Union soldier from Massachusetts named John D. Billings, who served in the eastern theater of the war and was awarded a medal of honor for his valor at the 1863 Battle of Gettysburg. The excerpt here discusses foraging, that is, the practice of soldiers living off the land or, in this case, off the food and other property of the enemy.

When the Civil War began in April 1861, both North and South expected it to be over quickly, with their side victorious. It did not work out that way, of course. While the North possessed greater numbers and economic might, the South had better officers and the strategic advantage of simply having to defend itself, rather than capture enemy territory.

By 1863, it had become apparent that this would be a war of attrition. Northern generals, most notably Ulysses S. Grant and William T. Sherman, came to the conclusion that the only way to win was to destroy the South's capacity to make war, and so it embarked on a policy of total destruction. Although the main purpose of foraging was to supply Union soldiers with additional food and materiel, it also served to destroy the Southern economy and thus its will and ability to fight on.

A Closer Look

Union soldiers were generally well provisioned, a testament to the great productive agricultural and industrial capacity of the North. Both in camp and on the march, the fighting man would be provisioned with meat—in the form of salt pork—beans, rice, sugar, coffee, salt, and hardtack, a kind of preserved hard bread. He also typically received a ration of soap and candles.

Early in the war, the soldiers would have to cook the rations themselves. But this proved inefficient and often unappetizing, as many of the young men had no experience preparing food, a female activity at home. Eventually, the army assigned cooks to most units, although some soldiers were fed by private commissaries that trailed the units as they moved about the country.

But when supply lines got stretched as the army moved into enemy territory and rations grew scarcer, it became necessary to forage, although, as Billings relates, there were a number of political and moral obstacles to doing so. At first, Northerners did not want to alienate Southerners, causing them to keep fighting. In addition, foraging seemed all too much like stealing, something these young men had been taught at home and in church never to do.

1   100 200 300   400   500   600   700   800   900   1000 1100 1200 1300   1400   1500   1600   1700   1800   1900   2000 CE

2.15.20 A Vietnamese Appeal to Resist French Occupation

Vietnam
1862

Let us now consider our situation with the French today.

We are separated from them by thousands of mountains and seas.

By hundreds of differences in our daily customs.

Although they were very confident in their copper battleships surmounted by chimneys,

Although they had a large quantity of steel rifles and lead bullets,

These things did not prevent the loss of some of their best generals in these last years, when they attacked our frontier in hundreds of battles. . . .

Our country has always been known as a land of deities; shall we now permit a horde of dogs and goats to stain it?

The moral obligations binding a king to his subjects, parents to their children, and husbands to their wives were highly respected. Everyone enjoyed the most peaceful relationships.

Our customs and habits were so perfect that in our country, in our ancestors' tombs, and in our homes, all things were in a proper state.

But from the moment they arrived with their ill luck,

Happiness and peace seem to have departed from everywhere.

Our heart cannot restrain its sadness when we look at the incense burner and the bowl of water: offerings on the altar.

A foot of our land and a shoot of our vegetables remind us of the humiliation our country endures.

Righteous conduct turns into a misdeed in their eyes.

Honest people become the basest culprits in their hands.

They execute our brave and loyal defenders while they feed and cherish gangs of scoundrels and hooligans.

Source: Hoang Ngoc Phach and Le Tri Vien. *So tuyen Van tho yeu nuoc va cachmang* (*A Preliminary Selection of Patriotic and Revolutionary Literature*). Hanoi: 1959, pp. 1, 95–100; Dinh Giang and Ca Van Thinh. *Tho van yeu nuoc Nam Bo cuoi the ky thu XIX* (*Patriotic Literature of South Vietnam in the Second Half of the 19th Century*). Hanoi: 1962, pp. 241–247.

TIMELINE   2000 1900 1800 1700 1600 1500 1400 1300 1200 1100 1000 900 800 700 600 500 400 300 200 100 1 BCE

What You Need to Know

This appeal or rather an amalgam of two appeals, believed to have been written by patriotic scholars, calls on resistance to the French in Vietnam. The French had invaded the country in 1858, gradually extending their control over much of Indochina by the end of the century.

Under the Nguyen dynasty, the last in Vietnam's history and which the French eventually propped up, the country was a starkly divided land, with an educated elite living in comfort in the nation's cities and an impoverished peasantry struggling in the countryside. Making things worse were heavy taxes imposed by the Emperor Tu Duc, who had reigned since 1847, to support his lavish court, which he had moved from Hanoi to Hue, building a palace complex there. This had triggered peasant uprisings up and down Vietnam in the mid-nineteenth century. Where the scholars saw the emperor as a symbol of national unity against outside forces, the peasantry saw him as the cause of their poverty and repression. It is no wonder that the appeal the scholars issued fell on deaf ears. It would not be until the first half of the twentieth century, when a new, more progressive-oriented nationalism was promulgated that ordinary Vietnamese began to stand up to the French.

A Closer Look

The appeals were written in 1862 at a time when France was first beginning to occupy the country, ostensibly to protect Vietnamese Christians who had been converted to the faith by French Catholic missionaries since the early years of the century. While the scholars writing the appeals believed that they were tapping into a deep fount of Vietnamese nationalism, they were unaware of the changes their society was undergoing. Confucian deference to social superiors and the emperor was already being undermined, and not just by missionaries and French forces.

In their appeal, the writers speak of traditional Vietnamese ways that the French occupation threatened. Under the Nguyen dynasty, the country had very much turned inward, averse to outside influences. Traditional values, based on Confucian principles, dictated Vietnamese life. Societal harmony was anchored in the obligations and duties every person had to one another—subject to emperor, wife to husband, children to parents. Ancestors were worshipped as a validation of these social relations, showing that they were anchored in the ancient past.

The intrusion of outside forces and the conversion of increasing numbers of Vietnamese to Christianity—which preached an equality of souls under God—threatened the social and political order of Nguyen dynasty Vietnam, which served the scholars well. As part of Confucian principles, they were seen as the rightful administrators of the country and so fought to ward off outside influences, such as the French.

1 100 200 300 400 500 600 700 800 900 1000 1100 1200 1300 1400 1500 1600 1700 1800 1900 2000 CE

2.15.21 Battle Hymn of the Republic

United States
1862

Mine eyes have seen the glory of the coming of the Lord:
He is trampling out the vintage where the grapes of wrath are stored;
He has loosed the fateful lightning of His terrible swift sword:
His truth is marching on.

(Chorus)
Glory! Glory! Hallelujah!
Glory! Glory! Hallelujah!
Glory! Glory! Hallelujah!
His truth is marching on.
I have seen Him in the watch-fires of a hundred circling camps,
They have builded Him an altar in the evening dews and damps;
I can read His righteous sentence by the dim and flaring lamps:
His day is marching on.
(Chorus)
I have read a fiery gospel writ in burnished rows of steel:
"As ye deal with my contemners, so with you my grace shall deal;
Let the Hero, born of woman, crush the serpent with his heel,
Since God is marching on."
(Chorus)
He has sounded form the trumpet that shall never call retreat;
He is sifting out the hearts of men before His judgment-seat:
Oh, be swift, my soul, to answer Him! be jubilant, my feet!
Our God is marching on.
(Chorus)
In the beauty of the lilies Christ was born across the sea,
With a glory in his bosom that transfigures you and me:
As he died to make men holy, let us die to make men free,
While God is marching on.
(Chorus)

Source: Howe, Julia Ward. "The Battle Hymn of the Republic." *Atlantic Monthly* IX, no. LII (February, 1862): 10.

TIMELINE   2000 1900 1800 1700 1600 1500 1400 1300 1200 1100 1000 900 800 700 600 500 400 300 200 100 1 BCE

What You Need to Know

These are the lyrics to the "Battle Hymn of the Republic," first printed in the *Atlantic Monthly* magazine in early 1862 and written by Julia Ward Howe, a Boston poet and abolitionist.

Howe was an active member of the abolitionist cause, the pre–Civil War movement to end slavery throughout the country. Such a position was most decidedly a minority one in the North. (Support for abolitionism in the antebellum South could land a person in jail or worse.) Although antislavery sentiment grew in the North in the years leading up to the Civil War, it was largely aimed at preventing that institution's spread into the West. Northerners felt that it would close off virgin territory to free farmers. But ending slavery in the South was seen as threatening, as it might unleash a tide of free blacks into the North who would undercut white workers' wages and force them to live alongside people they deemed racially inferior. Abolitionist meetings were frequently broken up by mobs, and a few abolitionists, such as publisher Elijah Lovejoy of Illinois, were murdered.

But the abolitionists were nothing if not determined. They kept the issue at the forefront of national politics. When the Civil War broke out, they pressured politicians and propagandized to make ending slavery—rather than simple preservation of the Union—the main objective of the struggle. Ward's lyrics were part of that successful effort.

A Closer Look

While the lyrics were written by Howe, the music, which was first notated in 1856, was derived from tunes popular at Christian revival camp meetings. Many Union soldiers, particularly in the early years of the Civil War, when the army was largely made up of volunteers, were familiar with such revival meetings; revivalism and antislavery politics were closely allied. They adopted the tune, the tempo of which is ideal for marching, and added lyrics of their own. These were dedicated to John Brown, who may have been a real sergeant. But soon they became associated with the historical John Brown, the abolitionist who, shortly before the war began, was hanged in Virginia for trying to foment a slave rebellion.

In 1862, Howe visited a Union Army camp and decided that the lyrics—which included a reference to a body "mouldering in the grave"—were not suitably uplifting and inspiring for such a noble cause as ending slavery and preserving the Union. The new lyrics caught on, first among more religious units and then throughout the massive Union Army, and became the most popular marching song of the war.

2.15.22 Cuban Cigar Box Label

Cuba
1865

Credit: Transcendental Graphics/Getty Images

What You Need to Know

This is a 1865 cigar box label from a Havana cigar factory known as La Indiana, Spanish for Indian woman. The image on the cover shows an Indian princess striding through a field of tobacco plants.

Tobacco is native to the Americas, and was widely smoked by indigenous peoples throughout hemisphere, including Cuba, long before Columbus's arrival. This was typically done in pipes, although Columbus notes in his journal that he saw the Taino people of the Caribbean smoking tobacco leaf rolled into palm and plantain leaves. Europeans, too, long preferred smoking tobacco in pipes but also smoked cigars from early on, though they used tobacco leaves themselves as a wrapper. By the early nineteenth century, however, most smokers in Europe and America enjoyed their tobacco in the form of cigars. This led to a ramping up of production in Cuba and elsewhere that brought prices down, further enhancing demand. By 1850, annual consumption in the United States alone topped 300 million, much of it coming from Cuba.

A Closer Look

Unlike sugar production, Cuba's largest industry, cigar making was not dominated by large factories and firms. Instead, Havana and other Cuban cities were dotted with small workshops, where a few dozen persons would sit at long tables making the product. Such workers—and both men and women labored in these workshops—were highly skilled. Producing a high-quality cigar required a good eye for the best tobacco leaf and skilled hands to roll the leaf tightly enough to produce a cigar that smoked evenly and in which the ember would not keep going out.

Cigar workers saw themselves as an elite within the laboring community—not just manual workers but educated ones. Typically, cigar workers would pay the salary of a *lector*, or reader, who would read to them as they worked. The readings could be light fare or, just as often, serious works of economics and philosophy, often of a left-wing bent. Cigar workers were also highly organized into unions, both in Cuban and in the Florida cigar-producing cities, such as Tampa, where Cuban emigres lived and worked.

Meanwhile, the Cuban industry also responded to demand by producing a wide variety of cigars for every pocketbook. This allowed cigar smoking to catch on among all classes of people. At the same time, cigars were largely the preserve of men. Indeed, indulging in the habit became a male ritual, indulged in all male saloons or in high-class drawing rooms after dinner, away from the women.

2.15.23 Description of a Berber Camp in Morocco

Morocco
1870

The duar is usually a settlement of ten, fifteen or twenty families, connected by some bond of relationship, each family having its own tent. These tents stand in two parallel lines, about thirty feet apart, so that a sort of rectangular space is left in the middle, open at both ends. The tents are almost invariably alike; they are made out of a large piece of black or chocolate-colored material, woven from the fibre of dwarf palms or from goats' or camels' hair; this is stretched over upright stakes or thick reeds, connected by a wooden cross-piece, on which the roof rests, their shape still resembling that of the habitations of the Numidians of the time of Jugurtha, which Sallust compares to overturned ships with their keels in the air. During the autumn and winter the covering is drawn down to the ground and held in place by means of cords and pegs, so as to effectually exclude both wind and rain. In summer a wide aperture is left all around, so that the air may circulate freely, and this is protected by a low hedge of rushes and dried brambles. Owing to these precautions the tent of the daar is much cooler in summer and better protected through the rainy season than the same class of Moorish dwellings in the cities, since the latter are without either proper ventilation or glazed windows. The maximum height of a tent is about eight feet, the maximum length about ten. . . . A partition made of rushes divides the dwelling in two parts, in one of which the father and mother sleep, and in the other the children and the rest of the family. A few osier mats, a brightly-colored and arabesqued wooden box, containing clothing; a small looking-glass, manufactured in Trieste or Venice; a high tripod, made of canes and covered with a haik, under which the family bathing is done; a couple of stones for grinding wheat; a loom, such as was used in the days of Abraham; a rough tin lantern, a few earthenware jugs, a few goat-skins, a few dishes, a distaff, a saddle, a gun, a big dagger, such is the entire furnishing of one of these dwellings. . . .

The life of the daar is of the simplest description. At daybreak every one gets up, says his prayers, the cows are milked, the butter made and the sour milk that is left, drunk; for drinking-cups they use conch and limpet-shells, which they purchase from people living on the coast. Then the men go to their work in the fields, not returning until towards nightfall. The women meanwhile carry wood and water, grind flour, spin the coarse fabrics in which they and their husbands are clothed, twist rope for their tents from the fibre of the dwarf palm; send their husbands' mid-day food to them and prepare the Kuskussú [couscous—a coarsely ground pasta popular in North Africa] for the evening. The Kuskussú is mixed with beans, gourds, onions and other vegetables; sometimes it is sweetened, spiced and dressed with a meat sauce, and on feast days meat is served with it. On the return of the men, supper is eaten, and at sunset everyone goes to bed; but sometimes one of the old men will tell a story after supper, seated in the middle of the family circle. Throughout the night the daar is plunged in profound silence and darkness; only a few families will occasionally leave lanterns burning before their tents to guide any wayfarer who may have missed his path.

Source: De Amicis, Edmondo. *Morocco: Its People and Places*. Translated by Maria Hornor Lansdale. Vol. I. Philadelphia: Henry L. Coates and Company, 1897, pp. 207–209.

TIMELINE   2000 1900 1800 1700 1600 1500 1400 1300 1200 1100 1000 900 800 700 600 500 400 300 200 100 1 BCE

What You Need to Know

This document comes from the writings of Edmondo De Amicis, an Italian journalist who traveled to Morocco in 1870. In this excerpt, he describes life in a *duar*, a camp of seminomads consisting of about a dozen or so families.

Duars largely consisted of Berber people, the original inhabitants of North Africa. In the seventh and eighth centuries, Arab armies conquered the region, bringing settlers with them, who soon came to dominate the urban centers of Morocco. While converting to Islam and often intermarrying with Arabs, the Berbers of the countryside maintained their own language, still spoken today, and their own distinctive culture. The term *Berber* was given to these people by the Arabs, who adapted the Greek word *barbarus*, or "foreigners," the origin of the English word *barbarians*. For their part, the Berbers referred to themselves as the *mazign'en*, or "free people," as they prided themselves on resisting the authority of their new Arab rulers.

A Closer Look

The Berbers were largely seminomadic peoples in the late nineteenth century, as De Amicis relates. In traditional Berber communities, men took care of the animals and sometimes farmed while women were in charge of handicrafts, which were often sold in town *souks*, or marketplaces, thereby earning the money needed to buy some of the European goods the Italian journalist observes in the *duar* he visits.

Together, these families represented a clan that traced its origins to a common ancestor in the distant past. That is, they considered themselves related but not so intimately that they could not marry among themselves. In fact, many members came from other *duars* and were adopted into the clan through marriage. Members of the *duar* lived seminomadic lives. During part of the year, they would settle in a fixed spot, where they could tend crops. At other times, they roamed their semidesert environment in search of pasturage for their cattle, goats, and other animals.

As De Amicis relates, life in the *duar* was a mix of the communal and the private. Every family had its own tent or tents and cooked for itself. But farmland was communally worked, with the crop being divvied up among the members of the *duar*. The community also lived on the edge of the emerging global trading system of the late nineteenth century. They largely lived off the food they themselves grew or raised and their tents were handmade from materials at hand. Yet De Amicis also notes the presence of items from afar, including mirrors manufactured in his homeland of Italy.

1 100 200 300   400   500   600   700   800   900   1000 1100 1200 1300   1400   1500   1600   1700 1800 1900 2000 CE

2.15.24 Portrait of a Maori Man

New Zealand
ca. 1875

Credit: Hulton Archive/Getty Images

What You Need to Know

The photo on the opposite page is of a Maori man, dating to around 1875. While the man, who appears to be elderly, is dressed in Western clothing, his faced is covered in the tattooing typical of his people.

The islands of New Zealand were the last large landmasses on Earth to be inhabited by humans, when the Polynesian ancestors of the Maori first sailed there around the year 1300 CE. The islands were first encountered by Europeans several centuries later. By the early nineteenth century, the British had begun to settle them. In 1840, the major Maori chiefs signed the Treaty of Waitangi, incorporating the islands into the British Empire. The treaty granted the Maori equal citizenship with British settlers.

But as settlers from Europe poured in during the nineteenth century, Maori lands were expropriated and the colony's economy and politics fell under settler control. This resulted in warfare that led to further land expropriation. Meanwhile, educators and reformers, many of them influenced by evangelical Christianity, attempted to wean Maori youth from their indigenous culture in boarding schools.

A Closer Look

Known as *ta moko* in the Maori language, such tattoos were made not by puncturing the skin, as is done in Western tattooing, but through the use of a chisel, known as an *uhi*. These were typically made from the bones of seabirds, which were strapped onto a wooden handle. Soot from the burning of fossilized resin—itself the residue of ancient forests long since cut down by earlier Maoris—was then placed on the tip of the *uhi* and gently tapped into the skin with a mallet.

Ta moko was done for several reasons. Typically, Maori boys and girls would receive their first tattoo as an initiation rite marking their passage to adulthood. The *ta moko* were applied to both body and face, although on women's faces it usually did not ascend above the lips. The tattoos served as a kind of visual history of the person and served as his or her identity card. By studying the tattoo, an observer could tell the person's social ranking and the clan they belonged to. They might also learn, for a man, what kind of warrior he was, and for a woman, how many children she had given birth to. Beyond providing this history and identity, the *ta moko* were seen as aesthetically enhancing a person's looks, making them more attractive to the opposite sex.

Tattooing was seen as a pagan custom by the British and so discouraged. As many Maori assimilated to colonial life, they gave up the practice. As this occurred, the techniques for making them went into disuse and became largely forgotten. It has only been with the revival of Maori culture since World War II, that the practice of *ta moko* has come back in a significant way.

1   100   200   300   400   500   600   700   800   900   1000   1100   1200   1300   1400   1500   1600   1700   1800   1900   2000 CE

2.15.25 Parsi Funerary Practices

British India
1878

The tower selected for the present funeral was one in which other members of the same family had before been laid. The two bearers speedily unlocked the door, reverently conveyed the body of the child into the interior, and, unseen by any one, laid it uncovered in one of the open stone receptacles nearest the central well. In two minutes they re-appeared with the empty bier and white cloth. But scarcely had they closed the door when a dozen vultures swooped down upon the body, and were rapidly followed by flights of others. In five minutes more we saw the satiated birds fly back and lazily settle down again upon the parapet. They had left nothing behind but a skeleton. Meanwhile the bearers were seen to enter a building shaped like a huge barrel. There, as the Secretary informed me, they changed their clothes and washed themselves. Shortly afterwards we saw them come out and deposit their cast-off funeral garments on a stone-receptacle near at hand. Not a thread leaves the garden, lest it should carry defilement into the city. Perfectly new garments are supplied at each funeral. In a fortnight, or at most four weeks, the same bearers return, and with gloved hands and implements resembling tongs place the dry skeleton in the central well. There the bones find their last resting-place, and there the dust of whole generations of Parsis commingling is left undisturbed for centuries.

The revolting sight of the gorged vultures made me turn my back to the towers with ill-concealed abhorrence. I asked the Secretary how it was possible to become reconciled to such a usage. His reply was nearly in the following words: "Our Prophet Zoroaster, who lived 6,000 years ago, taught us to regard the elements as symbols of the Deity. Earth, fire, water, he said, ought never, under any circumstances, to be defiled by contact with putrefying flesh. Naked, he said, we came into the world, and naked we ought to leave it. But the decaying particles of our bodies should be dissipated as rapidly as possible, and in such a way that neither Mother Earth nor the beings she supports should be contaminated in the slightest degree. In fact our Prophet was the greatest of health officers, and, following his sanitary laws, we build our towers on the tops of hills, above all human habitations. We spare no expense in constructing them of the hardest materials, and we expose our putrescent bodies in open stone receptacles, resting on 14 feet of solid granite, not necessarily to be consumed by vultures, but to be dissipated in the speediest possible manner, and without the possibility of polluting the earth or contaminating a single living being dwelling thereon. God, indeed, sends the vultures, and, as a matter of fact, these birds do their appointed work much more expeditiously than millions of insects would do if we committed our bodies to the ground. In a sanitary point of view nothing can be more perfect than our plan. Even the rain water which washes our skeletons is conducted by channels into purifying charcoal. Here in these five towers rest the bones of all the Parsis that have lived in Bombay for the last 200 years. We form a united body in life, and we are united in death. Even our leader, Sir Jamsetjee, likes to feel that when he dies he will be reduced to perfect equality with the poorest and humblest of the Parsi community."

Source: Monier-Williams, Monier. *Modern India and the Indians: Being a Series of Impressions, Notes, and Essays*. London: Trubner and Company, 1878, pp. 61–62.

TIMELINE   2000 1900 1800 1700 1600 1500 1400 1300 1200 1100 1000 900 800 700 600 500 400 300 200 100 1 BCE

What You Need to Know

The accompanying document comes from the writings of Monier Monier-Williams, an Oxford scholar of Sanskrit, born in India of British parents. In this excerpt, he describes the funeral customs of the Parsi people.

The Parsi were originally from Persia; indeed, their very name means "Persian" in Farsi, the language of Iran. When they came to South Asia around the year 1000, they settled in Gujarat, in the western part of India. The arrival of the British dramatically altered their history. In the late seventeenth century, the British East India Company took control of Bombay and soon developed a policy of religious tolerance. Being of a tiny minority religion, many Parsi decided to migrate there.

A trading people through much of their history, the Parsi, who as a minority people involved in trade, were more open to outside influences than their Hindu and Muslim compatriots. They learned the language and economic practices of the English, thriving commercially under British rule. For their part, the British preferred dealing with them. This was partially for racial reasons—the Parsi are fairer skinned than most Indians—and because they were more assimilated to British society. The Parsi also remained a people apart, choosing to live and marry among their own. This created a close-knit community, ideal for commerce. A Parsi felt he could trust another Parsi in business. Even today, the Parsi are disproportionately represented among India's middle and upper classes.

A Closer Look

The Parsi people at that time mostly lived—and still live—in and around the city of Bombay (now Mumbai). The Parsi are neither Hindu nor Muslim but practitioners of Zorastrianism, a pre-Islamic faith of Persia, from which they migrated near the end of the first millennium CE.

The Parsi believe that the world is divided into what is pure (good) and what is polluted (evil). Pollution can only be held at bay so long, eventually felling all of us with death. Thus, funerals are elaborate affairs for the Parsi, so that the pollution of the corpse does not affect the purity of the living. Traditional Parsi homes in the nineteenth century had a special room set aside for the dead. There, fire and rituals were employed to confine the pollution of death. Special prayers were said to purify the soul of the deceased. A line was drawn around the body; no one was to cross it, except for those who carried the corpse to funeral towers, where the flesh was eaten by vultures and the bones bleached by the sun, purifying them in the process.

2.15.26 Digging for Diamonds in South Africa

South Africa
1880

After our dinner we walked along the bank and found another "river" digger, though this man's claim might perhaps be removed a couple of hundred yards from the water. He was an Englishman, and we stood awhile and talked to him. He had one Kafir with him to whom he paid 7s. a week and his food, and he too had found one or more stones which he showed us,—just enough to make the place tenable. He had got upon an old digging which he was clearing out lower. He had, however, in one place reached the hard stone at the bottom, in, or below which there could be no diamonds. There was, however, a certain quantity of diamondiferous matter left, and as he had already found stones he thought that it might pay him to work through the remainder. He was a most good-humored, well-mannered man, with a pleasant fund of humor. When I asked him of his fortune generally at the diggings, he told us among other things that he had broken his shoulder bone at the diggings, which he displayed to us in order that we might see how badly the surgeon had used him. He had no pain to complain of,—or weakness; but his shoulder had not been made beautiful. "And who did it?" said the gentleman who was our Amphytrion at the picnic and is himself one of the leading practitioners of the Fields. "I think it was one Dr——," said the digger, naming our friend whom no doubt he knew. I need not say that the doctor loudly disclaimed ever having had previous acquaintance with the shoulder.

The Kafir was washing the dirt in a rough cradle, separating the stones from the dust, and the owner, as each sieveful was brought to him, threw out the stones on his table and sorted them through with the eternal bit of slate or iron formed into the shape of a trowel. For the chance of a sieveful one of our party offered him half a crown,—which he took. I was glad to see it all inspected without a diamond, as had there been anything good the poor fellow's disappointment must have been great. That halfcrown was probably all that he would earn during the week,—all that he would earn perhaps for a month. Then there might come three or four stones in one day. I should think that the tedious despair of the vacant days could hardly be compensated by the triumph of the lucky minute. These "river" diggers have this in their favor,—that the stones found near the river are more likely to be white and pure than those which are extracted from the mines. The Vaal itself in the neighborhood of Barkly is pretty,—with rocks in its bed and islands and trees on its banks. But the country around, and from thence to Kimberley, which is twenty-four miles distant, is as ugly as flatness, barrenness, and sand together can make the face of the earth.

Source: Trollope, Anthony. Excerpt from "The Story of the Diamond Fields." In *The Transvaal. Griqualand West. The Orange Free State. Native Territories.* Vol. II: South Africa. London: Chapman and Hall, 1878, pp. 166–168.

TIMELINE   2000 1900 1800 1700 1600 1500 1400 1300 1200 1100 1000 900 800 700 600 500 400 300 200 100 1 BCE

What You Need to Know

This excerpt on diamond mining in late nineteenth-century South Africa comes from Anthony Trollope, the famed British novelist who visited the colony a little more than a dozen years after diamonds were discovered there in 1867.

Diamonds and, later and more significantly, gold transformed South Africa forever. The modern history of the country begins with a Dutch settlement around Cape Town in the mid-seventeenth century, as a supply station for fleets sailing to the East Indies. The British seized the colony during the Napoleonic Wars of the early 1800s. Local Dutch farmers, known as Boers, chafed under British rule and flocked to the interior in the mid-nineteenth century, beyond the Vaal River, a territory that came to be called the Transvaal. There, they came into conflict with Zulus and other native people.

The discovery of diamonds and gold led to a mass influx of miners from around the world, and to British annexation of the Transvaal. In the 1880s and 1890s, the Boers fought back but were eventually forced to surrender, although retaining significant self-government. As mining operations became more sophisticated, requiring vast labor forces, native Africans were recruited, leaving the Boers and English as the ruling elite of the colony, a situation that would continue after South Africa achieved independence from Britain in 1910.

A Closer Look

Kimberly, deep in the South African veldt, or prairie, had the richest diamond deposit ever found. Still, that did not mean they were there for the picking. On average, there was one carat worth of diamond for every 2,000 pounds of rock. This meant miners had to sledgehammer for days on end until the rock was reduced to pebbles, which were then passed through a sieve and finally picked over to find the telltale glimmer of diamond.

What was astonishing about Kimberly was that the diamond bearing rock never seemed to end. Soon, miners were descending on ladders into deeper and deeper donut-shaped holes. It was safer to dig in rings. To raise funds to continue their operations, miners divided up their claims so that the ever-descending holes were full of men swinging pickaxes side by side. Not surprisingly, this led to frequent injuries, as Trollope relates. They also hired local Africans, whom they called Kaffirs, from an Arabic term for nonbelievers. Originally a neutral term, it is now considered very derogatory. Africans were also allowed to work their own claims, at least in the early years of the mining, but these were usually isolated ones with little prospect of finding riches. And should an African strike a good claim, they were usually quickly evicted from it by white miners.

Still, few struck it rich, although many stayed on to work for the larger mining concerns that took over the industry as it became more expensive to tap deeper veins. Initially, the miners were largely single men, but eventually some brought their wives and families to join them.

1   100   200   300   400   500   600   700   800   900   1000   1100   1200   1300   1400   1500   1600   1700   1800   1900   2000 CE

2.15.27 Colonial Boarding Schools in West Africa

French West Africa
1890s

It is regarded as futile to attempt to get any real hold over the children unless they are removed from the influence of the country fashions that surround them in their village homes; therefore the schools are boarding; hence the entire care of the children, including feeding and clothing, falls on the missionary.

The French government has made things harder by decreeing that the children should be taught French. It does not require that evangelistic work should be carried on in French, but that if foreign languages are taught, that language shall be French first. The general feeling of the missionaries is against this, because of the great difficulty in teaching the native this delicate and highly complex language. . . .

The native does not see things in this light, and half the time comes only to learn, what he calls "sense," *i.e.* white man's ways and language, which will enable him to trade with greater advantage. Still, I think the French government is right, from what I have seen in our own possessions of the disadvantage, expense, and inconvenience of the bulk of the governed not knowing the language of their governors, both parties having therefore frequently to depend on native interpreters; and native interpreters are "deceitful above all things and desperately wicked" occasionally, and the just administration of the country under these conditions is almost impossible. . . .

But to return to the Mission Evangelique schools. This mission does not undertake technical instruction. All the training the boys get is religious and scholastic. The girls fare somewhat better, for they get in addition instruction from the mission ladies in sewing, washing, and ironing, and for the rest of it they have an uncommonly pleasant and easy time, which they most bitterly regret as past when they go to their husbands, for husbands they each of them have.

Source: Kingsley, Mary Henrietta. *Travels in West Africa: Congo Francais, Corisco and Cameroons*. London: Macmillan and Company, Ltd., 1897, pp. 205–207.

What You Need to Know

In the early 1890s, the British ethnographer and travel writer Mary Kingsley traveled to Africa, writing of her experiences in her 1897 book *Travels in West Africa*. This excerpt touches on her observations of the boarding schools established by French colonialists for African youths.

Until the late nineteenth century, the European colonial enterprise in Africa was of a limited extent. Other than the slave trade, Europeans largely kept their distance from the tropical parts of the continent, fearing a host of diseases—the West African coast was known as the "white man's graveyard"—and well-armed tribes. But advances in public health measures and weaponry altered the equation. By the late 1880s, so many European countries were staking claims to the region that a conference was held in Berlin to sort out who got what. Needless to say, no Africans were invited.

Previously, European governments could claim ownership of a swath of Africa by merely showing that their nationals had explored the territory in question. After Berlin, it was decided that "pacification" was required to make a legitimate claim to ownership. This meant subjugating the local peoples militarily and politically. To do this effectively, and to exploit the resources for which the Europeans had come in the first place, the colonizers needed effective government, hence the establishment of native schools.

A Closer Look

As Kingsley notes in the accompanying excerpt, and not without a measure of criticism, the education of West Africans was largely along European lines. They learned to read and write European languages and they studied European history and ideas. One French text for African students famously included the line: "our ancestors, the Gauls." At the same time, African customs, traditions, and languages were disparaged. Severe punishment was doled out to any student who insisted on using his or her African name rather than the European one given to them by the teachers, most of whom were Christian missionaries. Indeed, colonial authorities preferred boarding schools because they allowed the student to be removed from influences of family and community.

The schools were largely set up to provide a corps of low-level civil servants Europeans could use to help administer their colonies. Thus, the French insisted on teaching the students in French and kept them to strict schedules, so that they would become more assimilated into the work regimes of colonial governments and enterprises.

Still, many African parents were eager to send their children to such schools, recognizing that in the new colonial order, such an education offered their children opportunities for a better life.

1   100   200   300   400   500   600   700   800   900   1000   1100   1200   1300   1400   1500   1600   1700   1800   1900   2000 CE

2.15.28 An American Missionary Describes Chinese Foot-Binding

China
1897

I am doing what little I can in my small sphere to show an applied Christianity. In the first place, I try always to be neat in dress. This invariably calls out complimentary remarks. The Chinese women at once compare my pretty and fresh, though cheap, dress with their silken (and generally soiled) robes. Then they notice my clean, short finger nails, and contrast them with their long ones,—often a finger in length,—which indicate that they are ladies of leisure. They at once want to know *why* I dress so differently from them. It is an easy step to tell them that God, who made us, has put women into the world for *use*, and not merely to live to adorn our bodies, and that there are many poor suffering children and others who need our help. If we have such long nails and bound feet, we cannot go about to help them.

They all assent to this, and generally there is an inquiry on the part of some one present if she cannot have her feet unbound. Then you should hear the clamor! A dozen will admonish the one who has been so bold as to propose such a thing. Had she lost all her modesty that she wanted to go about like a man? Now you will laugh, but all my arguments are as nothing compared with showing them a well-fitting pretty foreign boot or shoe. I have always thought, since feet are such a momentous question in this land, that we should be very careful to make our own as presentable as possible. To see us start off quickly and gracefully and go through the streets so independently often makes them desirous of imitating us, especially when they see women hobbling along painfully, or being carried on the backs of others.

The same is true of our homes. I try to make mine attractive in its simplicity. I have a weekly prayer meeting here just because I want to show my home to these women who have never seen cleanliness and order in their dark, damp, crowded quarters. I give them, after the meeting, tea and sponge cake, served in pretty cups and plates. Simple as all this is, it lifts them up and out of their sordid surroundings, for the time being, at least, and, I hope, will lead them to make their own houses more homelike. I always urge those coming under my influence to try and be as clean as possible, and I am happy to say that I observe year by year an increasing tendency to the use of foreign soap and handkerchiefs.

Source: Fulton, Mary H. In James S. Dennis, *Christian Missions and Social Progress: A Sociological Study of Foreign Missions.* New York: Fleming H. Revell Co., 1897, pp. 46–47.

TIMELINE   2000 1900 1800 1700 1600 1500 1400 1300 1200 1100 1000 900 800 700 600 500 400 300 200 100 1 BCE

What You Need to Know

This passage was written by Mary Fulton, an American Presbyterian missionary in China in the late nineteenth and early twentieth centuries. A trained medical professional, Fulton worked in a hospital and established a medical school in South China where she was stationed.

In this excerpt, Fulton discusses the differences between the dressing habits of herself and Chinese women, with an emphasis on the latter's practice of foot-binding. Foot-binding was widespread in China during the period Fulton worked there. Virtually every woman of means—middle class and aristocrat alike—had her feet bound. The point of the binding was to demonstrate that these were women of leisure, who did not need to work or even to travel about, as everything they might need was provided for them. Over time, bound feet were deemed aesthetically superior, and were considered to be quite erotic.

Going back about 1,000 years, foot-binding involved an excruciating process in which girls as young as five years old had their feet tightly wrapped to prevent their growth. The bones in the arch of the foot and toes were broken to compress the appendage even further. Periodically, the feet would be unbound, the toenails cut, and the toes folded back even further, preventing any further growth. Because the process cut off circulation to the feet, the women often suffered infections and even the loss of their feet altogether.

A Closer Look

In the early nineteenth century, Americans of a particularly religious bent experienced a passion for missionary work that would continue into the twentieth century. The idea was that Americans could spread a "benevolent empire," in contrast to the political and military ones of Europe, based not just on Christian principles but on spreading Western cultural values and customs, which the missionaries assumed were superior to those of non-Western peoples, such as the Chinese.

For American missionaries, such as Fulton, the secular and the sacred overlapped. As she tells her Chinese women friends, God did not intend for them to be mere adornments for their men. He wanted them to make the world a better place. Bound feet and excessively long fingernails prevented them from doing that. Fulton also uses her missionary activities to promote yet another ideal that fused the worldly and divine—cleanliness. Her well-kept home, which she used for prayer services, provided a real-world manifestation for the old English adage, much repeated in America, that "cleanliness is next to godliness."

1 100 200 300   400   500   600   700   800   900   1000 1100 1200 1300   1400   1500   1600   1700 1800 1900 2000 CE

2.15.29 *The White Man's Burden*

British Empire
1899

Take up the White Man's burden—
Send forth the best ye breed—
Go bind your sons to exile
To serve your captives' need;
To wait in heavy harness,
On fluttered folk and wild—
Your new-caught, sullen peoples,
Half-devil and half-child.

Take up the White Man's burden—
In patience to abide,
To veil the threat of terror
And check the show of pride;
By open speech and simple,
An hundred times made plain
To seek another's profit,
And work another's gain.

Take up the White Man's burden—
The savage wars of peace—
Fill full the mouth of Famine
And bid the sickness cease;
And when your goal is nearest
The end for others sought,
Watch sloth and heathen Folly
Bring all your hopes to nought.

Take up the White Man's burden—
No tawdry rule of kings,
But toil of serf and sweeper—
The tale of common things.

The ports ye shall not enter,
The roads ye shall not tread,
Go mark them with your living,
And mark them with your dead.
Take up the White Man's burden—
And reap his old reward:
The blame of those ye better,
The hate of those ye guard—
The cry of hosts ye humour
(Ah, slowly!) toward the light:—
"Why brought he us from bondage,
Our loved Egyptian night?"

Take up the White Man's burden—
Ye dare not stoop to less—
Nor call too loud on Freedom
To cloke your weariness;
By all ye cry or whisper,
By all ye leave or do,
The silent, sullen peoples
Shall weigh your gods and you.

Take up the White Man's burden—
Have done with childish days—
The lightly proferred laurel,
The easy, ungrudged praise.
Comes now, to search your manhood
Through all the thankless years
Cold, edged with dear-bought wisdom,
The judgment of your peers!

Source: Kipling, Rudyard. "The White Man's Burden." In *The Seven Seas Edition of the Works of Rudyard Kipling: The Five Nations and the Seven Seas*. Vol. XXII. Garden City, NY: Doubleday, Page and Co., 1915, pp. 66–68.

TIMELINE   2000 1900 1800 1700 1600 1500 1400 1300 1200 1100 1000 900 800 700 600 500 400 300 200 100 1 BCE

What You Need to Know

Short-story writer, novelist, and poet Rudyard Kipling was arguably the most widely read English writer around the turn of the twentieth century, a period that saw the British Empire reach its apogee, ruling over nearly 600 million people, or roughly one-third of humanity. The poem printed here—"The White Man's Burden" from 1899—is probably his most widely anthologized piece of verse.

The British were fond of saying that they acquired their empire by accident, or as one Victorian put it, "in a fit of absence of mind." A ridiculous contention in the main—Britain actively sought raw materials and markets for its manufactured goods, like other European countries—there was a kernel of truth to it, when it came to India. Britain began by establishing commercial outposts, largely through the government-chartered but privately owned British East India Company. Ultimately, to defend its interests, it gradually extended its sway over the subcontinent and then finally established government rule only after a massive mutiny in the British-officered but locally manned Indian army.

A Closer Look

"The White Man's Burden" is written in the imperative voice, appealing to his fellow countrymen to take up their God-given duty to lead the rest of the world's peoples to a civilized way of life. Although some scholars have asserted it may have been written in a satirical vein, to deflate the pretensions of colonial authorities, on its surface the poem reflects Kipling's firm faith in the righteousness of Britain's imperial mission.

Kipling was born in India to Anglo-Indian parents. The term Anglo-Indian at that time referred to Britons who had lived for long periods of time—in some cases, all their lives—in India. Small in number—just 3,500 in 1900—Anglo-Indians administered a colony of 300 million. They lived and socialized among themselves, viewing even the highest caste Indians as their cultural and racial inferiors. Winters would be spent doing administrative work in the major Indian cities; when summer heat descended on the subcontinent, they would retreat to more temperate hill stations and govern the colony from there. Still, many of them adopted elements of Indian culture, becoming attached to Indian cuisine, fabrics, art, and music. Although always viewing themselves as British, they nevertheless viewed India as their home.

The administrators sent to India, such as Kipling's parents, did not look on their mission as strictly exploitative. They felt they were uplifting the Indian people through education, the settlement of internal disputes, and the building of a modern infrastructure. That sense of duty, absorbed in Kipling's childhood, is evinced in every verse of the poem.

1 100 200 300   400   500   600   700   800   900   1000 1100 1200 1300   1400   1500   1600   1700   1800   1900   2000 CE

2.15.30 Blackfoot Tipis from the Great Plains

American Great Plains
Early Twentieth Century

Credit: Library of Congress

What You Need to Know

This photo from the early twentieth century depicts tipis of the Blackfoot Indians, a nomadic, bison-hunting people who inhabited the Great Plains of the northern United States and southern Canada.

The Blackfoot were, in fact, a group of linguistically related tribes that referred to themselves as the Siksika. The origins of the name Blackfoot is disputed but may come from the black ash from campfires on the moccasins they wore. This name was given to the Siksika by neighboring tribes.

The bison was central to Blackfoot life both before and after the adoption of the horse in the eighteenth century. Before, men would hunt the animal on foot, draping themselves with buffalo hides to disguise their presence and scent, so that they could approach them. Once the Blackfoot tamed the horses that were introduced by the Spanish and then escaped to run free on the Plains, they became much more effective hunters, and their numbers grew. But the golden age of the Blackfoot and other bison-hunting Great Plains Indians was short-lived. By the late nineteenth century, many had been forced onto reservations, and the bison were all but wiped out by white hunters and settlers.

A Closer Look

Tipis were a portable form of housing, constructed of wooden poles and covered in hides, typically of buffalo, but also elk and other large grazing mammals. They suited the hunting and gathering life of the Blackfoot because they could be set up and taken down quickly, and easily moved from camp to camp. The hides were sewn together using sinews from the guts of animals and attached to the poles with rope. As shown in the photo, the tipis had a small opening at the apex to allow smoke from cooking and heating fire inside to escape. Tipis were usually erected on top of packed earth, although as the Blackfoot and other Plains Indians came into contact with white settlers, gaining access to milled lumber, they might line the ground with boards. A door, also made of hide, was attached to the opening with pins, originally of bone but, after contact with settlers, of metal, too.

Blackfoot tipis were typically decorated with painted sacred symbols or images depicting heroic deeds of the owner. Like other North American tribes, the Blackfoot associated with life, nature, and the world. The animals on the tipi in the photo, probably elk, may have been totemic of the tipi owner's clan. Such animals were that clan's connection to the spirit world that infused all of nature.

2.15.31 Description of a Turkish Harem in the Ottoman Empire

Turkey
1903

There are many people in England whose ideas on the subject of the harem are but a confused misconception, based on what they may have heard about Eastern polygamy. In this chapter, that I may correct these mistaken conceptions, I will give some more exact information on the subject of the harem and its inmates, as well as on the position of women in Turkey in general. . . .

Although the word harem is known and used by the people of Western Europe, the true meaning of the term is understood by but few persons in this country. As a matter of fact, many subjects concerning the East are much misunderstood in the West, just as there are certain manners and customs of Western Europe that cause prejudice in the Eastern mind. When an Englishman uses the word harem, he means thereby the numerous wives whom a man in our part of the East is supposed to shut up in his house. He, moreover, believes that every man in the Mohammedan East may marry as many women as he pleases. This idea is not only mistaken, but grotesque. There are thousands of men who would consider themselves fortunate if they could marry even a single woman. . . .

After pointing out the absurdity of the notion that a man's harem is his collection of wives, I will now explain what it really is. In Mohammedan countries, where the seclusion of women is a deeply rooted and religiously observed custom, every house is divided into two separate parts. In Turkey the section of a house where the ladies reside is called the harem, and the men's portion is named the *selamlik*—that is to say, the reception-place. Though the female inmates of a house are also collectively called the harem, this does not mean that they are all the wives of the master of the house. A man's wife, his mother, his sister, his daughter, and such other women as may lawfully appear unveiled in his presence, belong to his harem. . . .

The life in most Turkish harems is very simple, and, if we leave out the case of the few polygamists who still remain, very peaceful and happy. The absolute authority of the husband does not interfere with the recognised privileges of the wife; while the obedience of the wife, which is regarded by more advanced women in Western Europe with such contempt, in most cases strengthens the affection and respect of the husband for her. Wives are not slaves of their husbands, as some people in this country fancy them to be. The inmates of harems live mostly indoors, but they are not entirely shut up. They go out in groups of two, three, and more to pay visits to other harems, and they receive visitors from the harems of friends and relations. . . .

The number of educated women was much less than it is now. The most learned among them used to read sacred legends, or religious tracts, or recite hymns to the other ladies, who would listen attentively for hours. I believe this social pastime is still in favour in the provinces.

Source: Halid, Halil. *Diary of a Turk*. London: Adam and Charles Black, 1903, pp. 46–49, 52–53.

TIMELINE   2000 1900 1800 1700 1600 1500 1400 1300 1200 1100 1000 900 800 700 600 500 400 300 200 100 1 BCE

What You Need to Know

This passage comes from the book *Diary of a Turk*, published in 1903. Its author was Halil Halid, a Turkish-born scholar and diplomat who lived much of his life in England and wrote in English. In this excerpt, he tries to explain the meaning of the Turkish harem to the English reading public.

Then as now, Europeans had many misconceptions of what the harem really was. This was understandable in that most associated it with the great sultans of the Ottoman Empire, whose harems were filled with concubines. In fact, as Halid relates, the harem, which comes from the Arabic term *haram*, or "prohibited place," was simply that part of the home reserved for women, including the wife, daughters, and mother of the male head of household. Turkish households—at least, those of wealthier families, which could afford the space—were divided into three parts, a space for men that was open to the public, a space for women, where only other women and male members of the family could enter, and a mixed area where cooking was done. Life in the typical Turkish harem was quite ordinary and routine, Halid emphasizes. It was no more or less than a place for sleeping, bathing, female household chores, and female socializing.

A Closer Look

Halid is also intent on dispelling English stereotypes of subjugated Turkish women. At a time when English women were beginning to assert their political, economic, and social rights, the status of Islamic women represented a kind of antithesis to Western progressive ideals. Indeed, at a time of European imperial supremacy, the colonial enterprise in general was rationalized as an effort to bring such ideals to the benighted peoples of the world.

And nothing seemed more backward or repressive to English readers than the Islamic institution of polygamy. In reality, says Halid, the practice was quite rare. Moreover, he says, Islamic women were not particularly repressed. They managed the household and left the home, although always in groups, to engage in business necessary to that end. Many of them were also educated, with harems serving as places where they could read and learn among themselves. As for Islamic strictures about obedience to husbands, Halid argues that rather than a source of dissatisfaction for women it was a means to ensure peaceful and harmonious relations within marriage.

1 100 200 300   400   500   600   700   800   900   1000 1100 1200 1300   1400   1500   1600   1700 1800 1900 2000 CE

2.15.32 Indian Cricket Batsman

British India
ca. 1905

Credit: Hulton-Deutsch Collection/Corbis

What You Need to Know

This photograph is of Kumar Shri Ranjitsinhji, a prince from Nawanagar State in British India and, according to historians of cricket, arguably the greatest batsman, or hitter, in the history of the game. Ranjitsinhji—better known as Ranji to his fans—played out his cricket career for various teams in England, including Britain's national team.

Britons of the nineteenth and early twentieth centuries referred to India as the "crown jewel" of the empire. After a major sepoy uprising in the 1850s, it was ruled directly by Parliament. As today, India had a vast population, around 300 million in 1900, who were administered by no more than 3,500 British-born officials. To staff the bureaucracy needed to run the colony, Britain set up a system for educating and recruiting the country's native elite, particularly among the high-born Brahmin castes. They set up a secondary school system modeled after their own and culled the most promising candidates for government positions. The very best and most elite were then sent to England for higher education. Ranji, for one, attended and played cricket for Cambridge University. With this corps of educated and able Indian bureaucrats, they set up a centralized government, which applied uniform laws across the colony and applying to both Hindu and Muslim communities and to all castes, although the most important decisions were always reserved for Parliament or British officials in the subcontinent.

A Closer Look

The game of cricket, which bears a vague resemblance to baseball, has been played since the early modern era, although the modern game, with its national sides and international competitions dates to the nineteenth century. As the British gradually colonized India, first through the British East India Company and then as a crown colony, in the eighteenth and nineteenth centuries, they brought cricket with them. At first, it was played on the subcontinent by Englishmen only. By the late nineteenth and early twentieth centuries, elite Indians, such as Ranji, brought to England to be educated, began to play the game there.

At the same time, the game was catching on in India, particularly among sepoys, or Indian soldiers serving in the British army in India. Cricket also became popular among India's growing middle class, particularly urban areas, as these people were the most likely to send their sons to English schools on the subcontinent, where they picked up a fondness for the sport. Colonial educators and administrators encouraged this activity, as they saw cricket embodying what for them were estimable British values of gentlemanly sportsmanship, discipline, and clean competition.

2.15.33 Apsaalooke (Crow) Mother with Child in Cradleboard

American Great Plains
1908

Credit: Library of Congress

What You Need to Know

Shown here is a photograph of an Apsaalooke mother and child. By the time this photograph was taken in 1908, the Apsaalooke, like the other tribes of the Great Plains, had been militarily subdued by the American government and forced to live on reservations. Aside from clearing lands for settlement, the reservations were meant to "civilize" the Indians—that is, replace their indigenous culture with a more European one. As with any assimilation process, the key to success was the children. To that end, government agents and educational reformers, most of whom were influenced by Christian ideals, required Apsaalooke and other Plains Indian children to attend boarding schools. Separated from their parents, the children were taught skills that fit the gender stereotypes of whites; boys were taught to farm and crafts, such as carpentry, while girls learned how to sew, clean an American-style house, and cook foods fit for a white palate. And, of course, they were taught to discard the spiritual beliefs of their people and adopt Christianity.

A Closer Look

Like many other Native American peoples, the Apsaalooke, known as the Crow in English, had a reverence for children. Indeed, the child-rearing practices of the Apsaalooke and other North American Indians surprised and often upset white observers for their leniency and indulgence of childhood needs. Unless unable to produce milk, Apsaalooke mothers never allowed other women to nurse their babies. In fact, when a mother was unable to feed the baby, the father might step in, by chewing corn in his mouth until it was a mush and then spitting it directly into his baby's mouth. Moreover, nursing continued until the child was three and four.

Nothing, however, surprised nineteenth-century whites more than the fact that Apsaalooke parents, like most other Native Americans, never physically punished their children. And mothers rarely left their children alone. Babies were carried on the back on cradleboards like this one. Such cradleboards featured a solid wooden back, lined with animal hide. The child was then wrapped tightly in another hide. Because Apsaalooke mothers often had to walk long distances to gather plants, firewood, and water, they carried the children on their back, but without boards, even after the latter could walk. They simply tied the child to their back with straps. As the image reveals, the cradleboards were elaborately decorated with beads and weaving, another sign of the respect they had for children.

2.15.34 Description of Native American Corn Dances

American Great Plains
1915

Among the Omaha tribe when the time came for planting, four kernels from a red ear of corn were given to each family by the keeper of this sacred rite. These four red kernels were mixed with the ordinary seed corn, that it might be vivified by them and made to yield an ample harvest. Red is the symbolic color of life. In this ceremony is preserved a trace of the far-away time when all the precious seed corn was in the care of priestly keepers. The ceremony of giving out the four red kernels served to turn the thoughts of the people from a dependence solely on their own labor in cultivating corn to the life-giving power of Wakon'da dwelling within the maize. . . .

DANCE I

INTRODUCTORY Note.—This ceremonial dance touches upon the mystery of the giving of life that life may be maintained; an exchange that links together the different forms of life and enhances the joy of living.

Properties.—Thin green mantles; yellow plumes like the corn tassel; bone clips; as many of these articles as there are dancers.

Directions.—This dance belongs to both sexes and a number of each should take part, if that is possible. Should there be trees near the open space where the dance takes place, one-half of the dancers, closely wrapped in their green mantles, should be grouped at one side among the trees and the other half similarly placed at the other side. In the center of the space a single dancer stands facing the rear, wrapped about the head and body with the green mantle, leaving only the face exposed.

All being in readiness, the central figure turns slowly, lifts a draped arm and says slowly and impressively: "Harken! The Corn speaks!"

The group of dancers on the right then sing softly the first line only of the Ritual Song in which the Corn speaks. . . .

> **Ritual Song No. 1**
> Fourfold deep lie my roots within the land;
> Clad in green, bearing fruit, Lo! here I stand!
> Pluck and eat, life for life, behold, I give!
> Shout with joy, dance and sing with all that live.

Source: Fletcher, Alice C. *Indian Games and Dances with Native Songs: Arranged from American Indian Ceremonials and Sports*. New York: C. C. Birchard and Co., 1915, pp. 9–12.

What You Need to Know

This excerpt comes from Alice Fletcher's 1915 book on the dances, songs, and games of Great Plains Native American groups, including the Omaha, the Osage, and the Pawnee tribes.

One of the reasons that scholars such as Fletcher ventured out to the Great Plains frontier in the late nineteenth century was because they believed that the Native Americans tribes who lived there represented dying cultures, and they wanted to record them for posterity. The cultures of the Great Plains Indians were under grave threat; the buffalo, on which many relied for protein and leather for clothing and housing, were being wiped out in wholesale fashion. White settlers were moving in, and to make room for them, the U.S. army was herding tribes onto reservations, where they could no longer practice their seminomadic way of life. There, Indians were being forced to adopt white ways even as their children were being taught to disparage their traditional culture.

A Closer Look

Fletcher was an American ethnologist who traveled to the Great Plains in the 1880s and 1890s to study the cultures of the Native American peoples there. Those years witnessed the final subjugation of the Plains Indians to U.S. government control. In fact, Fletcher used her observations as a means to teach white school children how to reenact such dances, as a means of raising awareness of Native American cultures among non-Indian peoples.

In this excerpt, Fletcher describes the songs and dances associated with the corn harvest of the Omaha, Osage, and Pawnee tribes. Such ceremonial dances were typically held out in the open around great bonfires, with men and women dancing separately. The dancers formed great circles, which represented the cycle of the corn crop—planting, tending, sowing, dormancy, and replanting. Most dances were a mix of ritualized body movements and impromptu performances. The dances might be led by a dance leader, who was usually the spiritual or war leader of the tribe. Because corn planting and harvesting was the purview of women, an elder matriarch would sometimes lead ceremonial dances related to this crop.

Alongside harvest dances such as the corn dances of the Omaha, Osage, and Pawnee described here, there were also dances celebrating victories in battle, offering general prayers to the spirits, or enacting the myths of the tribe.

Part 16:
The Industrial Revolution

Late Eighteenth–Early Twentieth Centuries

2.16.1 Description of a Mechanical Reaper

United States
1831

There are four vital elements in a reaper, none of which can even today be dispensed with; and yet all four were successfully embodied in the machine which Cyrus H. McCormick introduced to the world in the harvest of 1831:

I. A platform, or grain deck, one end of which is flexibly affixed to the master-wheel, while the other is supported by a small "grain" wheel, so that the platform may readily accommodate itself to the irregularities of the surface.

II. A reciprocating knife (operated directly from the master-wheel) having a serrated edge, with stationary teeth or guards projecting forward from the platform, immediately over the inner edge of the knife and bent backward beneath it—so that, as the knife reciprocates through them, the stalks will be sustained by the fixed teeth and sheared off.

III. A horizontal and adjustable reel, so situated as to rotate in the direction of the master-wheel, serving to sweep the standing grain towards the cutting apparatus, and delivering the several stalks parallel upon the platform, in a swath adapted to be raked off into bundles, ready for the binders.

IV. A divider, serving, as McCormick stated in his original description, to "divide and keep separate the grain to be cut from that to be left standing"—an operation in which the reel also takes part.

. . . In after years McCormick stated that, living in the then isolated Valley of Virginia, he had never seen or heard of any experiments in the mechanical reaping of grain save those made by his father. Such experiments were at the time not infrequently alluded to in English agricultural magazines, but none of these publications had as yet penetrated to Walnut Grove. Without doubt there was in this isolation a certain advantage, for the young inventor was free to approach the subject from a comparatively fresh and original point of view. Probably this was the reason why, contemplating only the failures of his father, he made a radical and most essential departure from all his predecessors, inventing a machine along entirely new lines.

As is usually the case with the first form of an invention, the McCormick reaper of 1831 was crude in construction; but there is nothing on record indicating that any prior invention embodied such a scheme of construction, or indeed any scheme that succeeded or survived; and despite all subsequent invention, and it has been lavish, no one has contrived a successful substitute for McCormick's original plan. From it has proceeded in unbroken succession, and with remarkable adherence to the primary arrangement—although subsequently enriched with many refinements in details and supplemental improvements—the reaper that has taken and still holds possession of the markets of the world.

Source: Thwaites, Reuben Gold. *Cyrus Hall McCormick and the Reaper*. Madison, WI: State Historical Society of Wisconsin, 1909, pp. 240–242.

What You Need to Know

This passage comes from a 1909 book by historian Reuben Gold Thwaites, entitled *Cyrus Hall McCormick and the Reaper*. In 1831, McCormick, an inventor from Virginia, demonstrated what most historians consider the world's first mechanical reaper, which is described in this excerpt. He was issued a patent for the device three years later. Although it took a decade or more for the device to catch on with farmers, the machine ultimately transformed American—and world—agriculture in the nineteenth century and made McCormick one of the richest men in the country.

As the excerpt illustrates, the reaper was a mechanical wonder. But it was not just the complexity of the machine that was so revolutionary but the way it was put together. Borrowing from developments in the gun industry, McCormick used standardized parts, so if one broke, it could be easily replaced from the inventory marketed by his sales force. These innovations provided a winning formula; by 1860, his company was selling more than 4,000 reapers a year.

A Closer Look

Wheat production was the mainstay of the Northern rural economy in the nineteenth century. Wheat is not a particularly-labor intensive crop, except at harvest time, when it must be reaped rapidly or be eaten by birds, destroyed by inclement weather, or simply rot in the field. Every able member of a farm family in the premechanical reaper era would be sent into the fields at harvest, but even that was not enough, forcing farmers to search desperately—and pay dearly—for outside help.

At $120 (about $3,300 in today's money) in 1850, or about half a year's profit for a small farmer, McCormick's horse-drawn reaper was not cheap. But it quickly paid for itself in that it allowed a single farmer to do the work of five men.

McCormick's reaper not only changed American agriculture, it helped revolutionize commerce as well. The McCormick Harvesting Machine Company—now, International Harvester—helped pioneer the installment paying plan, allowing farmers to put a small amount down and then pay for the machine over time. It set a fixed price for the machine, ending traditional bickering over price. McCormick set up a team of trained traveling sales agents, who not only sold the machine for him but educated the farmers in its use and even did repairs. And McCormick offered an ironclad guarantee: "15 acres a day" or a full refund.

1 100 200 300 400 500 600 700 800 900 1000 1100 1200 1300 1400 1500 1600 1700 1800 1900 2000 CE

2.16.2 Child Labor Conditions in Great Britain

United Kingdom
1833

Charles Harris, a boy working in the carding room of Mr. Oldacres's mill for spinning worsted yarn, testifies as follows:

I am twelve years old. I have been in the mill twelve months. I attend to a drawing machine. We begin at six o'clock and stop at half past seven. We don't stop work for breakfast. We do sometimes. This week we have not. Nothing has been said to me by Mr. Oldacres or the overlooker, or anybody else, about having any questions asked me. I am sure of that. The engine always stops for dinner. It works at tea time in the hot weather; and then we give over at half past seven instead of eight, which is the general time. We have generally about twelve hours and a half of it. On Saturdays we begin at six and give over at four. I get *2s. 6d.* a week [2 shillings 6 pence, roughly equivalent to $15 today]. I have a father and mother, and give them what I earn. I have worked overhours . . . at the rate of *2d.* for three hours. I have always that for myself. . . .

The boy. I am going fourteen; my sister is eleven. I have worked in Milnes's factory two years. She goes there also. We are both in the clearing room. I think we work too long hours; I've been badly with it. We go at half past five; give over at half past nine. I am now just come home. We sometimes stay till twelve. We are obliged to work overhours. I have *4s.* a week; that is for staying from six to seven. They pay for overhours besides. I asked to come away one night lately, at eight o'clock, being ill; I was told, if I went I must not come again. I am not well now. I can seldom eat any breakfast; my appetite is very bad. I had a bad cold for a week.

Father. I believe him to be ill from being overworked. My little girl came home the other day cruelly beaten. I took her to Mr. Milnes; did not see him, but showed Mrs. Milnes the marks. I thought of taking it before a magistrate, but was advised to let it drop. They might have turned both my children away. That man's name is Blagg; he is always strapping the children. I shan't let the boy go there much longer; I shall try to apprentice him; it's killing him by inches; he falls asleep over his food at night. I saw an account of such things in the newspapers, and thought how true it was of my own children.

Source: "Extracts from a Parliamentary Report on Child Labor." In *Readings in Modern European History. Volume II: Europe Since the Congress of Vienna.* Edited by James Harvey Robinson and Charles A. Beard. Boston: Ginn & Company, 1909, pp. 282, 284.

TIMELINE   2000 1900 1800 1700 1600 1500 1400 1300 1200 1100 1000 900 800 700 600 500 400 300 200 100 1 BCE

What You Need to Know

Excerpted here is the Parliamentary Report on Child Labor, also known as the Sadler Report, after Parliamentarian Michael Sadler who sponsored it in 1833. Two years earlier, Sadler had tried to get a bill passed, limiting working hours for children to 10 a day. Although he failed, he did get Parliament to agree to look into the matter, which included testimony from child workers and their parents. Excerpts of that testimony are reprinted here.

Before the introduction of factories, most spinning and weaving was done on a piecework basis by workers in their homes. The discipline and long hours of factory work did not appeal to them. To obtain enough workers, early factory owners turned to poorhouses, where there were many young children—both orphans and those whose families could not support them—who were already used to long hours of labor.

A Closer Look

Child labor was common before the industrial age. Most English people lived on farms, where children were expected to work long hours at key periods of the growing season. But factory labor was different. While children worked in a number of industries, including mining, they were most commonly employed in cotton mills. Conditions in these factories were harsh even for adults. Child workers—some apprenticed into the factories as early as five years of age—not only worked in the factories—up to 13 or 14 hours a day, six days a week—but lived there as well, locked up at night so they could not escape. Food was meager and of the coarsest variety. Mealtimes were not always honored, especially when a factory owner was trying to fill an order. The children were given low or no pay, beyond what little they received in room and board. To maintain discipline, overseers used harsh punishment, typically beatings for shirking, damaging equipment, or simply not working fast enough.

The coercion and exploitation of child labor offended many people's sensibilities, including Sadler's. The testimony he gathered helped convince his fellow parliamentarians to pass the Factory Act of 1833, banning child labor under the age of 9, limiting the workday for children 9 to 13 to 8 hours a day and adolescents from 14 to 18 to no more than 12 hours.

2.16.3 Description of the Early American Factory System

Lowell, Massachusetts
1830s–1840s

Before 1836 the era of mechanical industry in New England had hardly begun, the industrial life of its people was yet in its infancy, and nearly every article in domestic use that is now made with the help of machinery was then "done by hand." . . .

Their lives had kept pace for so many years with the stage-coach and the canal that they thought, no doubt, if they thought about it at all, that they should crawl along in this way forever. But into this life there came an element that was to open a new era in the activities of the country. This was the genius of mechanical industry, which would build the cotton-factory, set in motion the loom and spinning frame, call together an army of useful people, open wider fields of industry for men and (which was quite important at that time) for women also. . . .

At the time the Lowell cotton-mills were started, the factory girl was the lowest among women. In England, and in France particularly, great injustice had been done to her real character; she was represented as subjected to influences that could not fail to destroy her purity and self-respect. In the eyes of the overseer she was but a brute, a slave, to be beaten, pinched, and pushed about. It was to overcome this prejudice that such high wages had been offered to women that they might be induced to become mill-girls, in spite of the opprobrium that still clung to the "degrading occupation." . . .

The fourth class, lords of the spade and the shovel, by whose constant labor the building of the great factories was made possible, and whose children soon became valuable operatives, lived at first on what was called the "Acre," a locality near the present site of the North Grammar schoolhouse. Here, clustered around a small Catholic Church, were hundreds of little shanties, in which they dwelt with their wives and numerous children.

Source: Robinson, Harriet H. *Loom and Spindle, or Life among the Early Mill Girls*. New York: Thomas Y. Crowell and Co., 1898, pp. 2–4, 15, 61.

What You Need to Know

This description of some of the first textile mills in the United States comes from Harriet Robinson's memoir *Loom and Spindle, or Life among the Early Mill Girls*. Although published in 1898, the book recalls Robinson's experiences in the mills of Lowell, Massachusetts, during the first Industrial Revolution of the 1830s and 1840s.

When Robinson started working in them, the mills, as with the American economy generally, were experiencing flush times and owners offered many amenities to attract workers, including relatively good pay, modern boarding houses, healthy meals, and even cultural activities for their off time.

While many of the early factory owners considered themselves good Christians, there were motives behind the beneficence. Available labor was hard to come by, and the awful conditions in earlier factories in England, of which Americans were well aware from newspaper accounts, led many male workers to shun such work. Young women, with fewer options for paid labor, were then recruited. But living unmarried and apart from their families concerned parents. Factory owners thus promised that the young female workers would live in a wholesome and moral environment. However, with the economic downturn in the late 1830s and more competition, factory owners provided fewer amenities, even as they increasingly hired impoverished Irish immigrant girls and young women.

A Closer Look

A child of 10 when she started working in 1835 and a young woman of 23 when she stopped working there for the last time, Robinson was typical of the workers in the Lowell mills.

Work in the mills consisted largely of tending the spinning and weaving machines that were driven, via a series of gears and belts, by the water power produced by falls in the Merrimack River that ran through the city. It was a cacophonous place to work but relatively well lit and clean. The main duty of the primarily female workforce was to monitor the machines. When a thread broke or something got caught in the gears, the machine would automatically shut off. The worker would then fix the break or remove the foreign object, and restart the machine. More extensive repairs were handled by older male mechanics, who had specialized training.

The typical workweek consisted of six 12-hour days. Such long hours were not unusual for the time; the farms where most of the workers came from required lengthy workdays. What was different—and new—was the strict adherence to schedule. Bells rang throughout the day, announcing the start of the day, lunch, and quitting time.

1 100 200 300   400   500   600   700   800   900   1000 1100 1200 1300   1400   1500   1600   1700   1800 1900 2000 CE

2.16.4 Pollution in the Thames River

London, England
1855

I traversed this day by steam-boat the space between London and Hangerford Bridges between half-past one and two o'clock; it was low water, and I think the tide must have been near the turn. The appearance and the smell of the water forced themselves at once on my attention. The whole of the river was an opaque pale brown fluid. In order to test the degree of opacity, I tore up some white cards into pieces, moistened them so as to make them sink easily below the surface, and then dropped some of these pieces into the water at every pier the boat came to; before they had sunk an inch below the surface they were indistinguishable, though the sun shone brightly at the time; and when the pieces fell edgeways the lower part was hidden from sight before the upper part was under water. This happened at St. Paul's Wharf, Blackfriars Bridge, Temple Wharf, Southwark Bridge, and Hungerford; and I have no doubt would have occurred further up and down the river. Near the bridges the feculence rolled up in clouds so dense that they were visible at the surface, even in water of this kind.

The smell was very bad, and common to the whole of the water; it was the same as that which now comes up from the gully-holes in the streets; the whole river was for the time a real sewer. Having just returned from out of the country air, I was, perhaps, more affected by it than others; but I do not think I could have gone on to Lambeth or Chelsea, and I was glad to enter the streets for an atmosphere which, except near the sink-holes, I found much sweeter than that on the river.

I have thought it a duty to record these facts, that they may be brought to the attention of those who exercise power or have responsibility in relation to the condition of our river; there's nothing figurative in the words I have employed, or any approach to exaggeration; they are the simple truth. If there be sufficient authority to remove a putrescent pond from the neighbourhood of a few simple dwellings, surely the river which flows for so many miles through London ought not to be allowed to become a fermenting sewer. The condition in which I saw the Thames may perhaps be considered as exceptional, but it ought to be an impossible state, instead of which I fear it is rapidly becoming the general condition. If we neglect this subject, we cannot expect to do so with impunity; nor ought we to be surprised if, ere many years are over, a hot season give us sad proof of the folly of our carelessness.

I am, Sir, Your obedient servant,

M. FARADAY.

Source: Faraday, Michael. Letter to *The Times*, July 7, 1855. Reprinted in "Observations on the Filth of the Thames, Contained in a Letter Addressed to the Editor of the *Times* Newspaper, by Professor Faraday." *Report of the Committee for Scientific Inquiries in Relation to the Cholera-Epidemic of 1854*. Vol. 2. London: Eyre and Spottiswoode, 1855, p. 284.

What You Need to Know

This 1855 letter was written by Michael Faraday to the *Times* newspaper of London, concerning pollution in the Thames River that runs through the British capital. A scientist by training, Faraday is best known for his pioneering work in the study of electromagnetism.

In the summer of 1858, three years after Faraday wrote his letter, London was struck by what contemporaries referred to as the "great stink." So bad was the stench that Parliament, whose houses lay along the river in Westminster, even considered convening elsewhere, until a heavy rainstorm washed the smell from the city.

In the wake of this noxious episode, Parliament earmarked 4.2 million pounds (about half a billion dollars in today's money) for a new sewer system for the city. They also hired one of the premier civil engineers of the day, Joseph Bazalgette, to design and build it. Bazalgette dug up some 3.25 million cubic yards of earth and laid more than 300 million bricks in build 82 miles of underground sewers. People hailed his creation as one of the seven wonders of the nineteenth-century world. But, in fact, it merely shifted the problem downriver, below the city. It would not be until the early twentieth century that London would get its first sewage treatment plant.

A Closer Look

Nearly two-and-a-half million people lived in the London metropolitan area in the 1850s, making it the largest city in the world. They poured more than 400,000 tons of untreated sewage into the Thames every day, 150 million tons a year. Essentially an open sewer, the river was biologically dead.

There were many sources of pollution. Human and animal excrement flowed down gutters and through pipes directly into the river, in the middle of the city. The introduction of the flush toilet in the first half of the century only made things worse, as it added to flow of effluvia. This made the Thames a breeding ground for bacteria, including the one that caused several fatal cholera outbreaks in the first half of the century.

Although London was not Britain's main center of industry, there were still many factories that produced chemicals and other toxic wastes, which also went straight into the water. Another major source of pollution were laundries, which sent vast quantities of corrosive lye into the Thames. Once a place for fishing and boating, the water was largely avoided now, except for transport, and the riverfront became among the least desirable areas of the city to live, inhabited by the poor, itinerant sailors, houses of prostitution, and other illicit activities.

1 100 200 300 400 500 600 700 800 900 1000 1100 1200 1300 1400 1500 1600 1700 1800 1900 2000 CE

2.16.5 Life at an English Boarding School

United Kingdom
1857

The lower-fourth form, in which Tom found himself at the beginning of the next half-year, was the largest form in the lower school, and numbered upwards of forty boys. Young gentlemen of all ages from nine to fifteen were to be found there, who expended such part of their energies as was devoted to Latin and Greek upon a book of Livy, the "Bucolics" of Virgil, and the "Hecuba" of Euripides, which were ground out in small daily portions. The driving of this unlucky lower-fourth must have been grievous work to the unfortunate master, for it was the most unhappily constituted of any in the school. Here stuck the great stupid boys, who, for the life of them, could never master the accidence. . . . There were no less than three unhappy fellows in tail coats, with incipient down on their chins, whom the Doctor and the master of the form were always endeavouring to hoist into the upper school, but whose parsing and construing resisted the most well-meant shoves. Then came the mass of the form, boys of eleven and twelve, the most mischievous and reckless age of British youth. . . . The remainder of the form consisted of young prodigies of nine and ten, who were going up the school at the rate of a form a half-year, all boys' hands and wits being against them in their progress.

Source: Hughes, Thomas. *Tom Brown's School Days*. London: Macmillan and Co., 1868, pp. 151–152.

What You Need to Know

The accompanying document comes from *Tom Brown's SchoolDays*, an 1868 novel by Thomas Hughes. Although the account is fictional, it is based on Hughes's own youthful experiences at the Rugby School, an English public school, in the 1830s and 1840s. Traditionally, in England, private boarding schools were known as "public schools," because, their steep tuition aside, they were technically open to all young males, regardless of class or birth.

As Hughes notes, Rugby was filled with the typical rambunctious of young boys and teens living together away from their parents. Unmentioned by the author was the very stern discipline exercised, usually in the form of corporal punishment, by both faculty and prefects, higher form (grade) students assigned to keep order among the younger pupils. One master at Eton School, a Rugby rival, boasted of flogging no less than 80 students in one session (semester) in the early nineteenth century. Although not officially sanctioned, bullying was also common among the students. In addition, schools such as Rugby, employed the so-called "fagging" system, in which younger students spent part of each day doing chores and running errands for the older ones.

A Closer Look

The fagging system at public schools was rationalized on the grounds that it taught the younger students how to be obedient and in command of their emotions while inculcating lessons in how to exercise authority among the older students.

Indeed, while the teaching of the arts and sciences was an important component of a public school education, the main mission of elite academic institutions such as the Rugby School was in shaping the character of England's future leaders. Thus, the teaching of Latin and Greek texts that Hughes mentions was less focused on understanding the historical context of the works or the beauty of the languages they were written in but on the moral lessons they taught.

Religious observance was valued, too, and all schools required attendance at regular chapel services. Equally important, especially as the nineteenth century progressed, was an emphasis on athletics as a means to foster gentlemanly attributes, such as fair play, selflessness, and a sense of team spirit. In fact, the Rugby School is where the eponymous football game, involving a high level of team coordination and ability to withstand rigorous contact among athletes, was invented.

1   100   200   300   400   500   600   700   800   900   1000   1100   1200   1300   1400   1500   1600   1700   1800   1900   2000 CE

2.16.6 A British Servant's Diary

United Kingdom
1860

Opened the shutters & lighted the kitchen fire. Shook my sooty things in the dusthole & emptied the soot there. Swept & dusted the rooms & the hall. Laid the hearth & got breakfast up. Clean'd 2 pairs of boots. Made the beds & emptied the slops. Clean'd & wash'd the breakfast things up. Clean'd the plate; clean'd the knives & got dinner up. Clean'd away. Clean'd the kitchen up; unpack'd a hamper. Took two chickens to Mrs. Brewer's & brought the message back. Made a tart & pick'd & gutted two ducks & roasted them. Clean'd the steps & flags on my knees. Blackleaded the scraper in front of the house; clean'd the street flags too on my knees. Wash'd up in the scullery. Clean'd the pantry on my knees & scour'd the tables. Scrubbed the flags around the house & clean'd the window sills. Got tea at 9 for the master & Mrs. Warwick in my dirt, but Ann carried it up. Clean'd the privy & passage & scullery floor on my knees. Washed the dog & clean'd the sinks down. Put the supper ready for Ann to take up, for I was too dirty & tired to go upstairs. Wash'd in a bath & to bed.

Source: Cullwick, Hannah. Excerpt from diary entry on July 14, 1860, in *The Diaries of Hannah Cullwick, Victorian Maidservant*. Edited by Liz Stanley. London: Virago, 1984.

What You Need to Know

This excerpt is from the diary of Hannah Cullwick, who worked as a maid in various upper-class households from age 14 until well into her 50s. In 1860, when this diary entry was written, she was working for a barrister, or lawyer, named Arthur Munby, with whom she would eventually have an affair and secretly marry.

The late nineteenth and early twentieth centuries has been described as the golden age of domestic service in England. This is not because working conditions for servants were especially good but because domestic service was so ubiquitous in English society. In the early 1900s, roughly 1.5 million people in Britain worked as servants in homes. No other occupation, other than agricultural laborer, with about 1.2 million, even came close. Most servants did not work on fancy estates, where the domestic staff could number in the dozens, but rather in the homes of the rapidly expanding middle class.

A Closer Look

As the daily chores she describes make clear, Cullwick was what the people of the time called a "maid-of-all-work." That is, working in a household with a small servant staff, or sometimes singly, such maids were expected to do all manner of tasks—cleaning, cooking, serving at table. In larger households, such work was divvied out to specialized servants.

A typical workday for a maid such as Cullwick began before dawn and did not end until after the last dishes from supper were washed and put away, usually around 10 PM. Typically, a maid would get off just half a day each week, with every other Sunday free.

With virtually no mechanical appliances at her disposal, Cullwick's tasks were exhausting, backbreaking, and, in the case of cleaning out the privy, with its nonflush basins for urine and excrement, unpleasant as well.

The vast majority of the servants were from the working class; many were Irish. While the work of the servant could be both demeaning and full of drudgery, it was not the worst option for those who took it up. It usually paid less than unskilled factory work, although often more than agricultural labor, but a servant could hold onto most of his or her wages because room and board came with the job. This allowed young people to save up enough money to marry and start a household of their own.

2.16.7 American Woman Working on Singer Sewing Machine

United States
1860

Credit: Archive Photos/Getty Images

What You Need to Know

This photo from 1860 depicts a woman sewing on a Singer Sewing Machine. The machine sits on top of the crate it came in, with a label reading "Singer's Patent Sewing Machine."

As important as its products were to the everyday life of Americans, the Singer Sewing Machine Company revolutionized consumerism itself, both at home and abroad. Although much less expensive than previous devices, the machine, which sold for about $100 in its early years, or about four months' wages for the average unskilled worker, was still out of the price range of most consumers. To overcome this problem, the company introduced what historians say was the first installment buying program in history, which would later be imitated by the manufacturers of other household durables and eventually automobiles.

The company also aggressively marketed abroad, advertising in richer country newspapers and magazines and handing out pamphlets and postcards in less well-off places. Indeed, the Singer Sewing Machine Company became the first multinational marketer of manufactured goods in world history, paving the way for a host of other American multinationals. By 1890, it controlled roughly 80 percent of the world market in sewing machines and sold its products, through franchisees, on every inhabited continent.

A Closer Look

Before the machine's introduction in 1851, sewing was typically done by hand, which was slow and painstaking. Early mechanical devices were large, dangerous, and difficult to operate. The Singer Machine allowed almost anyone, to sew safely at a rapid pace with little training.

The machine was the first in a series of laborsaving devices that would ease the domestic workload of homemakers, offering them more leisure and time to devote to their children. But the machine had, possibly, an even greater impact on the clothing industry and the way people bought their clothing. Before its introduction, most garments were made by tailors for those who could afford them or at home by those who could not. With the machine in widespread use in sweatshops and factories, ready-to-wear clothing became the norm in many industrializing countries, such as the United States, in the second half of the nineteenth century. Thus, before the machine and its many imitators, one could tell much about a person by his or her clothing. A well-made garment was a sign that the wearer had money; a poorly made one signified poverty. With ready-to-wear widely available, it was harder to determine by outward appearance somebody's class, helping to erode such distinctions in everyday life.

1 100 200 300 400 500 600 700 800 900 1000 1100 1200 1300 1400 1500 1600 1700 1800 1900 2000 CE

2.16.8 Advice on How to Treat Cholera at Home

United Kingdom
1861

2624. THE CHOLERA AND AUTUMNAL COMPLAINTS.—To oppose cholera, there seems no surer or better means than cleanliness, sobriety, and judicious ventilation. Where there is dirt, that is the place for cholera; where windows and doors are kept most jealously shut, there cholera will find easiest entrance; and people who indulge in intemperate diet during the hot days of autumn are actually courting death. To repeat it, cleanliness, sobriety, and free ventilation almost always defy the pestilence; but, in case of attack, immediate recourse should be had to a physician. The faculty say that a large number of lives have been lost, in many seasons, solely from delay in seeking medical assistance. They even assert that, taken early, the cholera is by no means a fatal disorder. The copious use of salt is recommended on very excellent authority. Other autumnal complaints there are, of which diarrhoea is the worst example. They come on with pain, flatulence, sickness, with or without vomiting, followed by loss of appetite, general lassitude, and weakness. If attended to at the first appearance, they may soon be conquered; for which purpose it is necessary to assist nature in throwing off the contents of the bowels, which may be one by means of the following prescription:—Take of calomel 3 grains, rhubarb 8 grains; mix and take it in a little honey or jelly, and repeat the dose three times, at the intervals of four or five hours. The next purpose to be answered is the defence of the lining membrane of the intestines from their acrid contents, which will be best effected by drinking copiously of linseed tea, or of a drink made by pouring boiling water on quince-seeds, which are of a very mucilaginous nature; or, what is still better, full draughts of whey. If the complaint continue after these means have been employed, some astringent or binding medicine will be required, as the subjoined:—Take of prepared chalk 2 drachms, cinnamon-water 7 oz., syrup of poppies 1 oz.; mix, and take 3 tablespoonfuls every four hours. Should this fail to complete the cure, 1/2 oz. of tincture of catechu, or of kino, may be added to it, and then it will seldom fail; or a teaspoonful of the tincture of kino alone, with a little water, every three hours, till the diarrhoea is checked. While any symptoms of derangement are present, particular attention must be paid to the diet, which should be of a soothing, lubricating, and light nature, as instanced in veal or chicken broth, which should contain but little salt. Rice, batter, and bread puddings will be generally relished, and be eaten with advantage; but the stomach is too much impaired to digest food of a more solid nature. Indeed, we should give that organ, together with the bowels, as little trouble as possible, while they are so incapable of acting in their accustomed manner. . . . But our last advice is, upon the first appearance of such symptoms as are above detailed, have *immediate* recourse to a doctor, where possible.

Source: Beeton, Isabella. *The Book of Household Management*. London: S. O. Beeton, 1861, pp. 1073–1074.

TIMELINE   2000 1900 1800 1700 1600 1500 1400 1300 1200 1100 1000 900 800 700 600 500 400 300 200 100 1 BCE

What You Need to Know

This selection comes from *The Book of Household Management*, by Isabella Beeton, published in London in 1861. A wife and mother herself, Beeton was well known in Britain for her articles on cooking and household management published as monthly supplements to *The Englishwoman's Domestic Magazine*. The articles were then compiled in the book. As the excerpts here indicate, Beeton included basic medical advice, including instructions on how to treat cholera, in her columns.

While the first breakthroughs in the germ theory of medicine were being made even as Beeton wrote her columns, the vast majority of the medical establishment of the time, on which Beeton based her advice, believed that diseases such as cholera were caused by three basic factors. One was climate; a second was an inherited susceptibility to the illness; and the third were lifestyle choices, specifically, intemperance—too much alcohol, too much rich food, too much indulging of the senses. Thus Beeton's chief advice for avoiding cholera is to avoid an "intemperate diet" and maintain a clean and well-ventilated home.

A Closer Look

Although Beeton offered various home remedies for treating cholera, her main advice was for sufferers and those caring for them to immediately seek the advice of a doctor upon the first evidence of symptoms.

Physicians were a highly regarded profession in Victorian England. Doctors would see their patients in one of two settings. Those who were financially well off were usually treated through home visits; the poor largely saw them when confined to hospitals, if they saw them at all. One of the reasons the well-off avoided hospitals was because they were typically crowded and filthy places, notorious for their high death rates.

Even for the wealthy, it helped to be in the right place, as the vast majority of English physicians were situated in London, where there were enough patients with means to support a practice. While physicians, in the major cities at least, had to be licensed by the Royal College of Physicians, most did not attend the few medical schools and teaching hospitals that then existed in Britain. Most physicians and physicians-to-be held to the idea that medicine was best learned through books, rather than observation, and the more ancient the better, as the diagnoses and remedies in them were believed to have withstood the test of time.

1   100   200   300   400   500   600   700   800   900   1000   1100   1200   1300   1400   1500   1600   1700   1800   1900   2000 CE

2.16.9 Pony Express Poster

New York, New York
1861

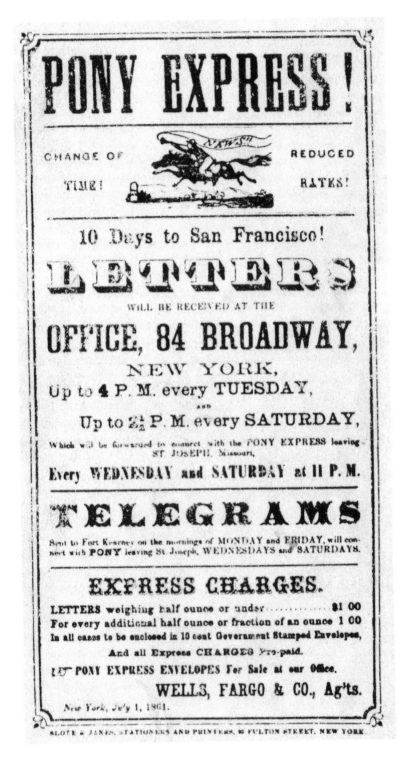

Credit: Three Lions/Getty Images

What You Need to Know

The poster shown here advertising the Pony Express was issued by Well, Fargo, & Company in 1861. In fact, other businessmen founded the Pony Express a year earlier; Wells Fargo, a New York–based banking and express delivery company, specializing in Western business, took over the company in 1861.

The Pony Express was operated as a private mail company that offered the fastest service available at the time for the delivery of mail, newspapers, and small packages from western Missouri—where the telegraphic network ended—to California and back. As the poster notes, it promised delivery in 10 days from New York to San Francisco. Before this service, it could take months for mail and news to reach the burgeoning state of California. Sending materials by Pony Express was not cheap—$10 for an ounce of mail (or about $250 today)—so it was primarily used by businesses.

To deliver on its promise, the service established more than 180 relay stations across the 2,000-mile route, which included stables and corrals of fresh ponies about every 10 to 15 miles, depending on terrain. Roughly every 75 miles, the stables included living quarters for riders. To save money and provide security, the facilities—which were manned by station keepers, stock tenders, and route superintendents—were usually attached to existing trading posts or army forts.

A Closer Look

The Pony Express chose both its men and its horses for speed. One wanted ad (for the former) read: "young, skinny, wiry fellows, not over 18. Must be expert riders. Willing to risk death daily. Orphans Preferred."

Riders and horses would stand ready at stations. As soon as another rider arrived, the bags, which were easily detachable from the saddle, would be passed to the new rider, who would take off as fast he could for the next stable, where he would change horses, about every half an hour to an hour, depending how rough the trail was.

Pay for the riders was quite good—about $125 a month, plus room and board, at a time when the average unskilled worker made about $50 a month. But then the riders put up with primitive living conditions, isolation from friends and family, a high injury rate, and the possibility of Indian attack.

Even as they galloped across the Plains, Pony Express riders were becoming national celebrities. Travelers on the route would raise a cheer as they saw the riders advance from a dot on the horizon to a whirl of dust as they passed. Further cementing the express's place in Western lore was its ephemeralness. Within 18 months of being launched, it had been rendered obsolete by technology, when the first transcontinental telegraph service offered communication at a speed not even the fastest pony could match.

1 100 200 300 400 500 600 700 800 900 1000 1100 1200 1300 1400 1500 1600 1700 1800 1900 2000 CE

United Kingdom
1861

Bubble-and-Squeak (Cold Meat Cookery).

Ingredients.—A few thin slices of cold boiled beef; butter, cabbage, 1 sliced onion, pepper and salt to taste.

Mode.—Fry the slices of beef gently in a little butter, taking care not to dry them up. Lay them on a flat dish, and cover with fried greens. The greens may be prepared from cabbage sprouts or green savoys. They should be boiled till tender, well drained, minced, and placed, still quite hot, in a frying pan, with butter, a sliced onion, and seasonings of pepper and salt. When the onion is done, it is ready to serve.

Time.—Altogether, 1/2 hour

Bengal Recipe for Making Mango Chetney.

Ingredients.—1 1/2 lbs. of moist sugar, 3/4 lb. of salt, 1/4 lb. of garlic, 1/4 lb. of onions, 3/4 lb. of powdered ginger, 1/4 lb. of dried chilies, 3/4 lb. of mustard seed, 3/4 lb. of stoned raisins, 2 bottles best vinegar, 30 large unripe sour apples.

Mode.—the sugar must be made into a syrup; the garlic, onion, and ginger be finely pounded in a mortar; the mustard seed be washed in cold vinegar, and dried in the sun; the apples be peeled, cored, and sliced, and boiled in a bottle and a half of the vinegar. When all this is done, and the apples are quite cold, put them into a large pan, and gradually mix the whole of the rest of the ingredients including the remaining half-bottle of vinegar. It must be stirred until the whole is thoroughly blended, and then put into bottle or use. Tie a piece of wet bladder over the mouths of the bottles, after they are well corked.

Note.—This recipe was given by a native to an English lady, who had long been resident in India, and who since her return to her native country, has become well celebrated among her friends for the excellence of this Eastern relish. . . .

Toad-in-the-Hole (Cold Meat Cookery).

Ingredients.—6 oz. of flour, 1 pint of milk, 3 eggs, butter, a few slices of cold mutton, pepper and salt to taste, 2 kidneys.

Mode.—Make a smooth batter of flour, milk, and eggs in the above proportion; butter a baking-dish, and pour in the batter. Into this place a few slices of cold mutton, previously well seasoned, and the kidneys, which should be cut into rather small pieces; bake about 1 hour, or rather longer, and send it to the table in the dish it was baked in.

Time.—Rather more than 1 hour

Source: Beeton, Isabella. *The Book of Household Management*. London: S. O. Beeton, 1861, pp. 190, 287, 351.

What You Need to Know

This selection of recipes come from *The Book of Household Management*, by Isabella Beeton. The 1861 volume was a compilation of advice columns Beeton had written on domestic tasks for *The Englishwoman's Domestic Magazine*, which was published by her husband Samuel.

England in the mid-nineteenth century was a society very much divided by class and wealth, and the food people ate reflected these divisions. The urban poor had perhaps the worst diet of all, often consisting of little more than potato scraps, old turnips, and rotten vegetables. If desperate enough, unemployed persons might seek sustenance in poorhouses, where they would be fed a diet of potatoes, bread, cheese, and oatmeal, although they would be required to work long hours to receive this basic fare. Poor people in the countryside usually had access to a wider variety of foods, including more types of vegetables and even some meat, usually in the form of sausages and smoked cuts.

Beeton, of course, was not writing for them, but for the burgeoning middle class, who tried to emulate their class superiors among the aristocracy and the merchant elite in their consumption of great quantities of carefully prepared dishes, served on fine china and eaten with silverware.

A Closer Look

The recipes in this excerpt from Beeton's book include bubble-and-squeak, a kind of hash made from the meats and vegetables leftover from a roast; mango chutney, a spiced fruity condiment of Indian origin; and toad-in-the-hole, a savory pie of meat and vegetables. The first and third are traditional British dishes, geared to middle-class budgets. Both involved the use of leftovers, food that the truly well-off would not touch. The second, mango chutney, was an exotic import, brought back from India, the so-called "jewel in the crown" of Britain's burgeoning overseas empire.

The economic prosperity of the Victorian age not only lead to the introduction of more variety and quantity of foods but caused changes in the way people ate. Better artificial lighting allowed suppers to be consumed later, leading to the introduction of late afternoon teas, with their light sandwiches and delicate savory pastries for the peckish. There was also a growing social distancing of the servants in the household. Whereas before the Industrial Revolution, families often ate at the same table with their help, a new emphasis on the nuclear family and new social proprieties saw the family eating in a formal dining room and the servants eating in the kitchen.

Nebraska
1867

Credit: Hulton Archive/Getty Images

What You Need to Know

This poster from 1867 advertises travel on the Union Pacific Railroad. The Union Pacific was the eastern leg of the first transcontinental railroad, connecting the eastern United States with California, and completed in 1869. Even before its completion, the railroad was open for service as far west as it went—in this case, from its starting point in Omaha to its then terminus in North Platte, Nebraska, about 300 miles west.

While traveling across the continent by rail was faster, safer, and more comfortable than earlier modes of travel—wagon train, steamship via the disease-ridden Isthmus of Panama, and sailing ship around stormy Cape Horn—it was not without its hardships, dangers, and delays, especially in its first years of operation. Although the trains could average 40 miles per hour, they seldom stayed at that speed for long. Mechanical failures were frequent as were track outages. To maximize government incentives for miles built, the railroads had often laid down shoddy track. Weather was a concern as well. Snowdrifts could stop a train, leading to food shortages and other discomforts, such as freezing cold when car heaters failed. Summertime journeys could be oppressive, as passengers had to choose between leaving windows open and being assaulted by smoke, dust, and grit, or closing them and being stifled by warm, still air.

A Closer Look

If riding on the transcontinental railroad was a series of annoyances and hardships, building the road could be grueling and even fatal. Days were long, from sunup to sundown, and the work of the most labor-intensive kind. Workers—largely Irish immigrants and Civil War veterans on the Central Pacific heading west, as well as similar contingents on the Union Pacific heading east, although supplemented with thousands of Chinese immigrants—spent most of their days laying heavy, fifty-foot lengths of iron track and four-foot-long crossties, then connecting the two with spikes driven into the ground by sledgehammers. And that was on the flatland. In the mountains, rock had to be blasted with unstable nitroglycerine, which, because of laws against its transport, had to be manufactured on site. (More stable dynamite, while invented in 1867, was not yet available in sufficient quantities in the American West at that time.) Several hundred workers are believed to have died actually constructing the railroad. But the real killer in the work camps was disease. Overwork, poor food, and crowded and unsanitary conditions are estimated to have killed 10 times the number of persons who died from accidents.

1   100   200   300   400   500   600   700   800   900   1000   1100   1200   1300   1400   1500   1600   1700   1800   1900   2000 CE

2.16.12 Deadwood Stagecoach

South Dakota
Late Nineteenth Century

Credit: Library of Congress

What You Need to Know

The accompanying photo shows a stagecoach en route between Cheyenne, Wyoming, and Deadwood, South Dakota.

Deadwood, South Dakota, the destination of the coach pictured here, was typical of Western mining towns. In 1874, Colonel George Custer—famously killed two years later at the Battle of the Little Bighorn—reported the discovery of gold in the Black Hills in the southwestern corner of what was then the Dakota Territory. The news brought a flood of prospectors to lands held sacred by the Sioux peoples of the region.

The gold ore at Deadwood proved substantial enough to sustain the town after the initial gold rush period. But now the mines were owned by wealthy individuals and larger companies because only they had the capital to dig the deep mines needed to get at it.

As Deadwood became a more settled community, it was increasingly linked to the nation's transportation network, first with stagecoaches and then, in the late 1880s, with a railroad. Both transported people and freight but were often kept afloat financially by lucrative government contracts to transport mail.

A Closer Look

In the late nineteenth century, when this photo was taken, stagecoaches were the primary form of long-distance travel between towns in the American West unserved by railroads. Stagecoach journeys were tests of endurance for the passengers. To maximize revenue, stagecoach lines tried to pack as many people into—and onto—the coach as possible, with the average passenger getting between 15 and 18 inches of sitting space. Adult male passengers were often asked to sit up top with the driver, where they were exposed to dust and the elements, although it did free them from the annoyances of their fellow passengers. Days on the road meant little bathing and much body odor.

The routes the coaches followed were little more than rutted tracks, and most vehicles lacked springs to cushion the ride because such devices were heavy and represented just one more thing to break down on the road. Thus, coaches rocked violently back and forth. Mark Twain, who rode to California on one in the 1860s, described the stagecoach, sarcastically, as "a cradle on wheels."

Riding the coaches also meant riding with fear. By the late nineteenth century, Indians represented little threat, but the coaches, slow moving and far from law enforcement, were fat targets for bandits.

1   100   200   300   400   500   600   700   800   900   1000   1100   1200   1300   1400   1500   1600   1700   1800   1900   2000 CE

2.16.13 Victorian Man with a Penny-Farthing Bicycle

United Kingdom
Late Nineteenth Century

Credit: Hulton-Deutsch Collection/Corbis

What You Need to Know

In this photo, a young British man poses in front of what was known as a "penny-farthing" bicycle. The image comes from the late nineteenth century.

Invented around 1870, the penny-farthing was named for the fact that its two wheels of very different sizes resembled the ratio between the tiny farthing and the much larger penny in British coinage. The enormous size of the front wheel, up to 60 inches in diameter, was a result of this early bicycle's limitation as a direct-drive vehicle. That is, the pedals the bicyclist used to propel the vehicle were directly attached to the front wheel. The bigger the wheel, the faster it could be pedaled.

The penny-farthing and its variants in other industrialized countries was the first vehicle to be called a "bicycle." Between the 1870s and the 1890s, when it was replaced by the so-called safety bicycle, which featured a chain drive that dispensed with the outsized front wheel, the penny-farthing and its variants proved enormously popular, in the United Kingdom, continental Europe, and the United States.

Although an improvement over earlier velocipedes, in which the cyclist was propelled by running along the ground while sitting on it, the penny-farthing was hard to mount, dangerous to ride, and very uncomfortable. Without pneumatic tires, the bicycle offered no resistance to shocks from rocks and uneven ground. It was thus a sport largely confined to adventurous young men, who were often seen riding through parks and the countryside, usually as part of bicycling clubs.

A Closer Look

The penny-farthing craze of the 1870s and 1880s was at the intersection of two larger social developments of the age, which were particularly noticeable in the Anglo-Saxon countries: physical health and new ideas about masculinity. By the late nineteenth century, older medical ideas about the dangers of overexertion were giving way to a new understanding that the human body needed exercise. This was, in part, a response to the growth of white-collar work, particularly among middle- and upper-class men. Such sedentary activity was increasingly seen as presenting health problems of its own.

At the same time, such work was viewed as undermining masculinity. That is, sedentary work was seen as somehow feminizing. In response, young men of the late nineteenth century took up all kinds of physical activities to reassert their manhood, including competitive sports, such as cricket in England and baseball in the United States, and noncompetitive activities, such as riding penny-farthing bicycles. The fact that they were so difficult to ride and so potentially dangerous—putting them outside the preserve of women—only added to their appeal.

1 100 200 300 400 500 600 700 800 900 1000 1100 1200 1300 1400 1500 1600 1700 1800 1900 2000 CE

2.16.14 American Temperance Crusaders Protest a Saloon

Pittsburgh, Pennsylvania
1880

We paused in front of the saloon [in Pittsburgh] that I have mentioned. The ladies ranged themselves along the curbstone, for they had been forbidden in any wise to incommode the passers-by, being dealt with much more strictly than a drunken man or a heap of dry-goods boxes would be.

At a signal from our gray-haired leader, a sweet-voiced woman began to sing, "Jesus the water of life will give," all our voices soon blending in that sweet song. I think it was the most novel spectacle that I recall. There stood women of undoubted religious devotion and the highest character, most of them crowned with the glory of gray hairs. Along the stony pavement of that stoniest of cities rumbled the heavy wagons, many of them carriers of beer; between us and the saloon in front of which we were drawn up in line, passed the motley throng, almost every man lifting his hat and even the little newsboys doing the same. It was American manhood's tribute to Christianity and to womanhood, and it was significant and full of pathos.

The leader had already asked the saloonkeeper if we might enter, and he had declined, else the prayer meeting would have occurred inside his door. A sorrowful old lady, whose only son had gone to ruin through that very death-trap, knelt on the cold, moist pavement and offered a broken-hearted prayer, while all our heads were bowed.

At a signal we moved on and the next saloonkeeper permitted us to enter. I had no more idea of the inward appearance of a saloon than if there had been no such place on earth. I knew nothing of its high, heavily corniced bar, its barrels with the ends all pointed towards the looker-on, each barrel being furnished with a faucet, its shelves glittering with decanters and cut glass, its floors thickly strewn with sawdust, and here and there a round table with chairs—nor of its abundant fumes, sickening to healthful nostrils.

The tall, stately lady who led us placed her Bible on the bar and read a psalm, whether hortatory or imprecatory I do not remember, but the spirit of these crusaders was so gentle, I think it must have been the former.

Then we sang "Rock of Ages" as I thought I had never heard it sung before, with a tender confidence to the height of which one does not rise in the easy-going, regulation prayer meeting, and then one of the older women whispered to me softly that the leader wished to know if I would pray. It was strange, perhaps, but I felt not the least reluctance, and kneeling on that sawdust floor, with a group of earnest hearts around me, and behind them, filling every corner and extending out into the street, a crowd of unwashed, unkempt, hard-looking drinking men, I was conscious that perhaps never in my life, save beside my sister Mary's dying bed, had I prayed as truly as I did then. This was my Crusade baptism. The next day I went on to the West and within a week had been made president of the Chicago W.C.T.U.

Source: Willard, Frances Elizabeth. *The Autobiography of an American Woman: Glimpses of Fifty Years*. Evanston, IL: Ruby I. Gilbert, 1904, pp. 340–341.

TIMELINE   2000 1900 1800 1700 1600 1500 1400 1300 1200 1100 1000 900 800 700 600 500 400 300 200 100 1 BCE

What You Need to Know

This excerpt is from *The Autobiography of an American Woman: Glimpses of Fifty Years*, written by Frances Elizabeth Willard and published in 1889. Willard was president of the Women's Christian Temperance Union (WCTU), the nation's leading organization in the fight against alcohol, although it also worked for broader social reforms and women's suffrage.

Willard, who took over the WCTU in 1879, was determined to fulfill the organization's mission to create a "pure and sober world." She was tireless in her efforts, which included organizing, education, lobbying, and protest, both of politicians who resisted demands to limit or outlaw alcohol consumption and, as described in the excerpt, at saloons themselves. There, the largely women demonstrators would sing hymns, pray, and pass out tracts to besotted patrons. More radical antialcohol crusaders, such as Carrie Nation, went further, engaging in direct action by smashing saloon property.

A Closer Look

Drinking establishments were ubiquitous in late nineteenth- and early twentieth-century America, an estimated 300,000 in all by 1900. They were particular prevalent in cities with large numbers of immigrants. San Francisco, for example, had one licensed saloon for every 96 residents in 1890.

They varied much in quality. Some were elegant establishments, with paintings on the wall—often lascivious in subject matter—and upholstered furniture; others were dark and dingy places, where customers lined up at plain wooden bars for steins of cheap beer or to bring the beer back to their homes in buckets. Many establishments enticed their primarily male, working-class clientele with generous buffets.

The saloons served multiple purposes. Many were more than just places to drink and eat, but community centers of a sort. Businessmen met there to strike deals and politicians to hear the grievances of their constituents. Indeed, saloonkeepers—respected members of their community with a wide network of acquaintances—often went into politics, serving as city councilmen.

All of this drinking, of course, came with a social cost, in lowered worker productivity, increased criminality and, worst of all to the women who filled the ranks of the WCTU, led to domestic abuse, broken marriages, and shattered families. Women, in and out of the organization, frequently complained that husbands wasted their earnings on drink, leaving their families in penury. In rural areas, drunken men often left fieldwork undone. Physicians spoke of the "syphilis of the innocent," a prevalence of venereal disease in the wives of husbands who took advantage of the prostitutes that hung around saloons.

2.16.15 Widow's Mourning Wear during the Victorian Era

United Kingdom
1888

The regulation period for a widow's mourning is two years; of this period crape should be worn for one year and nine months, for the first twelve months the dress should be entirely covered with crape, for the remaining three months trimmed with crape, heavily so the first six months, and considerably less the remaining three; during the last three months black without crape should be worn. After two years two months half-mourning is prescribed, but many people prefer to continue wearing black without crape in lieu of half-mourning.

The widow's cap should be worn for a year and a day.

Lawn cuffs and collars should be worn during the crape period.

After a year and nine months jet trimming may be worn.

Widowers should wear mourning for the same period as widows, but they usually enter society much sooner than widows. . . .

A widow is not expected to enter into society under twelve months, and during that time she should neither accept invitations nor issue them. Her visiting should be confined to her relations and intimate friends. After twelve months she should commence gradually to enter into society, but balls and dances should be avoided during the period that crape is worn.

Source: Anonymous ("A member of the aristocracy"). *Manners and Rules of Good Society or Solecisms to be Avoided*. London: Frederick Warne and Co.: 1888, pp. 223, 226.

What You Need to Know

The accompanying document comes from *Manners and Rules of Good Society or Solecisms to be Avoided*, a guidebook on etiquette written in 1888 by an anonymous author who simply signed himself or herself as "A member of the aristocracy."

Supplying mourning clothes was big business for Victorian tailors, especially as economic prosperity expanded the number of customers from the middle class who were able to buy them. Although all tailors were capable of supplying mourning clothes, some specialized in the business.

What made the trade especially lucrative was that people were expected to wear new sets of clothing every time they went into mourning. It was considered both disrespectful and unlucky to keep mourning clothes after the mourning period was over.

Nor were tailors the only Victorians to make a good living out of the dead. Victorian funerals were typically elaborate affairs, providing much employment for caterers and other service workers, as were the tombstones and mausoleums that marked the graves of the dead.

A Closer Look

Victorian England had elaborate rituals surrounding the mourning process. This document focuses on dress at different time periods following a death. Not only were widows in their earliest months of loss to wear black, which represented spiritual darkness, but they should wear materials that were not shiny. Crape—a hard and rough form of silk—was an important part of the mourning outfit because, according to fashion ideas of the time, it did not combine well with inappropriately luxurious fabrics, such as velvet or satin. In addition, widows were to limit their jewelry to items made of jet, a hard and polished form of coal, which, of course, was deep black in color.

Gradually, over a period of years, the widow could begin wearing lighter colors during her period of "half-mourning," first gray, then mauve, and finally white. The dress rituals for widowers were simpler, just dark suits and accessories. As for minor children, they were not expected to wear mourning clothing at all, though some families would not let their daughters wear colorful clothes during the mourning period.

The period of mourning varied by the closeness of one's relationship to the deceased. Widows were expected to mourn for two years, as the document indicates, while children and parents were to do so for one. More distant relatives such as grandparents, siblings, aunts, uncles, and cousins were to mourn for between six months and four weeks.

1 100 200 300 400 500 600 700 800 900 1000 1100 1200 1300 1400 1500 1600 1700 1800 1900 2000 CE

2.16.16 New York City Street Urchins

New York, New York
1890

Credit: Bettmann/Corbis

What You Need to Know

This image shows two homeless street children from journalist and photographer Jacob Riis's landmark 1890 exposé of life in poor immigrant neighborhoods, *How the Other Half Lives*.

Although some of New York's better-off residents viewed the "urchins" or, for that matter, the immigrant masses with disdain, others saw them as victims of circumstance, needing and deserving help. Among these reformers were the so-called muckrakers, journalists who sought to bring the awful conditions of immigrant neighborhoods to the attention of the larger public. Among these was the Danish-born social reformer Riis, although even he held that many of the young children he photographed and wrote about were "hardened little scoundrels."

Riis tried to tell his story in the city's major newspapers but was rejected because the images and descriptions he offered were considered too disturbing for polite readers. But there was another outlet, *Scribner's Magazine*, one of several publications that did not shy away from hard-hitting investigations of the darker sides of American life. The article was widely read, convincing Riis to expand on what he had found in *How the Other Half Lives*, which not only became a best seller but was critically praised by some of the papers that had initially refused to print Riis's original article and photos.

A Closer Look

Between the end of the Civil War and enactment of strict quotas in the early 1920s, immigrants poured into American cities by the millions, crowding into the poorer quarters where they struggled to make a living. New York City's Lower East Side, where these so-called street urchins resided, was the epicenter of this phenomenon. With 702 persons per acre, it was among the most densely populated spots on Earth.

Most of its inhabitants lived in tenements—poorly constructed, low-rise apartment buildings—where they packed into tiny rooms, with little access to outside air. With no indoor plumbing, residents were forced to use overwhelmed water pumps and outhouses in the tiny spaces behind the buildings. Death rates from disease were high, resulting in thousands of orphan children forced to live on the streets. Many other children, with living parents, were nevertheless pushed onto the streets because there was simply no room in the tenements for them. There they slept where they could, under bridges and in alleyways, eating food from street vendors or those offered by charity soup kitchens. While middle- and upper-class New Yorkers considered them a criminal class in the making, most of the urchins struggled to make an honest living doing odd jobs, such as peddling goods or selling newspapers.

1   100   200   300   400   500   600   700   800   900   1000   1100   1200   1300   1400   1500   1600   1700   1800   1900   2000 CE

2.16.17 Sumo Wrestlers

Japan
1890

Credit: Unidentified Author/Alinari via Getty Images

What You Need to Know

The accompanying photo from 1890 shows two Japanese sumo wrestlers locked in a bout. The picture is clearly posed. Cameras of the day did not have fast enough shutter speeds to capture rapid action, and the two men are consciously looking over their shoulders at the photographer.

Japan's long history has consisted of cycles of openness to outside influences, primarily from China and Korea, followed by periods in which it closed itself to outsiders. In 1853, the nation was abruptly jarred out of one of the latter periods by the arrival of an American naval armada, which demanded that Japan open up its ports to American ships. Japanese leaders recognized how vulnerable their closed-off nation had become to Western armaments, although it took another 15 years for a new government to come to power that opened up Japan to Western technology and culture.

The new leaders recognized that to defend themselves, they needed to modernize their economy and culture by borrowing from the West. The result was rapid industrialization, urbanization, and growth of the working classes, who in their off time sought mass forms of entertainment, such as sumo matches.

A Closer Look

Sumo is the national sport of Japan and grew out of rituals connected to the indigenous Shinto faith, although some of its elements have origins in mainland Asian cultures. The sport, in its modern form, dates to the Edo period from the early seventeenth century to 1868, a time when Japan was becoming unified under a central government. Originally, sumo wrestlers were *ronin*, or *samurai* knights without a lord to serve, who engaged in contests for extra income. At first, they were hired by wealthy individuals to put on private performances in their palaces or in local Shinto shrines. But as Japan became more urbanized in the Edo period, sumo-wrestling matches were put on for public audiences, and admission was charged. By the time this photo was taken, the sport was dominated by full-time professional wrestlers, who could earn substantial sums as they performed in specially built arenas that seated thousands of spectators. In the late nineteenth century, sumo organizations were largely local, with contestants usually competing with others from their home city. But by the 1920s, interurban organizations had formed, leading to national rankings and celebrity status for top wrestlers.

1 100 200 300 400 500 600 700 800 900 1000 1100 1200 1300 1400 1500 1600 1700 1800 1900 2000 CE

WASHING–DAY REFORM.

HARPER TWELVETREES'

UNRIVALLED LABOUR-SAVING

VILLA WASHER,

Wringer and Mangler combined, £5 5s. (Cash Price, £4 15s.), or without Wringer and Mangler, £2 15s. (Cash Price, £2 10s.)

Does the Fortnight's Family Wash in Four Hours, without RUBBING or BOILING, as certified by thousands of delighted purchasers.

The Rev. J. ROBINSON, Great Sampford, Braintree, writes—" With the aid of the servant, aged 14, the Fortnight's Family Washing for six in family is done in four hours."

Mrs. CHARLES PAMMENT, St. Saviour's Villa, Bury St. Edmunds—" Our Fortnight's Family Wash, which formerly occupied from 8 A.M. till 8 P.M., is now done in three hours, and the copper fire is out five hours sooner than it used to be."

Carriage paid; free trial; easy instalment payments, or ten per cent. cash discount.

New Illustrated Catalogue, 48 pages, post free, from
HARPER TWELVETREES, Laundry Machinist,
8o, FINSBURY PAVEMENT, LONDON, E.C.

What You Need to Know

This advertisement for a wringer and mangler, devices for washing clothes, ran in a British newspaper around 1890. Wringers squeezed the moisture out of clothes after they were laundered, while manglers pressed them to remove wrinkles. As the advertisement notes, the device being offered could reduce the washing time for a fortnight's (two weeks') family's laundry from 12 hours to a mere three or four hours.

Housework in the United Kingdom was exhausting and time-consuming in the nineteenth century, especially so when it involved the use of water. But, by late in the century, it was getting easier. Many middle- and upper-class homes were being fitted with indoor plumbing, ending the taxing chore of fetching water from an outdoor pump. The introduction of gas made for easier water heating as well.

Laborsaving devices, such as the combination wringer and mangler here, were also changing the composition of the household, lessening the need for live-in servants or, at least, for so many. As one of the testimonials in the ad notes, the Villa Washer was not meant to replace servants but to make it possible for them to do more work in less time. Although servants, notably from poverty-stricken Ireland, could be had for very low wages, falling prices for appliances—the five pound, five shilling price on this ad (about $600 today)—represented just a week's earning for a skilled worker, making the device accessible on even a lower-middle-class budget.

A Closer Look

While devices such as the washer advertised here made housework go faster and easier, they also raised expectations about what constituted a well-run household. With the introduction of such devices, advertisers in particular, but also the media generally, began to make the argument that a well-kept house—not to mention a well-maintained family—was a hygienic one. Anything less showed the homemaker in a bad light. Prior to the introduction of washers like this one, for example, clothing was laundered less frequently. Except for the very well-off, most people wore the same dirty and smelly clothing for days on end. That was deemed less acceptable as it became possible to do laundry more often. As with all such trends, the trend toward increased household and personal hygiene and cleanliness began among the upper middle class, and then, as prices for laundering devices and ready-to-wear clothing steadily fell, the lower middle class and even working class adopted this ideal and tried to put it into practice.

1 100 200 300   400   500   600   700   800   900   1000 1100 1200 1300   1400   1500   1600   1700 1800 1900 2000 CE

2.16.19 Description of Election Day in New York City

New York, New York
1896

Election Day morning is the earliest of the year. The polls open at six o'clock—long before day-light in that late and cloudy month of November. At three the policemen who are to serve at the polls (nearly three thousand of them on the last occasion) are aroused and sent to breakfast. An hour later they reassemble, are paraded before the desks of the station-houses, instructed, and despatched to their polls, taking with them all the ballot-boxes, ballots, and other furniture, for the safety of which they are held responsible. . . .

On the stroke of six the poll is declared open, and the voting immediately begins, the name and address of each applicant being called out by the inspector as soon as the voter presents himself. If he is reported as properly registered, and no one challenges his right, the ballots are given him, their number is recorded by the clerks and every one else interested, and he retires to a booth to select in secret the ticket or tickets he wishes to vote. This done, he returns, hands his ballots to the inspectors, so folded that no one can see their purport, the fact that he has voted is proclaimed and recorded, and he leaves the inclosure. If challenged, he "swears in" his vote, or refuses to do so, according as he is willing or not to take the responsibility of an oath. . . .

To many who are more or less visible all day there this is the most important occasion of the year. To be sure, it may be worth a few dollars to them, directly or indirectly; but plainly they look further than this. . . . It is these men who make the voting-places picturesque. In rough garb and with lordly swagger, they sandwich themselves between neat and dignified lawyers, merchants, and clergymen, proudly sensible of their equality at the polls. Sometimes the motley line reaches out of doors and down the street. . . .

The moment the polls close the liquor-saloons open, but the excessive drunkenness and brawl-ing common in former years are not now seen. . . .

The greatest of the indoor jollifications is that at Tammany Hall. Early in the evening the spacious auditorium becomes packed with tribesmen, a brass band is stationed in the gallery, the wives and daughters of prominent braves appear in the boxes, and the big and little sachems, wiskinskies, and all the rest, gather about a mythical council fire on the stage. A member with a stentorophonic voice reads telegrams from the district leaders and police headquarters, against a storm of cheerful yells and witticisms when the news is favorable, and of hoots and cat-calls when it is not.

Source: Ingersoll, Ernest. "Election Day in New York." *The Century Magazine* 53:1 (November 1896): pp. 3–4, 6–8, 12.

What You Need to Know

This description of voting in the pivotal presidential election of 1896 was written by Ernest Ingersoll. Although a naturalist who focused much of his writing on the environment and archaeology, he also worked as a journalist. In this article, he focuses his considerable observational skills on the less-than-seemly mechanics of voting in New York City, which was then under the control of the Tammany Hall political machine. The article was published in the *Century* magazine, which, in the 1890s, was a forum, largely read by educated middle- and upper-income persons, for political reform, including opposition to the corruption of political machines.

For working-class and immigrant New Yorkers, however, Tammany Hall was not a corrupt organization but one that offered them a deal. In exchange for their votes, Tammany politicians offered supporters the chance of a steady job on public works projects or in the city bureaucracy; when a family was in trouble, the local ward politician from Tammany could offer relief in the form of food or even cash. This was especially important in the 1890s. The city was flooded with impoverished immigrants at a time when private charities were overwhelmed by demand for help and government welfare agencies had yet to be created.

To ensure that voters kept their end of the bargain, Tammany Hall politicians created an elaborate infrastructure to oversee polling, making sure supporters came out and voted the right way. This was made easier by the fact that secret balloting—a goal of many reformer readers of the *Century*—had yet to be introduced in New York.

A Closer Look

Politics in the Gilded Age, the period between the end of the Civil War and the reformist Progressive Era of the early twentieth century, was very much about identity. Although ideology mattered to some extent—Democrats generally held to the idea that government should not interfere with personal liberties while Republicans argued that it should be a force for moral uplift—voters usually chose a party based on who they were. Immigrants and Catholics tended to vote Democratic, native-born Protestants typically sided with the Republicans.

In the rapidly growing urban centers of the country, the conflict was especially acute. Republicans pushed for laws restricting alcohol consumption and keeping the Sabbath a day of rest, policies much opposed by urban workers who enjoyed their beer and their Sunday entertainments as a respite from the long and grueling workweek. They resented Republican do-gooders and so flocked to the polls to defend their way of life by voting for Tammany Hall Democrats.

2.16.20 Advertisement for Kodak's Bullet Camera

United States
1897

Credit: Kean Collection/Archive Photos/Getty Images

What You Need to Know

Shown here is an advertisement for the patented "bullet camera," manufactured and sold by the Eastman Kodak Company. The ad ran in the March 1897 issues of *Ladies' Home Journal*, then the number one selling general interest magazine for women.

Eastman's box cameras were only one of the many new products enticing American consumers in the late nineteenth century, as mass manufacturers made the first hesitant steps away from industrial goods to consumer ones. Some of these were new products—the light bulb, the telephone, the phonograph—but most were old products, such as soap or preserved foods (now in cans) mass produced for a national market, rather than at home, or by local artisans.

To make their operations profitable, these new mass consumer goods manufacturers turned to advertising. As old as the press itself, advertising, before the Civil War, consisted of lists of goods being offered for sale. By the 1880s, advertising had become increasingly visual, focusing on the attributes of the product and why the consumer might want them. The ad here focuses on the camera's ease of use, an important attribute for potential consumers whose only experience with photography was having their picture taken by a professional and watching him laboriously set up his camera.

A Closer Look

In 1888, George Eastman, a former banker from Rochester, New York, introduced the first camera simple enough for nonprofessionals to use. Before Eastman's invention, taking photographs was a complicated process, requiring expertise in the use of lenses, film, and most important, the developing of negatives. Taking advantage of the latest innovations in focusing and the other internal mechanics of photography, Eastman introduced a box camera with 100-exposure roll of film. After taking the pictures, the amateur photographer sent the camera back to Kodak, where the pictures were developed and sent back to the consumer, along with a newly loaded camera. Eastman simplified the process with the new "bullet camera," which contained cartridges (hence, the name "bullet") that could be sent back by themselves for development.

Within a few years of their introduction, Americans were taking millions of pictures annually. Photography became less formal in the process. Staid studio poses gave way to more spontaneous imagery. Beyond photography, the ability to capture important landmarks in life, along with the simple joys of living, changed the nature of how people saw and remembered things.

1 100 200 300 400 500 600 700 800 900 1000 1100 1200 1300 1400 1500 1600 1700 1800 1900 2000 CE

2.16.21 French Opera Poster for Sapho

Paris, France
1897

Credit: DeAgostini/Getty Images

What You Need to Know

This is an 1897 poster for the opera "Sapho," being given its premiere that year at the Theatre de l'Opera Comique in Paris. With music by the French composer Jules Massenet, it was based on the novel of the same name by the popular French novelist Alphonse Daudet. It tells the story of a naïve young man from rural Provence who comes to Paris to study and falls in love with an artist's model with a notorious reputation. When he learns of it, he leaves her and returns to Provence. She follows, but he spurns her.

As the typography of the poster reveals, the biggest appeal for audiences, at least in the impresarios' opinion, was its star, Emma Calvé, the most famous French opera star of the late nineteenth and early twentieth centuries. Calvé represented a new phenomenon in French culture, the rise of the performing arts celebrity. With incomes rising and more leisure time available, people flocked to the theater to see these stars. At the same time, new mass production techniques allowed for more advertising. New illustration-heavy newspapers and magazines devoted whole sections of the paper to the doings of opera and theater stars. Posters with their image were pasted up on walls and fences throughout Paris and other cities.

A Closer Look

The period between the Franco-Prussian War of 1871 and the outbreak of World War I in 1914 is known in France as the Belle Époque, or "beautiful era," although the name was applied retrospectively during World War I as a contrast to the horrors and deprivation of that conflict.

It was a time of peace, prosperity, and a wave of new technological and scientific breakthroughs that gave people an optimism about the future. While the name Belle Époque applies to France, the same sense of optimism and progress permeated much of the Continent's culture, resulting in great artistic achievements. And the cultural capital of the age was Paris, a city that attracted artists, musicians, and writers from across Europe and even the Americas.

One of its main attractions was its nightlife—alive with bistros, cafés, music halls, and theaters featuring performances from variety-type shows to high opera—and its demimonde, a term encompassing a kind of underground society where artists, prostitutes, and others rejecting the mores and lifestyles of the bourgeoisie could mingle. Calvé was on the fringes of the real demimonde, while the tragic heroine Sapho that she portrayed on stage was fully immersed in it.

1 100 200 300   400   500   600   700   800   900   1000 1100 1200 1300   1400   1500   1600   1700   1800   1900 2000 CE

2.16.22 American Woman Modeling a Corset

United States
1899

Credit: Library of Congress

What You Need to Know

The accompanying photograph shows a young woman brushing her long hair and modeling a corset. It was taken in 1899.

Corsets were undergarments that were made from cloth and a semirigid material, such as cane, ivory or, most often, bone. Of the latter, whale bone was the most commonly used, a by-product of the thriving whale-oil industry of the nineteenth century. Corsets were designed to shape a woman's torso by lifting the breasts and tightening the stomach, to produce what was considered the ideal hourglass figure. (Corsets were also occasionally worn by men, to pull in the stomach.) Typically, the corset was worn over a chemise, or light undergarment, which absorbed sweat.

Putting on a corset was arduous and required the help of another person, who tightened the laces on the back to create the pressure that would reshape the wearer's figure, sometimes tightening the waist to a mere sixteen inches around. This process was known as tight-lacing. Corsets could be quite uncomfortable to wear; they often chafed and they could cause shortness of breath. This made it difficult for women wearing them to engage in strenuous physical activity, even walking fast. Worse, they could be dangerous to a woman's long-term health. The pressure they exerted on the lungs could cause mucus to form, resulting in a persistent cough and even infection.

Still, corsets remained popular in much of the industrialized West, through the nineteenth century and into the early twentieth. Mass production brought down the cost so that even working-class women could wear them.

A Closer Look

Not all women—or men—were fans of corsets or, more specifically, the tight-lacing process. Both in the United Kingdom and the United States, movements emerged to get women to give up such constrictive undergarments. Their main rationale concerned women's health and so was taken up by doctors. Journalists, too, inveighed against tight-lacing, as did preachers who used the argument that women were putting their own sinful vanity and pride before the healthful body they needed to take care of their families.

There were also a number of inventors and designers who tried to come up with alternatives. One was the "emancipation" or "reform" bodice, a tight sleeveless vest that offered some support to the waist and breasts but without the excessive constriction of the corset. Such bodices never really caught on. What finally put the corset back in the closet were changing ideals of women's beauty, which increasingly in the early twentieth century moved toward a slimmer shape, without hourglass curves.

1 100 200 300 400 500 600 700 800 900 1000 1100 1200 1300 1400 1500 1600 1700 1800 1900 2000 CE

2.16.23 Renault's First Saloon Car

France
1902

Credit: Hulton Archive/Getty Images

What You Need to Know

This photo shows the first "saloon" automobile produced in 1902 by the Renault brothers, who had founded what would become the Renault Corporation in 1898.

By 1902, France had long been a pioneer in automobile innovation and production. French inventor Nicolas-Joseph is believed to have built the first self-propelled vehicle there in 1769 while Jean Joseph Étienne Lenoir helped create the first internal combustion engine in the mid-nineteenth century. By the early twentieth century, France was the largest automobile manufacturer in the world; its more than 30,000 new cars in 1903 represented nearly half the total for the entire world and nearly three times the production of the United States.

At first, French automobile producers, like the Renault brothers, built their automobiles by hand, with each one constructed by a team of engineers and mechanics. No car was exactly the same. Such techniques kept cars expensive. Renault introduced some mass-production techniques before World War I and the conflict itself, which created an urgent need for ambulances, trucks, and tanks, sped up that process. Still, there were factors that slowed the transition to true mass production and sales of automobiles in France and Europe, especially compared with the United States, including low wages and productivity, the economic downturn of the Great Depression, and World War II.

A Closer Look

Saloon automobiles, also known as sedans, were fully enclosed vehicles, usually with a separate compartment for luggage. Saloon cars offered the obvious advantage of protection from the elements for passengers and goods alike. Aside from the enclosed cabin, the car pictured here featured a few key innovations, including kerosene headlights for nighttime driving and pneumatic tires, which cushioned the ride. Cars in turn-of-the-twentieth-century France were typically used for recreational purposes—such as attending special occasions or going on excursions in the countryside—rather than daily commuting. For that, most people still relied on urban rail transport.

At the turn of the twentieth century, automobiles had an exclusive clientele, made of the well-heeled and the adventurous. Before the introduction of the American Model T, mass produced on assembly lines by industrialist Henry Ford beginning in 1908, automobiles were expensive, costing upward of several years' wages for the average worker. They were difficult to operate, requiring hand-cranking to start and strong muscles to steer and brake, especially on the primitive roads that characterized France outside city centers until after World War I. They were also prone to frequent breakdowns, meaning that drivers had to have a solid understanding of automobile mechanics to fix them.

1 100 200 300 400 500 600 700 800 900 1000 1100 1200 1300 1400 1500 1600 1700 1800 1900 2000 CE

2.16.24 A English Traveler's Description of Marrakesh

Marrakesh, Morocco
1904

IN RED MARRAKESH

There are certain cities that cannot be approached for the first time by any sympathetic traveler without a sense of solemnity and reverence that is not far removed from awe. Athens, Rome, Constantinople, Damascus, and Jerusalem may be cited as examples; each in its turn has filled me with great wonder and deep joy. But all of these are to be reached nowadays by the railway, that great modern purge of sensibility. Even Jerusalem is not exempt. A single line stretches from Jaffa by the sea to the very gates of the Holy City, playing hide-and-seek among the mountains of Judea by the way, because the Turk was too poor to tunnel a direct path.

In Morocco, on the other hand, the railway is still unknown. He who seeks any of the country's inland cities must take horse or mule, camel or donkey, or, as a last resource, be content with a staff to aid him, and walk. Whether he fare to Fez, the city of Mulan Idrees, in which an old writer assures us, "all the beauties of the earth are united"; or to Mequinez, where great Mulai Ismail kept a stream of human blood flowing constantly from his palace that all might know he ruled; or to Red Marrakesh, which Yusuf ibn Tachfin built nine hundred years ago,—his own exertion must convoy him. There must be days and nights of scant fare and small comfort, with all those hundred and one happenings of the road that make for pleasant memories. So far as I have been able to gather in the nine years that have passed since I first visited Morocco, one road is like another road, unless you have the Moghrebbin Arabic at your command and can go off the beaten track in Moorish dress. . . .

For the rank and file of us the Government roads and the harmless necessary soldier must suffice, until the Gordian knot of Morocco's future has been untied or cut. Then perhaps, as a result of French pacific penetration, flying railway trains loaded with tourists, guide-book in hand and camera at the ready, will pierce the secret places of the land, and men will speak of "doing" Morocco, as they "do" other countries in their rush across the world, seeing all the stereotyped sights and appreciating none. For the present, by Allah's grace, matters are quite otherwise.

Source: Bensusan, S. L. *Morocco*. London: Adam and Charles Black, 1904, pp. 77–79.

What You Need to Know

The accompanying document comes from the book *Morocco*, published in London by Samuel Levy Bensusan in 1904. A popular writer of novels and books on the English countryside, Bensusan also penned a number of travel books. In this excerpt from his book on Morocco, Bensusan contrasts travel to the country in his own time to the country with what he expects it to be like in the future, once the kingdom, increasingly under French control, is fully connected to the outside world by railways. Specifically, he fears the onslaught of tourists "guide-book in hand and camera at the ready."

But although Bensusan prides himself on his willingness to go to places the ordinary English tourist would not, in fact travel even to popular locales outside Europe and a few other industrialized places was still quite onerous and harrowing in the early twentieth century. The middle- and upper-class Englishmen and women who were the most likely to venture abroad for pleasure were used to safe water, decent accommodations, and indoor plumbing. Few of these things were to be had overseas, even in many European countries. Complaints about all of these things, as well as crime, bribery, filth, lack of decent service, and the fact that foreigners did not understand English filled the diaries of Victorian- and Edwardian-era tourists.

A Closer Look

Still, for all of the complaints, travel for leisure was becoming ever more commonplace in the late nineteenth and early twentieth centuries, especially as rising economic prosperity expanded the middle and upper middle classes who were new to tourism. Aside from the larger cohort of potential travelers, better transport was the chief reason for the expansion in tourism. Railways allowed for relatively speedy and comfortable inland travel while steamships provided not just faster and more luxurious ocean travel but more predictable scheduling because they did not rely on fickle winds. Expanding telegraph networks permitted instant communication with the tourist's home country, in case of trouble. In addition, much of the world outside the Americas had been absorbed into empires, guaranteeing that tourists could find a fellow countryman or, at least, European with the authority to help them on site.

In response to these advances, a growing tourism industry had emerged. This included not only new hotels, restaurants, and guest houses in some of the more popular destinations but also an infrastructure geared to the needs of the traveler. In the 1890s, American Express introduced the traveler's check. Meanwhile, Thomas Cook & Son, arguably the world's first modern travel agency, had expanded from modest origins in excursions to the English countryside in the 1840s to offering a variety of tours to the edges of the Earth.

1 100 200 300 400 500 600 700 800 900 1000 1100 1200 1300 1400 1500 1600 1700 1800 1900 2000 CE

2.16.25 Preamble to the Industrial Workers of the World Constitution

United States
1905

The working class and the employing class have nothing in common. There can be no peace so long as hunger and want are found among millions of the working people and the few, who make up the employing class, have all the good things of life.

Between these two classes a struggle must go on until workers of the world organize as a class, take possession of the earth and the machinery of production and abolish the wage system.

We find that centering of the management of industries into fewer and fewer hands makes the trade unions unable to cope with the ever growing power of the employing class. The trade unions foster a state of affairs which allows one set of workers to be pitted against another set of workers in the same industry, thereby helping defeat one another in wage wars. Moreover the trade unions aid the employing class to mislead the workers into the belief that the working class have interests in common with their employers.

These conditions can be changed and the interest of the working class upheld only by an organization formed in such a way that all its members in any one industry, or in all industries if necessary, cease work whenever a strike or lockout is on in any department thereof, thus making an injury to one an injury to all. Instead of the conservative motto, "A fair day's wage for a fair day's work," we must inscribe on our banner the revolutionary watchword, "Abolition of the wage system." It is the historic mission of the working class to do away with capitalism. The arm of production must be organized not only for the everyday struggle with capitals, but also to carry on production when capitalism shall have been overthrown. By organizing industrially we are forming the structure of the new society within the shell of the old.

Source: "Preamble of the Industrial Workers of the World." In Erik Bruun and Jay Crosby, *Our Nation's Archive: The History of the United States in Documents*. New York: Black Dog, 1999, pp. 547–548.

TIMELINE   2000 1900 1800 1700 1600 1500 1400 1300 1200 1100 1000 900 800 700 600 500 400 300 200 100 1 BCE

What You Need to Know

This is the preamble to the 1905 constitution of the Industrial Workers of the World (IWW), a national union that attempted to organize unskilled laborers in the early decades of the twentieth century. Members of the IWW were known as Wobblies, supposedly after the mispronunciation of the name IWW by a Chinese immigrant worker.

Organized out of the Western Federation of Miners union in 1905, the IWW differed significantly from the leading labor organization of its day, the American Federation of Laborers (AFL). The latter organized by craft, focusing on skilled workers, who were largely white, male, and native-born. While reflecting the prejudices of the day against immigrants, African-Americans, and women, the strategy also had a solid rationale. Skilled workers were harder to replace, making management more likely to negotiate with their representatives.

The Wobblies took a different approach. They had no racial or gender restrictions on membership. And they focused on organizing every worker in a given industry or worksite, whether skilled or unskilled, typically getting their best reception among the latter. This, as noted, presented an inherent problem; the unskilled could easily be replaced by strikebreakers. That is why the IWW eschewed arbitration for direct action. But such radical measures produced a backlash among industrialists and governments, which actively tried to suppress the union.

A Closer Look

While the IWW was active across the country, it was particularly strong in the West, especially among unskilled and semiskilled laborers in the lumber, mining, and dock-working industries. The Wobblies eschewed arbitration of labor disputes, preferring the direct action of strikes, boycotts, and propaganda instead. Indeed, their house press organ was called *Direct Action*. Often, when a strike occurred at a Wobbly worksite, hundreds of members would flock to the community, often by illegally hitching rides on freight trains. Once there, they would begin speaking out in favor of the strikers on street corners. Inevitably, they would get arrested, as local governments passed laws against such activities. This would only bring more union members, who would take their places. The goal was to overwhelm the jails with union members, making it so expensive for town leaders that they would urge company owners to settle. But this could backfire disastrously, as in the 1916 lumber strike in Everett, Washington, when vigilantes shot down five union members, helping to bring the labor action to an end.

The attacks on the IWW was only a more exaggerated version of the general hostility toward all unions—even conservative craft unions—held by business, the upper class, and many members of the middle class. Although unions were legal, judges frequently issued injunctions against them for engaging in strikes or boycotts, penalizing their leadership with large fines. As for members of the working class, they were divided about unions. Most appreciated what they offered but feared that joining them would cause them to lose their jobs.

2.16.26 Prison Conditions in Siberia

Siberia
1905

A fortnight later I was informed that a party of convicts would start for Moscow that evening. I was to accompany them, and accordingly must assume the convict garb. After eighteen years I think of that day with a shudder.

First of all, I was taken into a room where was stored everything necessary to the equipment of a convict under sentence. On the floor lay piles of chains; and clothes, boots, etc., were heaped on shelves. From among them some were selected that were supposed to fit me; and I was then conducted to a second room. Here the right side of my head was shaved, and the hair on the left side cut short. I had seen people in the prison who had been treated in this fashion, and the sight had always made a painful impression on me, as indeed it does on everyone. But when I saw my own face in the glass a cold shudder ran down my spine, and I experienced a sensation of personal degradation to something less than human. I thought of the days—in Russia not so long ago—when criminals were branded with hot irons.

A convict was waiting ready to fasten on my fetters. I was placed on a stool, and had to put my foot on an anvil. The blacksmith fitted an iron ring round each ankle, and welded it together. Every stroke of the hammer made my heart sink, as I realised that a new existence was beginning for me.

The mental depression into which I now fell was soon accompanied by physical discomfort. The fetters at first caused me intolerable pain in walking, and even disturbed my sleep. It also requires considerable practice before one can easily manage to dress and undress. The heavy chains—about 13 lbs. in weight—are not only an encumbrance, but are very painful, as they chafe the skin round the ankles; and the leather lining is but little protection to those unaccustomed to these adornments. Another great torment is the continual clinking of the chains. It is indescribably irritating to the nervous, and reminds the prisoner at every turn that he is a pariah among his kind, "deprived of all rights."

The transformation is completed by the peculiar convict dress, consisting—besides the coarse linen underclothing—of a grey gown made of special material, and a pair of trousers. Prisoners condemned to hard labour wear a square piece of yellow cloth sewn on their gowns. The feet are clad in leathern slippers nicknamed "cats." All these articles of clothing are inconvenient, heavy, and ill-fitting.

I hardly knew myself when I looked in the glass and beheld a fully attired convict. The thought possessed me—"For long years you will have to go about in that hideous disguise." Even the gendarme regarded me with compassion.

"What won't they do to a man?" he said. And I could only try to comfort myself by thinking how many unpleasant things one gets used to, and that time might perhaps accustom one even to this.

Source: Deutsch, Leo. *Sixteen Years in Siberia: Some Experiences of a Russian Revolutionist.* Translated by Helen Chisholm. London: J. Murray, 1905, pp. 95–96.

What You Need to Know

This excerpt is from Leo Deutsch's *Sixteen Years in Siberia: Some Experiences of a Russian Revolutionist*, published in London in 1905. Deutsch (also transliterated as Deich) was a socialist revolutionary convicted of terrorism by the government of Tsar Alexander III in 1884. Sent to a prison camp in Siberia, he escaped in 1901. He returned to Russia during 1905 revolution, when he was sentenced again. This time, he escaped while on his way to prison. He became an exile in London, until the Bolshevik Revolution of 1917, when he returned to Russia.

Until the late nineteenth century, Russia lagged well behind the West in economic development. Rapid industrialization in the western third of the country—while addressing that shortcoming— also created a large class of workers, many of whom gravitated toward socialism. Tsar Alexander II, a reformer who abolished serfdom early in his reign, tried to open up the political system by allowing more representative government, at least at the municipal level. But he was assassinated by antitsarist terrorists in 1881.

His successor, Alexander III, immediately rescinded the political reforms of Alexander II, reasserted the absolute power of the tsar, and launched a crackdown on political dissidents, such as Deutsch. In the meantime, economic modernization continued, even as the political system allowed no outlet for the discontent of the working classes, angry at awful working conditions, low pay, and the ancestral privileges of the nobility, as manifested in an archaic legal system that granted them special favors and immunities.

A Closer Look

The tsarist government chose to imprison political and other prisoners in Siberia for two reasons— the awful conditions of life there and the difficulty of surviving escape in such a vast and inhospitable wilderness. Yet as Deutsch notes, the government took additional precautions by shackling prisoners and cutting their hair and dressing them in uniforms so they could not blend into whatever civilian population was around.

Conditions in Siberian prisons were terrible. Most prisoners were put to hard labor for most of the day, usually in mines, where they would work 12 hours at a stretch, rarely seeing sunlight. Meals consisted of brown bread and cabbage. Medical facilities were primitive, with prisoners forced to lie on cold floors for lack of beds. Moreover, sick prisoners were not culled out of the general population, so diseases spread rapidly and, because of the poor diet, frigid climate, and terrible working conditions, often had fatal consequences.

Still, Deutsch was fortunate in that he was sentenced after railroads connected Siberia to more populous western Russia. Before that, prisoners sometimes spent months and even years marching to the camps.

1 100 200 300 400 500 600 700 800 900 1000 1100 1200 1300 1400 1500 1600 1700 1800 1900 2000 CE

2.16.27 Description of a Chicago Meatpacking Plant

Chicago, Illinois
1906

One curious thing he [Jurgis Rudkus, a meatpacking worker] had noticed, the very first day, in his profession of shoveler of guts; which was the sharp trick of the floor bosses whenever there chanced to come a "slunk" calf. Any man who knows anything about butchering knows that the flesh of a cow that is about to calve, or has just calved, is not fit for food. A good many of these came every day to the packing houses—and, of course, if they had chosen, it would have been an easy matter for the packers to keep them till they were fit for food. But for the saving of time and fodder, it was the law that cows of that sort came along with the others, and whoever noticed it would tell the boss, and the boss would start up a conversation with the government inspector, and the two would stroll away. So in a trice the carcass of the cow would be cleaned out, and the entrails would have vanished; it was Jurgis's task to slide them into the trap, calves and all, and on the floor below they took out these "slunk" calves, and butchered them for meat, and used even the skins of them.

One day a man slipped and hurt his leg; and that afternoon, when the last of the cattle had been disposed of, and the men were leaving, Jurgis was ordered to remain and do some special work which this injured man had usually done. It was late, almost dark, and the government inspectors had all gone, and there were only a dozen or two of men on the floor. That day they had killed about four thousand cattle, and these cattle had come in freight trains from far states, and some of them had got hurt. There were some with broken legs, and some with gored sides; there were some that had died, from what cause no one could say; and they were all to be disposed of, here in darkness and silence. "Downers," the men called them; and the packing house had a special elevator upon which they were raised to the killing beds, where the gang proceeded to handle them, with an air of businesslike nonchalance which said plainer than any words that it was a matter of everyday routine. It took a couple of hours to get them out of the way, and in the end Jurgis saw them go into the chilling rooms with the rest of the meat, being carefully scattered here and there so that they could not be identified. When he came home that night he was in a very somber mood, having begun to see at last how those might be right who had laughed at him for his faith in America.

Source: Sinclair, Upton. *The Jungle*. New York: The New American Library, 1906, pp. 66–67.

TIMELINE 2000 1900 1800 1700 1600 1500 1400 1300 1200 1100 1000 900 800 700 600 500 400 300 200 100 1 BCE

What You Need to Know

This passage is from Upton Sinclair's classic 1906 novel about the meatpacking industry, *The Jungle*. While of course fictional, the descriptions of Chicago's meatpacking factories in the book were based on Sinclair's six months of investigative reporting for the socialist newspaper *Appeal to Reason*.

Sinclair was a muckraker. The term, first popularized by President Theodore Roosevelt, was applied to journalists, many of them writing for popular national magazines, with a reformist agenda. Pioneers of the investigative form of journalism, they wrote exposés of industry and government that was meant to rouse public concern and result in legislative action. Their articles covered such topics as working conditions, unethical business practices, and governmental corruption.

The best of the muckrakers did much of their work in the field, interviewing workers, government officials, and ordinary citizens to get at the facts. They were often compelling storytellers as well, offering vivid descriptions and strong characters in the magazines that were sold on newsstands and through subscriptions. Many even went undercover to penetrate institutions that resisted exposure. Nellie Bly, the pseudonym of muckraker Elizabeth Cochrane, pretended to be a mental patient to expose conditions in a New York insane asylum, while Sinclair himself spent seven weeks working undercover in a Chicago meatpacking plant.

A Closer Look

Meatpacking plants in the early twentieth century were unregulated, unsanitary, and extremely dangerous for those who worked inside them, including young children. Workdays were long, up to 15 hours at a stretch. Little was done to keep the meat from becoming contaminated. The roughly 25,000 workers in the Chicago meatpacking plants of the early twentieth century—mostly newly arrived, young immigrant males from Eastern and Southern Europe—did not wear hairnets or gloves, and there were almost no facilities for washing hands.

The cutting machinery was largely unprotected; loss of fingers and even limbs were a frequent occurrence. As production lines rarely stopped for such accidents, much of this human flesh, along with that of the numerous rats and insects that infested the factories, ended up in the various meat products that were shipped off to stores across the country. Thousands of people died each year from contaminated food and drugs across the country.

Ironically, Sinclair, a socialist, wrote *The Jungle* to expose the awful working conditions in the plants. But what his largely middle-class readers took from the book was just how contaminated the conditions were in the plants that produced the meat products they consumed every day.

1 100 200 300 400 500 600 700 800 900 1000 1100 1200 1300 1400 1500 1600 1700 1800 1900 2000 CE

2.16.28 Account of the Triangle Shirtwaist Company Fire in New York City

New York, New York
1911

Men and Girls Die in Waist Factory Fire; Trapped High Up in Washington Place Building; Street Strewn with Bodies; Piles of Dead Inside. . . .

Nothing like it has been seen in New York since the burning of the General Slocum. The fire was practically all over in half an hour. It was confined to three floors the eighth, ninth, and tenth of the building. But it was the most murderous fire that New York had seen in many years. The victims who are now lying at the Morgue waiting for some one to identify them by a tooth or the remains of a burned shoe were mostly girls from 16 to 23 years of age. They were employed at making shirtwaist by the Triangle Waist Company, the principal owners of which are Isaac Harris and Max Blanck. Most of them could barely speak English. Many of them came from Brooklyn. Almost all were the main support of their hard-working families. There is just one fire escape in the building. That one is an interior fire escape. In Greene Street, where the terrified unfortunates crowded before they began to make their mad leaps to death, the whole big front of the building is guiltless of one. Nor is there a fire escape in the back. The building was fireproof and the owners had put their trust in that. In fact, after the flames had done their worst last night, the building hardly showed a sign. Only the stock within it and the girl employees were burned. A heap of corpses lay on the sidewalk for more than an hour. The firemen were too busy dealing with the fire to pay any attention to people whom they supposed beyond their aid. When the excitement had subsided to such an extent that some of the firemen and policemen could pay attention to this mass of the supposedly dead they found about half way down in the pack a girl who was still breathing. She died two minutes after she was found. . . .

Girls had begun leaping from the eighth story windows before firemen arrived. The firemen had trouble bringing their apparatus into position because of the bodies which strewed the pavement and sidewalks. While more bodies crashed down among them, they worked with desperation to run their ladders into position and to spread firenets. One fireman running ahead of a hose wagon, which halted to avoid running over a body spread a firenet, and two more seized hold of it. A girl's body, coming end over end, struck on the side of it, and there was hope that she would be the first one of the score who had jumped to be saved. Thousands of people who had crushed in from Broadway and Washington Square and were screaming with horror at what they saw watched closely the work with the firenet.

Source: "141 Men and Girls Die in Waist Factory Fire." *The New York Times* (March 26, 1911): 1.

What You Need to Know

This account comes from the *New York Times*, dated March 26, 1911. It describes the fire at the Triangle Shirtwaist Company, a New York City clothing factory, which killed 146 workers.

The Triangle Company's operation was, in fact, a sweatshop, a factory where workers put in long hours for low pay under unhealthful and unsafe conditions. While the company was owned by businessmen Max Blanck and Isaac Harris, most of the work in their factory was actually done by subcontractors, who then hired hands to do the actual garment making, taking a cut of their earnings as profit. This was a typical arrangement in New York City sweatshops at the time. It allowed owners to avoid paying wages and maintaining conditions they had agreed to after settling a 1910 strike, organized by the International Ladies Garment Workers Union. Subcontractors were not signatories to the agreement and so could pay whatever they wanted and work their employees long hours, under substandard conditions.

In the wake of the disaster, Blanck and Harris were found negligible in civil court and were forced to pay out to the families of victims just $75 each (about $1850 today). Blanck, who was also found criminally liable for keeping the doors locked, was fined just $20, and never served a day in jail.

A Closer Look

Sweatshops were commonplace in the American garment industry of the late nineteenth and early twentieth centuries, the epicenter of which was New York City. Most of them were located in high-rise buildings in the industrial sections of Lower Manhattan. Their workers came from desperately poor families, who relied on the income of every able family member to survive. Complaining to a boss might mean immediate dismissal and even the loss of wages not yet paid.

In sweatshops like the Triangle Shirtwaist Company, young immigrant women—primarily Italian and Jewish, many still in their teens—sat at long tables, bent over sewing machines or doing finer stitching by hand. There were some men in the shops, usually overseers, fabric cutters, and mechanics to fix the machines. The air in the factories was filled with lint and dust, the floors covered in flammable scraps. Workers typically put in 12 hours a day, six days a week, and breaks were few, even to go to the toilet. Discipline was tight. The doors of such factories were often locked, to prevent shirking and pilfering. Indeed, it was the locked doors at the Triangle factory—along with piles of old textile scraps, never cleaned up—that contributed to the high death toll, as women jumped from the factory's eighth, ninth, and tenth story windows to escape the flames and smoke.

1 100 200 300 400 500 600 700 800 900 1000 1100 1200 1300 1400 1500 1600 1700 1800 1900 2000 CE

2.16.29 Automobile Business Opportunities in America

Detroit, Michigan
1915

A good many years ago, a famous preacher addressed a gathering of six hundred boys. He spoke to them of their future and among other things, said: "Boys, you can be just what you want to be in this world. You can become a great merchant. You can become a successful doctor, or a lawyer. You can accomplish anything you set out to accomplish, but you will have to pay the penalty. And the penalty is work, concentration, and application."

And this rule applies with equal truth to all men and to any business, including the automobile business. . . .

There are opportunities in every branch of the business. There is plenty of room for good salesmen, a lot of it, in fact.

There is room for garagemen, for dealers, and for all who have a desire to work faithfully and who are willing to attend to the duties in hand and make every effort to secure the maximum results.

Fortunes have been made in a short time in the retail field.

Money has been made and is now being made in the wholesale distribution of automobiles.

Salesmen, men who attend to business and who try to find out all about the details of successful automobile selling, are making money. No matter what branch you contemplate entering, there are plenty of opportunities providing you concentrate and do business according to the standards demanded of the successful business man of today.

The business has not altogether been ideal, but better automobile days are coming.

The time is not far off when the relationship between the factory, dealer and consumer is going to change for the better and this will be because the owner is going to have a better understanding of an automobile. He will understand its limitations, what to expect and what not to expect of it, and let us hope that he will take better care of his car and treat it with more consideration than he has in the past.

Since the beginning of the industry the owner, in a certain sense, has been erroneously educated.

He has been given false ideas of what a piece of mechanism will do and has attached altogether too much sentiment to his machine. He has been given to understand that it will go on and on without care, without attention and without breakdowns. The average owner seems to forget that his car is made up of a collection of metal parts.

This idea is changing, of course, and it is time that it should. The dealer will profit by it, too, for he is the one who has suffered most by this method of selling automobiles.

Source: Newmark, Jacob H. *Automobile Business: A Guide.* Detroit: Automobile Publishing Company, 1915, pp. 1–5.

What You Need to Know

This excerpt is from the book *Automobile Business*, which was published in Detroit in 1915. In it, the author addresses the reader on the many opportunities to be had in the burgeoning American automobile industry of the early twentieth century, whose epicenter was Detroit.

Almost from the beginning, American automobile manufacturers relied on dealerships to sell their cars in far-flung markets. Most of these were owned by franchisees, independent businessmen who agreed to market automobiles under conditions set by the manufacturers. Initially, dealers simply sold cars. Manufacturers set the prices but, from early on, dealers offered discounts to customers and dickered over price. Eventually, as this document reveals, they came to understand that servicing the cars, and providing parts, was a lucrative business as well, and dealerships began to add service garages behind their open lots of cars for sale.

Early dealerships also offered financing, often at relatively low interest rates, because the car could be repossessed should the borrower default. Eventually, in 1919, General Motors introduced the General Motors Acceptance Corporation to offer credit straight from the manufacturer. This practice was soon taken up by other companies, although Ford proved a laggard. Still, many dealerships continued to offer their own credit terms, as this proved often more lucrative than the selling of the cars themselves.

A Closer Look

In the early 1900s, engineer and entrepreneur Henry Ford had applied the assembly-line process to automobile manufacturing, thereby bringing down the cost of a car to within the budget of a skilled worker. By the mid-1910s, Ford's company alone was selling a quarter of a million automobiles and, in the process, creating a host of new businesses, jobs, and opportunities.

Mass production of automobiles not only created new prospects within the industry itself, it spawned business opportunities far and wide. Service stations, not affiliated with dealerships, employed tens of thousands of mechanics, as well as unskilled attendants to fill tanks and change oil. Motels and auto camps, roadside facilities for travelers to pitch tents, proliferated along America's roads and, after the Federal Highway Act of 1921, a spreading highway network. Diners sprung up to feed drivers and their passengers.

As a transformative new technology, however, the automobile also proved destructive of existing occupations. Saddlers, blacksmiths, and stable owners saw business dry up, as the use of animals for transport declined. And although it would not occur until after World War II, the automobile—as well as the airplane—undermined both commuter and long-distance rail travel. Whereas some 1.5 million people worked on the railroads at the beginning of the twentieth century, less than 200,000 were employed on them at century's end, and those mostly on freight trains.

1 100 200 300 400 500 600 700 800 900 1000 1100 1200 1300 1400 1500 1600 1700 1800 1900 2000 CE

Part 17:
The World at War

1914–1945

2.17.1 Description of Trench Life in World War I

Western Europe
1914–1918

So I examine my domain. It is not very extensive, one hundred and twenty metres at the most, occupied by my sixty men. My trench is composed of the communication trench and two large salients, each containing half a section or two squads. Its general arrangement is as follows:—

Each of the salients is divided in the middle by a bomb-shield, and contains therefore two squads, whose dugouts, rather deep, are at the right and left ends of the salient. In front, in shell holes, the listening-patrols are posted during the night. There are machine guns in each of the salients. My headquarters are so placed that I am in immediate touch with both my half-sections. A little winding trench leads to my dug-out, which is about two metres underground. It is comfortable and contains a rather dilapidated hair mattress which the Germans, formerly proprietors of this trench, brought over from the village of Perthes. A set of shelves made of three boards has on it some old tin cans, along with the things I have taken out of my haversack. Two or three pegs stuck in the dirt wall serve as clothes hooks. The furnishing is completed by a wooden stool brought from the village, and by a brazier in which charcoal is burning. In one corner are some trench rockets and a large case of cartridges.

This domicile is not at all bad; it is almost luxurious. The dugouts of my soldiers are large undergrounds holding fifteen men comfortably. Straw helps ward off the dampness of the soil of Champagne, and discarded bayonets stuck in the walls serve as hooks for canteens and haversacks. Meanwhile, as the cold was a bit sharp, I had some braziers made for the men by piercing holes in old tin cans with bayonets. Charcoal was brought up from the kitchens.

So life was sufficiently endurable. We felt pretty secure. The loopholes were well protected, and one could fire comfortably. The machine guns were always in readiness, and in short, the Germans over opposite did not seem malicious. All that could be seen of them were white streaks across the land, many and intertwined, with wire entanglements alongside. That was all—nothing that budged or had the least human semblance, only here and there a sort of ragged, bluish heap that seemed a part of the earth on which it lay—a corpse. There were not many dead directly in front of us, but to the west, on our left, much higher up, in front of the skeleton remnant of a wood, lay a number of those motionless bundles, bearing witness to recent attacks.

Source: Nicolas, René. Excerpt from *Campaign Diary of a French Officer*. Reprinted in *The World's Story: A History of the World in Story, Song and Art*. Vol. 15. Edited by Eva March Tappan. Boston: Houghton Mifflin, 1918, pp. 286–287.

TIMELINE   2000 1900 1800 1700 1600 1500 1400 1300 1200 1100 1000 900 800 700 600 500 400 300 200 100 1 BCE

What You Need to Know

This description of trench life was written by a French military officer in World War I.

Trench warfare was necessitated by advances in technology, particularly in defensive weaponry. Barbed wire, land mines, and the machine gun made frontal assaults against the enemy, the main-stays of offensive warfare before World War I, virtually suicidal.

Not that desperate generals did not try them. Early in the war, the belligerents attempted to outflank the enemy on the Western Front in northern France. Each side responded by building ever more complicated networks of trenches. With Germans in control of French territory, it was up to the allies to dislodge them. In the lead up to offensive thrusts, allied forces would unleash a merciless artillery barrage against German trenches. Then, soldiers by the tens of thousands, led by junior officers, would "go over the top," into "no man's land." The resulting slaughter was appalling. In the summer of 1916, for instance, French and British troops launched the Battle of the Somme. After weeks of fighting, the allies had sacrificed 600,000 dead and wounded for a gain of just 125 square miles of territory. Not until the widespread deployment of the tank in 1917 did the allies find an offensive weapon capable of breaking the stalemate.

A Closer Look

After gains by the Germans in the early months of the war, the conflict in Western European settled into a stalemate, with neither side able to shift the front significantly in one direction or another. Both the Allies and the Central Powers, which included the Germans, began to build a network of defensive trenches on both sides of the front, where soldiers settled in for months and even years at a time.

Life for soldiers in the trenches was a mix of misery and terror. Although protected from small arms fire, soldiers were subject to artillery shells raining down on them; there was almost nothing that could be done to protect oneself, and death came randomly.

The soldiers shared the trenches with all kinds of vermin, including rats, lice, and even frogs. Mud was ever present, as were collapsing walls. A constant complaint was "trench foot," a fungal infection caused by sustained exposure to cold and wet, which could lead to gangrene and amputation.

But mostly there was boredom and fatigue. Getting little sleep at night and with little to do most of the day, many soldiers became disoriented and slightly crazed, which explains why some would purposefully expose themselves to enemy fire, either in suicide attempts or to simply liven up their day.

2.17.2 African and Asian Soldiers in the British Army

British East Africa
1916

Credit: Culture Club/Getty Images

What You Need to Know

The accompanying photo shows three soldiers serving in the British military during World War I. The man in the middle was a member of the 2nd Kashmir rifles of India; the two soldiers flanking him served in the King's African Rifles Battalion out of Uganda, then a British Protectorate. The year is 1916.

Before the late nineteenth century, Europe's impact on Africa was limited, aside from the slave trade. But in the 1880s and 1890s, various European countries—most notably, Britain, France, and Germany—divided up virtually the entire continent among themselves. The eastern half of the continent was turned into colonies of Britain and Germany.

After World War I broke out, both sides mobilized their African troops—bolstered by new recruits as well as, in the case of the British, native forces from the Indian subcontinent, in the case of the British—to oust the other; the British were the more effective in this, driving the Germans out of the region by 1917.

A Closer Look

The new colonial order utterly transformed the lives of ordinary Africans, and not necessarily for the better. Peasants were now required to pay head or hut taxes, for government services they rarely enjoyed, aside from police (which were often a force of oppression rather than security) and schools for a tiny elite needed to man the colonial bureaucracy.

Most African peasants, however, did not have the money to pay the taxes and so were forced to work, either on public infrastructure projects, which were largely built to service European-owned plantations and mines, where other peasants were forced to labor. European regimes subsidized pliant chiefs, who would then order and supply the necessary labor. Forced to work on distant projects, the men would go months or even years without seeing their families, while women would be required to raise the subsistence crops their families and villages relied on.

Unlike in the case of forced labor, most of the estimated 200,000 African troops in British East Africa were volunteers, motivated to join by money and the respect of being fighting men. The British were especially effective in recruiting among the more martial peoples of the region. The troops were both sent to the European fronts and used in the minor battles that took place in Africa itself.

2.17.3 Spalding Official Baseball Guide Cover

United States
1917

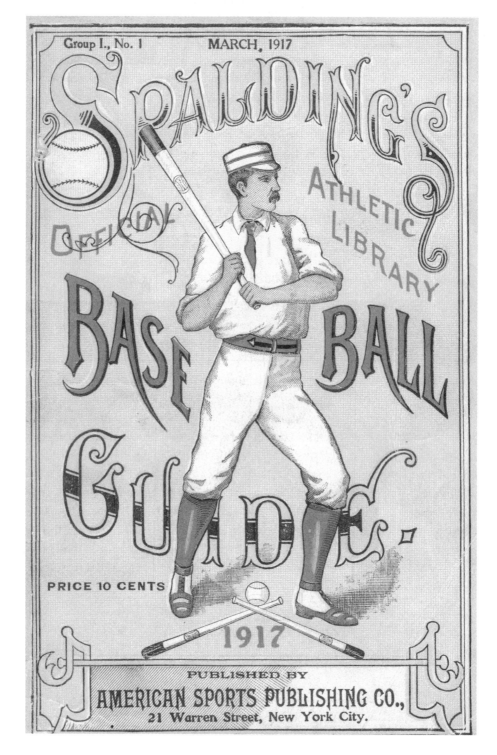

Credit: Transcendental Graphics/Getty Images

What You Need to Know

This cover of *Spalding's Official Baseball Guide* was published by the A. G. Spalding and Bros. Company of Chicago in 1917. While still a pitcher for the Chicago White Stockings (now the Chicago Cubs), Spalding helped organize the National League in 1876.

The growing popularity of baseball, and sports in general, reflected broader economic and social changes in American life in the late nineteenth century. The first was rising levels of disposable income, a result of increased productivity, successful labor union organizing among skilled workers, and greater numbers of middle-class professionals and managers. The second was more leisure time. Agitation among workers and mechanization shortened workweeks, from nearly 70 hours in 1860 to less than 60 by 1890, including half-days on Saturday. Adding to leisure time was the easing of old social and legal restrictions, particularly in urban areas, on keeping the Sabbath as a day of rest. Finally, improved manufacturing techniques made sports equipment less expensive, allowing more people to play games such as baseball that required gloves, bats, balls, and special apparel. Not coincidentally, Spalding made his own fortune by opening up a chain of sporting goods stores after his retirement from baseball in 1878.

A Closer Look

First popular among wealthy Northeastern men in the 1850s, and later catching on across all classes of men from around the country during the Civil War, by the 1880s baseball was both a participatory game and a well-organized professional sport, with codified rules, leagues of teams, and salaried players.

Heavily covered in the mass press, top baseball clubs attracted thousands of fans to their games. Still, there were no dedicated stadiums at the time, so most games were played in large vacant lots, around which owners built fences and gates to make sure fans paid admission. The baseball field itself, however, was still a work in progress, and would not take its present dimensions until after the turn of the twentieth century.

The guide shown here was widely popular, selling thousands of copies annually on newsstands and through subscription sales. It featured articles on top players and teams, and analyses of the previous season and was heavy with illustrations and, later, photos. It also offered the first rudimentary collection of what would become a central element of fans' appreciation of the sport: statistics.

1　100　200　300　400　500　600　700　800　900　1000　1100　1200　1300　1400　1500　1600　1700　1800　1900　2000 CE

2.17.4 Description of German Submarine Warfare

Atlantic Ocean
1917

A submarine conceals within its small compass the most concentrated technical disposition known in the art of mechanical construction, especially so in the spaces reserved for the steering gear of the boat and for the manipulation of its weapons.

The life on board becomes such a matter of habit that we can peacefully sleep at great depths under the sea, while the noise is distinctly heard of the propellers of the enemy's ships, hunting for us overhead; for water is an excellent sound conductor, and conveys from a long distance the approach of a steamer. We are often asked, "How can you breathe under water?" The health of our crew is the best proof that this is possible. We possessed as fellow passengers a dozen guinea pigs, the gift of a kindly and anxious friend, who had been told these little creatures were very sensitive to the ill effects of a vitiated atmosphere. They flourished in our midst and proved amusing companions.

It is essential before a U-boat submerges to drive out the exhausted air through powerful ventilating machines, and to suck in the purest air obtainable; but often in war time one is obliged to dive with the emanations of cooking, machine oil, and the breath of the crew still permeating the atmosphere, for it is of the utmost importance to the success of a submarine attack that the enemy should not detect our presence; therefore, it is impossible at such short notice to clear the air within the boat. These conditions, however, are bearable, although one must be constantly on the watch to supply in time fresh ventilation. . . .

When everything is in readiness, the crew is given a short leave on land, to go and take the much coveted hot bath. This is the most important ceremony before and after a cruise, especially when the men return, for when they have remained unwashed for weeks, soaked with machine oil, and saturated with salt spray, their first thought is a hot bath. At sea, we must be very sparing of our fresh-water supply, and its use for washing must be carefully restricted.

Source: Forstner, Georg-Günther Freiherr von. *The Journal of Submarine Commander von Forstner*. Translated by Anna Kneeland Crafts Codman. Boston and New York: Houghton Mifflin, 1917, pp. 6–8, 56–57.

What You Need to Know

This document comes from the *Journal of Submarine Commander von Forstner*, which was published in the United States in 1917, the year America entered World War I. Georg-Günther von Forstner came from an aristocratic family, with a long history of service in the army and navy of Prussia and its successor state, Germany.

Both the Allies and the Central Powers, of which Germany was one, launched submarines to disrupt the enemy's trade, but Germany was the most prolific in their use. France and especially Britain were highly reliant on overseas food imports to feed their populations and raw materials to feed their war industries. Much of this came through the Mediterranean or across the North Atlantic and North Sea, and so that is where Germany dispatched its hundreds of submarines. The U-boats proved extremely effective. Over the course of the war, they sank some 5,000 ships, in the process losing 178 submarines and 5,000 men.

But the U-boat also proved Germany's undoing, or at least played a role in it. To keep America out of the war, Berlin had agreed to restrictions on its submarine warfare aimed at sparing U.S. ships. But by early 1917, Germany was desperate to cut off supplies to its enemies and announced unrestricted submarine warfare in the Atlantic. That decision helped prompt President Woodrow Wilson to declare war on the Central Powers in April 1917. The arrival of hundreds of thousands of American troops over the next 18 months turned the tide of war, forcing Germany to surrender in November 1918.

A Closer Look

Despite von Forstner's assurances, life on a German submarine, or U-boat, in World War I was both uncomfortable and terrifying. (The "U" stood for *untersee*, or "undersea.") The quarters were extremely cramped; berths were so narrow that men had to lay sideways on them to sleep. Equipment lay everywhere or protruded from walls and bulkheads; crew members experienced frequent bruising when the ship surfaced and was rocked by waves. Fumes from the diesel engines produced steady headaches.

The fact that the inside of the vessel was warmer than the water outside meant that condensation was a constant annoyance. Water dripped so steadily on the crew that they went about in rain gear, even to sleep. The seepage also caused electrical circuits to burn out on a regular basis, which shocked crew members. The submariners often gave up trying to use the tiny electric oven and burners on the boat and cooked their food on paraffin stoves on the deck above, although this entailed the risk of being swept overboard into frigid North Atlantic waters.

Unpleasant as it was, being underwater was actually safer, at least early in the war, before the development of depth charges. But submarines had to spend a lot of time on the surface, recharging the batteries for their electric motors because diesel engines could not operate underwater. There, the U-boats were subject to the fire of warships.

2.17.5 German War Bond Poster

Germany
1917

Credit: IBL Bildbyra/Heritage Images/Getty Images

What You Need to Know

This 1917 German poster asks people to subscribe to, that is, buy, war bonds.

By 1917, the country's war prospects grew dimmer as the arrival of hundreds of thousands of fresh troops from America turned the tide in favor of the allies. Germany was forced to surrender, even though its territory was never invaded. This led many after the war—including Adolf Hitler—to speak of treachery at the top.

In fact, the desperation on the German home front in the last year of the war had led the government to conclude that carrying on the fight risked sparking a revolution. Workers struck in industries across the country; moderates in the German parliament—and protest marches on the streets—were calling for immediate peace without any territorial gains. In response to the unrest, the German military established a virtual dictatorship but even this could not hold things together. Inspired by the Bolshevik Revolution a year earlier, German sailors, soldiers, and workers began to establish antiwar, revolutionary councils across the country in early November 1918. On the eleventh of that month, Germany surrendered.

A Closer Look

Like all of the major belligerents, the German government raised revenues for the war effort by issuing such bonds, or debt obligations. As they typically offered yields below-market rates, the bonds were sold through appeals to patriotism. In this poster, the appeal is to support the troops by showing what they were up against. The soldier is depicted with a gas mask around his neck, reminding civilians back home of the horrors of modern warfare. The appeal would have hit home to many, as roughly 11 million persons served in the armed forces in World War I or about one in six Germans. The words above the illustration read, "Help us triumph!"; those below say, "Subscribe to war bonds."

Life was hard on the German home front, especially as the war progressed. With millions of men on the country's two fronts, many families were reduced to living off government handouts. Some income was gained as women and youth went to work—the latter as schools shortened their semesters because so many teachers were in uniform—but they were generally paid far less than adult men.

There were also shortages of food and other consumer goods—a result of an ever-tightening allied blockade—causing prices to rise, as welfare payments from the government grew skimpier as the war went on.

1   100   200   300   400   500   600   700   800   900   1000   1100   1200   1300   1400   1500   1600   1700   1800   1900   2000 CE

2.17.6 American Poster Urging Women to Work

United States
1917–1918

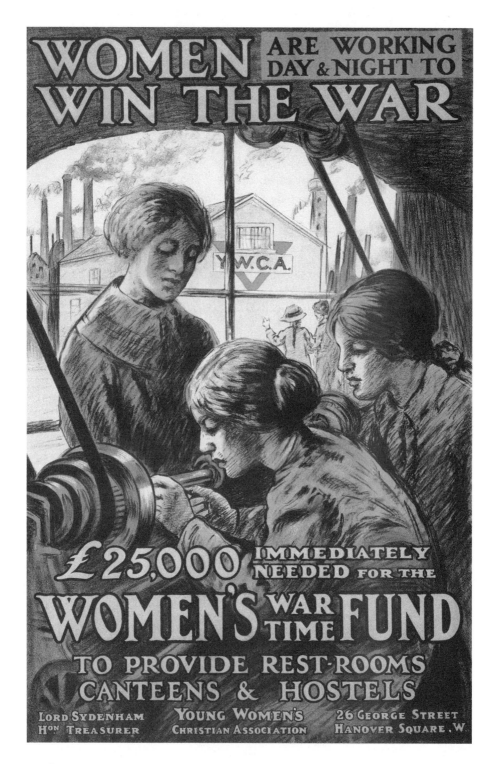

Credit: Library of Congress

What You Need to Know

This World War I era poster, put out by the Young Women's Christian Association (YWCA), urges women to enter the workplace. The poster emphasized the economic home front as the nation's "second line of defense."

Women served in many ways in World War I. Thousands volunteered for the armed services, where they performed all kinds of support duties, most notably as nurses. The many social welfare groups, set up during the Progressive Era that immediately preceded the war effort, rolled and packaged bandages for the war front and sold bonds to pay for the war.

In terms of numbers, however, the most significant contribution women made was by going to work, filling jobs left open when men joined or were drafted into the military. Between 1914 and 1918, adult female participation in the workforce climbed from about 23 percent to more than 40 percent. Equally important, hundreds of thousands left domestic service to work in factories, railroads, farms, and mines.

Among the most crucial industries they poured into was the manufacturing of munitions. Thousands of women packed millions of artillery shells, breathing in acidic fumes and risking death from explosions. After the war, however, participation fell by half, to levels seen before the conflict.

A Closer Look

Not all Americans were as supportive as they could be of women joining the labor force. Despite all of the agitation for women's rights before—and during—the war, culminating in the vote, there was a widespread sentiment that women were either unsuited by temperament and physique for manufacturing and other traditionally male occupations or that participation in the workforce would undermine their femininity.

Businesses, although desperate for labor, especially as the flow of working-class immigrants from Europe dried up, nevertheless often refused to grant women time off to care for their children or to provide on-site day care. Some even failed to put in women's bathrooms. Unions were hostile as well, many having a history of excluding women as members. Typically, women working in nontraditional jobs during World War I were paid a fraction of the wages men received. Although the federal government imposed equal pay regulations on businesses that received government war contracts, employers got around them by either hiring several part-time women to replace one full-time man or dividing higher-paid skilled tasks into several lower paying semiskilled or unskilled tasks.

2.17.7 Margaret Sanger on Birth Control in America

United States
1920

The most far-reaching social development of modern times is the revolt of woman against sex servitude. The most important force in the remaking of the world is a free motherhood. . . .

Only in recent years has woman's position as the gentler and weaker half of the human family been emphatically and generally questioned. Men assumed that this was woman's place; woman herself accepted it. It seldom occurred to anyone to ask whether she would go on occupying it forever. . . .

Caught in this "vicious circle," woman has, through her reproductive ability, founded and perpetuated the tyrannies of the Earth. Whether it was the tyranny of a monarchy, an oligarchy or a republic, the one indispensable factor of its existence was, as it is now, hordes of human beings—human beings so plentiful as to be cheap, and so cheap that ignorance was their natural lot. . . .

To-day, however, woman is rising in fundamental revolt. Even her efforts at mere reform are, as we shall see later, steps in that direction. Underneath each of them is the feminine urge to complete freedom. Millions of women are asserting their right to voluntary motherhood. They are determined to decide for themselves whether they shall become mothers, under what conditions and when. . . .

Even as birth control is the means by which woman attains basic freedom, so it is the means by which she must and will uproot the evil she has wrought through her submission. . . .

Two chief obstacles hinder the discharge of this tremendous obligation. The first and the lesser is the legal barrier. Dark-Age laws would still deny to her the knowledge of her reproductive nature. Such knowledge is indispensable to intelligent motherhood and she must achieve it, despite absurd statutes and equally absurd moral canons.

The second and more serious barrier is her own ignorance of the extent and effect of her submission. Until she knows the evil her subjection has wrought to herself, to her progeny and to the world at large, she cannot wipe out that evil. . . .

What effect will the practice of birth control have upon woman's moral development? . . . It will break her bonds. It will free her to understand the cravings and soul needs of herself and other women. It will enable her to develop her love nature separate from and independent of her maternal nature.

It goes without saying that the woman whose children are desired and are of such number that she can not only give them adequate care but keep herself mentally and spiritually alive, as well as physically fit, can discharge her duties to her children much better than the overworked, broken and querulous mother of a large, unwanted family.

Source: Sanger, Margaret. *Woman and the New Race*. New York: Truth Publishing Co., 1920, pp. 1–3, 5, 7, 179–180, 183.

What You Need to Know

This excerpt is from Margaret Sanger's *Woman and the New Race*, published in 1920, the same year American women won the vote. Originally a visiting nurse in the immigrant ghettoes of New York City, Sanger came to the realization that one of the greatest impediments to the health and well-being of poor immigrant women were their frequent pregnancies and overly large families. She became an advocate for birth control, demanding an end to laws that banned the sale and use of contraceptives as well as pushing to change hostile public attitudes.

The primary form of birth control in early twentieth-century America was the condom, for men, and the diaphragm and cervical cap for women. Condoms were outlawed in some states and federal law banned their advertising and distribution through the mail. As for female contraceptive devices, they had to be fitted by doctors, who were often opposed to them. Meanwhile, the rhythm method of avoiding sex during ovulation, which required no devices, was poorly understood and thus ineffective.

Thus, for many women, particularly the poor and uneducated, there was almost no way to prevent unwanted pregnancies. Desperate, some women resorted to abortions, induced by toxins and crude efforts to extract the fetus from the womb. Because few doctors would perform them, the women were forced to seek out untrained help or to perform the procedures themselves. This often led to grave health complications and death.

A Closer Look

There were several factors behind the anticontraceptive laws and the broad public's opposition to birth control, mostly based in moral and religious teachings. For some, preventing pregnancy was seen as thwarting God's natural order; for others, it seemed to divorce sex from procreation. This highlighted the pleasurable aspects of the former, at a time when public prudity about sex prevailed. Finally, there were many who feared that making contraceptives widely available would encourage unmarried women and men to engage in sex, a grave sin.

Sanger dismissed all of this. Although she did not condone sex outside of marriage, she believed that lifting the fear of unwanted pregnancy would empower women, allowing them greater fulfillment in life as they were freed from constant child-rearing.

But there were also less positive reasons for birth control, at least to modern sensibilities. Sanger and other birth control activists were advocates of eugenics, the idea that selective breeding could improve the human race. With better educated people already having access to birth control, it was imperative, she believed, that the less successful classes of society gain access as well, or they would overwhelm their biological and social superiors with their higher birth rates.

2.17.8 European Micro Telephone with Receiver

France
1920

Credit: DEA /A. Dagli Orti/DeAgostini/Getty Images

What You Need to Know

Shown here is a French telephone from 1920. The device pictured has a number of improvements on the earliest telephones from the late nineteenth century, including its relatively small size; its portability; a receiver that includes both earpiece and mouthpiece, allowing it be held away from the phone's base; and most significant, a rotary dial, which allowed users to bypass operators and dial parties directly, although only for local calls.

Before the early twentieth century, telephones, which were leased from telephone companies as part of an expensive service, were largely the preserve of businesses and wealthy individuals, usually to connect their homes to their businesses. Early telephone directories were replete with business numbers but few residential ones.

Immobile and attached to the wall, and producing low-quality sound, phones were usually placed in a separate and closed off room or booth within a business or residence, so that they could be better heard. Personal calls were largely reserved for special announcements, such as a birth or the death of a loved one.

A Closer Look

Falling costs for telephone service, the growing ubiquity of the telephone in industrialized countries, such as France, as well as the innovations just noted, began to change the way the technology was perceived and how it was used, especially in the home. Before these developments, a telephone call was almost a special event, used for important announcements. Traditional etiquette applied. Just as wealthier households had servants answer the door to visitors, so they were charged with responding to phone calls in a similar fashion.

By the early twentieth century, however, the telephone—at least, for those who could afford it—was becoming more a part of daily life. The better sound quality and portability—at least as far as the wire would let the user move about—allowed the device to be moved out of its special room into the bedroom, living room, and kitchen. Not needing to go through an operator, people began making more routine calls.

As with many path-breaking technologies, the telephone made old ways of doing things obsolete and, in the process, changed social attitudes as well. As calls became more routine, people began answering the phone themselves and with less formality. The old practice of sending out servants with calling cards—similar to business cards but for personal use—to announce visits came to an end.

1 100 200 300 400 500 600 700 800 900 1000 1100 1200 1300 1400 1500 1600 1700 1800 1900 2000 CE

2.17.9 War Poems by English Poet Rupert Brooke

United Kingdom
1920

III. THE DEAD

Blow out, you bugles, over the rich Dead!
There's none of these so lonely and poor of old,
But, dying, has made us rarer gifts than gold.
These laid the world away; poured out the red
Sweet wine of youth; gave up the years to be
Of work and joy, and that unhoped serene,
That men call age; and those who would have been,
Their sons, they gave, their immortality.
Blow, bugles, blow! They brought us, for our dearth,
Holiness, lacked so long, and Love, and Pain.
Honour has come back, as a king, to earth,
And paid his subjects with a royal wage;
And Nobleness walks in our ways again;
And we have come into our heritage.

V. THE SOLDIER

If I should die, think only this of me:
That there's some corner of a foreign field
That is for ever England. There shall be
In that rich earth a richer dust concealed;
A dust whom England bore, shaped, made aware,
Gave, once, her flowers to love, her ways to roam,
A body of England's, breathing English air,
Washed by the rivers, blest by suns of home.
And think, this heart, all evil shed away,
A pulse in the eternal mind, no less
Gives somewhere back the thoughts by England given;
Her sights and sounds; dreams happy as her day;
And laughter, learnt of friends; and gentleness,
In hearts at peace, under an English heaven.

Source: Brooke, Rupert. *The Collected Poems of Rupert Brooke*. New York: John Lane Company, 1920, pp. 109, 111.

TIMELINE   2000 1900 1800 1700 1600 1500 1400 1300 1200 1100 1000 900 800 700 600 500 400 300 200 100 1 BCE

What You Need to Know

The preceding poems—III. The Dead and V. The Soldier—were written by Rupert Brooke and first published in 1915 as part of a sonnet sequence entitled *1914 and Other Poems*. Just 27 years old when World War I broke out, Brooke was already a celebrated English poet when he volunteered for the British Army, where he participated in an early defensive battle in Belgium. In 1915, he was part of the expedition sent to Gallipoli, an allied effort to knock the Ottoman Empire, one of the Central Powers, out of the war. His death from blood poisoning aboard a transport ship symbolized to many of his countrymen the war's terrible toll on the most promising youth of the nation.

The poems here capture both the early commitment many Britons felt for the war effort early on and the sense of despair that would descend on the nation once the conflict's terrible toll in lives became evident.

When Britain declared war on Germany in early August 1914, the British people responded with enthusiasm, aside from socialist groups who argued the war was launched by capitalists and pitted the working classes of European countries against each other. Most agreed, however, with the government's propaganda claims that the war was in defense of empire and to halt German aggression. As bands played in town squares across Britain, hundreds of thousands of young men descended on recruitment offices; indeed, the more than 2.6 million who did so represented the largest volunteer fighting force in world history, up to that time.

A Closer Look

Well received at the time of its publication, *1914* became a best-selling collection of poems in the wake of Brooke's untimely death, and they remained popular well after the war. This was partly because they captured a moment in time, when the sense of a noble purpose to the war first gave way to questions about its human cost.

The sense that the war was avoidable, if not for the ineptitude and venality of the country's statesmen, and that the slaughter was caused by irresponsible and incompetent military leadership, left British people of all classes with a deep sense of melancholy after the war. And they were not alone in this feeling.

Artists across Europe best captured the spirit of the times. German historian Oswald Spengler's majestic *The Decline of the West* (1918) became an immediate best seller. Critics widely hailed Anglo-American poet T. S. Eliot's *The WasteLand* (1922), which depicted a world of alienation and desolation. Europeans of the 1920s and 1930s looked on what they called the Great War as a break from nineteenth-century certainties about the progress of Western civilization.

1   100   200   300   400   500   600   700   800   900   1000   1100   1200   1300   1400   1500   1600   1700   1800   1900   2000 CE

2.17.10 Weighing Harvested Rubber in Brazil

Brazil
1925

Credit: Library of Congress

What You Need to Know

In this image, a man is weighing a cake of latex, the raw ingredient from which rubber is derived. The photo was taken on a rubber plantation in the Amazonian region of Brazil in 1925. Surrounding the man with the scales is a group of *seringueiros*, or rubber tappers. Most of them are in the dress of Brazilian peasants, but the man in the foreground wears his hair in the style of an indigenous inhabitant of the rain forest.

The Brazilian rubber industry had experienced many booms and busts since it was founded in the middle of the nineteenth century, just a few decades after American inventor Charles Goodyear discovered the vulcanization process to render rubber more durable and useful.

The latex rubber was made from came from a number of plants, but the most prolific was the *hevea brasiliensis*, native to the Amazon. With the spread of the automobile in the early twentieth century came a soaring demand for rubber tires. Brazilian planters prospered greatly, as various Amazonian towns became major commercial centers. The chief one, steamy Manaus, had, in the early twentieth century, one of the richest concentrations of millionaires in the world.

However, the boom years did not last. By the 1920s, most of the world's rubber was being produced far more efficiently on plantations in British- and French-controlled Southeast Asia, the rubber trees there grown from *hevea brasiliensis* saplings smuggled out of the Amazon.

A Closer Look

Rubber was obtained in two ways in Brazil—from plantations and from the forest itself, where workers tapped native latex-producing trees. Because it was scarcely populated and because many indigenous people kept their distance from outsiders, rubber entrepreneurs recruited thousands of workers from Brazil's impoverished northeast, with promises of free passage to the Amazon and hefty advances on wages. In fact, the owners of the *seringais*, or rubber estates (which designated either plantations or stretches of native latex-producing forest) typically debited the workers' accounts for both the passage and advance. This left the workers in perpetual debt to the owners.

Located in work camps far from any town, they were forced to purchase their food and other necessities from the planters at exorbitant prices. *Patraos*, or the labor bosses who actually recruited the men, maintained harsh discipline over the workers, using frequent applications of the whip to get them to work. And situated deep in the Amazon forest, hundreds of miles from their homes, the workers had little chance of escape. In addition to importing labor from other parts of Brazil, planters and their *patraos* captured thousands of natives, holding them at gunpoint in work camps.

2.17.11 Portrait of an American Flapper

Chicago, Illinois
1929

Credit: Chicago History Museum/Getty Images

What You Need to Know

This photo shows Lita Grey Chaplin, the second wife of director and actor Charlie Chaplin, posing in front of an expensive touring sedan parked on a Chicago street in 1929. Chaplin is shown in a slim, form-fitting dress and cloche hat, typical of the style worn by women contemporaries referred to as *flappers*.

The origin of the term is disputed. Some historians say it derives from the actions of a young bird first leaving its nest; others argue it is derived from the British slang for a woman of loose morals. What it meant in common usage was a young woman liberated from the strictures of Victorian dress and propriety. Flappers wore revealing clothing, lots of makeup, and bobbed their hair. They smoked, drank (illegal) alcohol, listened and danced to the latest risqué jazz tunes, went out unescorted on dates—often in their boyfriends' automobiles, and treated sex in a much more casual fashion than their mothers had.

In fact, the vast majority of America's young women—and those of other industrialized countries undergoing many of the same social changes in the 1920s—did not engage in such behavior, even if they dressed the part and enjoyed following the doings of Hollywood flappers, such as Chaplin, in the movie magazines that had recently gained a wide readership.

A Closer Look

Flappers aside, the 1920s saw a number of significant changes in the way many women lived their lives. Most important, they were having far fewer children, a result of more widespread use of birth control and more liberal attitudes about it. Whereas well over half of married women who lived to the age of 50 in the late nineteenth century had five or more children, by the 1920s, the figure was down to one in five. And, as women were living longer, this meant even less of their lives devoted to raising children.

There were also more single women, especially divorcees. In 1920, roughly 1 in 7.5 marriages ended in divorce; by decade's end, it was up to 1 in 6. In urban areas, it climbed to 1 in 4. For middle-class women who could afford them, a range of new appliances—from toasters to washing machines—was freeing them from some of the drudgery of housework.

Still, most women stayed in their socially prescribed roles of mother and homemaker, although the latter involved less cleaning and sewing and more shopping and chauffeuring. But as for becoming employees themselves, the numbers barely budged. Between 1920 and 1930, the female percentage of the labor force only climbed from 20.4 to 22 percent.

2.17.12 Line outside a Charity Soup Kitchen during the Great Depression

New York, New York
1932

Credit: Fotosearch/Getty Images

What You Need to Know

The accompanying photo shows a line of men formed alongside Bryant Park in Midtown Manhattan in the winter of 1932. They are waiting to receive a free meal at a restaurant run by a charity. The sign at the front cajoles better-off passersby to contribute to the kitchen. A one-dollar donation (about $17 today) will feed 20 needy persons a lunch, it says.

The Great Depression, which began with the Stock Market Crash of 1929 and continued, albeit in somewhat attenuated form, until the outbreak of World War II in the early 1940s, was the worst and longest lasting economic downturn in American history. At its depths in 1932 and 1933, roughly one in four workers was unemployed. Another 10 percent could not obtain full-time work.

Want spread across the land, as even necessities became luxuries. When food from soup kitchens was unavailable, people scraped for food in garbage cans or city dumps. Adding to the frustration was the fact that because prices for crops fell below the cost of raising and shipping them, farmers ended up dumping food in the countryside rather than transporting it to urban areas where it was so desperately needed.

A Closer Look

Churches and private charities ran such donation-based restaurants in the early years of the Great Depression; government did not get involved until the mid-1930s, nearly half a decade into the downturn. Contemporaries referred to them as "soup kitchens" because that's what they mainly served, along with a side of bread. Soup was the preferred meal because it was cheap to make and could always be watered down to feed the ever-growing numbers of poor people showing up at the kitchens.

In many towns, the soup kitchens consisted of tents set up in parks and vacant lots. Patrons would line up cafeteria style to be served and then would eat their soup in the open air, regardless of the weather, although many churches made use of their basements to serve food and accommodate diners. In some cases, the charities would raise money separately then, as shown in this photo, supplement the donations by raising money at the site of the kitchen.

Nevertheless, malnutrition became common, particularly in urban areas, and with it came increased illness. Unable to pay rent, people doubled up in apartments, which were often freezing cold as many could not pay for coal to heat them. Thousands of people, mostly young men, became homeless, establishing shanty towns made from crates and discarded lumber, and called "Hoovervilles" after widely reviled President Herbert Hoover.

1   100   200   300   400   500   600   700   800   900   1000 1100 1200 1300   1400   1500   1600   1700 1800 1900 2000 CE

2.17.13 1930s Refrigerator in the United States

United States
1935

Credit: Sherman Clark/Hulton Archive/Getty Images

What You Need to Know

This is a publicity photo put out by the General Electric Corporation in 1935 to sell its line of home refrigerators. The round device on top is the unit's compressor, and the tiny box beneath is the freezer section. Typical for advertising of the day, the model is dressed somewhat formally, inappropriate for housework. The fact that she is wearing an overcoat is no doubt meant to convey the refrigerator's ability to generate cold temperatures.

Traditionally keeping food cold meant obtaining ice and putting it into insulated containers, so-called iceboxes. City streets were filled with horse-drawn carts covered in hay for insulation, making regular deliveries to homes and apartments, muscle-bound icemen lugging the large and heavy blocks to people's kitchens using oversized tongs.

Various technological breakthroughs in mechanical refrigeration in the nineteenth and early twentieth centuries led to the development of the household refrigerator just before World War I. But it was a large, noisy, and dangerous device, as early refrigerants were toxic. Thus, the compressor was typically placed in the basement with the cold air, piped to the box in the kitchen. In 1928, Frigidaire, a General Electric competitor, discovered the far less toxic refrigerant, chlorofluorocarbons (CFC).

A Closer Look

Such advances made refrigerators smaller, safer, and more convenient, but they remained expensive. Through the 1930s, refrigerators typically cost more than a basic automobile, making them the preserve of the wealthy and upper middle class, especially as hard times during the Depression put the devices out of reach of most Americans' budgets.

Still, when people could afford them, they changed the way they bought and prepared food, reducing the time and bother of both. Food manufacturers responded to the spread of the refrigerator with new convenience products, such as frozen foods and bottled orange juice. Consumers could now buy a week's worth of groceries at a time, instead of just enough for the next few meals. Leftovers could be safely saved, allowing people to cook more food at once. Refrigerators also contributed to better health, especially for babies and young children, because milk did not spoil in them.

Although still considered a luxury item in the late 1930s, falling production costs and rising prosperity turned them into a household necessity after World War II. In 1935, about one in four urban households had one; in 1950, the figure was nine in ten.

2.17.14 American Tabletop Radio

United States
1937

Credit: DEA/G. Cigolini/DeAgostini/Getty Images

What You Need to Know

Shown here is a "cathedral" style radio, manufactured by America's Emerson Radio and Phonograph Corporation in 1937. The tabletop design, which became the most popular style of radio in the 1930s, got its name from its resemblance to the elaborate facades of Gothic cathedrals. (They were also called "tombstone" radios, although not by manufacturers, because of their distinctive shape.) The radio here was made from Bakelite, an early form of plastic, but colored to look like an expensive tropical wood.

Radio dates to the end of the nineteenth century, although during its first two decades, it was primarily used for two-party transmissions, such as from ship to shore. With the development of broadcast radio after World War I and technology improvements, including the amplification of sound through speakers rather than individual headphones, the medium came into widespread use. In 1920, there were virtually no consumer radios in America; by the late 1930s, roughly 6 of every 10 households were, to use the contemporary expression, "radioized homes."

Still, radios were not cheap, so most homes had just one, usually placed in the main room of a house, where the family would gather in the evenings to listen to their favorite shows. While the sets were a major expense, about a month's wage for a typical worker in the Great Depression, listening to them was free, making them the most popular form of home mass entertainment in the 1930s.

A Closer Look

In 1920, the nation's first radio station, KDKA of Pittsburgh, went on the air; by 1937, there more than 600 commercial radio stations broadcasting out of all 48 states. Unlike in Europe, radio in America was a largely capitalist enterprise; instead of the government sponsoring broadcasts, private companies did, recouping their costs by selling advertising. By the 1930s, many of the stations were linked to networks, which allowed for more expensively produced programs than a single radio station could afford to make.

For Americans during the 1930s—the so-called golden age of radio—there were all kinds of entertainment available, usually on programs sponsored by a single advertiser. Orchestral and big band music, often broadcast live from big-city ballrooms, were popular, as were soap operas during the afternoon—so-called because they were typically sponsored by detergent companies and aimed at stay-at-home mothers. But the most widely followed were the action shows, such as the *Lone Ranger* and *Dick Tracy*, and comedies, such as *Amos 'n' Andy*, about characters in an African-American neighborhood in Chicago (although voiced by white actors) and *Burns and Allen*, featuring the antics of the real-life married couple of George Burns and Gracie Allen.

1 100 200 300 400 500 600 700 800 900 1000 1100 1200 1300 1400 1500 1600 1700 1800 1900 2000 CE

2.17.15 American Ticker Tape Operator

United States
1938

Credit: Chaloner Woods/Getty Images

What You Need to Know

This photograph shows an operator at a telegraph office in the United States in 1938, receiving ticker tape showing price changes on corporate securities listed on the New York Stock Exchange.

Since its origin in the late eighteenth century, the New York Stock Exchange had been the preserve of large investors, typically located in and around the financial hub of Wall Street. But in the 1920s, all that changed. New brokerage firms, such as Merrill Lynch, specializing in the marketing of securities to small investors, capitalized on rising prosperity and soaring stock prices to entice millions of middle- and working-class people to purchase shares.

All of this new money, along with the solid economic growth of the decade, itself built on new mass technologies, such as the radio and automobiles, as well as rising productivity, produced steadily climbing stock prices, bringing more people into the market.

At brokerage houses around the country, small investors would sit in rows of chairs, as the ticker tape clicked and young boys wrote up the latest price changes on chalkboards. Other investors would call in their purchase and sell orders to brokers, who would then wire them to New York to be executed.

A Closer Look

Between the end of the brief but sharp recession that hit the United States in 1921 and 1922 and the peak of the stock market in 1929, the Dow Jones Industrial Average, a composite index of major stocks, rose from around 70 points to more than 380.

Share price gains were trumpeted in the nation's press, with stories featuring quotes from leading investors and economists talking of permanent prosperity and ever-rising values for corporate securities. There were tales of ordinary people making fortunes overnight. Conversations about the stock market could be heard everywhere, in barbershops, grocery stores, and dinner parties.

Contributing to the frenzy were the policies of the new retail brokerage firms, as well as investment banks, which allowed people to buy shares on margin, sometimes with as little as 10 percent down, secured by the collateral of the stocks themselves, which were expected to continue rising in value.

The boom inevitably proved unsustainable, as the Great Crash of 1929 proved. But it did not stop speculation in the stock market. Savvy investors understood that the best time to buy was when everyone else was selling. Although small investors stayed away from the market in the 1930s, enough investors remained to keep the volume of shares traded at roughly one-third to one-half of what they had been in the 1920s.

1 100 200 300 400 500 600 700 800 900 1000 1100 1200 1300 1400 1500 1600 1700 1800 1900 2000 CE

2.17.16 Victory Garden Poster from the United States

United States
1940s

Credit: National Archives

What You Need to Know

In this World War II–era poster, issued by the National War Garden Commission, people are urged to plant what were known as Victory Gardens. Such gardens, planted and tended by families and communities, provided fruits and vegetables that could be immediately consumed or preserved by canning or drying for later consumption.

At the height World War II, the United States had more than 16 million men and women in uniform and was spending $100 billion annually ($1.4 trillion in today's money) on the war effort. It was a total war and, as such, required full mobilization of the civilian sector. A key component of this mobilization was propaganda, organized by the Office of War Information and primarily aimed at promoting patriotism, commitment, and sacrifice.

Posters, more than 200,000 varieties, including the one shown here, and published by the government, businesses, and other organizations, decked the interiors and exteriors of buildings across the country. Americans were inundated by print and radio advertising, sometimes directly promoting the war effort; in other, less altruistic cases, businesses used patriotism to sell goods and services. Comic books and cartoons featured patriotic themes, and moviegoers watched thousands of newsreels, which tried to put the best spin on how the war was going. Even when the main feature came on, it was often about the heroic efforts of American fighting men and women and the treachery and brutality of the country's enemies.

A Closer Look

Victory Gardens had several basic purposes: to allow more of the food grown on U.S. farms to be devoted to military personnel; to ease the inflation that continued despite government price controls; to stretch family budgets suffering from the loss of male wage earners; to provide needed nutriments at a time when commercially grown vegetables and fruits were often in short supply or rationed; and to create a shared sense of purpose for the civilian population and solidarity with the troops overseas.

Americans responded to the call with enthusiasm; some 20 million people participated in the volunteer program. Sales of pressure cookers, needed for home canning, exploded from 62,000 units in 1942 to 315,000 the following year. Victory gardens could be found everywhere, in the public squares of small towns, in suburban backyards, even on the rooftops of urban tenements. They even became fashionable. Working families and socialites alike could be found digging, planting, sowing, and preserving some 9 to 10 million tons of home- and community-grown vegetables during World War II, roughly the same amount grown and processed commercially.

2.17.17 World War II British Ration Book

United Kingdom
1943

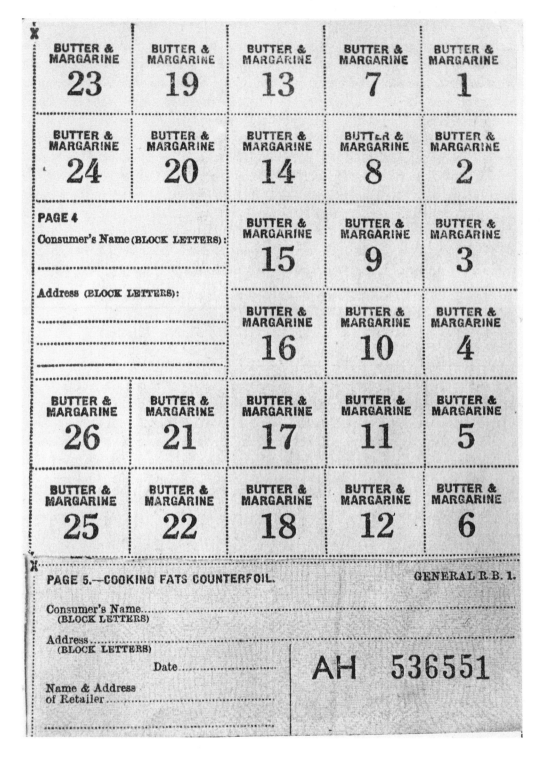

Credit: Hulton Archives/Getty Images

What You Need to Know

Shown here is a ration book, issued by the British government during World War II.

At the beginning of World War II, Britain imported roughly two-thirds of the food its people consumed. The supplies largely came from imperial holdings in Asia and Africa, and especially from the United States and other countries in the Americas. The war affected the food supply—both imported and domestic—in several ways. First, with much of the British economy devoted to the war effort, there were fewer funds to pay for imports. Second, gas rationing and railroads devoted to war transport made it more difficult to get farm goods to urban markets. The countryside also saw the loss of tens of thousands of farmers and farm laborers recruited into the military. But the most devastating blow came at sea. Recognizing Britain's dependence on imports—both to feed itself and to supply necessary materiel to its troops—Germany embarked on a massive campaign of U-boat, or submarine, warfare. Until the practice of sending ships across the Atlantic in armed convoys went into full effect in 1943, allied shipping losses were appalling. In 1942, more than 1,500 U.S. merchant ships alone were sunk in the crossing to Britain.

A Closer Look

The page shown here is for butter and margarine; the numbers are for administrative purposes. The page is divided into perforated squares. A customer, who typically received his or her set of ration cards annually, would present one of these squares to a merchant, who would then sell them the amount indicated. The varying amounts allowed consumers flexibility, depending on how many people they had to feed at a given time and the kinds of food they wanted to prepare. Merchants were required to keep the stamps, so that the government could keep tabs on how many rationed goods were sold and check that against the amount of goods the merchant had been issued to sell. This was designed to prevent goods showing up on the black market at inflated prices.

Rationing dominated almost every aspect of British life during the war. With petrol in particularly short supply, people curtailed unnecessary automobile trips. Consumer durables, such as refrigerators and radios, were essentially rationed out of existence. Furniture and clothing became utilitarian in design; elegant fabrics were unavailable, and frills and cuffs disappeared from clothing. With silk needed for parachutes, women painted their legs in lieu of unavailable stockings.

Ironically, however, the British diet may have improved during the war, as unhealthy ingredients such as fats and sugars were limited, forcing people to consume more locally grown fruits and vegetables. The Ministry of Food, which was responsible for rationing rules, also took account of the special needs of pregnant women, children, and the ill, who were given access to more milk, cod liver oil, and coveted citrus fruits.

1 100 200 300   400   500   600   700   800   900   1000 1100 1200 1300   1400   1500   1600   1700 1800 1900 2000 CE

2.17.18 Survey of American Combat Bomber Crews

United States
1944

A. Belief in the Value of Strategic Bombing:

1. Most officers and men in heavy bomber crews express strong belief in the overall *value of their own part in winning* the war. The proportion of men who think their own type of outfit will play a "very important part" is considerably higher among men in combat crews than among ground troops recently surveyed in ETO.
2. The majority of men feel that the *targets selected* for bombing are usually as important as any that could be chosen. However, a sizeable minority question the value of bombing certain targets.
3. The majority feel that their most recent raids did *serious damage* to important targets. But the number who have doubts about damage done on recent raids is not negligible.
4. Sixty per cent say they *sometimes* have had the feeling that a particular mission was *not worth the cost*, and 6% say they have quite often felt this. About three men in ten say they have never felt that a mission was not worth the cost.
5. Men who have flown *a large number of combat missions* are more likely than those with less combat experience to have some doubts about the *selection of targets* and the value of *particular missions*.
6. Men who *think their targets as important as any that could be assigned* are much more likely than men who are critical of the choice of targets to *feel that their missions are worth the cost*. . . .

D. Difficulty of missions:

1. Six men in ten believe that their present missions are about as difficult as when they began combat flying in ETO, and two men in ten think the missions now are *more* difficult than the first ones they flew. One man in ten says that missions are now *less* difficult than when he began combat flying (and one man in ten has no opinion).
2. There are no differences in the opinions of officers and enlisted men regarding the relative difficulty of missions now and in the past.
3. The opinions of the fliers are substantiated by available statistics, which show that the work load and personnel losses among combat crews increased from November 1943 through April 1944. During May the work load continued to rise whereas the rates of personnel loss and battle damage decreased.

Source: Headquarters, European Theater of Operations. Research Branch. "Survey of Combat Crews in Heavy Bombardment Groups in ETO." *Preliminary Report*. Special Services Division Headquarters, June 1944, pp. 3, 5.

What You Need to Know

This document comes from the "Survey of Combat Crews in Heavy Bombardment Groups in ETO [European Theater of Operations]," part of a report issued by the United States Army Air Forces. Released in June 1944, it consists of conclusions drawn from interviews of bomber crews about the effectiveness of the U.S. air war against Germany.

Over the course of World War II, the United States, along with its ally, Great Britain, unleashed a bombing campaign from bases in England of unprecedented ferocity against the cities, transportation network, and manufacturing facilities of German-occupied Europe. Up to 1,000 heavy bombers—mostly B-17s and B-24s—would participate in a single raid.

Manned by a crew of between 10 and 15, the American bombers would take off in formation, usually in the morning, led by brightly colored "lead-ships," which would direct them to their targets.

Aside from the sheer terror of being hit by enemy aircraft (although this diminished over the course of the war as the German air force was destroyed) and antiaircraft fire from the ground, known as *flak*, conditions on the planes were trying at best. Flying at up to 30,000 feet, the unpressurized and unheated planes subjected crews to painful earaches and temperatures falling to 60 degrees below zero, their only protection electrically heated suits and bulky oxygen masks.

A Closer Look

Between them, the U.S. and British air forces dropped nearly 2.8 million tons of bombs over the course of the war; the average German city saw roughly 50 percent of its structures destroyed.

As the survey reveals, the crews, although often critical of their mission, were generally convinced that the bombing raids were effective. Subsequent studies have offered a more nuanced picture of the effect of the raids on Germany. Although it is true that German war production peaked in 1944, as the bombing reached its apex, the output was nonetheless one-third less than the Nazi government planned it to be. Much of this had to do with higher absenteeism, as workers stayed away from plants they knew to be targeted or used their days to scrounge for food and rebuild damaged homes.

Aside from absenteeism, the effect on German civilian morale, a key justification for the attacks, is harder to measure but seems to have been more deeply affected than industrial output. Surveys immediately after the war found more than 90 percent of Germans agreeing that the bombing did negatively affect their morale; roughly 70 percent said that the intensity of the bombing led them to conclude that Germany would lose the war fully a year before it actually surrendered.

1 100 200 300   400   500   600   700   800   900   1000 1100 1200 1300   1400   1500   1600   1700   1800   1900 2000 CE

2.17.19 Japanese Soldiers' Experiences during World War II

Japan
1945

On Negros Island in the Philippines. At daybreak on March 29, 1945, the main American forces landed. Our 77th Infantry Brigade's 354th Independent Infantry Battalion held our position at 1,100 meters on Higashitaroyama (later renamed Dolan Hill by the U.S. forces).

The fierce bombardment from air and land by the main American forces had scorched the densely foliated deep jungle encampment, rendering it as barren as a volcano. When the artillery bombardment ended, the enemy infantry approached to 30 meters and threw hand grenades in close combat. We struck nightly into the enemy encampment. One after another my war buddies went through the gates of Yasukuni Shrine. We were left with many heavily wounded soldiers. Maggots hatched in our bandages, writhing on our flesh and exuding a foul stench.

Food supplies were cut off. Having eaten up all the stalks of grasses and plants, and all the insects and reptiles, we became malnutrition cases. One's entire body swells, one's strength gives out, and it becomes impossible to control one's bodily functions. Hunger gnawed at people's spirit. There were those who ate human flesh. With the onset of the rainy season, men suffered from malaria, dengue fever, tropical ulcers, and chronic amoebic dysentery. There were those among the seriously wounded and ill soldiers who despaired so much that they killed themselves. Their gunshots echoed in the valley. Some deserted on their way to attack the enemy, or attacked the supply base, fighitng against other Japanese soldiers to obtain food.

Higashitaroyama had held out for 52 days against a heavy siege. By May 23, a mere dozen or so men were left under company commander Ishizuka. After ordering his men to assemble at battalion headquarters, Commander Ishikuza received a heavy gunshot wound, which perforated his stomach. I was ordered to escape alone with important documents—reports to battalion headquarters. Giving a sidelong glance at the 200 heavily wounded and ill soldiers left behind, I made my escape. I thought of the poems "Eyes hot with tears, I see the round eyes of the infant clinging to its mother's dead body"; and "I overtake Japanese women and children carrying children on their backs, pulling children along by the hand and carrying baggage."

I reached brigade headquarters. There they had food—plenty of it. It shocked me to see the well-fed men of the headquarter units line up like ants and carry off provisions into the distance. At the front we had not been sent even a grain of unhulled rice.

Source: Kobuko Yumio. Letter to the *Asahi Shimbun*. Reprinted in *Senso: The Japanese Remember the Pacific War: Letters to the Editor of* Asahi Shimbun. Edited by Frank Gibney. Armonk, NY: M. E. Sharpe, 1995, pp. 152–153.

TIMELINE   2000 1900 1800 1700 1600 1500 1400 1300 1200 1100 1000 900 800 700 600 500 400 300 200 100 1 BCE

What You Need to Know

This 1986 letter was written by Kobuko Yumio to the *Asahi Shimbun*, among the largest national newspapers in Japan. In it, Yumio, who served in the Imperial Japanese army from his teens to his early 20s, recalls the fighting he experienced in early 1945 as American forces retook the Philippines, which had been seized by Japan four years earlier.

Japanese soldiers were highly disciplined and motivated, although not always for the best of reasons. From an early age, Japanese boys were indoctrinated in the ancient principles of *bush-ido* or samurai code of ethics. This dictated that a samurai, or soldier, be willing to sacrifice and even die for his *daimyo* or lord. By the twentieth century, the lord had been replaced by the concept of the nation, as embodied by the emperor.

If to die in the name of a higher cause was glorious, then to surrender and return home in defeat was shameful. Japanese soldiers were well aware that after previous conflicts, those who had been taken prisoners of war became social outcasts, unable to find good jobs or even wives. Finally, there was fear of the Americans. While the U.S. military's official policy was to take prisoners, many American soldiers—motivated by anti-Japanese racism and convinced that their enemies were fanatics who preferred death over surrender—made little effort to solicit their surrender before massacring them. All of this motivated many Japanese soldiers to fight to the death.

A Closer Look

With their supply lines destroyed by American submarine warfare and the home islands subjected to constant aerial bombardment, Japanese soldiers stationed around the Pacific were subject to incredible privations. Food rations—typically rice and miso (soy) powder—were scarce, leading to hunger and even famine. One Japanese veteran, rescuing survivors from Guadalcanal, described them as "skin and bones dressed in military uniform, thin as bamboo sticks." Near starvation conditions, and a lack of medicine, meant that the soldiers were prey to the host of diseases endemic to their tropical outposts.

Making things worse was the harsh discipline of the Japanese army. As it became clear that they were losing, officers became increasingly savage in punishing ordinary soldiers, whom they blamed for Japan's battlefield setbacks, with beatings for the most trivial of offenses. There were even reports of men being kicked to death for failing to serve dinner to their officers fast enough.

Part 18:
The Cold War

1945–1990

2.18.1 President Truman Announces Dropping of Atomic Bomb

Washington, DC
August 6, 1945

Sixteen hours ago an American airplane dropped one bomb on Hiroshima, an important Japanese Army base. That bomb had more power than 20,000 tons of TNT. It had more than 2,000 times the blast power of the British "Grand Slam," which is the largest bomb ever yet used in the history of warfare.

The Japanese began the war from the air at Pearl Harbor. They have been repaid manyfold. And the end is not yet. With this bomb we have now added a new and revolutionary increase in destruction to supplement the growing power of our armed forces. In their present form these bombs are now in production, and even more powerful forms are in development.

It is an atomic bomb. It is a harnessing of the basic power of the universe. The force from which the sun draws its power has been loosed against those who brought war to the Far East. . . .

We are now prepared to obliterate more rapidly and completely every productive enterprise the Japanese have above ground in any city. We shall destroy their docks, their factories, and their communications. Let there be no mistake; we shall completely destroy Japan's power to make war. . . .

The fact that we can release atomic energy ushers in a new era in man's understanding of nature's forces. Atomic energy may in the future supplement the power that now comes from coal, oil, and falling water, but at present it cannot be produced on a basis to compete with them commercially. Before that comes there must be a long period of intensive research.

It has never been the habit of the scientists of this country or the policy of this government to withhold from the world scientific knowledge. Normally, therefore, everything about the work with atomic energy would be made public.

But under present circumstances it is not intended to divulge the technical processes of production or all the military applications, pending further examination of possible methods of protecting us and the rest of the world from the danger of sudden destruction.

I shall recommend that the Congress of the United States consider promptly the establishment of an appropriate commission to control the production and use of atomic power within the United States. I shall give further consideration and make further recommendations to the Congress as to how atomic power can become a powerful and forceful influence towards the maintenance of world peace.

Source: Truman, Harry S. "Statement by the President Announcing the Use of the A-Bomb at Hiroshima," August 6, 1945. Online at The American Presidency Project by Gerhard Peters and John T. Woolley. http://www.presidency.ucsb.edu/ws/?pid=12169.

TIMELINE   2000 1900 1800 1700 1600 1500 1400 1300 1200 1100 1000 900 800 700 600 500 400 300 200 100 1 BCE

What You Need to Know

This excerpt from an announcement given by President Harry Truman on August 6, 1945, informed the American people and the world that the United States had just dropped an atomic bomb on the Japanese city of Hiroshima.

For nearly four years, following the Pearl Harbor attack, the United States had been waging war against Imperial Japan across the far-flung Pacific. Numerous battles had been fought as the United States launched bloody amphibious assaults on tiny coral atolls and in the heavily populated Philippines.

In many of the battles, Japanese soldiers—inspired by both patriotism and motivated by fear of the Americans, who, their government told them, were barbarians and torturers—had fought to the death, rather than surrender. By the summer of 1945, the Americans had tightened the noose around Japan and began contemplating an invasion of the country's home islands, which, it was expected, the Japanese would defend even more fiercely than their possessions abroad. The army put forth projections of hundreds of thousands of American casualties, and millions of Japanese ones.

For Truman that was enough to justify dropping the bomb on Hiroshima, and another one on Nagasaki three days later. Still, say opponents of his decision, the attacks were unnecessary; a devastated Japan, they insist, was already prepared to surrender.

A Closer Look

The United States had been at war with Japan since the latter had attacked the naval base at Pearl Harbor, Hawaii, on December 7, 1941. As Truman noted, the bomb had the equivalent explosive power of 20,000 tons of TNT. Unmentioned was an even deadlier component of atomic weaponry—radiation—which killed more than half of the 140,000 and 180,000 victims of the Hiroshima attack.

During much of the war, the people of Hiroshima had been relatively lucky. Lacking military and manufacturing targets, despite Truman's claims to the contrary, they had been spared the incessant bombing that had reduced many other Japanese cities to rubble. So when the citizens looked up that sunny summer morning and saw a single American airplane in the sky—by then the Japanese air force had been all but destroyed—they assumed it was a reconnaissance flight and ignored it.

Then came a flash as bright as the sun, literally burning out the retinas of those who were looking directly at it. Depending on how close they were to the explosion, people were either vaporized, set aflame by the heat flash, killed by flying debris, or burnt in subsequent fires. And these were, in one sense, the lucky ones. For those who died of acute radiation poisoning in the following weeks and months, symptoms included nausea, vomiting, internal bleeding, the loss of hair and teeth, all of which were often accompanied by debilitating pain.

2.18.2 Safe Conduct Pass for North Korean Soldiers

Korea
1950

Credit: Keystone/Getty Images

What You Need to Know

The "safe conduct pass" shown here was dropped behind by United Nations forces behind North Korean lines in December 1950, calling on enemy soldiers to surrender and promising to treat each one "as an honorable prisoner of war."

When Japan surrendered to Allied forces in the late summer of 1945, the Korean Peninsula, which had been occupied by Japan since early in the century, was divided between American and Soviet forces at the 38th Parallel. North of that line, Moscow sponsored the regime of communist Kim Il Sung; in the south, Washington put anticommunist general Syngman Rhee in power.

The division was supposed to be temporary. But as Cold War divisions hardened in the 1940s, reconciliation seemed increasingly impossible. Both sides were frustrated, each provoking the other with small raids. Then, in June 1950, Kim launched a massive invasion that nearly captured all of the peninsula. Operating under a UN Security Council order, the United States sent in hundreds of thousands of troops. This turned the tide and pushed the fighting into North Korea, nearly to the border with newly communist China, which then sent in a large force of its own to push back. By mid-1951, the front had stabilized near the 38th Parallel, where it remained for the next two years until a truce was signed. After all of the fighting and death, that is roughly where Korea would remain divided down through the present day.

A Closer Look

At the time it was dropped, anticommunist South Korean and United Nations forces, the latter largely composed of U.S. troops, had pushed back a North Korean offensive and were fighting deep in enemy territory. Indeed, during the first year of the war, which began in June 1950, the front lines had shifted wildly up and down the Korean Peninsula. The impact on Korean civilians was devastating.

Thousands of people fled southward as internal refugees, seeking to escape the fighting and North Korean forces. The latter, inspired by communist ideology, often set up so-called "people's tribunals," in the villages and towns they captured. There, the so-called bourgeoisie, typically merchants, landlords, and even peasants with land of their own, were put on trial. Some were executed; others were forced to labor for the North Korean army. Virtually anyone with property had it taken away.

Over the course of the three-year conflict, roughly 2.5 million civilians were killed, or about one 1 of every 12 Koreans. While the North Korean army committed more of the atrocities, North Koreans suffered from the overwhelming firepower of UN forces. Indeed, 60 percent of civilian casualties were in the north.

1 100 200 300 400 500 600 700 800 900 1000 1100 1200 1300 1400 1500 1600 1700 1800 1900 2000 CE

2.18.3 Workers on a Central American Banana Plantation

Guatemala
ca. 1950

Credit: Three Lions/Getty Images

What You Need to Know

The accompanying photo shows workers hauling bananas on a plantation in Guatemala in 1950.

The presence of United Fruit Company, a U.S. corporation, in Guatemala went back to the beginning of the twentieth century. Known to locals as *El Pulpo*, or "the octopus," the company not only controlled the best tracts of land but had minority and controlling interests in the companies that ran the country's transportation and communications systems. It charged a tariff on all goods that moved out of the country's main, which it controlled. It even got itself exempted from virtually all Guatemalan taxes.

It was able to maintain this control because it gave unconditional financial support to a string of right-wing presidents, who helped supply the company with its labor force and violently crushed potential union organizing efforts.

In 1950, however, Guatemalan voters elected the left-wing Jacobo Arbenz as president, on a platform of land reform. Arbenz nationalized much of United Fruit's land that lay unused. He paid for it but at the very low valuation the company declared it to be worth for the purposes of avoiding property taxes. But the company had friends in high places in Washington, who, amid Cold War fears of communism, orchestrated a successful coup against him.

A Closer Look

By 1950, roughly 30,000 Guatemalans worked on banana plantations, most of them owned by the United Fruit Company with the fruit they raised destined largely for the U.S. market. Most of them were virtual slaves, forced to work on the plantations under a 1934 law that allowed the government to arrest landless peasants for vagrancy and then contract them out to private growers for months at a time.

There was almost no end to the supply of labor, as Guatemala suffered from one of the most inequitable distributions of land in the world. Between them, foreign corporations and the wealthiest 2 percent of Guatemalans—mostly persons of European descent—owned approximately 70 percent of the land, with another 20 percent controlled by the 8 percent of the population that might qualify as middle class. The other 90 percent of the population, largely indigenous Mayan Indians, owned just 10 percent.

On the plantations, the landless peasants were forced to work 12-hour days, six days a week, largely in weeding and keeping the trees free of insects and vermin, as well as wielding machetes to cut paths through the jungle and planting new trees. It was backbreaking and dangerous work, made worse by the fact of its locale in the humid tropical lowlands of the nation's Caribbean coast. Most of the laborers came from the country's cooler highlands. Not only were they unused to such heat, they were prone to tropical diseases, such as yellow fever.

1 100 200 300 400 500 600 700 800 900 1000 1100 1200 1300 1400 1500 1600 1700 1800 1900 2000 CE

2.18.4 *Brown v. Board of Education* Decision

United States
1954

In approaching this problem, we cannot turn the clock back to 1868 when the Amendment was adopted, or even to 1896 when *Plessy v. Ferguson* was written. We must consider public education in the light of its full development and its present place in American life throughout the Nation. Only in this way can it be determined if segregation in public schools deprives these plaintiffs of the equal protection of the laws.

Today, education is perhaps the most important function of state and local governments. Compulsory school attendance laws and the great expenditures for education both demonstrate our recognition of the importance of education to our democratic society. It is required in the performance of our most basic public responsibilities, even service in the armed forces. It is the very foundation of good citizenship. Today it is a principal instrument in awakening the child to cultural values, in preparing him for later professional training, and in helping him to adjust normally to his environment. In these days, it is doubtful that any child may reasonably be expected to succeed in life if he is denied the opportunity of an education. Such an opportunity, where the state has undertaken to provide it, is a right which must be made available to all on equal terms.

We come then to the question presented: Does segregation of children in public schools solely on the basis of race, even though the physical facilities and other "tangible" factors may be equal, deprive the children of the minority group of equal educational opportunities? We believe that it does. . . .

Segregation of white and colored children in public schools has a detrimental effect upon the colored children. The impact is greater when it has the sanction of the law; for the policy of separating the races is usually interpreted as denoting the inferiority of the negro group. A sense of inferiority affects the motivation of a child to learn. Segregation with the sanction of law, therefore, has a tendency to [retard] the educational and mental development of negro children and to deprive them of some of the benefits they would receive in a racial[ly] integrated school system.

Whatever may have been the extent of psychological knowledge at the time of *Plessy v. Ferguson*, this finding is amply supported by modern authority. Any language in *Plessy v. Ferguson* contrary to this finding is rejected.

We conclude that in the field of public education the doctrine of "separate but equal" has no place. Separate educational facilities are inherently unequal. Therefore, we hold that the plaintiffs and others similarly situated for whom the actions have been brought are, by reason of the segregation complained of, deprived of the equal protection of the laws guaranteed by the Fourteenth Amendment. This disposition makes unnecessary any discussion whether such segregation also violates the Due Process Clause of the Fourteenth Amendment.

Source: Supreme Court of the United States. *Brown v. Board of Education of Topeka*, 347 U.S. 843 (1954).

What You Need to Know

This selection comes from the U.S. Supreme Court case of *Brown v. Board of Education of Topeka*.

In the immediate wake of emancipation during and immediately after the Civil War, African-Americans in the South made significant advances politically and socially, under the protection of the federal government. But this period, known as Reconstruction, proved short-lived. By the late 1870s, conservative whites had retaken control of every state government in the South. They disenfranchised virtually all black voters and imposed a comprehensive system of segregation, allowing for the separation of races in public facilities, both those operated by the government, such as schools and parks, and those owned by individuals and companies, such as hotels and restaurants. Few blacks challenged the system in its first 75 years, for to do so invited severe retaliation—from the loss of employment to being lynched.

World War II, however, began a transformation in race relations. How could America claim to be fighting against racist regimes in Germany and Japan when it perpetuated racism at home? African-Americans, having fought to defend democracy abroad, demanded change. The federal government began to respond, with the desegregation of the military and a series of court cases undermining segregation in higher education.

A Closer Look

The unanimous decision, written by Chief Justice Earl Warren, overturned the 1896 *Plessy v. Ferguson* decision, which stated that "separate but equal" public facilities for black and white Americans, including schools, was constitutional. "Segregation of white and colored [a non-pejorative term at the time] children in public schools," Warren wrote, "has a detrimental effect upon the colored children" and was therefore unconstitutional.

In saying that even where schools were "equal," segregation was unconstitutional, Warren was being charitable to state governments in the South. In fact, black schools were almost always inferior and underfunded. The physical structures were old and poorly maintained, with leaky roofs, sagging floors, and windows without glass. Books were in short supply and, where they were available, they were usually the torn and dirty hand-me-downs of white schools. There was even censorship of the curriculum, particularly when it came to civics classes and lessons from the Declaration of Independence and Constitution about equality before the law.

Black schools were almost inevitably overcrowded, with student-to-teacher ratios far higher than white schools, and teachers who were there far less well-trained than their white counterparts. Often, a single teacher had to instruct children in several grades in the same classroom, a relic from the nineteenth century that had largely disappeared in white schools.

But as sweeping as the *Brown* decision was, the struggle to end segregation was only the beginning. The decision read that states should desegregate "with all deliberate speed," which southern governments took to mean as slowly as possible.

Fix that thirst _but_ good...here's your
real thirst-quencher!

It's the surest way for any home handyman (and his helpers, too!) to nail down a thirst. One bottle of sparkling 7-Up does the job in a jiffy—all by itself!

Seven-Up has a lively, tingling flavor. This drink gets right at the very cause of thirst. Thirst comes when the natural flow of moisture in your mouth stops. Seven-Up has a quenching quality that stimulates this flow—makes your mouth literally water. When you finish the bottle, you feel no stickiness . . . no come-back thirst.

And after you've savored that last lively sip of 7-Up, you get something more —you get a quick, refreshing lift. There is just enough sugar in 7-Up to go to work in from 2 to 6 minutes to renew your energy. Have a 7-Up and see!

Nothing does it like Seven-Up!

You like it...
it likes you!

Credit: Apic/Getty Images

What You Need to Know

Pictured here is a 1956 magazine advertisement for the soft drink 7-Up.

As this advertisement reveals, much of American culture was devoted to domesticity in the 1950s. The man, after all, is spending his leisure hours in his workshop garage with his family nearby, not out drinking or hunting with his male friends. Rather than going out to the movies in the evening, people increasingly stayed home to watch television.

The emphasis on the family had dramatic demographic repercussions. Reversing a century-old trend, birth rates soared from 80 per 1,000 women of reproductive age (15 to 44 years) in 1940, to 123 in 1957. The average number of children per married couple went from 2.3 to 3.5. The so-called baby boom generation was the largest in American history, and its effects would be felt over the next half century and beyond. It initially resulted in suburban growth, as well as a vast school-building expansion program and a whole new consumer culture of toys, fads, and popular entertainment geared to young children and teenagers.

A Closer Look

The scene in the ad shows a young father in his home workshop; the ad copy below touts how 7-Up quenches the thirst of the "home handyman (and his helpers, too!)," the latter presumably his children. Although the dad is featured, the main target audience is the wife, the suburban mother, who did most of the family shopping.

In the years after World War II, newly prospering Americans were eager to put 20 years of economic depression and wartime rationing behind them. Buying a home was a key way to do that. Owner-occupied housing climbed from 43.6 percent of all housing in 1940 to 61.9 percent in 1960. Most of the new housing was in the suburbs, which went from constituting 18 percent of the American population in 1930 to fully 30.7 percent in 1960. Coming from various neighborhoods, they tried to create new social communities, through child- and family-centric activities, such as PTA events, block parties, and Little League baseball games.

To meet the demand for suburban housing, developers applied the principles of mass production to home construction, creating instant neighborhoods of look-alike homes. They were affordable, partly because of government programs that made it easier and cheaper to obtain a mortgage, but they were also quite small and plain. Almost immediately, new homeowners, presumably like the one featured in the ad shown here, went to work on home remodeling and expansion projects.

1 100 200 300 400 500 600 700 800 900 1000 1100 1200 1300 1400 1500 1600 1700 1800 1900 2000 CE

Credit: Central Office of Information. "If You Think It's Hopeless, You're Wrong." September 1957 national press advert. UK National Archives: INF 2/122. Online at Civil Defence is Common Sense: The National Archives. http://www.nationalarchives.gov.uk/education/resources/fifties-britain/civil-defence-common-sense/.

What You Need to Know

This civil defense poster was issued by the British Government's Central Office of Information in 1957.

British scientists were important participants in the Manhattan Project, the U.S.-led and -based program to develop an atomic bomb during World War II. One of the main motivations for the project was the realistic fear that the Nazis might develop their own bomb first. Britain was a more likely target than the United States, as it was within reach of the early missiles Nazi Germany had developed before the end of the war. Indeed, Nazi Germany had already unleashed the missiles, albeit with conventional warheads, to devastating effect on London.

After the defeat of the Nazis in 1945 came fears of a new enemy—the communist Soviet Union. With Moscow's development of an atomic bomb in 1949 and the far more devastating hydrogen bomb in 1953, Britons were forced to live with the possible doom of nuclear attack.

But in its efforts to show that nuclear war was survivable, the British government met much resistance from antinuclear weapons groups, such as the Campaign for Nuclear Disarmament, founded the same year this pamphlet came out. With its "ban the bomb" slogan, the CND ridiculed notions of survivability, insisting instead that by getting rid of nuclear weapons Britain would be less likely to be attacked in the first place.

A Closer Look

Entitled "If You Think It's Hopeless, You're Wrong," it provides a summary of the services available to Britons in the case of nuclear war and encourages people to participate in civil defense so that should such a war occur, they will be better able to survive it.

As one of the most important countries in the anti-Soviet alliance during the Cold War, Great Britain, which developed its own atomic bomb in 1952, lived with the same Cold War fears of nuclear Armageddon that gripped much of the West from the 1950s through the 1980s.

Such fears expressed themselves in popular culture, government propaganda, and personal behavior. People built civil defense shelters under their backyards and in their basements, which they stocked with canned foods and other goods needed to survive the initial attack. The government tried to convince people that nuclear war was survivable and did not mean the end of civilization, as most people assumed.

Meanwhile, films, TV shows, and popular literature dealt with nuclear radiation obliquely and often fantastically. With the odd exception of books such as *On the Beach* (1957; made into a movie in 1959), a realistic account of nuclear war survivors, radiation was portrayed as a mysterious force that created mutants and monsters bent on humanity's destruction. Meanwhile, the British media hardly talked about actual nuclear policy at all, partly because various secrecy acts did not allow it to discuss what kinds of nuclear weapons and strategy the government was developing.

2.18.7 People Greeting Families Members across the Berlin Wall

Berlin, Germany
1962

Credit: Pictorial Parade/Archive Photos/Getty Images

What You Need to Know

This photo from 1962 shows a family in East Berlin holding a baby aloft so that other family members in West Berlin, on the other side of so-called Berlin Wall can get a glimpse of it. The year before, the communist East German government, backed by the Soviet Union, had erected the wall through the city, which had been divided into Soviet- and Western-controlled sectors since the end of World War II, to prevent East Germans from fleeing to West Germany.

Over the course of the 1950s, as West Germany prospered, and its citizens came to enjoy democratic freedoms, the country became a draw for many in East Germany, especially the more educated citizens. Between 1949 and the construction of the wall, some 2.7 million people—or about 15 percent of the population—fled East Germany for the West.

By the early 1960s, it was becoming clear that the authorities would have to put a stop to the flow or face permanent demographic and economic decline. In anticipation, East Berliners took jobs in the western part of the city and rented apartments there, so that they would be able to escape if the internal border was closed.

A Closer Look

At first, the Wall, which started going up in August 1961, was somewhat porous. In some cases, the authorities used existing buildings, so that people could enter a front door in East Berlin and exit a back door in West Berlin. Eventually, the holes were sealed and armed guards were placed along the Wall's length, given orders to shoot anyone who tried to go over or under it. Between 1961 and 1989, when the Wall came down, some 136 persons were killed trying to make the passage.

The contrast between the two Berlins of the 1950s and 1960s was stark. West Berlin was thriving economically and culturally. Standards of living were orders higher there than in East Berlin, with most people able to afford cars, modern household appliances, and trips abroad. The streets were lined with shops, nightclubs, and movie theaters, and brightly lit at night. By contrast, East Berliners, although better off than most people in communist Eastern Europe, could afford few luxuries, when they were even available. The city itself was drab, its streets lined with monotonous rows of gray apartment buildings.

Making things even worse for East Berliners was the fear under which they lived. The East German government had established a pervasive security system—which included hundreds of thousands of civilian informants—to keep tabs on its citizens, sending dissenters to jail. People avoided criticizing the government, even in private and amongst friends and relatives.

1 100 200 300 400 500 600 700 800 900 1000 1100 1200 1300 1400 1500 1600 1700 1800 1900 2000 CE

2.18.8 Fans Lining Up for Beatles Concert Tickets in London

London, England
1963

Credit: Evening Standard/Getty Images

What You Need to Know

In this photo from November 1963, a group of young fans were lining up to buy tickets to a concert by the Beatles at a South London arena. The three teenage-looking girls in the foreground enthusiastically display the much-coveted items. By 1963, the Beatles, formed in Liverpool three years before, were easily the most popular musical act in the United Kingdom. Within a few months, they would become a pop sensation on both sides of the Atlantic and across the European continent, as they combined England's music hall traditions with African-American rhythm and blues in a series of infectious number one hits.

In 1962, the Beatles returned to England from a two-year hiatus playing in West Germany. Late that year, they recorded "Please, Please Me," which went to the top of music charts. They then went on a concert tour of Britain that drew thousands of enthusiastic fans, many of them teenage girls, who would often scream their excitement through the entire concert. By late 1963, the media was talking of "Beatlemania," a cultural phenomenon never before seen in Britain or nearly anywhere else. The "Fab Four," as they came to be called, could hardly go out in public, without being mobbed by fans. Men began to adopt their "mop top" hairstyle, slim cut suits, and ankle-high, Cuban heel boots. The group's commercially savvy promoters marketed an endless array of Beatles paraphernalia.

With several more number one songs under their belts—including "She Loves You (Yeah, Yeah, Yeah)" and "I Want to Hold Your Hand"—The Beatles arrived in the United States in February 1964, reproducing the Beatlemania phenomenon on an even greater scale.

A Closer Look

The group's undeniable musical talents aside, Beatlemania was very much a product of demographic trends, specifically, the huge growth in the number of young people in Britain and other Western countries in the 1960s. In 1940, England and Wales experienced just under 600,000 live-births; in 1947, the figure was close to 900,000. And those nearly one million babies were turning 15 and 16 when The Beatles recorded their first hit records.

As in much of the West, the United Kingdom saw the emergence of a unique teenage culture in the late 1950s and early 1960s. First and foremost, there was the music of The Beatles and a host of other groups influenced by American rock and roll, including the Rolling Stones and the Dave Clark Five. But there were also new fashions, notably, the "mod" look of miniskirts and space-age outfits, personified by reed-thin, English model Twiggy, as well as a host of youth-oriented films, some of them by the Beatles themselves, celebrating music, hedonism, and a lives lived outside the bounds of respectable middle-class culture.

1 100 200 300 400 500 600 700 800 900 1000 1100 1200 1300 1400 1500 1600 1700 1800 1900 2000 CE

2.18.9 Mao Zedong's "Little Red Book"

China
1964

Credit: Carl De Souza/AFP/Getty Images

What You Need to Know

Shown here is the cover of the *Quotations of Chairman Mao Tse-Tung* (now transliterated as Mao Zedong), first published in 1964. Mao had been the leader of the Chinese Revolution and served as chairman of the Chinese Communist Party from 1945 to 1976.

In 1949, after years of civil war, the Chinese Communist Party, under the leadership of Mao Zedong, took power in Mainland China. Civil and political rights, already limited under the precommunist nationalists, were effectively abolished.

The new government collectivized agriculture and industry through long-term, centralized economic planning, which for a time, produced significant gains in economic output, if few consumer goods. Then, in the late 1950s and early 1960s, Mao launched the Great Leap Forward, a radical economic and social initiative to create a purer socialist model of communal living and production. It failed, and Mao lost influence within the party.

He responded by launching a crusade to purge China of "feudalism" and "bourgeois culture" known as the "cultural revolution." Brigades of youthful zealots, known as the Red Guards and chanting quotations from the Little Red Book, would attack intellectuals and other perceived elites, forcing them into the countryside to work alongside peasants. But the social and economic chaos the revolution engendered ultimately led to a backlash against such radicalism and the rise to power of more moderate forces. Under their leader, Deng Xiaopeng, they would introduce market economics, although not political liberalism, into the country from the early 1980s onward.

A Closer Look

The book, popularly known in the West as the "Little Red Book," for its cover and size, contained hundreds of sayings by the ideological leader of China. Most of these were on political and military matters, specifically, exhortations on how to promote, defend, and govern by socialist principles.

At more than five billion copies, it is the second most widely printed book in human history, after the Bible. Almost immediately after its first release, the book became interwoven into Chinese daily life. Schoolchildren would memorize its quotations and chant them in class. It would be waved aloft at prosocialist rallies and marches. It was frequently given as a gift at weddings and other life events. People would quote it frequently to answer questions that seemingly had little to do with politics, such as those concerning the proper care of children and what kinds of food to serve at a public function. At the height of communist ideological purity in the late 1960s, the physical object itself was treated with a reverence typically reserved for religious books. It was always to be held in the right hand, custom went, and must never placed on the ground. To own a soiled or torn copy was considered shameful.

1 100 200 300   400   500   600   700   800   900   1000 1100 1200 1300   1400   1500   1600   1700 1800 1900 2000 CE

2.18.10 Jeep Assembly Line at a Mitsubishi Factory

Japan
ca. 1965

Credit: Hulton Archive/Getty Images

What You Need to Know

The accompanying photo shows a worker at a Mitsubishi factory in Japan driving a Willy's Jeep off an assembly line sometime around 1965.

World War II devastated the Japanese economy. Incessant American bombing had destroyed nearly half of the nation's industrial capacity. Production levels in 1950 stood at the same level that they had been on the eve of the global depression of the 1930s. But the war also offered Japan certain advantages. Rebuilding the country fostered enormous demand. New factories with the latest technology and equipment gave the country a leg up on its competitors. America, its erstwhile enemy, contributed to the "Japanese economic miracle" by purchasing large amounts of military equipment, such as the Jeeps in this photo, to foster prosperity. In the midst of the Cold War, America did not want an economically frustrated Japanese people turning to communism.

That policy, along with Japan's own industrial tradition and emphasis on education, produced the rapid growth of the period, largely driven by domestic demand. By the 1960s, Japan had become a consumer society, as families bought appliances, televisions, and cars, with income levels rivaling those of Western Europe, also rebuilding from the devastation of World War II.

A Closer Look

Japan was a nation undergoing a dramatic social transformation in the 1960s, propelled by growth rates approaching 10 percent annually. Although roughly one-third of the population still lived in rural areas and made a living from agriculture, growing numbers of people were moving to urban areas and working in the manufacturing sector.

Nothing was more coveted than a job with one of the nation's big corporations. While salaries started low, the companies offered steady promotions, a guarantee of lifetime employment, and an array of social amenities. A worker could shop in the company supermarket with its discounted goods and obtain home mortgages from the company's internal bank; their children would be taken care of in company-provided day care and educated in company schools. The businesses also offered cultural amenities, such as swimming pools, gyms, and recreational centers; arts and crafts classes; chances to perform in theatrical and music groups; or to play on company baseball teams. Indeed, a worker's entire life might center around his (or, more rarely, her) employer. In return, the companies demanded discipline, hard work, and above all, loyalty to the company's interest. Very few workers were fired and very few quit.

2.18.11 Promotional Postcard for Rock Concert at the Fillmore

San Francisco, California
1966

Credit: Blank Archives/Archive Photos/Getty Images

What You Need to Know

The 1966 postcard shown here promotes a concert by the Grateful Dead and other rock groups at San Francisco's Fillmore Auditorium.

Various things about the poster—the long hair of man in the photo, the rock music groups featured, and the flowing script and floral design—reveal its origins in the burgeoning counterculture of the time. From the mid-1960s through the early 1970s, millions of primarily younger Americans rebelled against what they saw as the conformity of mainstream culture—its perceived materialism, corporatism, and militarism, the latter manifested in conscription into the armed forces and deployment in the Vietnam War.

Many of the often middle-class youth felt frustrated by the emphasis society put on getting a college education, pursuing a career, getting married, buying a home, and settling down in the suburbs.

Instead, they sought an escape in what contemporaries called the "counterculture." Defined in different ways by different people, the counterculture could take the form of politics (usually radical), economics (such as, cooperative stores), social (new ways of living, such as communes), religious (typically non-Western beliefs), lifestyle choices (long hair, nontraditional clothing, use of illicit drugs), and artistic (such as, psychedelic, or hallucinogen-influenced, art and music).

A Closer Look

Founded in the Bay Area in 1965, the Grateful Dead became one of the most popular musical groups from the 1960s onward, playing a genre of music known as psychedelic rock. The music, either performed live or listened to on records, served as an accompaniment to the emerging counterculture in America and other advanced industrial nations in the 1960s and 1970s. A major component of the counterculture experience was the use of psychedelic drugs, most notably lysergic acid diethylamide, also known simply as "acid," or LSD.

Young people would gather at parties, concerts, and "happenings"—large gatherings that featured music, art, and sometimes politics—and "drop acid," usually in the form of drug-infused sugar cubes or pieces of paper. LSD produced a sense of euphoria as well as hallucinations, in an experience known as a "trip." At the larger events, such as the one advertised here, the psychedelic music—featuring electric guitars, free-form rhythms, and lyrics, often with surrealistic content—would be accompanied by colorful, shape-shifting light shows and free-form dancing.

Although participants claimed LSD expanded consciousness and the lifestyle accompanying it promised a new sense of community to users, the drug had its downside. Illegal in most states from 1966 onward, it was sold on the black market, often of unknown strength and including dangerous additives. Users talked of "bad trips," and there were a number of suicides associated with the drug.

2.18.12 NOW's Bill of Rights for Modern Women

United States
1967

We Demand:

I. That the U.S. Congress immediately pass the Equal Rights Amendment to the Constitution to provide that "Equality of rights under the law shall not be denied or abridged by the United States or by any State on account of sex," and that such then be immediately ratified by the several States.

II. That equal employment opportunity be guaranteed to all women, as well as men, by insisting that the Equal Employment Opportunity Commission enforces the prohibitions against sex discrimination in employment under Title VII of the Civil Rights Act of 1964 with the same vigor as it enforces the prohibitions against racial discrimination.

III. That women be protected by law to ensure their rights to return to their jobs within a reasonable time after childbirth without loss of seniority or other accrued benefits, and be paid maternity leave as a form of social security and/or employee benefit.

IV. Immediate revision of tax laws to permit the deduction of home and child care expenses for working parents.

V. That child care facilities be established by law on the same basis as parks, libraries, and public schools, adequate to the needs of children from the pre-school years through adolescence, as a community resource to be used by all citizens from all income levels.

VI. That the right of women to be educated to their full potential equally with men be secured by Federal and State legislation, eliminating all discrimination and segregation by sex, written and unwritten, at all levels of education, including colleges, graduate and professional schools, loans and fellowships, and Federal and State training programs such as the Job Corps.

VII. The right of women in poverty to secure job training, housing, and family allowances on equal terms with men, but without prejudice to a parent's right to remain at home to care for his or her children; revision of welfare legislation and poverty programs which deny women dignity, privacy and self-respect.

VIII. The right of women to control their own reproductive lives by removing from penal codes laws limiting access to contraceptive information and devices and laws governing abortion.

IX. Amendment of Title II of the Civil Rights Act and state laws to include prohibition of sex discrimination in places of public accommodation, housing.

X. Revision of marriage, divorce and family laws to equalize the rights of men and women to own property, establish domicile, maintain individual identity and economic independence, etc., and promote marriage as an equal partnership of shared responsibility in all its aspects.

Source: Reprinted with permission of the National Organization for Women. This is a historical document (1967) and may not reflect the current language or priorities of the organization.

TIMELINE   2000 1900 1800 1700 1600 1500 1400 1300 1200 1100 1000 900 800 700 600 500 400 300 200 100 1 BCE

What You Need to Know

The accompanying document, "A Bill of Rights for Modern Women," was issued by the National Organization of Women (NOW) in 1967.

The history of the women's rights movement dates back to the mid-nineteenth century, when women first began to demand equality before the law. This "first wave" of feminism culminated in the winning of the vote in 1920. Then, the movement went into a hiatus. While women joined the workforce in huge numbers in World War II, it was deemed a wartime necessity. After the war, most women quit or were ousted from their jobs, as politicians and the media reemphasized traditional ideas about the proper role for women in society.

Still, women's wartime experiences had a lingering effect, as did the participation of many women in the struggle for African-American civil rights in the 1950s and 1960s. Then, in 1963, Betty Friedan, a mother and writer, published *The Feminine Mystique*, which examined the discontent felt by many college-educated housewives, frustrated at the limited role they were allowed to play in society. Many historians cite the best-seller status of the book as the beginning of the "second wave" of feminism, of which NOW, cofounded by Friedan, was the institutional embodiment.

A Closer Look

Founded the year before, NOW's initial mission was to get the federal government to enforce the anti–sexual discrimination clauses in the Civil Rights Act of 1964, particularly those concerning equal rights in the workplace. As this document indicates, NOW interpreted the law broadly, meaning that women could not achieve that equality unless they were provided child care, reproductive rights, and equal access to a wide array of government programs.

Before the women's liberation movement of the 1960s and 1970s, of which NOW was a prominent participant, women faced discrimination both in law and life. In 1967, they earned just 57.8 cents for every dollar a man earned in comparable employment. Despite laws to the contrary, employers openly discriminated in both hiring and employment; wanted advertisements typically stated that only men would be considered for many jobs.

In the mid-1960s, women's participation in the paid workforce remained below 40 percent. And, according to polls, most Americans, including a majority of women, preferred it that way. Putting career before family was considered unfeminine and even unpatriotic. In the Cold War atmosphere at the time, government-provided child care, which NOW deemed necessary for women to gain equality in the workplace, was seen as a step on the road to socialism, undermining the God-given sexual order of things and allowing the government to indoctrinate young minds.

2.18.13 Women Leaning against a Fiat Automobile

Mallorca, Spain
1967

Credit: Chris Ware/Keystone Features/Getty Images

What You Need to Know

The accompanying photo shows a fashionable young woman standing next to a Fiat 850 automobile, which is parked in front of a post office on the Spanish resort island of Mallorca in 1967.

Although World War II laid waste to Western Europe manufacturing capacity and led to the deaths of roughly 10 million people there, it did not impact the less tangible assets of the continent—namely, its people's skills and business acumen. Building on those, as well as hefty American aid through the Marshall Plan, Western Europeans rapidly rebuilt their region's economy in the quarter century after Nazi Germany's surrender, in the process moving millions from farms to cities and from the peasantry and working class to the middle class.

Contributing to what contemporaries called the "Western European miracle" was the integration of the continent's economies. With the establishment of the European Coal and Steel Community (predecessor to the European Union) in 1957, tariffs on goods and restriction on cross border travel fell among member countries. While Spain, where this photo was taken, was not a member of the Community in 1967—as a dictatorship it was not eligible—it benefited from the general European integration, which created a vast consumer market, allowing for economies of scale, as well as those open borders and the mass tourism to which they gave rise.

A Closer Look

The Italian-made Fiat was one of a number of small and economical cars put out by European manufacturers in the decades after World War II.

Before that conflict, Western Europeans had lagged behind Americans in developing a consumer culture, of which the automobile was central. But in the prosperous 1950s and 1960s, they caught up with a vengeance. Whereas just five million cars rode Western European roads in 1948, there were more than 44 million by 1965. Once the exclusive preserve of the wealthy, cars were now within the budgets of almost every European family, save the very poor. Making cars even more affordable was the spread of consumer credit and installment buying, both rare before the war.

One of the most frequent uses to which Europeans put their cars was travel, motoring down a new network of highways from the northern parts of the continent to sunny vacation spots along the Mediterranean coast in the summer and ski resorts in winter. Government mandates and healthy profit margins pushed—and allowed—companies to offer long paid vacations.

1   100   200   300   400   500   600   700   800   900   1000   1100   1200   1300   1400   1500   1600   1700   1800   1900   2000 CE

2.18.14 American Anti-Vietnam War Flyer

New York, New York
1968

Credit: Blank Archives/Getty Images

What You Need to Know

This flyer advertises an "International Student-Faculty Strike" against the War in Vietnam, to take place on the campus of New York University, on April 26, 1968.

In early 1965, President Lyndon Johnson decided to escalate American involvement in Vietnam—which, up to then, had largely consisted of providing advisors to the anti-communist South Vietnamese military and conducting air sorties against communist North Vietnam—by sending in U.S. ground troops. First dispatched to protect American air bases, they were soon going out into the field on "search and destroy" missions. But they had little effect in stopping the communist insurgency, leading U.S. commanders in Vietnam to keep demanding more men, insisting that their strategy of flooding the country with troops was working. By early 1968, there were roughly 550,000 U.S. military personnel in Vietnam, most of them conscripts.

As the war escalated, so did the antiwar movement. Still, most Americans at the beginning of 1968 supported the war, believing it necessary to stop the spread of communism. But in late January, North Vietnam and South Vietnamese communist insurgents launched the massive Tet Offensive. Ultimately a military failure, it nevertheless exposed the fact that the enemy was not giving up. Public opinion in the United States began to shift. While most Americans did not approve of the long-haired protesters of the antiwar movement, nor their claims that Vietnam was an "immoral" war, they nevertheless began coming to the conclusion that it might be an "unwinnable" one.

A Closer Look

The event being advertising included a walkout on classes and a march up Fifth Avenue. The demands of the strike's organizers included bringing Americans troops home from Vietnam, stopping the draft, or military conscription and, somewhat more vaguely, ending "racial oppression." The strike was part of the "ten days of protest," organized by the National Mobilization to End the War, known to followers as "the Mobe," and Students for a Democratic Society, a radical youth organization established in the early 1960s to challenge political conformity, racial oppression, and capitalist inequities.

As the antiwar movement intensified over the course of the late 1960s, it changed not only in size but in its tactics. Teach-ins, in which students and faculty would meet to discuss why America was at war, gave way to marches and demonstrations, some featuring protesters illegally burning their draft cards and thereby announcing they would not serve if conscripted.

Peaceful demonstrations turned violent, as protesters refused to heed police demands to disperse. The rhetoric of the movement changed as well. Gone were appeals to the rationality and humanity of the nation's government and military leaders, replaced by *ad hominem* attacks on their character, usually phrased as offensive epithets.

1   100   200   300   400   500   600   700   800   900   1000   1100   1200   1300   1400   1500   1600   1700   1800   1900   2000 CE

2.18.15 "America Salutes" Button Commemorating Moon Landing

United States
1969

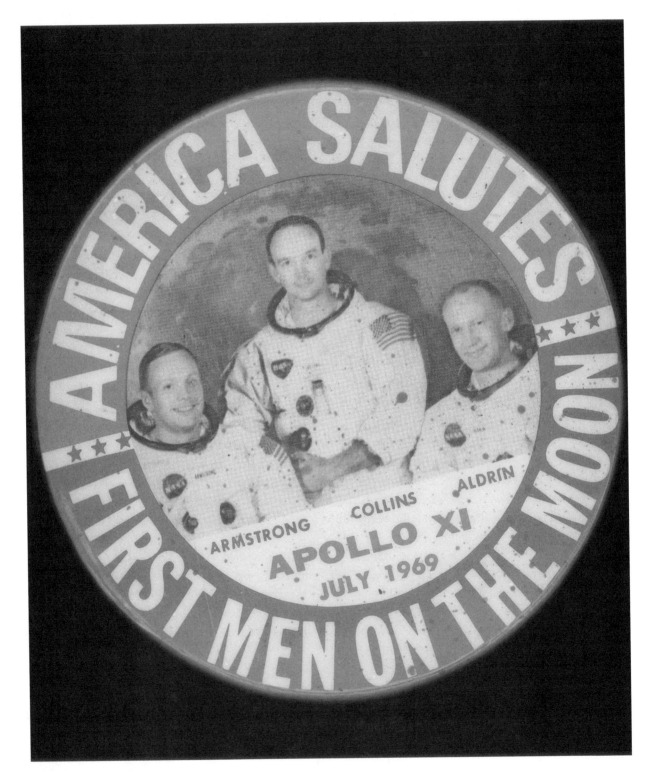

Credit: Blank Archives/Getty Images

What You Need to Know

This button commemorates the first Moon landing by the crew of Apollo 11—Neil Armstrong, Michael Collins, and Edwin "Buzz" Aldrin"—on July 20, 1969.

Much of the impetus for America's ambitious space program was political. Since just after the end of World War II, democratic and capitalist America had been locked in a global ideological struggle with the communist Soviet Union. An aspect of the so-called Cold War was convincing the rest of the world—particularly, the non aligned Third World of former European colonies—that its system was superior.

Both sides competed in space to demonstrate that fact. The Soviets got off to an early lead, becoming the first to put a satellite and man in space, in 1957 and 1961, respectively. The former particularly shook the American people, who became obsessed with the idea that a communist satellite was circling over their heads for who knew what purposes. President Eisenhower responded by committing more funds to math and science education and establishing NASA.

In 1961, Eisenhower's successor, President John Kennedy—a fierce Cold Warrior—pledged to have America put a man on the Moon before decade's end. No expense was spared. At its height in the late 1960s, the U.S. space program was consuming fully 1 federal government dollar in 10.

A Closer Look

Americans were obsessed with all things space related in the 1960s. Rocketry influenced industrial design well beyond aerospace to products such as household appliances and automobiles. Comics were filled with space stories that children sometimes read while munching on Space Food Sticks, a kind of early energy bar modeled after those consumed by astronauts in space. The elite corps of astronauts were celebrated as all-American heroes—clean-cut, patriotic, and willing to challenge obstacles and defy death to lead the country into space. Those who engaged in special missions—such as John Glenn's first orbits around the Earth and the trio of the Moon landing—were given ticker-tape parades upon their return. The nation's three broadcast television networks regularly broke into scheduled programming—which included several space-related prime time shows—to televise launches and other achievements, such as the first American space walk in 1965.

Media savvy NASA (National Aeronautics and Space Administration) contributed to the phenomenon by making the launches as theatrical as possible and parading the astronauts around the country as the agency's ambassadors.

Still, nothing captivated Americans—and the world—quite like the Moon landing. It is estimated that roughly 70 percent of Americans—and fully 600 million people around the world—gathered around their televisions sets to watch the grainy, black and white images of Armstrong becoming the first human to set foot on the Moon.

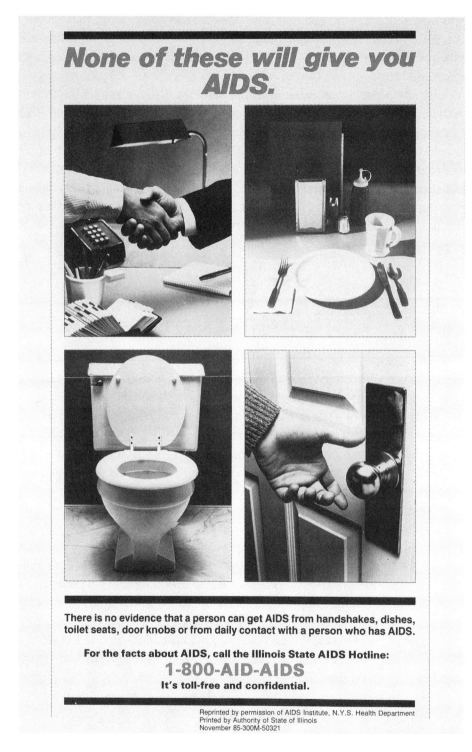

Credit: National Library of Medicine

What You Need to Know

Shown here is an AIDS (acquired immune deficiency syndrome) awareness poster put out by the State of Illinois in the 1980s. The explicit aim of the poster is to educate people on how AIDS is *not* contracted; implicitly, the poster's message is that people should not shun or ostracize people who have the disease.

Since the advent of antibiotics during World War II, Americans had come to believe that epidemics of communicable disease had become a thing of the past. AIDS, the first observable U.S. case occurring in 1981, challenged such complacency. Fear gripped the nation as 57,000 cases of AIDS were reported over the next seven years, resulting in 32,000 deaths.

A stigma lay over those who contracted it, especially because most of them engaged in behavior that many Americans considered immoral and irresponsible, including intravenous drug abuse and homosexual sex. Those engaging in the latter were especially blamed, as many conservative religious leaders, and their millions of followers, argued that AIDS was sent by God to punish homosexuals for their supposedly deviant behavior and lifestyle. In addition, many people feared contracting AIDS precisely because they did not understand how it was transmitted from person to person.

The spread of AIDS also contributed to changing attitudes about sexuality even among heterosexuals. The permissive atmosphere toward casual sex that had marked the "sexual revolution" of the 1960s and 1970s gave way to more traditional views that sex was for married couples only. Under prodding from conservative politicians and religious leaders, high schools curtailed sex education programs—other than advocacy of abstinence—and stopped dispensing out condoms, even though the latter were among the best means to avoid contracting AIDS, because it was felt this would encourage promiscuity.

A Closer Look

The homosexual community was utterly transformed by the AIDS epidemic. The ebullience of the early years of the gay liberation movement in the 1970s gave way to a new somberness and sense of tragedy, as virtually everyone in the community came to know someone with the disease, which at the time was usually fatal. A sexually permissive culture gave way to a more conservative one, and gay men increasingly committed themselves to monogamous relationships.

There was also a renewed activism, as a perception spread through the community that because the disease largely affected homosexuals and drug users the government and society generally did not want to hear—or do anything—about it. To challenge such attitudes, as well as to demand more research money into the cause of, and cures for, AIDS, gays and their supporters organized into activist groups, such as the media savvy ACT UP (AIDS Coalition to Unleash Power), which staged highly publicized protests and acts of civil disobedience to demand action from the government and pharmaceutical companies.

2.18.17 Students Protest in the Streets of Tehran

Tehran, Iran
1981

Credit: Kaveh Kazemi/Getty Images

What You Need to Know

The accompanying photo shows a street scene in Tehran, the capital of Iran, in the spring of 1981, two years after the country had undergone an Islamic-inspired revolution. The students, left-wing opponents of the new theocratic regime, have piled up newspapers to be burnt in case of attack by Revolutionary Guards, members of the Iranian military charged with enforcing public order at home.

In power nearly continuously since World War II, Shah Reza Pahlavi had used Iran's vast oil revenues to modernize his country, especially after the price of petroleum skyrocketed in the early 1970s. While the so-called White Revolution brought advances in education, health care, and infrastructure, it also led to corruption and growing inequalities of wealth. As noted, political dissent was not tolerated, and protesters often found themselves tortured by the notorious SAVAK, or secret police. The shah was also determined to secularize and modernize Iranian culture, which offended many more traditional members of society.

In the late 1970s, both religious and left-wing Iranians began to protest the regime, leading to a brutal crackdown. Religious opponents rallied around the exiled Ayatollah Khomeini, leader of Iranian Shiism, a branch of Islam. Ultimately, the opposition overwhelmed the regime, forcing the Shah himself into exile. The new regime imposed Islamic law and attempted to export the idea of Islamic revolution around the Muslim world, to mixed success.

A Closer Look

Daily life in the Islamic Republic of Iran bore a number of resemblances to what it had under the secular regime of the Shah, which the revolution had overthrown, and some important differences. In both cases, the government put severe limitations on free expression; criticisms of the old regime had brought jail and torture. While both had diminished after the revolution, they were replaced by Revolutionary Guard patrols, which rigorously enforced dress codes, especially for women, and any signs of alcohol consumption, public displays of affection, or anything else the Islamic regime deemed of decadent Western origin or counter to Islamic morality.

The country was also poorer than it had been under the Shah. International sanctions, imposed after government-inspired militants had seized the American Embassy in November 1979, caused a shortage of consumer goods, as well as spare parts for factories, which triggered rapid inflation, even as wages fell. Meanwhile, having been attacked by neighboring Iraq, much of the government's social welfare programs were starved for revenues, which were being redirected to the war effort.

1   100   200   300   400   500   600   700   800   900   1000   1100   1200   1300   1400   1500   1600   1700   1800   1900   2000 CE

2.18.18 Desmond Tutu's Speech on the Struggle against Apartheid

South Africa
1984

I speak out of a full heart, for I am about to speak about a land that I love deeply and passionately; a beautiful land of rolling hills and gurgling streams, of clear starlit skies, of singing birds, and gamboling lambs; a land God has richly endowed with the good things of the earth, a land rich in mineral deposits of nearly every kind; a land of vast open spaces, enough to accommodate all its inhabitants comfortably; a land capable of feeding itself and other lands on the beleaguered continent of Africa, a veritable breadbasket; a land that could contribute wonderfully to the material and spiritual development and prosperity of all Africa and indeed of the whole world. It is endowed with enough to satisfy the material and spiritual needs of all its peoples.

And so we would expect that such a land, veritably flowing with milk and honey, should be a land where peace and harmony and contentment reigned supreme. Alas, the opposite is the case. For my beloved country is wracked by division, by alienation, by animosity, by separation, by injustice, by avoidable pain and suffering. It is a deeply fragmented society, ridden by fear and anxiety, covered by a pall of despondency and a sense of desperation, split up into hostile, warring factions.

It is a highly volatile land, and its inhabitants sit on a powder-keg with a very short fuse indeed, ready to blow us all up into kingdom come. There is endemic unrest, like a festering sore that will not heal until not just the symptoms are treated but the root causes are removed. . . .

I visited one of the trouble-spots near Johannesburg.

In this black township, we met an old lady who told us that she was looking after her grandchildren and the children of neighbors while they were at work. On the day about which she was speaking, the police had been chasing black schoolchildren in that street, but the children had eluded the police, who then drove down the street past the old lady's house. Her wards were playing in front of the house, in the yard. She was sitting in the kitchen at the back, when her daughter burst in, calling agitatedly for her. She rushed out into the living room. A grandson had fallen just inside the door, dead. The police had shot him in the back. He was six years old. Recently a baby, a few weeks old, became the first white casualty of the current uprisings. Every death is one too many. Those whom the black community has identified as collaborators with a system that oppresses them and denies them the most elementary human rights have met cruel death, which we deplore as much as any others. They have rejected these people operating within the system, whom they have seen as lackies and stooges, despite their titles of town councilors, and so on, under an apparently new dispensation extending the right of local government to the blacks.

Source: Tutu, Desmond. "The Question of South Africa." Statement to the United Nations Security Council, October 23, 1984. In *Africa Report* 30 (January/February 1985): 50–52.

What You Need to Know

This excerpt is from a 1984 speech delivered by Desmond Tutu, then a priest—soon to be the first black Archbishop of Cape Town—in the Anglican Church of South Africa.

South Africa's history of race relations was a tortured one. Initially settled by the Dutch, the territory was absorbed into the British Empire following the discovery of gold and diamonds in the late nineteenth century. In 1948, the descendants of the early settlers, known as Afrikaners, took control of the South African government and turned a relatively informal system of racial segregation and discrimination into the rigid and comprehensive apartheid system.

Meanwhile, from the early twentieth century and the founding of the antiracialist African National Congress (ANC), blacks began to demand their rights in the country, a struggle that intensified with the outbreak of township unrest in the mid-1970s, which was met by brutal police crackdowns. Faced with rising protests, a series of costly wars against hostile states on its periphery, and crippling international economic sanctions, the white minority government was eventually forced to cede power to the black majority in the early 1990s. This led to the first truly democratic voting in 1994 and the election of ANC leader Nelson Mandela as president.

A Closer Look

Tutu received the Nobel Peace Prize for his leadership in the struggle against apartheid ("separateness," in the Afrikaans language, spoken by most white minority South Africans), a system of government-sanctioned racial segregation and discrimination against South Africa's black majority, as well as its Asian and mixed-race minorities.

Virtually every aspect of daily life for South African blacks was shaped by apartheid laws and practices. Blacks were required to carry passbooks with them wherever they went, which dictated those places they were permitted to go and at what times of day. Blacks were forced to live in the overcrowded and underserviced townships that surrounded South African towns and cities, available to work in urban areas but not allowed to enjoy the amenities those jurisdictions offered their white inhabitants.

Many were declared citizens of "Bantustans," supposedly independent countries within South Africa, but unrecognized by any other government in the world. Hundreds of thousands of black men were forced to leave their families behind for months at a time to work in South African mines, as there were few jobs in the overcrowded Bantustans, which were inevitably situated on the least productive lands in the country.

1 100 200 300 400 500 600 700 800 900 1000 1100 1200 1300 1400 1500 1600 1700 1800 1900 2000 CE

799

2.18.19 Child Soldier from Chad Posing with a Libyan Helmet

Kalait, Chad
1987

Credit: Dominique Faget/AFP/Getty Images

What You Need to Know

In this photo from 1987, a Chadian soldier, who looks to be about 12 years old, poses with an AK-47 automatic rifle and a helmet captured from a Libyan soldier. Between 1978 and 1987, Chad and Libya fought a series of conflicts over the Aouzou Strip, a 43,000 square mile territory of Saharan Desert in northern Chad that Libya claimed as its own.

In the winter of 1886–1887, the leaders of Europe met in Berlin to divide up the African continent between them. When drawing up colonial borders, they took virtually no countenance of existing ethnic and linguistic groups, dividing culturally akin peoples between the various colonies and placing various others, sometimes with long histories of competition and even enmity, in the same jurisdiction. The independent African states that emerged in the late 1950s and early 1960s, largely along old colonial lines, were nation-states in name only.

Various groups within them competed for power, leading to an endless series of military coups and civil wars. Poverty was another legacy of the colonial era that contributed to conflict. Leaders of the new governments did not always help the situation, often rewarding members of their own ethnic group, contributing to internal tensions. Modernization and urbanization broke down old cultural norms and morals; older ideals of respect for elders broke down among many youth, making them easy recruits for unscrupulous military and rebel leaders.

A Closer Look

Children have been used as soldiers for thousands of years but they became especially prevalent in the numerous civil wars that tore apart countries in Asia and Africa from the 1960s through the early twenty-first century. UNICEF, the United Nations agency dedicated to the welfare of the world's children, estimated that there were roughly 200,000 soldiers under the age of 18 fighting in the late 1980s, roughly half of them in various African conflicts.

Child soldiers are typically recruited by rebel forces, although governments use them as well. Although some are recruited with promises of food and the chance to loot, many others are simply abducted. Recruiters sometimes hook children on drugs, both to make them dependent on their commanders and less fearful in battle. In worst-case scenarios, the children are ordered to commit atrocities, sometimes killing their own parents, binding them to their abductees through guilt and making it impossible for them to escape and return home.

Both girls and boys are recruited. While the boys do much of the fighting, both are used in support capacities, as spies, porters, cooks, and guards.

1 100 200 300 400 500 600 700 800 900 1000 1100 1200 1300 1400 1500 1600 1700 1800 1900 2000 CE

2.18.20 Food Line in the Soviet Union

Moscow, Soviet Union
1990

Credit: Igor Gavrilov/The LIFE Images Collection/Getty Images

What You Need to Know

The accompanying photo shows a line of people waiting on a rainy street in Moscow to buy food from a local store sometime in the 1990s.

When the communist Bolsheviks seized power in the 1917 Revolution, they inherited a country that was already economically behind much of the rest of Europe. Under Josef Stalin, the Soviet dictator from the 1920s to the early 1950s, the country rapidly industrialized but the thrust was toward building infrastructure and manufacturing industrial goods.

After Stalin's death, his successors emphasized more consumer goods production, and for a time from the late 1950s to the early 1970s, they delivered, as the standard of living of the average Soviet citizen improved. But centrally planned and controlled, the economy simply could not meet the increasingly sophisticated wants of Soviet consumers. Meanwhile, without the discipline of the marketplace, companies failed to innovate and workers—guaranteed a job for life—remained unproductive. A popular Soviet era joke went: "We pretend to work and they pretend to pay us."

Ultimately, the system proved untenable. When reformer Mikhail Gorbachev came to power in the mid-1980s, he tried to liberalize both the Soviet economy and political system, but all he did was unleash forces that ultimately caused the system to collapse and the Soviet Union to pass into history.

A Closer Look

Before the fall of communism in the early 1990s, all wholesale and virtually all retail trade in the Soviet Union, including food, was under the control of the state. In cities, such as Moscow, there were two types of stores in which to buy most food and articles of daily life—the so-called Universal Stores, or Universams, equivalent to supermarkets/department stores and local grocery stores, bakeries, butchers, and the like.

At first glance, the system—aside from its government ownership—seems akin to that of the capitalist West. But there were profound differences. Soviet stores had far fewer packaged foods; most groceries were sold in bulk, and shoppers were required to bring their own bottles, bags and boxes to take them home. There was also much less variety. Typically shoppers would find an abundance of one item, but little else, forcing them to stock up on something that they might not have wanted so that they could barter it for something they did.

But mostly, particularly as the system failed to keep up with demand by the 1970s and 1980s, there were shortages. When a particular product became available, word would spread through the neighborhood and people would line up, sometimes for hours, to get a chance to buy it.

1 100 200 300 400 500 600 700 800 900 1000 1100 1200 1300 1400 1500 1600 1700 1800 1900 2000 CE

Part 19:
A New Millennium

1990s to the Present

2.19.1 China's One-Child Policy Statement

China
1995

The population problem is an important question that touches upon the survival and development of the Chinese nation, the success or failure of China's modernization drive as well as the coordinated and sustained development between the population on one hand, and the economy, society, resources and environment on the other. It is a natural choice that the Chinese government has made to implement family planning, control population growth and improve the life quality of the population a basic state policy on the basis of a wish to make the state strong and powerful, the nation prosperous and the people happy. . . .

Since the implementation of the policy of family planning in China, profound changes have been taking place in people's concepts of marriage, birth and family along with the reform and opening to the outside world as well as socio-economic development; the traditional ideas of "early marriage and early births," "more children, greater happiness," and "looking up on men and down on women" are being discarded by more and more people at the child-bearing ages. Late marriage and late births, fewer and healthier births, viewing male and female children as the same, establishing happy, perfect and harmonious small families and seeking a modern, scientific and civilized way of life have become an irresistible trend of the times. . . .

Voluntary participation is mainly manifested in the fact that, under the guidance of the state's relevant policies and legislation, the right of all couples and individuals to carry out family planning is protected and respected. While exercising their right of child bearing, couples and individuals must take into account their responsibilities and duties to the state and community, and the health and happiness of the family and all its members. . . .

One child for one couple is a necessary choice made under China's special historical conditions to alleviate the grim population situation. One child for one couple does not mean to "have one child" under all circumstances, but rather, while encouraging couples to have only one child, to plan arrangements for couples who have real difficulties and need to have a second child to do so. In China's cities and towns where family planning was introduced earlier and the economic, cultural, educational, public health and social security conditions are better, the overwhelming majority of couples of child-bearing age who are pleased with a small family have responded to the government's call and volunteered to have only one child.

Source: Information Office of the State Council of the People's Republic of China. Beijing: August 1995. Online at Permanent Mission of the People's Republic of China to the United Nations Office at Geneva and Other International Organizations in Switzerland: Family Planning in China. http://www.china-un.ch/eng/bjzl/t176938.htm.

What You Need to Know

This is an official statement from the Office of the State Council of the People's Republic of China on the whys, hows, and effects of its family planning program, including its controversial "one-child" policy.

The one-child policy was not communist China's first effort at social engineering on a mass scale. Mao Zedong, who served as the ideological leader of China from the revolution in 1949 until his death in 1976, instituted a number of policies, in an attempt to transform the country into both a modern industrial state and one based on pure socialist practices. The 1950s-era Great Leap Forward moved tens of millions of peasants into huge communes, then had them build thousands of small factories and mills in their backyards, with disastrous economic and human consequences, including a famine that wiped out millions. In the late 1960s came the Great Proletarian Revolution, known in the West as the Cultural Revolution, in which radical brigades purged government agencies, schools, and businesses of so-called bourgeois and intellectual elements, causing much disruption.

Meanwhile, believing that a growing population translated into national security strength, the government discouraged family planning and birth control and even set incentives for large families. Following Mao's death, more moderate leaders came to power. Recognizing that population growth was overtaxing the country's ability to feed itself and leading to severe environmental degradation, the government radically reversed course in a fashion only available to totalitarian states—a coercive and unpopular, but effective, program to limit the size of families.

A Closer Look

First instituted in 1979, the policy requires most couples to limit themselves to a single child. Violators are fined or, if they work in the public sector or for one of China's many government-run businesses, have their pay garnished in some fashion. These monetary penalties are graduated based on a couple's income.

The impetus for one child was population control and, to that end, it succeeded. By 2010, roughly 30 years into the policy, the fertility rate in China—that is, the number of children per woman—had fallen to 1.65, below the level of population replacement.

Meanwhile, the one-child policy had a number of unintended consequences. Because boys are more highly valued in most Chinese families, some couples chose to abort female fetuses. That, and the fact that the law allowed rural families to have a second child if their first was a girl, has created a growing gender imbalance. By 2012, there were 40 million more males in the country than females. This gave a certain advantage to women seeking marriage partners, but it promised to leave many young men, unable to find a mate, frustrated.

The one-child policy also led to changing attitudes toward children. The Chinese began to talk of the "little emperors," spoiled only children on whom increasingly prosperous parents lavished attention and gifts.

1 100 200 300   400   500   600   700   800   900   1000 1100 1200 1300   1400   1500   1600   1700   1800 1900 2000 CE

2.19.2 Afghan Women Wearing Burqas

Kabul, Afghanistan
2001

Credit: Chris Hondros/Getty Images

What You Need to Know

The accompanying photo from 2001 shows two Afghan women wearing burqas, loosely fitting garments that cover the body from head to foot. The Taliban regime, which took power that year, required all women to wear the burqa when in public. The garb was only one of many burdens the conservatively Islamic Taliban put on women.

Fractured by ethnic divisions, the people of Afghanistan have also been fiercely independent, fending off various invading forces through their history. In 1979, the Soviet Union became the latest outside power to try to control the country. A religiously inspired guerrilla force, known as the *mujahideen*, rose up to challenge them. Backed by Pakistan and the United States, they ousted Moscow's forces within a decade.

The country was then embroiled in civil conflict, both among the various ethnic groups and between rebel forces and the government installed by the Soviets. Among the rebels were the Taliban—the name means "students" in the Pashtun language of the largest of the country's ethnic groups—a highly discipline, largely youthful force that seized power in 1996. They offered law and order, but at the price of severe oppression—not just for women, but any who disagreed with their austere form of Islamic rule. They also invited the anti-Western, Islamist terrorist network, al-Qaeda, to set up its headquarters in the country. This latter decision proved their undoing. After al-Qaeda launched the 9/11 terrorist attacks on Washington and New York in 2001, the United States responded by invading the country and throwing the Taliban out of power.

A Closer Look

The Taliban strictly limited women's education. Under the regime, girls were only allowed to study the Koran, and after the age of eight, even that was denied them. Any girl who tried to get around the rules, and any teachers who participated, were threatened with execution. Male doctors were not allowed to treat women unless the latter were accompanied by a male relative. Given the dearth of female doctors in Afghanistan, the restriction severely undermined women's access to health care. Women were also effectively excluded from the workforce.

International critics of the regime likened it to "gender apartheid," after the outlawed system of racial segregation in South Africa. But in many ways, it was worse. The Taliban essentially tried to exclude women from all public life. The regime set up an informal spying system to make sure women did not speak loudly in the streets or appear in any part of a home that could be seen from outside. Women's images were banned from print media, outdoor advertising, and film.

The Taliban rationalized these rules by claiming they were sanctioned by Islam and that they protected the chasteness and dignity of women. In fact, such edicts contradicted Islamic scripture and were, instead, based on the medieval South Asian concept of *purdah*, or women's seclusion from public life.

1   100   200   300   400   500   600   700   800   900   1000   1100   1200   1300   1400   1500   1600   1700   1800   1900   2000 CE

2.19.3 Brazilian Favela and High Rises

Belo Horizonte, Brazil
2000s

Credit: Rogério Medeiros Pinho

What You Need to Know

This photo shows a favela, or shanty town, in the Brazilian city of Belo Horizonte, taken sometime in the early 2000s. Above the impoverished neighborhood loom modern high-rise office and apartment buildings, where the country's middle and upper classes work and live.

Most favelas emerged after World War II, as hundreds of thousands of peasants fled the poverty of the Brazilian countryside for urban jobs, largely in the domestic service and manufacturing centers. Then as now, Brazil topped the international charts for wealth and income inequality. But whereas in the early postwar period, the discrepancy was most notable between urban and rural Brazil—and between the relatively rich south and poor north—inequality is now a part of Brazilian urban life in both regions, though the same racial imbalance of poorer blacks and richer whites prevails.

Brazil's inequality, partly a product of its slave past and longtime reliance on plantation agriculture, was barely affected by the various efforts at rapid economic modernization, undertaken by both civilian and military governments, through the 1980s. But rising economic prosperity, as well as a host of social welfare programs launched by the government of Luiz Inácio da Sula, known popularly to Brazilians as Lula, reduced the percentage of the population living in poverty from more than 40 percent in 1990 to less than 20 percent in 2014.

A Closer Look

Life in the favelas can be economically trying but culturally rewarding. Housing is poor and overcrowded. The typical favela home is jerry-built from brick or concrete, often the discards from more formal construction sites, and topped with sheets of zinc and tin. Most house large families, living together in one or two rooms, with a single bed for the children and another for the parents.

Favelas are usually situated on marginal lands, such as river banks or steep hillsides, prone to flooding and avalanches in the wet season. Disease is often rampant, and hunger common. Life expectancy in the favelas is 48 years, compared with 68 for Brazil as a whole. Violence, fueled by gangs and the drug trade, is ever present, although somewhat diminished since a nationwide police crackdown on favela crime in 2008; this push has led to many cases of police abuse and killings, however.

Still, many Brazilians would argue, the favelas are where Brazilian culture truly flourishes, as new trends in music, dance, and the visual arts on the streets and in the impromptu clubs of these vibrant slums.

1 100 200 300 400 500 600 700 800 900 1000 1100 1200 1300 1400 1500 1600 1700 1800 1900 2000 CE

2.19.4 Foreclosure Sign about American Home

Winchester, Virginia
2009

Credit: Chris Rank/Bloomberg via Getty Images

What You Need to Know

Shown here is a foreclosure sign posted outside a home in the town of Winchester, Virginia. The photo was taken in May 2009 at the height of America's so-called foreclosure crisis.

From the five or so years between the end of the brief recession of 2001–2002 and the beginning of the foreclosure crisis in 2006, housing prices soared in many parts of the United States, particularly in the Sunbelt states of the South and West. The boom was fed by easy credit.

With interest rates low, which kept monthly mortgage payments down, homeowners were encouraged to upgrade to bigger and better homes. Those looking to enter the housing market for the first time were drawn in by subprime mortgages, aimed at those with little or poor credit. Many of these offerings were adjustable-rate mortgages; borrowers paid exceptionally low interest rates at first, with much higher rates to come. Few worried. With housing prices going up, people could refinance easily before the higher rates kicked in.

Borrowing to buy or refinance a home became a kind of national frenzy; people could not answer their phone or open their mailbox—virtual or real—without being hit with solicitations. Millions of ordinary people began to buy homes simply for the purpose of fixing them up and quickly reselling them at a profit, a process known as "flipping," many of them encouraged by reality TV shows on the subject.

Inevitably, the bubble burst. As interest rates rose, housing prices declined, causing many people to go "underwater"—that is, to owe more than their house was worth. With the housing crisis came an economic slump and higher unemployment. Out of a job, people could not meet their higher adjustable rates, leading to a wave of foreclosures.

A Closer Look

Reflecting the polarized political climate of the era, two visions of what caused the housing crisis emerged as foreclosures rose from less than 40,000 monthly in mid-2005 to more than 200,000 in mid-2009. Conservatives aimed their fire at both the government and the homeowners themselves. Federal policies to encourage home ownership among the poor pushed banks to offer mortgages to those who could not afford them. Meanwhile, reckless homeowners bought properties they could not otherwise afford.

For those on the left, the culprits were the banks and other financial institutions involved in the home mortgaging market, as well as the government. The banks offered mortgages to those they knew could not pay back the loans. They engaged in such irresponsible behavior because they typically bundled and sold the loans, as financial products, to other institutions. The government's role in the debacle, say liberals, was to ease financial regulations, often at the bequest of financial industry lobbyists, that otherwise would have prevented the housing bubble.

1 100 200 300   400   500   600   700   800   900   1000 1100 1200 1300   1400   1500   1600   1700 1800 1900 2000 CE

2.19.5 Maldives President's Speech on Climate Change

Maldives Islands
2009

We gather in this hall today, as some of the most climate-vulnerable nations on Earth. We are vulnerable because climate change threatens to hit us first; and hit us hardest. And we are vulnerable because we have modest means with which to protect ourselves from the coming disaster.

We are a diverse group of countries. But we share one common enemy. For us, climate change is no distant or abstract threat; but a clear and present danger to our survival. Climate change is melting the glaciers in Nepal. It is causing flooding in Bangladesh. It threatens to submerge the Maldives and Kiribati. And in recent weeks, it has furthered drought in Tanzania, and typhoons in the Philippines. We are the frontline states in the climate change battle.

Ladies and gentlemen, developing nations did not cause the climate crisis. We are not responsible for the hundreds of years of carbon emissions, which are cooking the planet. But the dangers climate change poses to our countries, means that this crisis can no longer be considered somebody else's problem. Carbon knows no boundaries. Whether we like it or not, we are all in this fight together. . . .

Ladies and gentlemen, when we look around the world today, there are few countries showing moral leadership on climate change. There are plenty of politicians willing to point the finger of blame.

But there are few prepared to help solve a crisis that, left unchecked, will consume us all. Few countries are willing to discuss the scale of emissions reductions required to save the planet. And the offers of adaptation support for the most vulnerable nations are lamentable. The sums of money on offer are so low, it is like arriving at a earthquake zone with a dustpan and brush. We don't want to appear ungrateful but the sums hardly address the scale of the challenge. We are gathered here because we are the most vulnerable group of nations to climate change. The problem is already on us, yet we have precious little with which to fight. Some might prefer us to suffer in silence but today we have decided to speak. And so I make this pledge today: we will not die quietly.

Source: Nasheed, Mohamed. Speech delivered at the Climate Vulnerable Forum, November 9, 2009. Online at Policy Innovations: A Publication of Carnegie Council. http://www.policyinnovations.org/ideas/innovations/data/000152.

TIMELINE   2000 1900 1800 1700 1600 1500 1400 1300 1200 1100 1000 900 800 700 600 500 400 300 200 100 1 BCE

What You Need to Know

This excerpt comes from a speech given by Mohamed Nasheed, president of the Maldives, an island nation situated off the southeastern coast of India in the Indian Ocean. The speech was delivered at the Climate Vulnerable Forum, established by the Maldives government and consisting of leaders of low-lying nations, such as the host country, that were especially vulnerable to rises in ocean levels.

Climate change, which includes a gradual warming of global temperatures, promises to raise ocean levels significantly in coming decades even as it causes increases in the frequency and intensity of cyclones (Indian Ocean hurricanes) that could flood much of the Maldives even before the rise in sea levels is fully experienced.

The Maldives is a medium-income country, with a per capita GDP of about $8,700. Most of its inhabitants make their living from fishing, tropical agricultural products, and tourism. All are threatened by climate change. Higher ocean temperatures kill off coral reefs, on which both sea life and much tourism depends. Rising ocean levels contaminate the fresh water sources needed for agriculture.

The Maldives consists of roughly 1,200 coral islands, about a sixth of which are inhabited. It is the lowest country on Earth, with roughly 80 percent of its landmass less than a meter above sea level. With ocean levels expected to rise by about .6 meters in this century, much of the country will have to be abandoned. Nor are only low-lying countries like the Maldives vulnerable. Recent studies have suggested that more than 600 million people living along coastlines on every inhabited continent are vulnerable to sea level rises and intensified storm surges.

A Closer Look

Experts specializing in the impact of climate change on human society predict drastic and even catastrophic effects. Climate change, say scientists, tends to make current climate patterns more extreme. That is to say, regions that suffer from periodic droughts are likely to experience more sustained dry spells; well-watered regions are more likely to experience floods. Both conditions are likely to disrupt agriculture and food supplies, even if some of the shortfall is made up for by longer growing seasons in high latitude regions. Warmer temperatures are likely to spread infectious diseases and insect pests, which cause diseases in humans and livestock, as well as damage to crops, from tropical regions to more temperate ones.

Such disruptions are bound to increase the number of environmental refugees, that is, those fleeing regions suffering from the effects of climate change. There are even national security implications to climate change, say experts, as all of these disruptions to human life and agriculture trigger civil and international conflicts.

1 100 200 300 400 500 600 700 800 900 1000 1100 1200 1300 1400 1500 1600 1700 1800 1900 2000 CE

2.19.6 Hydrogen Fueling Station in Southern California

Torrance, California
2011

Credit: Tim Rue/Bloomberg via Getty Images

What You Need to Know

In this photo from 2011, a man filling up his automobile with hydrogen at a Shell fueling station. The car, manufactured by Honda, uses fuel cell technology to run its engine. Fuel cells turn the chemical energy in hydrogen and oxygen into water, providing electricity in the process. Fuel cell technology, along with batteries charged with electric power from the grid and hooked up to electric motors, have offered the first significant alternative to the gas-burning internal combustion engine, which, along with its kin the diesel engine, have powered virtually all motorized vehicles since their introduction in the late nineteenth century.

Invented in the late nineteenth century, the internal combustion engine and its diesel kin remain the source of power for virtually all motor vehicles on the road. Although both have been much improved in the past 150 years, their basic operation remains essentially the same. They burn fossil fuels, converting the energy they contain into kinetic force and heat, while producing by-products a host of harmful by-products. Experts agree, however, that, alternative fuel infrastructure costs notwithstanding, America may be on the verge of an alternative fuel revolution that, along with driverless, computer-operated cars, will revolutionize private ground transport in coming decades.

A Closer Look

Fuel cells are essentially batteries that can be continually refilled with their chemical components—oxygen from the surrounding atmosphere and hydrogen from filling stations like the one pictured here. Because their only by-product is water, vehicles using fuel cells produce no exhaust pollutants or carbon dioxide, which exacerbates climate change. Of course, if the factories that make the hydrogen are powered by fossil fuels, then the use of fuel cells merely shifts the production of carbon dioxide and atmospheric pollutants from the vehicle to the fuel production site.

Vehicles powered by fuel cells and electric motors have the advantage of producing no atmospheric pollutants or climate-changing carbon dioxide in their exhaust. Thus, they have piqued the interest of those concerned about the environment, including some consumers. But most car buyers have remained hesitant because of what is known as "range anxiety," the fear that they will not be able to find places to recharge or refuel their vehicles and thus become marooned far from home. Addressing the problem presents something of a conundrum: while "range anxiety" causes consumers to avoid alternative fuel vehicles, businesses hesitate to invest the substantial sums needed to create an alternative fuel infrastructure until there are enough customers ready to take advantage of it.

Range anxiety has been a particularly acute concern in the United States, where a lack of inter-city public transit—aside from airplanes—requires people to make long-distance trips in their cars. Indeed, Americans in the early twentieth century live a good part of their lives in cars; urban sprawl has lengthened commutes even as more people seek to avoid overcrowded, security-intense airports for short- and medium-length trips.

1 100 200 300 400 500 600 700 800 900 1000 1100 1200 1300 1400 1500 1600 1700 1800 1900 2000 CE

2.19.7 Egyptian Man Holding Up Protest Sign

Cairo, Egypt
2011

Credit: Khaled Desouki/AFP/Getty Images

What You Need to Know

The accompanying photo from February 1, 2011, shows a young man in Cairo, Egypt's capital and largest city, holding up a sign that reads in Arabic and English: "Facebook . . . against every injustice." The man is standing in the city's Tahrir Square, epicenter of a popular movement that, within 10 days, would force Hosni Mubarak, the nation's authoritarian president for more than three decades, to resign from office. The Egyptian protests were part of the so-called Arab Spring, a series of antiauthoritarian uprisings that swept the Arab world in late 2010 and early 2011.

As the sign indicates, the initial success of the protests was attributable, in part, to the global rise of social media, which consists of a number of social networking websites, of which the American-based Facebook is the most prominent.

In most Arab countries, traditional broadcast media were—and are—strictly controlled by the government. They aired the news as they saw fit; indeed, even as the protests spread across the country, Egyptian TV stations virtually ignored it. And when that was no longer possible, they tried to portray the protesters as violent anarchists or Islamic radicals.

But social media outlets allowed people to pass on news and information independently of government censors. They also allowed people to better organize. Instead of handing out mimeographs or making phone calls, they could communicate via Facebook and Twitter, a popular microblogging website, to thousands of like-minded people at the push of a button.

A Closer Look

Important as it was in allowing ordinary people to pass on information and organize protests, social media was simply a tool—albeit, a particularly effective one—to channel Egyptian frustration with their lives and with the existing regime. Indeed, most of the nonyouthful, noneducated protesters around the country were not mobilized through social media but through traditional word of mouth.

Egyptians had good reason to be frustrated and angry. Years of population growth had produced a surging youth population that the economy was incapable of providing employment for. With no jobs, Egyptian men were forced to live with their parents in crowded housing, unable to marry and start families of their own.

Moreover, what wealth the country did have was monopolized by a small elite, with familial and political connections to either the Mubarak regime or the all-powerful military. Thus the protesters were demanding not only political change—more democracy—but also economic improvement in their lives. In the end, they got neither. After a brief democratic experiment, which led to an unpopular Islamist-led government, the army reasserted its control, as Egypt seemed destined to return to its authoritarian, crony capitalism past.

1 100 200 300 400 500 600 700 800 900 1000 1100 1200 1300 1400 1500 1600 1700 1800 1900 2000 CE

2.19.8 Kenyans Banking by Phone

Nairobi, Kenya
2013

Credit: Trevor Snapp/Bloomberg via Getty Images

What You Need to Know

This 2013 photo shows a customer conducting a banking transaction via his cell phone and the M-Pesa banking service at a store in Nairobi, Kenya.

The success of the pioneering M-Pesa and subsequent imitators in other countries reveals just how pervasive and influential mobile telephony has become in the twenty-first century.

While the origins of cellular phone technology date back to the first two-way radios of the early twentieth century, their use took off with the development of cellular transmission in the 1970s and 1980s. At first mobile, or cell, phones were the preserve of wealthy individuals or businesses in the developed world. Today, there are almost as many cell phone subscriptions—6.9 billion—as there are people in the world, 7.3 billion, although many people own more than one subscription, so the penetration is not quite as universal as the statistics make it seem.

A Closer Look

M-Pesa ("m" for mobile; *pesa* from the word for "money" in Swahili, one of Kenya's two official languages) is a mobile phone banking and microfinancing institution, begun in 2007 by East Africa's two largest mobile phone providers. M-Pesa has no branches; instead, as the photo illustrates, it uses agents, who are typically store owners, to interact with customers.

To begin using the service, a person registers with M-Pesa for free, then a simple app is sent to the person's cell phone. To fill up his or her account, a customer visits one of the country's thousands of agents, who takes the money and registers the amount on the person's phone. People can then use the service to pay bills, buy cell phone airtime, get cash, or wire money, the latter a popular service in a country where a father or mother often work in a town or city far from the rest of their family back in a rural homestead.

In just seven years of operation, M-Pesa has been adopted by roughly 70 percent of all Kenyans, including 50 percent of those living below the poverty line. M-Pesa is popular because it offers basic banking services in a simple format and at very low cost to customers who did not have access to a full-service bank before, kept away by high fees and a lack of education of how banks worked.

Cell phones have been revolutionary in poorer parts of the world like Kenya, where landline service was historically limited and of poor quality, as is computer access to the Internet today. Mobile phones there are not just for communication but provide all kinds of economic services beyond M-Pesa-style banking, such as providing merchants with the latest commodity prices or farmers with timely weather forecasts.

1 100 200 300 400 500 600 700 800 900 1000 1100 1200 1300 1400 1500 1600 1700 1800 1900 2000 CE

2.19.9 Cell Phone User Communicating Via Twitter

Kiev, Ukraine
2014

Credit: Dreamstime.com

What You Need to Know

This image from 2014 shows a cell phone displaying the Twitter social media network. Founded in San Francisco in 2006 by four young Internet entrepreneurs, Twitter allows users to send brief, 140-character messages—known as "tweets"—to other users, called "followers."

Originally created in 1969, the Internet came into widespread use in the 1990s, with the development of the World Wide Web, a graphical interface for interlinked hypertext documents, which allowed for the transmission of text, images, videos, and other media. Around the same time came chat protocols, which allowed for the sending of messages in real time between Internet users.

By the end of the 1990s, users began to "blog"—shorthand, for web-logging—or the maintaining of online personal journals accessible to Internet users. Blogging was both enhanced and made more user-friendly by early social-networking sites (SNS), which allowed users to create online profiles. Facebook, which debuted in the late 2000s, became the predominant SNS, partly because it allowed users to restrict access to their profiles, creating self-selected affinity groups. Twitter was, in part, a response to the movement of Internet users to mobile phones. The limited word count was ideal for the devices small screens and miniature keypads. By the middle of 2014, Twitter had more than 700 million active users around the world, sending more than 60 million "tweets" on an average day.

A Closer Look

Twitter is one of a number of social networking services—the most prominent being Facebook—made possible by the Internet and the widespread use of Internet-capable computers, including tablets, and smartphones. Social media, as these services are collectively known, allows for relational connections and social arrangements among users, who can be individuals, informal social networks, nonprofit organizations, businesses, and even government agencies.

Social media has had a transformative effect on the way people—particularly young people—interact with one another, both in the developed and increasingly in the developing world. Distance is no longer an issue; people can socially interact with anyone anywhere, as long as they have access to the Internet. Instead, people increasingly group themselves online, typically based on activities, things, and values that interest them—sports, hobbies, politics, and so on. Social media also has an impact on the real world, allowing people to set up spontaneous social events.

Tweets, in particular, because of their limited character count, have contributed to the rise of new forms of abbreviated written communication and the use of "emoticons," simple text-derived icons to convey the emotion of the message's sender.

1 100 200 300   400   500   600   700   800   900   1000 1100 1200 1300   1400   1500   1600   1700 1800 1900 2000 CE

2.19.10 Sudanese Refugees Wait in Line for Water

Sudan
2014

Credit: Ashraf Shazly/AFP/Getty Images

TIMELINE   2000 1900 1800 1700 1600 1500 1400 1300 1200 1100 1000 900 800 700 600 500 400 300 200 100 1 BCE

What You Need to Know

The accompanying photo from January 2014 shows a group of women and children waiting to fill up plastic water containers at a refugee camp in Sudan. The camp, operated by the Red Crescent of Sudan, part of the International Red Cross/Red Crescent network of aid agencies, was set up to house refugees fleeing civil strife in neighboring South Sudan. That country had emerged as an independent country just three years before, breaking away from Sudan after three decades of nearly continuous civil war between a largely Arab and Muslim north and a black African, animist, and Christian south. It then succumbed to internal strife of its own.

Since independence came to most of sub-Saharan Africa in the late 1950s and early 1960s, the region has been torn by war, largely in the form of civil conflicts based on a host of factors. These include ethnic and religious differences, political infighting, and struggles over natural resources. Some of these are the legacy of European imperialism, which often thrust various and sometimes historically hostile groups into a single polity and left very little in the way of a viable political and economic infrastructure when various colonial powers granted their possessions independence. But much has to do with the greed and incompetence of political leaders after independence, who stole their countries resources for themselves and small circles of loyalists, offering little in the way of economic development. The leaders also exploited ethnic and religious differences to maintain themselves in power.

A Closer Look

Life in Sudanese refugee camps, some of which house as many as 40,000 persons, is miserable for inhabitants, who overwhelm their limited facilities. Often situated on marginal lands with little shade, the people are exposed to the extreme heat of the Saharan sun. Latrines overflow, flooding the pathways with sewage and contaminating local wells. Diseases, notably dysentery, are rampant. Nongovernmental organizations, such as the French-run Médecins sans Frontières (Doctors without Borders), provide health care providers, but not nearly enough. And there are virtually no mental health services available for a population that includes thousands of children traumatized by war, the loss of parents and other immediate family members, and forced treks to escape the fighting.

The human cost of these African civil wars has been appalling. The various civil conflicts that rocked the Democratic Republic of the Congo in the 1990s and early 2000s is estimated to have killed as many as five million people, while the civil war in the Sudan left roughly 1.5 million dead. Altogether, Africa's civil wars of the past fifty years are said to have turned more than 10 million persons into refugees—that is, people fleeing across international borders—and internally displaced persons.

1 100 200 300 400 500 600 700 800 900 1000 1100 1200 1300 1400 1500 1600 1700 1800 1900 2000 CE

Further Reading about Daily Life from ABC-CLIO

Aldrete, Gregory S. *Daily Life in the Roman City: Rome, Pompeii, and Ostia*. Santa Barbara, CA: Greenwood, 2004.

Anderson, James M. *Daily Life during the Spanish Inquisition*. Santa Barbara, CA: Greenwood, 2002.

Bianchi, Robert S. *Daily Life of the Nubians*. Santa Barbara, CA: Greenwood, 2004.

Cohen, Elizabeth S., and Thomas V. Cohen. *Daily Life in Renaissance Italy*. Santa Barbara, CA: Greenwood, 2001.

Eaton, Katherine. *Daily Life in the Soviet Union*. Santa Barbara, CA: Greenwood, 2004.

Johnson, Claudia Durst. *Daily Life in Colonial New England*. Santa Barbara, CA: Greenwood, 2002.

Kia, Mehrdad. *Daily Life in the Ottoman Empire*. Santa Barbara, CA: Greenwood, 2011.

Lane, George. *Daily Life in the Mongol Empire*. Santa Barbara, CA: Greenwood, 2006.

Malpass, Michael. *Daily Life in the Inca Empire*. Santa Barbara, CA: Greenwood, 1996.

Nash, Alice, and Christoph Strobel. *Daily Life of Native Americans from Post-Columbian through Nineteenth-Century America*. Santa Barbara, CA: Greenwood, 2006.

Perez, Louis. *Daily Life in Early Modern Japan*. Santa Barbara, CA: Greenwood, 2001.

Schlotterbeck, John. *Daily Life in the Colonial South*. Santa Barbara, CA: Greenwood, 2013.

Schulz, Carol D., and Eve N. Soumerai. *Daily Life during the Holocaust*. Second edition. Santa Barbara, CA: Greenwood, 2009.

Sharer, Robert J. *Daily Life in Maya Civilization, Second Edition*. Santa Barbara, CA: Greenwood, 2009.

Stern, Pamela R. *Daily Life of the Inuit*. Santa Barbara, CA: Greenwood, 2010.

Index

Abbasid caliphate, 257
abolitionism, 635
absolutism, 561
Abu-Bakr, 239
Acatharti, 268
Achaeans, 75
Achaemenid Empire, gold model chariot from ancient Persia, 42–43
Adams, Abigail to John Adams on "Remember the Ladies": Adams, John, 569; American Revolution, causes of, 569; date and place of, 568; demands for equality, 569; empowerment of women, 569; Paine, Tom, 569; the Revolutionary War and women, 569; status of women, 569; text of, 568; on tyrants, 569
Adams, William, 485, 493
advertising: American soft drink advertisement, 772–773; Kodak's bullet camera, 702–703; 1930s refrigerator in, 748–749; Pony Express poster, 680–681; Union Pacific Railroad, advertisement for, 684–685; wringer and mangler, 698–699
Afghan women wearing burqas: al-Qaeda in Afghanistan, 809; burqa, definition of, 809; civil and international conflicts in, 809; date and place of, 808; "gender apartheid," 809; Islam and, 809; the *mujahideen*, 809; photograph of, 808; Taliban regime on women and girls, 809; U.S. invasion of Afghanistan, 809
Africa: African and Asian soldiers in the British Army, 726–727; bronze relief of Benin warriors, 270–271; colonial boarding schools in West Africa, 646–647; Democratic Republic of the Congo, 825; description of Timbuktu and its people, 278–279; digging for diamonds in South Africa, 644–645; Egyptian New

Kingdom fresco depicting Nubian Servants, 266–267; Ethiopian Orthodox gospel book, 276–277; human cost of African civil wars, 825; hunters of the Horn of Africa, 268–269; Neolithic arrowhead, 6–7; role of women in Islamic West Africa, 596–597; Saharan prehistoric cave painting, 264–265; a slaver's description of the Middle Passage, 524–525; Sudanese refugees wait in line for water, 824–825; Tellem rain sculpture, 274–275; Timbuktu and its people, description of, 278–279; travel and trade around the Red Sea, 62–63; Yoruba ancestor monolith, 272–273
African and Asian soldiers in the British Army: 2nd Kashmir rifles of India, 727; African peasants and taxes, 727; date and place of, 726; effectiveness of, 727; Europe's impact on Africa, 727; forced labor, 727; King's African Rifles Battalion out of Uganda, 727; military volunteers, 727; photograph of, 726; World War I and, 727
African chiefs: British instructions on negotiating with, 618–619
African National Congress (ANC), 799
African slave trade, Olaudah Equiano on: conditions of slave passage, 539; date and place of, 538; Equiano (Gustavo Vassa), 539; *The Interesting Narrative of the Life of Olaudah Equiano, Or Gustavus Vassa, The African*, 539; risk of, 539; text of, 538; the Triangle Trade, 539
African wild cat, 47
Afrikaners, 799
aging gracefully in rural America: condemnation of city life, 623; date and place of, 622; Emerson, Ralph Waldo, 623; the "Over-soul," 623; quality of life in New York City, 623; text of, 622;

foreclosure sign about American home, 812–813; gold solidus, 226–227; the great fair at Thessalonica, 230–231; guilds: charter for a butchers' guild, 384–385; Industrial Workers of the World (IWW) constitution, preamble to, 712–713; Kenyans banking by phone, 820–821; Marco Polo on Chinese paper money, 340–341; markets in the Aztec capital of Tenochtitlan, 472–473; M-Pesa banking service, 821; nautical signals of correspondence, 559; Pony Express poster, 680–681; running a manorial estate in England, 396–397; Song dynasty metal coin, 330–331; trade/trading, 187; Triangle Shirtwaist Company fire, an account of, 718–719; weighing harvested rubber in Brazil, 742–743; Western European miracle, 789

Busiris festival, 53

buying a farm in the country: aqueduct systems, 169; the *assidui*, or "hardworking ones" plan, 169; Cincinnatus, example of, 169; date and place of, 168; effective agriculture, 169; expansion of the Roman Empire, 169; farm yields, 169; irrigation, 169; *latifundia*, or plantations, 169; Pliny the Younger on, 169; private land ownership, 169; text of, 168

Byzantine Empire and Russia: *The Book of the Eparch* on economic regulation in Constantinople, 222–223; Byzantine Pilgrimage Flask, 212–213; description of the Rus from the *Risala*, 220–221; *Digest of Justinian* on fugitive slaves, 214–215; gold solidus, 226–227; the great fair at Thessalonica, 230–231; *Homilies on the Virgin*, illuminated illustrations from, 228–229; icon of Saint Eudocia, 224–225; *Institutes of Justinian* on marriage, 216–217; racing factions in the Byzantine capital, 218–219

Byzantine pilgrimage flask: advantages of pilgrimages, 213; the Christian faith and, 213; date and place of discovery, 212; image of, 212; peasants of the Byzantine Empire, 213; pilgrimages, undertaking up, 213; purpose of, 213; Saint Menas, 213

cacao consumption, 557

California: hydrogen fueling station in Southern California, 816–817; Pomo cooking basket, 310–311; promotional postcard for rock concert at the Fillmore, 784–785

Callcott, Lady Mary, 585, 587
Calle, Richard, 415
Calvé, Emma, 705
Calvin, John, 427, 515
Campaign for Nuclear Disarmament, 775
Canaan/Israel/Palestine, 61
Canadian frontier, building a log barn on: amount of time to build, 601; Canadian history paralleling U.S. history, 601; commercial farming, 601; date of, 600; the Great Lakes, 601; "raising bee," 601; *Reminiscences of a Canadian Pioneer for the Last Fifty Years* (Thompson), 601; socializing and, 601; text of, 600; Thompson, Samuel, 601
candomblé, 587
the Caribbean: Christopher Columbus's notes on the Carib and Taino peoples, 298–299
Carpenter, Helen, 629
Carthage/Carthaginians, 55
caste system, 77, 87, 89. *See also* Indian caste system in the *Vishnu Purana*
Castillo, Bernal Díaz del, 473
catgut, 33
the Catholic Church, 387, 447, 463, 467, 595
Catholicism, 479, 481
Catiglione, Baldasare, 421
Cato, 158, 159, 160, 161, 169
Cato the Elder on uppity women: about Cato the Elder, 153; conservative viewpoint of women, 153; date and place, 152; *History of Rome* (Livy), 153; Lex Oppia, 153; minority viewpoint of, 153; text of, 152; women's roles in Roman society, 153
Cato the Elder's philosophy on slave ownership: about Cato the Elder, 160, 161; agriculture and, 161; date and place of, 160; importance of slaves, 161; Plutarch, 161; slaves and Roman life, 161; slaves buying slaves, 160, 161; text of, 160
cats, 47
cavalry officer's sabretache: the bourgeoisie, 577; date and place of, 576; the French Revolution, 577; image of, 576; the nobility, 577; sabretache, definition of, 577; slogans of, 577; the storming of the Bastille, 577; urban poor and peasants, 577
Cavendish, Margaret, 465
cell phone user communicating via Twitter: blogging, 823; chat protocols, 823; date of, 822; emoticons, 823; Facebook, 823; the Internet,

image of, 602; legality of opium, 603; opium
dens, 603; opium poppy, 603; percentage of
adult Chinese population using, 603; price of
opium, 603; smoking opium, 603
Qing dynasty pewter altar set: date and place of,
518; description of, 519; Gelugpa School of
Buddhism, 519; image of, 518; Kangxi, 519;
pewter, definition of, 519
Qing dynasty play *The Peach Blossom Fan*, a
scene from: date and place of, 510; downfall of
the Mongol Yuan dynasty, 511; Kong Shangren,
511; Qing dynasty, 511; storyline of, 511; text
of, 510; theater in the Qing dynasty, 511; Zhu
Yuanzhang, 511
the Quakers (Religious Society of Friends), 529
Quintilian on how an orator should dress: arbitrary
comments, 163; clothing and status, 163;
clothing in ancient Rome, 163; date and place
of, 162; fastidiousness and, 163; femininity
and, 163; *Institutio Oratoria*, or Instructions on
Oratory, 163; sumptuary laws, 163; text of, 162;
the toga, 163; the tunic, 163
Quintilian's prescription for educating a child: for
boys, 191; date and place of discovery, 190; for
girls, 191; home education, 191; image of, 190;
Institutes of Oratory (Quintillian), 191; on the
responsibility of fathers and mothers, 191;
underlying philosophy and, 191
Qurnet Murai, 33

Ra, 37
race and class in colonial Lima: Ampuero family,
527; date of, 526; de Ulloa, Antonia, 527;
Europeans and European descendants in Lima,
527; Indians and poor mestizos, 527; Juan,
Jorge, 527; mestizos, 527; Negros, Milano, and
other descendents, 527; population of the
Spanish Empire, 527; text of, 526; *A Voyage to
South America* (Juan and de Ulloa), 527
racial classification: first treatise on, 501
racing factions in the Byzantine capital: as capital
of the Roman Empire, 219; chariot racing, 219;
date of, 218; geographic location of, 219; the
green and blue camps, 219; *History of the Wars
of Justinian* (Procopius), 219; infrastructure and
institutions of, 219; language of Constantinople,
219; political purpose of, 219; text of, 218
Ranjitsinhji, Kumar Shri, 657
the *Reconquista*, 479
Red Sea, 63

religion: accusation of heresy during the Spanish
Inquisition, 462–463; in ancient Rome, 197;
book of Deuteronomy, clean and unclean foods
according to, 40–41; Brahmanism, 75; Byzantine
pilgrimage flask, 213; *candomblé*, 587; the
Catholic Church, 427; church law from the
Council of Trent, 424–425; colonial tombstone
epitaphs, 514–515; the English word "religion,"
197; Ethiopian Orthodox gospel book, 276–277;
the fall of Jerusalem during the Crusades, 376–
377; funerary stele from the Athenian Necropolis
of Kerameikos, 128–129; heaven and hell
according to the Koran, 234–235; *Homilies on
the Virgin*, illuminated illustrations from, 228–
229; icon of Saint Eudocia, 224–225; Inca
religious beliefs, 305; Indian caste system in the
Vishnu Purana, 94–95; Islam, 235, 237, 239, 243,
251, 255; a Jesuit missionary's expedition to the
Sonoran Desert, 504–505; Jupiter, tasks of the
priests of, 196–197; the *Kojiki* on cosmic origins,
320–321; Koran, heaven and hell according to,
235–236; the Koran judgment day, 255; the
Koran on women and inheritance, 236–237;
Koran scroll fragment, 244–245; laws governing
Mecca, 246–247; Luther, Martin, criticism of the
church, 427; Maya, Bishop Diego de Landa's
account of the mistreatment of, 480–481; Mexica
religion, 297; monastic life according to *The Rule
of St. Benedict*, 360–361; monasticism, 361;
moral precepts from the Mahabharata, 74–75;
Muslim views on marriage, 252–253; *Ordinances
for the Regulation of the Churches* (John Calvin),
426–427; plaques for a caskets, small, 254–255;
Pliny the Younger and Trajan discuss how to
punish Christians, 202–203; predestination, 427;
pre-Inca and Inca religions, 308–309; priests of
Jupiter, tasks of, 196–197; the Prophet
Muhammad, 239, 241, 245, 246, 247, 257; Qing
dynasty pewter altar set, 518–519; the Quakers
(Religious Society of Friends), 529; the
Reformation, 427; Roman worship in pagan
times, 197; Saint Benedict of Nursia, 361;
Sharia on funerary ritual, 255; Shintoism, 315,
321; Spanish-Nahuatl dictionary, 478–479; the
Sunnah on charity, 238–239; the *Sunnah* on
prayer, 240–241; the *Sunnah* on women and
slaves, 242–243; syncretic faiths, 587; of the
Taino and Carib peoples, 299; *Tirukural* on
renunciation of flesh, 86–87; Visigoths and
Ostrogoths, 209

About the Author

James Ciment, PhD, is an independent scholar and an editor of reference works in history and the social sciences. His published works include *Another America: The Story of Liberia and the Former Slaves Who Ruled It.* Ciment received his doctorate in American history from the City University of New York.